The Vision,
The Struggle

How Metropolitan State University of Denver Began

The Vision,
The Struggle

How Metropolitan State University of Denver Began

ROBERT E. BOWEN

Foreword by Doug Holcombe

The Vision, The Struggle: How Metropolitan State University of Denver Began
Published by REBALS Press
Centennial, CO

Cover Photo: Courtesy of Metropolitan State University of Denver
State Legislature Photo: KFI Photography

Library of Congress Control Number: 2015935663
Bowen, Robert, Author
The Vision, the Struggle: How Metropolitan State University of Denver Began
Robert Bowen

ISBN: 978-0-9960055-1-7

EDUCATION / Organizations & Institutions
HISTORY / Social History

QUANTITY PURCHASES: Schools, companies, professional groups, clubs, and other organizations may qualify for special terms when ordering quantities of this title. For information, email info@rebalspress.com.

DEDICATION

This book is dedicated to my son, Rob, who I miss tremendously;
to my daughter, Christine, who I love dearly;
to my late parents, Ray and Helen Bowen, who gave me life
and shaped my values; and lastly to my sisters,
Raelene, Patricia, and Elizabeth who have always had my back.

Table of Contents

Acknowledgments   xiii
Foreword   xvi
Prologue   xvii

CHAPTER 1: IN THE BEGINNING: THE INEVITABLE CREATION OF MSC   1
The torch was passed   1
A perfect storm made MSC inevitable   4
Legislative groundwork   7
The struggle begins   10
1963: The die was cast   12
MSC is conceived: HB 349 is adopted   14

CHAPTER 2: THE STRUGGLE CONTINUES   21
More studies...seriously?   21
The stop-MSC coalition strikes   23
The visionaries fight back   25
The legislature's cold feet and Love's flip-flops   27

CHAPTER 3: MSC IS FINALLY BORN   35
'65 and barely alive   35
A long time coming   XX

CHAPTER 4: MSC IS FUNDED: NOW WHAT?   47
How would the vision be actualized?   47
The visionaries wanted an urban-oriented college   50

So, who was MSC supposed to serve?   55
The open door   60
How MSC defined itself   65

CHAPTER 5: IT FINALLY OPENS   67
So much to do, so little time   68
October 4, 1965: It begins   80
Open a month and already a controversy   84

CHAPTER 6: THE COLLEGE FIGHTS TO ADVANCE   91
Retention presents a challenge   91
Another attempt to make MSC a junior college   93
The spring of '66   97
Year 2: Enrollment doubles   104

CHAPTER 7: THEY DIDN'T THINK WE'D MAKE IT   111
Winter 1967: A student center, a year book, and student lobbyists   111
MSC becomes a four-year college   120
Addressing the problems of the city   124
The spring of '67: First student election; first graduation   126

CHAPTER 8: THE TIMES THEY ARE A-CHANGIN'   133
The winds of change   133
The Summer of Love and the counterculture   134
Blame it on the music   139
The counter culture and generation gap at MSC   141
Fall of '67: MSC after the Summer of Love   144

CHAPTER 9: STUDENT ACTIVISM GROWS   157
We've got those legislative blues again   157
Winter quarter 1968: Calm before the storm   158
Activism hits MSC   160
Martin Luther King's assassination shocks MSC   164
Spring quarter 1968: Race, athletics and war   167

CHAPTER 10: PROTEST, DISSENT AND DIVERSITY   177
Something was happening   177
Protests turn violent   180
The fall of 1968: Bombshells drop   181
The election of 1968   188

CHAPTER 11: TURMOIL, STUDENT POWER AND ATHLETICS   195
  The winter of '69   195
  Chicanos struggle for respect   198
  Protests grow   200
  Student power: 18-year-old vote, intercollegiate athletics   202
  The spring of '69: First class graduates   205

CHAPTER 12: WE HAVEN'T SEEN THIS VINTAGE HERE SINCE 1969   217
  The summer and fall of '69 and all was fine, maybe   217
  The Auraria campaign   222
  Uprising: Revolt against intercollegiate athletics   231
  The Vietnam Moratorium   236
  Meanwhile back at the ranch   240

CHAPTER 13: A BAD MOON RISES   245
  Winter of 1970: Fox building, loans, and day care   245
  Auraria the Sequel: Slum University…seriously?   248
  Spring: In like a lamb, out like a lion   254
  Kent State and Jackson State   261

CHAPTER 14: RIDING OUT THE STORM   269
  Summer and fall of '70   269
  The 1970 elections   278
  A horse with no name   281
  Another newspaper controversy   283

CHAPTER 15: CHANGES   287
  A big change is coming   287
  The Auraria battle continues   292
  Metro is accredited   296
  Salaries, women, interim president   296
  Crisis at *THE PAPER*   *299*
  The end of an era   301

Epilogue   303
Tables   305
Bibliography   307
Notes   309
Index   339

Acknowledgments

I want to acknowledge the people who made this book possible.

First, I want to thank my friend Angela Schnaubelt who convinced me that I could do this. Without her encouragement, I would not have taken on this enormous project, nor seen it through to completion.

Secondly, I want to acknowledge my friend, Doug Holcombe. His assistance in this effort was invaluable. More importantly, were it not for Doug, I would never have gotten involved in MSC's student government to begin with.

I want to acknowledge the assistance I received from the Special Collections Department of the Auraria Library, particularly Rosemary Evetts. Without her knowledge, assistance and guidance, I would not have been able to do the research required for this book.

Also, I want to thank and acknowledge Nathan Kenworthy, a student intern from Metropolitan State University of Denver. I could not have completed this book without his very professional expertise, assistance and guidance. Nathan assisted with research and editing. He gave invaluable editorial suggestions, most of which I actually listened to.

In addition, I want to acknowledge another MSU Denver intern, Aly Albert. She helped me with research and APA citations. Her unique perspective on the content made the book better.

I learned more from these student interns than they learned from me.

I also owe special thanks to Gini Mennenga, Scott Houck, Steve Haigh, Dr. Steve Leonard.

Dr. Charles Angeletti, Professor Joseph Sandoval, Professor Ken Phillips and members of the MSU Denver Institutional History Committee for their help and assistance. Also, I want to thank all the individuals who consented to be interviewed for this book.

I want to thank Dr. Stephen Jordan, president of Metropolitan State University of Denver for granting permission to use photos from the school's archives.

Lastly, I want to acknowledge Metropolitan State College for giving me an opportunity for a college education— an education I would not have received were it not for MSC. Furthermore, my professors and instructors at Metro taught me to think critically, to question and dare to try.

Foreword

This book tells a story that is as old as the Bible, and yet it is as current as the headlines in today's news. The story of David and Goliath comes to mind as I think of the early days when Metro State College was struggling to open its doors, and then keep them open.

There were powerful opponents who did not want Metropolitan State College to come into existence, and they did everything in their power to stop it. When it did open, they worked tirelessly to limit its funding and make it fail. They even worked to prevent it from becoming a four-year college despite the intent of the founders. Yet, just like Goliath, they lost in the end.

This book tells the story of that epic battle and of the cast of characters who fought in the early days. Like the exodus of the Israelites from Egypt, after a struggle, they finally reached the Promised Land.

The author of this book has a great handle on this story. He was there during the early years of the school and participated in that battle. He was the founder of Colorado's 18- year-old vote movement and lobbied it through the state legislature. Eventually, he became a legislator himself as well as a grass-roots organizer for many worthwhile causes.

If you like the story of the underdog then read on and you will see a modern day triumph of the first order involving many of the elements of a good novel, except this was not fiction— it happened.

If you know our history, you know the 1960s was a very active time for students— some good and some not so good. But the story of student involvement in Metro's early days has not been told. Bob Bowen is uniquely qualified to tell that story.

Let's face it the story of any institution of higher learning is only validated and truly told by the students and alumni explaining how they made something of value out of the education they received. One illustration of how it felt in those early days is that of Don Quixote as he tilted with windmills. We did our share of tilting and we actually won a few bouts. It is amazing what can be accomplished by a few dedicated people. This book will tell it all in detail. Enjoy!

Doug Holcombe

First graduating class, Metropolitan State College

Student Body President

Former president MSC Alumni Association

Prologue

A sage once said, "History is simply the context for what we are doing right now."

This book tells the story of how Metropolitan State University of Denver began. Originally called Metropolitan State College (MSC), it started with a vision and came to be through a difficult struggle. In 2015, the school celebrates its 50th anniversary.

With 23,000 students, Metropolitan State University of Denver (MSU Denver) currently has the highest number of undergraduate students of any institution of higher education in Colorado. It is not the numbers that make the school special; it's the institution's unique spirit. That "Metro spirit" has been present since the day it opened in 1965. Dr. Sheldon Steinhauser, a professor in his 45th year at MSC, summed it up this way: "Metro does not connote buildings or an historical landmark, but instead it is the spirit that has pervaded Metro since its inception."

Metropolitan State College was conceived by visionaries—educators and legislators including: Roy Romer, Allen Dines, Palmer Burch, Mark Hogan, Frank Kemp, Herrick Roth and countless others in the community with a vision. Their vision was to create an institution in the city, to solve the city's problems and serve the needs of the city's people.

They envisioned a college that would provide an opportunity for higher education to all who wanted it, and were willing to put forth the effort to achieve it. This included those who traditionally lacked an opportunity for a college education, or the means to afford one.

MSC was born through struggle and molded by adversity. Nothing was easy for those visionaries, the first administration, or the early students of the new college. Thanks to their struggle and perseverance, a unique institution emerged. It was an institution made special by its spirit—a spirit that developed because administrators, faculty, and students were all determined that this noble experiment would succeed.

The Arapahos—the first people to occupy the land on which MSU Denver now sits— believed that we, the present generation, are the beneficiaries of the seven generations that came before us; furthermore, we have a responsibility to the seven generations that come after us. If we want to meet our responsibilities, we need to understand where we came from. We need to know our history—our complete, uncensored, un-revised history.

It is often said that people who do not learn from history are condemned to repeat it. That is certainly true. Implied in that saying is this: if we learn from history, we won't repeat it. We can shape our history, but only if we understand the lessons of the generations that came before us. That is why this book is needed.

Alums of Metropolitan State have shaped history. As students, they played a major role in the early years of the school and its struggle for a permanent campus. MSC graduates have served in governors' cabinets, the state legislature, city councils, and other offices. Alumni have been police chiefs, newspaper editors, and bank executives. MSC graduate Omar Hurricane is achieving major breakthroughs in physics namely inertial confinement fusion.

Rich Castro was a legislator and headed a city agency. Kathleen Archuletta served as top aide to Denver's Mayor Peña and at the time of this writing, she is a key member of the Obama Administration. Betty Kenna served as controller under Governor Owens at the Office of Economic Development. Molly Markert is in her 34th year as an elected official in Aurora. Rosemary Rodriquez, a former Councilwoman, is currently State Director for U.S. Senator Bennet.

Metro graduates, as students and as alumni, have played major roles in the struggle for equal opportunity for the Latino, African-American and Native-American communities in Colorado and the nation. Dr. Daniel Valdes, a Metro professor and department chairman, was a nationally recognized leader in the Hispano community. Several Metro professors, including Charles Angeletti, Gwen Thomas, Rachel Noel and Wilt Flemon, were pioneers in the development of ethnic studies at MSC.

MSC students changed the face of politics in Denver in the 1970s, busting up long-established political machines and adding racial and ethnic balance to many governmental bodies.

Denver's light rail system, which thousands of students ride to campus every day, would probably not exist had an MSC graduate, Representative Robert Bowen, not fought for years to pass the legislation that created it, along with three other MSC alumni in the legislature.[1]

Metro alums were active in re-vitalizing several decaying inner-city Denver neighborhoods in the 1970s and '80s. Mary Bleecher was responsible for placing the downtown Federal Building and others on the Natural Register of Historic Places. Metro grads are leaders in business, the banking, industry, government, politics, health care, the sciences, and many other fields. Many graduates have returned to the school as faculty members and department heads.

Students changed the negative public perception of the struggling new college that existed in the early years. Were it not for students, MSC would be a footnote in the history of the University of Colorado at Denver.

Today, MSU Denver takes great pride in its intercollegiate athletic program and the very successful teams and players it has produced. Yet, athletics were not allowed at MSC in the beginning. Doug Holcombe, student body president at the time, Roger Braun and other students had to lobby the legislature and convince MSC's governing board to allow athletics at the school in 1969. Were it not for their efforts, there would be no Rowdy, championships, trips to the finals, winning coaches, and no intercollegiate trophies.

And one thing is certain; the Auraria Higher Education Center would not exist today were it not for MSC students. That is a fact.

Great things have only happened by efforts of great and humble people who made sacrifices for the greater good. In the words of the ancient Greek proverb, "a society grows great when old men plant trees whose shade they know they will not rest under."

Early MSC students are case studies of how a few determined individuals working together can change things. What better validation of the success of a college is there than the achievements of its students and graduates?

Behind every successful student there were one or more faculty members who inspired them, encouraged them, mentored them and taught them to think independently and critically. Faculty members at Metro were active in the community, serving as role models, making changes all the while earning less than they would have at another institution. Yet many have never been acknowledged for their contributions. For example, Dr. Angeletti has never been honored for his work pioneering the school's first African-American studies courses. Other outstanding faculty and staff have also gone unrecognized until now.

This book tells the stories of just a few of the individuals who helped make MSU Denver what it is today, but countless others also made a contribution. Everyone who walked through its doors—students, faculty members, administrators and staff—contributed something to the school's history.

An alumnus of Metropolitan State College, Anthony J. Garcia, wrote the following lyrics that are so true. His poem tells us, we must teach future generations who must learn in order to grow:

> *Seven generations of history*
> *Seven generations yet to be*
> *Seven generations that went before*
> *And seven generations yet to come.*
> *Seven generations that we must teach*
> *Seven generations our voice must reach*
> *Seven generations that learn to grow*
> *So seven generations will know.*
> *Within ourselves their spirit lasts*
> *The songs they sing of voices past*
> *The earth one day will reclaim itself*
> *Where we begin we will end.*

- Anthony Garcia[2]

Winston Churchill once said, "History will treat me well because I intend to write it."

History books have not treated the early MSC students and the pioneer faculty well. This book is written by a former student, assisted by former students, who were involved in the early days of MSC. Current student interns have added their knowledge, expertise, assistance and their unique perspective to tell the complete story of their university. Current faculty members and staff have greatly assisted this effort as well.

This work intends to tell the complete but heretofore untold story of how MSC/MSU Denver and the Auraria Higher Education Center began. It is time that students, faculty, administrators, legislators and staff are written into the history they helped create.

Roy Romer, one of the visionaries who fought hard for years to
pass legislation that created Metropolitan State College.

Photo Courtesy of Metropolitan State University of Denver.

CHAPTER 1

In the Beginning...
the Inevitable Creation of MSC

*Let the word go forth from this time and place... that the
torch has been passed to a new generation of Americans—
born in this century, tempered by war, disciplined by a hard
and bitter peace, proud of our ancient heritage—and unwill-
ing to witness or permit the slow undoing of those human
rights to which this nation has always been committed, and
to which we are committed today...*
John F. Kennedy January 20, 1961

THE TORCH WAS PASSED

At 11:56 AM on May 5, 1963, the torch was passed to men and women with a radical
new concept of higher education. With legislators gathered around him, Colorado Governor
John Love signed House Bill 349 into law. This bill authorized the creation of the first public
four-year institution of higher education in the Denver metropolitan area, called Metropolitan
State College. It was not intended to be just another state college.

Legislators and others at the ceremony probably did not recognize the full significance of
the day. They could not have known that this new school would become one of the largest
four-year state-supported colleges in the nation.

Until Metropolitan State College opened, many high school graduates in Denver were un-
able to go to college because they could not afford the costs of housing on top of the tuition.
Many others were working and needed a college nearby so they could continue to work while
they attended school. Married persons could not uproot their families to live in Greeley, Gunnison, or Ft. Collins while they sought a degree.

Still others were denied a college education because they either messed up in high school, or were just "late bloomers," as Roy Romer, the chief proponent of MSC, called them. Disproportionately, children in minority households and poor families were the ones who were being denied an opportunity for a college education. Help was on the way.

The battle to pass HB349 was fierce. Even though Denver was home to over half of Colorado's population, it did not have a state-supported four-year college. Institutionalized self-interest, parochialism, benign neglect, and competition for scarce state tax dollars are the reasons that it took 103 years after Colorado became a Territory before its largest city would get a public four-year, degree-granting institution of higher education.

The struggle to create Metropolitan State College began long before that bill signing; and the struggle did not end with that ceremony. Even after the legislature created MSC, there were a string of attempts to keep it from being opened, and after it opened, multiple attempts to close it or merge it with the University of Colorado's Denver Center. Governor Love, who beamed from ear to ear while he signed HB349, flip-flopped several times before he signed that bill, and again before he allowed it to open, and even after it started operations.

Every roadblock that could possibly be put in the path of MSC was actually put in place. There were continual efforts by state legislators, spurred on by other institutions of higher education—most notably the University of Colorado—to hasten its demise.

Despite all those efforts, the fledgling institution survived, grew and prospered. A lesser institution populated by weaker people would not have survived; a less determined group of students, faculty, administrators, and legislators would have given up.

To understand the story of how Metropolitan State College came to be, we need to briefly examine the historical context in which it was created.

The period after the end of World War II brought about major changes in American society. Where and how Americans lived changed. In more and more families, both the husband and wife worked. The middle class was in ascendancy. People began moving from inner cities to suburbs to raise their children. Freeways began sprouting up to move people from suburbs to jobs in the city. A rise of commercialism meant many new products were invented every year that changed life in the home.

Television replaced radio as the main means of information and entertainment. Americans replaced their portable black and white TVs with 21-inch console models. If they could afford it, they bought a color TV, but few programs were broadcast in color. Still, in 1963, only 60 percent of the households in the nation even had a TV and very few homes had more than one.

Phones had dials, not buttons, and in some neighborhoods, party lines still existed. The term "party line" referred to a single phone line shared by several homes. One knew if the call was for them by the distinctive ring—a long and short, two longs, etc. Occasionally nosey neighbors eavesdropped. Cell phones only existed in science fiction movies and the Dick Tracy comic strip. Computers were new, few, and usually took up whole rooms.

The closest thing to a laptop was a TV tray with an electric typewriter on it. The Mickey Mouse Club and Sheriff Scotty were must-see-TV for boomers after school. Lucky boomers got a fancy new transistor radio for Christmas or their birthday. I-phones were not invented.

The Cold War was raging; nuclear war a possibility; Russia was a feared enemy. Young Vladimir Putin was still in diapers in 1963, possibly playing with a Stalin action figure. China was totally isolated from the West. American's TV cameras seldom got even a censored glimpse into what life was like in the world's most populous nation.

Back then, married women were often referred to by their husband's name, not their own; an unmarried women's name was usually followed by "daughter of...," especially in newspapers. In polite terms at least, African-Americans were called Negroes; Latinos were identified as Spanish-Americans. If your name appeared in a newspaper, it was always followed by your address. Few worried about privacy or identity theft in those days.

Segregation and Jim Crow were the law in southern states, and silently practiced in many localities in the North. The KKK was burning "Negro" churches; lynching was commonplace and un-punished. The Civil Rights Movement was just beginning to crest. Boycotts and sit-ins were occurring in the South at lunch counters and bus stations; freedom riders were attempting to register black voters and were being killed in the process.

It was shortly after HB349 passed in 1963 that the famous March on Washington took place at which Dr. Martin Luther King delivered the now famous "I Have a Dream" speech. The brutal attack on peaceful demonstrators and children in Birmingham inspired President Kennedy to introduce the Civil Rights Act that he would not live to see enacted.

By 1958, the Denver Tramway Company had replaced the last clean, quiet electric trolley with modern, smoke-belching diesel busses, in the name of progress. They abandoned their downtown car-barn at 13th and Lawrence for a new garage complex on South Santa Fe. That move freed up the space for the CU Denver Center to open a bookstore and classrooms in the old garage.

The Valley Highway was nearly finished from Colorado Blvd to 84th Ave—four lanes, two in each direction. They were building a turnpike to Boulder that cost 25 cents each way. The first passenger jet flew into Stapleton airport in 1961. Women were starting to drive in much greater numbers than their mother's generation.

In 1963, if someone said publically that there would be an African-American president in their lifetime, or that gays would be allowed to marry, or marijuana would be legal, they would be laughed at or maybe placed on a three-day hold in the psyche ward.

It was in this context that Colorado legislators took up the notion of Metropolitan State College. In the words of Bob Dylan in his 1963 hit: "The times, they are a changin'."

A PERFECT STORM MADE MSC INEVITABLE

Sometimes, events are more powerful than the men and women who seek to shape them. That was the case with Metropolitan State College. A perfect storm of demographic changes made the school inevitable. Regional politics, institutional jealousies and insufficient budgets made the opposition to Metro State inevitable as well.

The first element of the perfect storm was Colorado's post-war population growth. In 1940, the population of Denver was 322,412. Before the war, however, many people had moved to other states to find work, so population growth slowed to a trickle—adding fewer than 40,000 in the decade. As a result, development of infrastructure, especially educational facilities, slowed down.[3]

During World War II, however, Denver's population skyrocketed. In the decade between 1940 and 1950, the population grew almost 29 percent, from 322,412 to 415,786 residents. Many people moved to Denver during the war to work in the arms plant located where the Denver Federal Center is today. They liked it and stayed as did many in military who had been stationed at Fitzsimmons and Lowery.

After the war, the growth continued. The heroic 10th Mountain Division trained in Colorado during World War II. After the war, many veterans of that Division decided to move to Colorado. Some opened ski resorts, kicking off an economic boom no one could have imagined before the war.

During the 1950s, President Eisenhower located his second White House in Fraser, Colorado, and consequently the state was treated well by his administration. Ike, as the president was affectionately called, located the Air Force Academy in Colorado Springs and awarded many post-Sputnik rocket contracts to the Martin Company (now Lockheed Martin) in Littleton. This all helped spur new population growth in Colorful Colorado.

The Great Migration was also swelling the population of Colorado. African-Americans left the South and moved to the North and West, some to Denver. Likewise, there was a migration of people from rural areas to cities and suburbs. Young Americans were leaving farms to get an education and find work in the city. A large number of these moved to Colorado from Nebraska, Kansas, New Mexico, and Wyoming.

By 1960, Colorado's population had grown to 1,750,000, up 56 percent from 1940. Growth in the suburbs was even more phenomenal—Adams County's population increased nearly 79 percent; Arapahoe County, 62 percent; Boulder County, 29 percent; and Jefferson County, 83 percent.[4]

Denver had the most non-military federal employees of any city outside Washington DC by 1960. There was even talk of moving the U.S. Capitol to Denver—out of reach of Russian missiles. National TV coverage of Eisenhower fishing in the Fraser River, with a backdrop of the snow-capped mountains, was free publicity for the state.

This growth also meant a shift in where people lived. Twenty years earlier, one third of Colorado's residents lived in Denver, but by 1960 it was up to half. Denver residents contributed about half of the state's taxes but got back less than any other county in the state per capita.

The inequity was beginning to anger Denver residents, but despite having half the state's population, Denver had only 27 percent of the sixty five seats in the legislature. Small rural counties were disproportionately over-represented in the legislature. The principle of "one man, one vote" did not apply to the Colorado legislature in those days.

The second element of the perfect storm was the baby boom. After World War II, millions of GIs returned home, found jobs, and started families. That generation of postwar babies, subsequently called "baby boomers," entered first grade between 1952 and 1958. By 1963, the first wave began graduating from high school. The peak of the first wave was predicted to hit colleges and universities between the years 1965-1967.

The baby boom generation hit local school districts hard in the mid-1950s. School boards were forced to find money to expand existing schools and build new ones to accommodate this wave of new students. They had to recruit thousands of new teachers. Bond issues were passed and counties and towns appropriated money to get elementary and high schools through this first wave of boomers. Colorado was hardly prepared for the baby boom.

Something else was occurring: the baby boom generation was more highly motivated to attend college than previous generations. In 1960, the Institute of Public Opinion conducted a poll of college age students across the nation and found that 63 percent of them said they intend to go to college.[5]

In the 1960 survey, 64.8 percent of the boys and 61.3 percent of girls wanted to go to college. However, just three years later, 72 percent said they were going—75 percent of the boys and 69 percent of the girls. Only 14 percent of boys and 19 percent of girls said they did not want any higher education. The rest were undecided.

So, not only were there more young people graduating from high school, but a higher percentage of them wanted to go to college.

There was a third element in that perfect storm: the demand for a more educated work force. While Americans were rocking and rolling to Elvis, the Russians launched Sputnik into space, leaving America in the dust. The embarrassment forced the Eisenhower Administration and Congress to place a new emphasis on higher education. They realized the U.S. had to catch up, and it needed a better-educated work force to do so.

Since Colorado had the Martin Marietta Company and the Buckley Naval Air Station (as they were called back then), many support operations for the space program were located in Denver. Therefore, the demand for an educated workforce in Denver became acute. But, high school graduates in Denver were not enrolling in college in the numbers required to meet the demands of employers. The inability of the state to convince kids to enroll in college threatened commerce, industry, and private enterprise throughout the state, but especially in Denver.

In 1956, to meet this demand, the state legislature recommended increasing the number of two-year colleges in the state. Junior colleges were a "relatively inexpensive way for the state to satisfy the education cravings of Colorado without spending too much money, and equally important, without posing a threat to the state's senior institutions."[6]

Denver had the Emily Griffith Opportunity School, but kids in suburbs had no place to go for vocational training after high school. However, the space race between the U.S and the Soviet Union meant the state needed a work force with more than a two-year degree. It needed graduates with at least four years of college to compete in the new, rapidly changing world.

A fourth factor contributed to the perfect storm: the growing demand for equal educational opportunity and the inequities of opportunity at the time. When a legislative committee looked at the issue of equality of educational opportunity in Denver it found that high schools in more affluent white neighborhoods enrolled a higher percentage of their graduates in college than schools in poorer neighborhoods with a higher minority population.[7]

There were nearly twenty times as many graduates of George Washington High School, in the mostly white, upper-middle-class South Denver area that went to college than did graduates of West High, located in a poor, largely Hispanic inner-city neighborhood.

The percentage of Denver high school graduates who enrolled in college in 1962 from predominately white schools was: George Washington 77%, Thomas Jefferson 74%, East 64%, South 55%, and North High 42%. From low income or minority schools: Manual 26%, West High 4%.

There was also a collar-gap in college attendance. The legislative committee found that 83 percent of students in *the metropolitan* area whose parents were white-collar workers said they were going to enroll in college after graduation. On the other hand, only 41 percent of those whose parents were blue-collar said they were going to college. It also discovered that the high school dropout rate was higher among "Negro and Spanish-American kids," due to a number of factors including lack of funds for tuition and books.[8]

The committee's study found that college attendance was significantly more prevalent in the Colorado counties that had a tax-supported college than ones that did not. Only a handful of Denver's high school graduates enrolled in college. In counties with a state college, by contrast, the percentage of high school graduates who went to college was 25 percent higher than in Denver.[9]

There were no state-run institutions in Denver to educate students beyond high school in 1960. The nearest state-supported school was the Colorado School of Mines in Golden—an engineering school. The University of Colorado was in Boulder—considered a long drive back then. There was an extension of the University of Colorado in Denver, but its program was limited and it did not offer degree programs—a student had to go to Boulder for that.

The only other colleges in Denver were private schools—University of Denver, Regis College, Loreto Heights, Colorado Woman's College (which became Temple Buell), and the Westminster School of Law. These schools were small, and tuition was high. Many of the students enrolled in them were from out-of-state.

In earlier times, this inequity of educational opportunity was acceptable. In the early 1960s, however, it wasn't. African-Americans had decided that the days of legal and institutional racism were over. They began demanding more equality of opportunity for higher education. Chicanos, as many of Hispanic heritage preferred to be called at the time, also began demanding equal educational opportunity. And the parents of middle-class baby boomers were not content to see their children denied a college education either.

So, the rapid population growth in the state from migration and the baby boom; the fact that baby boomers wanted to go to college in higher numbers than their parents' generation; the need of the business community in Denver for an educated work force; and the demands for more equality of opportunity for higher education during the civil rights era all combined to make Metropolitan State College inevitable. The only way this was going to be addressed was for Denver to have its own state-run college.

LEGISLATIVE GROUNDWORK

Metropolitan State College can trace its roots back to 1958 when two state legislators—Representatives John Mackie from Boulder County and Allen Dines from Denver—proposed House Joint Resolution 6, which created the "Legislative Committee on Education Beyond High School." Its charge was to make a broad comprehensive study of the whole field of education beyond high school in the state of Colorado. The resolution was passed on January 31, and the new committee started work that spring.[10]

Elections had an impact on higher education in Colorado that year. Republicans had put a measure on the ballot in 1958 that would have made Colorado a right-to-work state. To their surprise, that issue fired up labor unions and Democratic voters who turned out at the polls in unusually large numbers and swept many Republicans out of office. Democrats gained control of both houses of the state legislature and re-elected Democrat Steve McNichols as governor.

This was significant for Metropolitan State College because one Democrat who came to the legislature in the wave of 1958 was Roy Romer.

Newly elected Representative Romer was a Denver attorney when he won his seat in the Colorado House of Representatives. Romer was born in Kansas, but his family moved to Holly, Colorado, where he was raised. He received a degree in agricultural economics from CSU and a law degree from CU. He had served as a legal officer in the Air Force before moving to Denver to practice law.

With majorities in both Houses of the legislature, Democrats concerned with education were able to get more aggressive. In the 1960 session, the legislature created a sub-committee to the Legislative Committee on Education Beyond High School to study the need for higher education in metropolitan Denver. Representative Romer was chosen to head that subcommittee.

This was significant because legislators from rural districts had historically blocked development of institutions of higher education in Denver, choosing instead to keep colleges and universities, and the money they generate, in rural counties.

Representative Romer and his colleagues had to deal with the demographic changes occurring in Denver. They had a vision for a new college. As early as 1960, still in his first term, Romer said that it would be better for his constituents to create a four-year college in Denver that the state would fund rather than a junior college which would be the responsibility of local property taxpayers. Romer was aware it would take great political skill to accomplish this, but he and his colleagues were up to the task.

While the sub-committee deliberated in the summer and fall of 1960, other things diverted attention away from higher education. Adolph Coors, heir to the famous brewery, was kidnapped and murdered. A team called the Denver Broncos was among eight teams selected for the start-up American Football League. On September 9, the Broncos went to Boston and defeated the Boston Patriots 13-10 in the first official AFL game in history. The big take-aways from that game were the Pats' deflated footballs and the Broncos' vertically striped socks.

The next week, the Broncos made their Denver debut in Bears Stadium in front of a crowd of 18,732 fans where they defeated the hated Oakland Raiders. However, the Broncos only won one more game that season, finishing with the worst record in the AFL at 9-4-1. Nevertheless, Broncomania now occupied Sunday afternoons during the fall.

That October, presidential candidate John F. Kennedy visited Denver. His motorcade travelled from Stapleton Airport to downtown Denver via E.32nd avenue, now Martin Luther King Blvd., past Curé d' Ars Catholic school. The nuns let the students out to watch the motorcade pass. The convertible in which Kennedy was riding slowed allowing students to touch or shake hands with the senator. One of those was a sixth grader, Robert Bowen. He made eye contact with the youthful John Kennedy, and from that moment he became politically active.

Roy Romer was re-elected in 1960. In early 1961, the legislature determined that the state needed more junior colleges but not more four-year schools. Their goal in pushing junior colleges was to pass the buck and shift the costs to local school districts.

In the spring of '61, while the subcommittee was working, the East Germans, with Russian assistance, built a wall to seal off West Berlin from Germany. President Kennedy responded by increasing the U.S. military presence, thus forcing the East Germans and Russians agree to allow access to West Berlin through East Germany.

In May that same year, Alan Shepherd became the first American to go into space for a 15-minute ride in a capsule he named "Freedom." On May 25, President John F. Kennedy addressed a Joint Session of Congress and stated that the United States should set as a goal "landing a man on the moon and returning him safely to the earth by the end of the decade." Kennedy urged the U.S. to work diligently to lead the achievements of space travel because, as he said, "in many ways space may hold the key to our future here on earth."[11]

Colorado's Martin Marietta Company and other suppliers played a major role in the moon shot. They and other business groups began putting pressure on the legislature to do something about the higher educational system in the Denver metro area. The editorial pages of the two daily newspapers, however, were still advocating for new junior colleges in Denver. In the fall, a new class of baby boomers entered high school.

By the end of 1961, the Sub-Committee on Education Beyond High School in Denver had completed studies showing that that there was a shortage of trained manpower in math and science in the Denver area and it was hurting business. The Denver Chamber of Commerce, headed by insurance company executive Shelby Harper, was pressing the legislative committee to recommend a new four-year college be opened in Denver to increase the number of people trained in math and science.

In the 1962 session, legislators on the sub-committee were concerned that the crush of baby boomer high school graduates was actually greater than expected. Romer told the sub-committee the state was "running out of time." They responded by setting up the Task Group on Education Beyond High School in Denver to make recommendations to the legislature.

One of the members of that task group was a new state representative from Denver named Mark Hogan. He would later play a key role in the establishment of the college.

While the task group was doing its work in 1962, other things once again grabbed the attention of all Americans. In mid-October, the U.S. military flew a U2 spy plane over Cuba and noticed suspicious activity. As it turned out, the Russians were in the final stages of building a nuclear missile base capable of launching missiles that could hit major U.S. cities. This set off the Cuban Missile Crisis. For a few days, nuclear war was a very real possibility. In fact, today we know that we were closer to nuclear war than we thought at the time.

Mid-term elections were being held across the country that fall. In Colorado, there was a major contest for U.S. Senate and Governor. Governor Steve McNichols was defeated by an unknown newcomer, Republican John Love. Voters also passed a ballot issue to re-apportion the state legislature and Republicans took back control. The election of Love and the Republican majority would have an impact on MSC. Despite the fact it was a Republican year, Romer was elected to the State Senate.

The task group predicted the new explosion of students graduating from high school would come in two waves. The first wave would occur in 1964 and 1965; the second between

1970 and 1971. They reported that the 8,300 high school grads in 1961 would increase to 18,600 by 1971. For this reason they wanted the new college in Denver up and running by 1964 and to graduate its first class in 1968.[12]

On November 26, 1962, Senator Romer got his wish. The task group, with Rep. Mackie of Boulder dissenting, agreed to recommend to the full sub-committee, the creation of a new four-year college in Denver and also establish a "graduate center" to be operated by the Denver Extension of the University of Colorado. The new four-year institution would be called Metropolitan State College.

In the fall of 1962, Doug Holcombe was a senior at Adams City High School, Roger Braun was a junior at Norton High School in Kansas, and Richard Castro was a sophomore at Annunciation High School in Denver. Unbeknownst to these future MSC students, things were about to happen that would change their futures.

THE STRUGGLE BEGINS

This was the beginning of the fight to create MSC—a fight Roy Romer said was the toughest fight of his entire career. "We overcame that [opposition] over a year or two or three, but it was one of the tougher fights I had in my Colorado political career," Romer recalled in a conversation with is friend Sheldon Steinhauser in 2012.[13]

"This was a real fight, and I'm not the only one involved. It was a bipartisan effort, but I was the point person in a fight with a very good friend of mine. The University of Colorado tried to kill this institution multiple times. I just have to be frank about it," Romer stated.

Since the voters had elected a new governor, John Love, and a Republican legislature, the task group decided to delay the release of their recommendations until February 1963, in order to allow time to consult with the new governor and the new legislative leaders.[14]

The University of Colorado immediately began a systematic campaign attacking the unreleased recommendations of the task group. CU used its connections to get articles printed in the objecting to the proposal to pre-empt the task group.

Jack Gaskie's article in the *News*, "Denver College Feared Mecca for Rejects," was critical of the proposed college's open door admission policy. He wrote, [Metro] "...unlike the state's colleges it would admit any and all high school graduates. All other colleges follow the two-thirds rule, only admitting students from the top two thirds of their class." He was reflecting the opinion of many at that time that the students in the bottom third were not entitled to a college education.[15]

A few days later, Robert Chase filed a piece the *News* entitled, "Back Door Sneak." He said that Colorado had too many colleges and scattered them over the state for geographical and political considerations rather than in the interest of better education. He suggested building a new college in Denver was "playing the same political game." He reminded readers that Boulder was part of metropolitan Denver, inferring metropolitan Denver already had a university, so why did it need a college?[16]

On December 4, the Colorado University regents said they were opposed to a new four-year school because their Denver Extension could serve any needs that Denver had. This irritated Senator Romer, who replied, "If the University of Colorado is to attain its announced goal of becoming a great university with greater emphasis on graduate programs and research, it should not be asked to run a general college in downtown Denver."[17]

Undaunted, CU spoke to the editorial boards of the daily newspapers and planted concerns that the new college would be second class, even though no one had any way to know that. As a result, on December 16, *The Denver Post* printed an editorial saying that more junior colleges would be a much better alternative for the state and Denver than a new four-year college.[18]

Three days later, the CU newspaper, *The Colorado Daily*, reported that the Board of Regents had voted to oppose the recommendations of the task group.[19] Next, the CU Faculty Senate added their half a cent's worth to the discussion, passing a resolution stating that the establishment of any college in Denver, independent of the University of Colorado, was "unrealistic and not economically or academically feasible."[20]

On December 22, the student government of the CU Denver Extension passed a resolution opposing creation of the new four-year school in Denver. "We will not tolerate a second-class degree from a second-class institution when a first- class degree from a first-class institution is more readily available," CU's Student Council President, Allan Sheline, said. He blasted Roy Romer and the task group for not soliciting the students' opinion at the CU Extension, but he admitted that students had not attended any open hearings of the task group.[21]

This CU claim about accreditation was not true, however. It was reported on New Year's Day that the body that accredits colleges and universities, the North Central Association, said that if the CU Extension began offering degrees, and not just classes, it might threaten CU Boulder's own accreditation. In fact, CU's accreditation might be in jeopardy whether the new college was created or not. So, this showed that the opposite of CU's claim was actually true.[22]

Representative Palmer Burch responded, saying that the new Denver college could get accredited in one year because the rules had been changed. "The gentlemen [CU regents] have not done their homework," he asserted. While CU was fighting the new college, their own accreditation was on shaky grounds, Burch pointed out.

The North Central Association had, in fact, changed the rules the previous year. Under the new rules, a new institution could obtain accreditation as early as the first year of operation, so long as all work completed by students was equivalent to that of a fully accredited institution. Burch noted correctly that university branches like the CU Denver Extension were questioned.[23]

In the waning days of 1962, Romer and his task group members won a battle against the behemoth in Boulder. The Association of State Supported Institutions in Colorado released a blueprint for higher education that detailed the functions of each higher education institution in Colorado. Romer said that this was the first time all the institutions agreed in writing what their functions would be.

"The task group's recommendation for a four-year college in Denver is consistent with that blueprint," Romer said. "However, establishing a branch of the University of Colorado with an open-door admissions policy is not consistent with the blueprint," he said. The blueprint stated that institutions with a doctorate program shall not have an open admission policy.[24]

As 1962 ended, the University of Colorado Buffaloes finished their season with a 2-8 record, in contrast to their 9-2 season and Orange Bowl appearance in 1961. The big news, however, was that the Broncos had been sitting in first place at 7-2 through the first nine games of the season. However, they would lose their final five games and finish with a 7-7 record. Coach Jack Faulkner was named Coach of the Year despite the record

In 1962, 16,000 military advisors celebrated New Year's Eve in Saigon. On the recommendations of the Pentagon and Vice-President Johnson, President Kennedy had authorized 15,000 additional military advisors to bolster the 900 sent by Presidents Truman and Eisenhower, beginning in 1950. He should have listened to his gut.

1963: THE DIE WAS CAST

As 1963 began, Roy Romer launched a counterattack against CU's opposition to the proposed new college. He told *the Rocky Mountain News* that only one percent of the freshmen entering CU Boulder were from the bottom third of their class, but at the CU Denver Extension, the number was 43 percent. Turning the Extension into a degree-granting institution would create a disparity between it and the Boulder campus. The current admissions policy at the Extension would violate the blueprint, Romer said.[25]

Romer continued his offensive at a debate with CU Regent Dick Bernick before the Denver Young Democrats. Romer said, "We can no longer think of education beyond high school as being only for the academic elite."

On January 8, Attorney General Duke Dunbar stunned CU when he made an official ruling: a four-year branch of the University of Colorado in Denver was unconstitutional. Despite his ruling, the attorney general said that the matter should be submitted to the Supreme Court, due to the contention surrounding CU's Denver Extension. Until then, he said, neither the regents nor the legislature could establish a four-year, degree-granting institution at the Denver Extension.[26]

CU's president, former Denver mayor Quigg Newton, urged the regents to appeal the Dunbar ruling to the state court. The student council at the CU Denver Center said Attorney General Dunbar "did not understand the constitution." [27]

Things looked hopeful for supporters of the new college in light of the attorney general's ruling. That hope lasted only 10 days, however. On January 11, newly-elected Governor Love gave his first State of the State message to the legislature. He said emphatically that he would "oppose funding for any new four-year schools until a new master plan to examine duplication was done." [28]

Love was clearly rejecting years of detailed and exhaustive studies the legislature's Committee on Education Beyond High School had done. The CU regents whispered in his ear.

Democratic legislators blasted Governor Love for his position. *The Rocky Mountain News* reported that Senator Roy Romer was shaken by Love's declaration against the new four-year Denver State University, as the *News* called it. "This is the most important decision the state faces," Romer said. "To delay a decision will close college doors on hundreds of students in the four-county area." College enrollments would triple in the next ten years, with half of the new students coming from the Denver area. [29]

Supporters of the new college fought back. They lined up a group of endorsements. Palmer Burch persuaded Kenneth Oberholtzer, the Superintendent of Denver Public Schools, to speak out in favor of the college. Various other organizations also came out in support. Romer told Denver's prestigious City Club that the legislature needed to act fast. [30]

The CU propaganda machine was not sitting still. Eleven members of the staff of the CU Denver Extension sent a letter to the legislature opposing the recommendation of the task group that a new four-year college be established. They said the economics of the proposal were "unrealistic."

They were trying to scare people, saying that a degree issued by Metropolitan State College would be of questionable value for at least five years because of accreditation problems. The letter claimed the proposed programs of the college do not meet the needs of *the metropolitan* area. They also panned the task group's recommendation of a Denver graduate program at the CU Extension, calling it unworkable. The CU staff ignored the fact North Central had changed the rules on accreditation.

Eleven days after Governor Love threw water on any new four-year schools in his State of the State address, he told *the Rocky Mountain News* that he predicted that Denver would have an "institute of learning before his term ends in 1967." That, of course, was four years away. Yet the first baby boom wave was only one year away. [31]

The Committee on Education Beyond High School met on February 5, and voted to accept the Denver Task Group proposal and advance that recommendation to the legislature. The report stated in part: "By acting now, the margin of time can be used for well-planned, wisely developed, integrated educational response. What is done must meet distinctive metropolitan needs and provide for stable growth and development of the state educational system as a whole." [32]

Representative John Mackie of Boulder dissented from the task group's recommendation because, he said, the legislature should not set up a "second rate" institution at the outset. It was now apparent that the tactic of CU was to continually refer to Metropolitan State College as inferior, even though it had not even been established. It is not clear how much of this was pure arrogance and elitism and how much was simply a tactic.[33]

Then, the Association of State Institutions of Higher Education in Colorado (the precursor to the Colorado Commission on Higher Education CCHE), announced its support for the new college. CU regent Quigg Newton dissented from the resolution of support. The Association also recommended the legislature phase out the CU Extension in Denver as Metropolitan State College advanced.

Senator Romer hailed the support of the Association as a "significant event," and stated that never before had there been such agreement on need of a new state college in Colorado. Romer noted the group recommended that Metro State open in 1963—a year earlier than his own task force suggested.[34]

Ray Jenkins, Chairman of the Downtown Denver Master Plan Committee (DDMPC), also set the stage for the launch when he said the legislature should establish the college in downtown to meet needs of *the post*-high-school bulge. This support from a business group would help firm up some Republican votes.[35]

MSC IS CONCEIVED: HB349 IS ADOPTED

On February 25, two Denver legislators—Representative Palmer Burch, a Republican, and Senator Roy Romer, a Democrat—introduced House Bill 349 (HB349). That bill would authorize the creation of Metropolitan State College as a four-year state college to be located in Denver.

The initial House sponsors of the bill in addition to Rep. Burch were: Representatives Alan Dines (D-Denver), Frank Evans (D-Pueblo), William Griffith (R-Denver), Don Friedman (R-Denver), Jean Bain (R-Denver), Joseph Albi (R-Denver), Thomas Dameron (D-Pueblo), Vince Massari (D-Pueblo), and Mark Hogan (D-Denver).

The bill provided for creation of a two-year school in Denver which would become a four-year, degree-granting institution by 1970, subject to legislative approval. The legislation, as introduced, provided a $100,000 appropriation for planning, and stipulated that it would open in the fall of 1964.

HB349 called for the curriculum to be "liberal arts and sciences as well as voc-tech," and would be governed by the Trustees of State Colleges. It was to be an urban-oriented school with no dormitories, fraternities, sororities, or inter-collegiate athletics, and have an open-door admission policy.

The bill, however, omitted one of the Task Group's recommendations—that Metropolitan State College acquire the University of Colorado Extension in Denver and house graduate programs offered by CU. Representative Burch and Senator Romer feared that provision would give ammunition to CU to sink the bill.[36]

The battle to pass HB349 began immediately after introduction. Burch and Romer knew that there were some natural enemies including legislators who represented towns and counties with existing state colleges or universities. Those included Boulder, Larimer, Weld, and Pueblo counties along with, Trinidad, the San Luis Valley and the Western Slope. These legislators were under pressure in their districts to prevent a new college from diverting students and state money away from the institutions in their districts.

Other enemies of the bill were rural and suburban legislators that voted against everything they saw as benefiting Denver. In addition, many Republicans simply opposed any new program that cost money.

This list of natural enemies did not leave many votes in play. A strategy had to be developed to take votes from the enemy camp, in part by old-fashioned horse trading (not to be confused with "vote trading," which is against the law). The MSC supporters won backing from Democrats in southern Colorado by supporting the four-year college in Pueblo. Since the bill establishing MSC put it under the Trustees of State Colleges, the trustees helped deliver support from legislators representing other colleges they governed.

As soon as the bill was introduced, however, CU pulled out all stops to derail it. Four faculty members from the CU Denver Extension (John Chapman Jr., Assistant Dean of Arts and Sciences; Michael Mandell, a math instructor; Dr. Wayne Marshal, Assistant Professor of Chemistry; and William Petrowski, a history instructor) held a news conference opposing the bill.

They wanted the legislature to expand the CU Denver Extension instead. The university's regents and its president worked the legislature behind the scenes, meeting with legislators—particularly CU alumni—lobbying them on the bill.[37]

CU had another stalling tactic up its sleeve. In response to the attorney general's constitutional concerns, they arranged for a constitutional amendment to be introduced in the legislature that would ask voters to allow CU to offer a four-year degree program at the Denver Center.

The Dean of Law at CU, Edward King, assumed that this would delay the Metro bill for two years until voters decided on that constitutional question. As we will see, the legislature didn't buy the dean's argument.[38]

The advocates of MSC were working hard as well. The superintendent of Jefferson County Schools and task group member, Dr. Forbes Bottomly, spoke out in support of the bill. He said there will be "three times as many college-bound students in 1971 as there were in 1962," and the existing state-supported schools could not handle this kind of surge.

The House Education Committee took up the bill on March 23, and as anticipated, the opposition was ready. Representative William Lennox (R-Colorado Springs) offered an amendment to strike the language in the bill that required that the CU Denver Extension be phased out as Metropolitan State College advanced. Lennox supported the regents because there was a CU Extension in his hometown of Colorado Springs.

The Committee chair, Representative Ruth Clark (R-Ft. Collins), argued against eliminating the phase-out of the Denver Center because the state couldn't afford two state-supported colleges in Denver—the CU Denver Center and MSC. Consequently, the Lennox amendment failed. Then Rep. Ted Rubin (R-Denver) offered an amendment to require that the CU Denver Extension develop any new school in Denver and operate it as a branch of CU. That amendment failed as well. With Chairwoman Clark's support, the committee passed the bill out of the committee.[39]

Unfortunately, eight committee members from the Denver metropolitan area voted for the Lennox amendment. They were: Representatives Bob Eberhardt (D-Denver), Ben Klein (D-Denver), Andrew Kelley (D-Denver); Joseph Scheifflein (R-Jeff), Ruth Stockton (R-Jeff), William Myick (R-Arapahoe) Bill Armstrong (R-Arapahoe) and Reginald Howard (R-Boulder). Representatives Andrew Kelley, Ben Klein, Joseph Scheifflein and Ruth Stockton ended up voting for the bill.

After the bill advanced out of the Education Committee, *The Denver Post* wrote an editorial urging support, citing Representative Clark's declaration that the state could not afford two schools in Denver. *The Post* said that CU was moving toward offering advanced professional graduate programs and MSC would have liberal arts and voc-tech programs, which Denver sorely needed. Was this a permanent change in *The Post's* position? Not really, as we'll see.[40]

Suddenly, it looked like supporters of the Metro bill were getting another big break. Governor Love surprisingly flip-flopped again and gave his support to the MSC bill. The Governor said in an interview that there had been "some amelioration in his feelings." He admitted that he had previously said "no new colleges until he completed a master plan," but now he was persuaded that delaying MSC too long would "prevent us from having the facilities ready when large numbers of students arrive—and they are quickly on us." [41]

Many did not understand that Love foreshadowed the future, however, when he added: "This is an acceptable compromise. It will not commit us to establishing a college. But it will give us the flexibility to move quickly if our study shows need."

HB349 came to the floor for second reading on March 30. Representative Lennox introduced the same amendment he offered in committee. It failed again on a 31-31 tie—three representatives did not vote. The hearts of MSC supporters were racing because it was not clear the Senate would have removed that amendment if it had passed. When the speaker announced that the motion failed, there was a sigh in the House gallery and lobby.

Rep. Ted Rubin then re-offered the amendment he had previously offered in committee, to designate that the CU Denver Extension would operate the new four-year college. Just as in committee, however, Rubin's amendment failed by a large margin. After amendments were dealt with, the bill passed second reading on a voice vote.

The newspapers showed their bias by characterizing the passage of the bill as "the death knell for the CU Denver Extension Center," rather than something like "Bill to Advance Metropolitan State College Passes."[42]

Two days later, on April 1, HB349 came up for third reading. Permission was granted for a third reading amendment that reduced the $100,000 planning appropriation by half. That money was intended for the trustees to use for planning the opening the college. After adoption of the amendment, the House, by a 52-10 vote, passed the bill creating Metropolitan State College. The bill then went to the Senate.

In the end, 22 Democrats and 30 Republicans voted for the bill; one Democrat and nine Republicans voted no, three were absent. In *the metropolitan* area, 20 representatives voted yes and five voted no with one absent. Among out-state representatives, 31 voted yes, six no, and 2 were absent.[43]

Senator Romer expressed his feelings about the victory saying, "Forget the fight. What was important is did we create an institution that enabled a bigger slice of America to get an opportunity to have good education? And we've done that."

An angry buffalo is hard to stop, and the CU regents were certainly angry. After HB349 passed the House, the regents voted to request a meeting with Governor Love to brief him on the ramifications of the bill.[44]

Two hundred irate CU Extension students showed up at the Capitol and protested on the steps, carrying signs and shouting slogans. They were supporting an expansion of the Denver Extension and opposed to establishment of MSC. They were angry because the bill required CU to phase out the under-graduate operations at the Denver Center as Metro State moved forward.[45]

Representative Lennox addressed the angry students, and riled them up when he told them that Governor Love flip-flopped. He said that, initially, Love stated he was against any new colleges but now he favored the bill. Lennox suggested students let the governor know their opinion. This was the beginning of student activism concerning Metropolitan State College, even though these student activists intended to stop the new college in its tracks.

This was one of those moments when the old saying, "it isn't over until it's over" rings true. The seemingly lopsided victory in the House did not necessarily insure victory in the Senate.

When the bill reached the Senate, it got off to a rough start. On April 4, the bill came before the Senate Finance Committee, chaired by Senator Harry Locke, (R-Hartsel). The CU regents came to the committee armed with a resolution supported by Regents Phillip Danielson, Charles Bromley, Richard Bernick and Dale Atkins. The resolution specifically opposed the provision that required the phase-out of the CU Denver Extension as an undergrad school.

In testimony, the regents said that the CU Denver Extension could meet the educational demands of Denver "better, cheaper, and quicker" than a separate college. Regent Bernick said Metro was a terrible plan and what they were doing to replace CU Denver Center wouldn't be good for the people of Denver. "They won't be able to offer the variety and quality of subjects that the Denver Center can."[46]

Regent Atkins said the plan was a "great injustice to the 6,000 kids down there [at the Denver Center]. I hope they don't do this until we get a chance to meet with the governor and discuss it." Regent Bromley said he would fight it and he thought it should be decided in a general election. Bromley complained that for four years the regents were trying to get the university to support the Denver Center, but they had not gotten enthusiastic support.[47]

Several CU Extension students and faculty members also testified against the establishment of Metropolitan State College. Their testimony generally mimicked the regents', but they seemed to have more standing since they were students. Their pitch: the CU Denver Center could do a better job than a new college.

Senator Locke brought the bill up for a vote and to the chagrin of Metro supporters; it failed to advance on a 7-7 tie. Chairman Locke said the Committee Report would be sent to the Senate and if there was enough support, the Senate could amend the Committee Report to say it actually passed.

Although a rarity, that is exactly what happened. The next morning the Report of the Senate Finance Committee was read. A motion was made to amend it, showing that HB349 did indeed pass. The motion carried. The bill was then debated on second reading; it passed by a voice vote, after it was amended to reduce the planning money to $25,000. The following day, April 6, 1963, HB349 was adopted on third reading 22-11 and sent to the governor.

In the Senate, eleven Democrats and eleven Republicans voted yes, two Democrats and eight Republicans voted no and three were absent. Out of the senators from *the metropolitan* area, nine voted yes, two voted no and one was absent.

A month later, on May 5, 1963, Governor John A. Love signed the bill creating Metropolitan State College in Denver, Colorado. Less than five months earlier Love said he was opposed to the creation of any new four year colleges.[48]

The thinking of the visionaries that day could be summed up in Simon and Garfunkel's future hit:

> *"And I think it's gonna be all right. Yeah, the worst is over now.*
> *The morning sun is shining like a red rubber ball."*

- "Red Rubber Ball" Simon, Paul/Woodley, Bruce 1966

That month, Doug Holcombe graduated from Adams City High School and enrolled in Colorado State College in Greeley, the first leg of his journey that would bring him to Metropolitan State College where he would make significant contributions.

HB 349 was signed into law May 5, 1963. It created Metro State College.

Photo Courtesy of Metropolitan State University of Denver.

BY REPRESENTATIVES BURCH, DINES, EVANS, BYRNE, GRIFFITH, FRIEDMAN, BAIN, ALBI, DAMERON, V. MASSARI, and HOGAN; also SENATOR ROMER.

HOUSE BILL NO. 349

CONCERNING THE SYSTEM OF HIGHER EDUCATION IN THE STATE OF COLORADO, AND "METROPOLITAN STATE COLLEGE" AS A COMPONENT PART OF SUCH SYSTEM.

BE IT ENACTED BY THE GENERAL ASSEMBLY OF THE STATE OF COLORADO:

SECTION 1. Chapter 124, Colorado Revised Statutes 1953, as amended, is hereby amended BY THE ADDITION OF A NEW ARTICLE 20, to read:

ARTICLE 20

METROPOLITAN STATE COLLEGE

124-20-1. PURPOSE. The general assembly hereby declares that this act is passed in conformity with the plan for the development of higher education in this state, which includes a system of state general colleges, whose functions shall principally be those of undergraduate education, a system of universities and special-purpose institutions conducting extensive graduate and research programs, as well as providing courses in undergraduate education, and a system of junior colleges. In conformity with such general plan, Metropolitan State College shall be a part of the state general college system.

124-20-2. CONTROL, OBJE... AND PURPOSES. Metropolit... ...llege shall be under the con... ...trustees of the... ...do and its

19

CHAPTER 2

The Struggle Continues...

Mama, take this badge off o' me
I can't use it anymore
It's gettin' dark, too dark to see
I feel I'm knockin' on Heaven's door
"Knockin' on Heaven's Door"
Bob Dylan[49]

In May of 1963 the groups that supported Metropolitan State College were gleeful. The governor had just signed the bill creating the institution. The legislature appropriated money for planning so Metro State could open in the fall of 1964. MSC's new governing board, the Board of Trustees, was anxious to find a temporary campus to open a new institution of higher education. One year was a short time. The trustees were knocking at heaven's door, thinking the battle was over and that they had won.

Then, Governor Love threw a knuckle ball. He refused to release the planning money the legislature appropriated because he had yet to see the master plan his higher education consultant was working on.

MORE STUDIES...SERIOUSLY?

It is typical behavior for politicians to demand a new study before they actually do something. Higher education in Colorado had already been studied extensively by the bi-partisan committee of legislators, educators, and members of the business community. Tax dollars were spent on exhaustive demographic studies and the latest education programs that were achieving success. The committee determined what the educational needs were in Colorado and came up with a comprehensive plan to address those needs.

Then there was an election in 1962 and all the work, all the money, and all the time that had been spent went in the Capitol's trash dumpster, so to speak.

All that Governor Love needed to do was to execute the legislature's plan. There was no reason to waste time and money on a new study—particularly when, as we shall see, the new study concluded the same things as the legislature's comprehensive study. But, he wanted to make more work for consultants.

Love named Dr. John Dale Russell to advise him on higher education, and produce a new master plan. There was a lot of noise floating around that the state should just help school districts build junior colleges to solve the influx of baby boomers. Love asked Dr. Russell to investigate that issue in particular because he did not want to waste money on a new four-year college if an expanded system of junior colleges was really the way to go.[50]

Dr. Russell gave his report to the Governor on June 30 and it seemed to contain good news for MSC. He examined a Michigan study that found that the cost of a junior college was just as high as a four-year college.

Russell found the cost for educating freshman and sophomores was $745 per year in a university and $700 per year in a state college. This compared with $700 per year for academic studies in a junior college and $945 per year for vocational education in a junior college. As a result, there was no big savings to be gained by replacing Metropolitan State College with a junior college, despite the hopeful expectations of the governor.

Russell also found that building junior colleges would not absolve the state from needing to build four-year colleges as well. He said a junior college is intended to increase *total attendance* in higher education, not drain off students from four-year colleges. A four-year college would still be needed in Denver even if junior colleges were built. This backed up the Legislature's Task Group on Post High School Education in Denver, which made the same points.[51]

Furthermore, Russell indicated that building junior colleges to provide the first two years of higher education for students wanting a four-year degree short changed those students. He found that students who transferred to the University of Colorado from junior colleges made lower grades and dropped out in greater numbers than those who started their freshman year there.

Russell said the notion of junior colleges sharing facilities with high schools did not work out well either. This debunked another notion floating around at the time that Metro could use high schools at night and on weekends rather than renting its own buildings.

Even though the master plan was completed, Governor Love still refused to release the $25,000 planning money the legislature appropriated for MSC. Love liked it both ways. He appeased MSC supporters when he said that he supported planning for Metro; then he appeased CU by not cutting loose with the funds. Already, two crucial months had been lost by this indecisiveness.

THE STOP-MSC COALITION STRIKES

MSC's proponents may have missed the storm clouds building up on the horizon after their legislative victory. The CU regents were busy working to derail Metro's planned opening and the governor was on board.

Before he received his first report from Dr. Russell, Governor Love told a group in Lamar that state's four-year colleges would have to tighten admission requirements to deal with the influx of new students. The cheapest way to avoid building a new school to handle the influx of baby boomers was simply do not let them in.[52]

Love's statement was a rebuke of Metro's anticipated open door admissions policy. The bill authorizing MSC had provided for open enrollment for anyone with a high school diploma or a GED. During the Metro debate, Love had said he wanted to expand the number of junior colleges to accommodate the influx of students. When his master plan was complete and he learned there was no huge savings in doing that, he looked to tighter admission policies to solve the baby boom problem.

On July 18, Senator Roy McVicker of Jefferson County wandered into the mix when he told *The Denver Post* he thought building a four-year college in Denver would cause a "money squeeze" for the other colleges and universities in the state. Nothing stirs up resentment faster than hearing a legislator say the new school was going to take money away from an existing school's budget.[53]

Responding to these developments, the Legislative Committee on Education Beyond High School voted unanimously to demand that Governor Love release the money the legislature appropriated for Metro's planning.[54]

A little over a week later, Dr. Joseph Smiley, CU's newly appointed president, said in an interview that people in America "attach too much credit to a college degree. "We need to realize *everyone* does not need a degree," Smiley said, taking a shot at the argument that Metro was needed to provide the un-served graduates in Denver an opportunity for a college education. His comments insinuated that poor kids and minorities did not need a degree.[55]

The next day, Dr. Smiley attacked Russell's plan—particularly the provisions arguing against any branches for CU. Senator Woody Hewitt, a Republican from Boulder, also took another shot at the whole concept of the new college in Denver, even though it was thought to be a settled issue.[56]

To counter the unexpected CU blitz, Bernard Houtchens, the new Chairman of the Board of Trustees of State Colleges, did an interview with the *Colorado Daily*—CU's student newspaper at that time. He reminded everyone that it was the intent of the legislature to eventually eliminate the University of Colorado's Denver Extension and the trustees were obligated to follow the legislature's intentions. His remarks went over like a lead balloon.[57]

The attacks by CU continued throughout the summer. Every few days there was a new statement by some CU official, or a news release, all pushing back against the implementation of HB349.

As the summer dragged on, legislators, the trustees, and certain Denver business and labor leaders began putting pressure on Governor Love to release the planning money. Finally, on August 10, Love relented and released the funds. As they began reading the governor's statement, MSC supporters were delighted because he said this:

> *"In 1965 there will be a greatly increased number of people just out of high school clamoring for post high school educational opportunities. More than half of them live in the Denver metropolitan area which at present does not have any state-supported facilities necessary to care for them. Many of these boys and girls will be financially unable to attend already established state institutions in the region. The prime need in the Denver area by 1965 will be for a publically supported college with a strong emphasis on technological and vocational courses of two years extent, and an open door policy permitting any high school graduate to take the first two years of college academic work in an attempt to qualify for a further college or university career."*

But Love didn't end his statement there. He flip-flopped again. After making a strong case for opening Metro, he said "never mind" by adding, "As for Metro, I want to delay it so the people and my office can deliberate and debate the matter." The governor said that he only released the funds so that if the decision was made to go ahead with Metro, more time would not be lost waiting for the planning to be completed. [58]

The announcement stunned MSC supporters. They held strategy meetings over the next few months to decide a course of action while the trustees moved ahead with planning—an exercise made very difficult by this uncertainty. As the fall semester drew to a close, hundreds if not thousands, of Denver high school students in the class of 1964 began applying for college. They did not know whether to apply to other colleges or wait for MSC. Now they were uncertain whether it would open in 1964, if ever.

In early November, CU's president Smiley took another poke at the proposed Metropolitan State College. Addressing a luncheon of the Colorado Association of School Boards and Administrators in Colorado Springs he said Metro would be an "unnecessary duplication of facilities" in Denver. He said Denver needed a junior college instead, claiming they were the best solution to booming enrollments. He added that the costs of the four-year school would be "staggering." He apparently did not read the Russell report. [59]

CU's President Smiley repeated the CU position at a CU alumni meeting in Denver, "It would be possible to have two degree-granting schools in Denver without conflict, however the University of Colorado is in a better position to expand the Denver Center to fulfill Denver's needs for a degree-granting college," Smiley said answering a question asked by a CU alumnus—Senator Roy Romer.[60]

A few days later, Smiley asked the Legislature to allow the University of Colorado to establish a technical institute in Denver. He did not state exactly what a technical institute was. Smiley's plan would make Metropolitan State College unnecessary because this undefined institute would be identical to Metro State, except it would not have an open door policy. The CU regents adopted that plan the very next day.[61]

Three days later, on November 22, President John F. Kennedy was assassinated. Vice-President Johnson was sworn in to replace him. The nation was in shock and grieving. The war of words subsided—for a while.

THE VISIONARIES FIGHT BACK

In early December, the Trustees of State Colleges completed the plan for Metro State College, which HB349 required. The trustees sent it off to be printed for the legislature. The dean of Adams State College, Dr. Keats McKinney, prepared the report with assistance from his secretary, Sandi Jones. It had a green cover and thus ended up being called the "Green Report." [62]

In the report, the trustees said they planned to open Metropolitan State College in September 1964 as called for in HB349. Grant Vest, secretary of the trustees, said in the news conference that the likely site for the college would be the old Security Life Building at 14th and Stout in downtown Denver. He said it could be purchased or leased with an option to purchase. The trustees needed $1.4 million to operate for the first year.

The plan called for two separate-but-equal functions—degree-length programs in liberal arts, business, and teacher preparation, and a technical program of less-than-degree length. Metro State would be "strictly an urban institution-meaning, among other things, it would not have varsity athletic teams, marching bands, baton twirlers, or dormitories."

MSC would operate year-round on the quarter system, thus allowing 43 percent more students to occupy the same space. It would have an "open door as modified by reality." CU would retain responsibility for post-graduate education, extension courses, and some upper division work. It indicated that the CU Denver Center would drop its freshman and sophomore courses per the legislature's intent. Tuition was proposed at $100 a quarter. The trustees asked for the money immediately so it could start planning for the fall.[63]

Herrick Roth, president of the Colorado Labor Council AFL-CIO, endorsed Metropolitan State College and urged the legislature to fund it so it could open. *The Littleton Independent* wrote an editorial saying that Metro State would not hurt CU, but it would help students at West and Manuel High get a college education.[64]

By mid-December, however, backers of Metropolitan State knew they had to make a push to get the legislature to overrule the governor and appropriate the funds to allow Metro to open in the fall of 1964. Hundreds of high school students had already made plans to enroll.

On Sunday, December 22, *The Denver Post* published an editorial urging the legislature to authorize a two-year Metro College in 1965, saying it would be the most "practical answer" to Denver's needs.

State Senator Roy McVicker (D-Jefferson County) responded to *The Post's* editorial with a guest editorial opposing Metro State College altogether, saying it would be a serious mistake. McVicker's position is hard to understand given the fact he was on the committee that recommended building Metro to begin with and kids from his home county would benefit from it, too.[65]

As the 1964 session of the General Assembly drew closer, encouraged by *The Post*, the opponents of Metro State were mobilizing to block funding for MSC. The CU regents had a new partner—the boards of the six junior colleges. They held a joint news conference with CU to oppose the opening of the college, demanding yet another master plan for higher education before any new college opened its doors in Denver.

Dr. W.L. McDivitt, president of Otero Junior College, claimed the new college would cost up to $100 million and he said the voters were being "fooled" by the supporters of Metropolitan State. If at first you don't succeed, plan, plan, and plan again.[66]

To rebut the regents and McDivitt, Representatives Palmer Burch and Allen Dines held their own news conference. They accused the regents and McDivitt of "throwing up a smokescreen of shifting offers to confuse the public." The end result, they said, would be to deny students in *the metropolitan* area an opportunity for education by making it more costly. They called the regent's move "*empire* building."[67]

On New Years' Eve, *The Denver Post* published a large feature by Walt Lindenmann entitled "Metro College Problem for Assembly." It began, "Higher Education is in a state of flux and a state of confusion." Quoting others, Lindenmann stated, "We've reached a new low in Colorado education when colleges start denouncing other colleges just to make themselves look good. It will be the death knell for junior colleges in Colorado if a new state-financed college is established in Denver."

Lindenmann said these were not his words, but rather statements made by three legislators, and they presented a dilemma for the legislature and the governor to decide what to do about Metropolitan State College in January. Many thought the battle over Metropolitan State

College was finished when HB349 was passed. Obviously, the battle had really just begun.[68]

1963 had been a watershed year. Prominent civil rights leader Medgar Evers was murdered on his front lawn in Jackson, Mississippi by a Klansman. TV screens were filled with images of Bull Conner and his police force beating the heads of young civil rights marchers in Birmingham, Alabama. Dr. Martin Luther King Jr. delivered his "I Have a Dream" speech in Washington. Four young black girls were murdered in Alabama when the KKK blew up a black church just before services.

These events finally led President Kennedy to go on national TV to announce that he was sending a civil rights bill to Congress. Kennedy himself would be murdered before he could see it enacted.

In November 1963, the new president of South Vietnam, Ngo Dinh Diem, was assassinated, which led to a coup. He had been propped up by the U.S. government. Many believed that the CIA was behind his murder, leading to further distrust of the U.S.

Things didn't go well for the Broncos in 1963, either. They were winless in their final 10 games and finished with a 2-11-1 record. Nonetheless, fullback Billy Joe was the AFL Rookie of the Year.

The CU Buffs ended the season 2-8 again. Perhaps CU was too focused on trying to squash Metro and took its eyes off the football.

THE LEGISLATURE'S COLD FEET AND LOVE'S FLIP-FLOPS

When Coloradoans awoke on January 1, 1964 and picked up *The Rocky Mountain News*, they were greeted by this front-page headline: "House Speaker Nixes Denver Metro College." Speaker John Vanderhoof, who had voted to authorize Metropolitan State College in April, told the *News*, "I can't see where the state's finances, without a major increase in taxes, can afford another four-year college."

He said that Governor Love only released $25,000 in planning money because he did not want to delay the planning of the college should it go forward. Johnny Van, as he was called, was implying that releasing the funds did not commit the legislature to proceed with opening the college in the fall.

Vanderhoof broke with Republican community leaders by saying Denver needed to establish a couple of junior colleges first to demonstrate a need for a new institution of higher education in Denver. He said the legislature had done this elsewhere in the state noting the first four-year college in Pueblo was not yet fully developed.[69]

Four days later, the Denver Chamber of Commerce flip-flopped and turned thumbs-down on Metro State College. This was surprising because in 1962, Chamber president Shelby Harper urged the Task Force to recommend a four-year college in Denver. The Chamber said it took a survey and the overwhelming opinion of business leaders was that instead of Metro, what was needed in Denver was a "vocational high school." That sounded a lot like CU's proposed technical institute.[70]

Senator Romer was shocked, saying that the survey was unfair because it "asked broad questions requiring great knowledge without providing even a skeleton of the necessary knowledge." Romer said this sort of approach can only elicit reactions unfounded on fact. He added the "spate of personal opinion now being released does not meet the needs of the people of Colorado and particularly the youth of the area."[71]

A few days into the 1964 legislative session, House majority leader John Mackie of Boulder introduced House Concurrent Resolution 1002 (HCR 1002) to allow the CU Extensions in Denver and Colorado Springs to grant degrees—ignoring Attorney General Dunbar's comments about the constitutionality of such a measure. Representative William Lennox, a Republican from Colorado Springs, introduced HCR 1003 to do essentially the same thing.[72]

The interesting thing is that both of these legislators, like Vanderhoof, had voted to create Metropolitan State College eight months earlier. It is easier to understand Lennox's position, since he had offered that same amendment in committee the previous spring, so, he was being consistent. Since the University of Colorado had an extension in Colorado Springs, he thought the branch in his district should also issue degrees.

The Denver Post quickly editorialized in favor of the Mackie and Lennox measures—whether MSC was opened or not. *The Boulder Daily Camera,* to no one's surprise, printed an editorial claiming the establishment of a new four-year school in Denver was not the best way to meet the educational needs of the state.[73]

Then, on January 21, *The Denver Post* front page headline read, "Metro College Killed." They had advance information on what Governor Love was about to say as he flip-flopped once again—this time turning against MSC.

In his State of the State message the next day, Love told the General Assembly, "With the higher priority I assign to this type education, it seems we are premature at this time in considering a new four-year college for *the metropolitan* area. I am therefore not asking the legislature at this session to implement plans which have been developed for Metropolitan State College." Love killed Metro while the "Green Report," was still in the print shop. One can only speculate that the CU lobby got to him. [74]

Sen. Romer immediately accused Love of playing "Russian roulette with the educational future of Denver area high school graduates." "I am amazed Governor Love can change his position so rapidly and as often as he has on this question," Romer said. He went on to say that six months earlier Love called for an end to the "long and involved controversy over this matter." Romer said Love was prolonging the debate without providing "specific practical and immediate solutions to the educational problems."[75]

Rep Allen Dines, who also sponsored the legislation creating Metropolitan State College, said that Governor Love's education message was a "rudderless presentation," and the governor "turned his back on sixty percent of the high school graduates of this state, those in *the met-ropolitan* area, by delaying the college." Dines said that most top educators in Colorado were critical of Love but did not want to use their names, fearing retribution. He pointed out that the "governor's own figures show that by 1970 there will be a desperate need for a four-year institution in Denver."

Then the CU-dominated power structure decided to finish the job. The regents and the president of CU came out against establishing Metro altogether. This was followed by the Denver Chamber of Commerce who agreed, citing opposition from businesses, even though they said earlier that there was an urgent need for a four-year college in Denver.

Finally, the two Denver daily newspapers weighed in by publishing editorials praising the governor for killing MSC. *The News* praised Governor Love for telling the General Assembly that Metropolitan State College was premature and beyond our reach financially. The insisted more study was needed to ensure that it fit into the fabric of higher education in Colorado.[76] (Apparently, the five years of study done by the legislature prior to passage of HB349 was not enough, in their opinion.)

Not to be outdone, *The Denver Post* editorial board wrote: "Now that 'Metro' has been sidetracked we believe the governor and the General Assembly should act to fill the gap." They acknowledged the need for an educational facility in Denver was tremendous but CU's Denver Extension was the best short-term answer.[77]

The Denver newspapers and the Denver Chamber flip-flopped about as often as Governor Love on the subject of Metropolitan State College. One needed a computer to keep track. Perhaps an invisible puppeteer was pulling the strings.

Despite the propaganda campaign, when the 1964 session convened, legislators still de-bated the issue. According to the provisions of HB349, MSC was still scheduled to open in the fall but it needed an appropriation to do so. Senator Wilkie Ham, a member of the legislature's task group, said that Metro State was still the only sensible answer to higher education in Den-ver. He told fellow legislators that Metro State "was not a local issue no more than CSU was a Fort Collins issue."

Senator Ham reminded legislators that one in four high school seniors in rural areas planned to move to Denver after graduation and Metropolitan State College would offer rural kids a chance to get an education and jobs. However, Speaker Vanderhoof still insisted Metro-politan State College needed to be at postponed for at least a decade.[78]

Metro supporters did not fade away. The Denver School Board urged the legislature to open Metropolitan State College as soon as possible. Representative Palmer Burch, president of the Denver School Board, said, "The studies recommending the establishment of Metro

State were the deepest he had ever seen as a legislator, and gave the best analysis and the best solution to the problem."[79]

The trustees appeared before a legislative committee and said that if MSC opened on schedule in September, there would be at least 665 students. They said Metro would operate between 8 a.m. to 10 p.m., five and a half days a week year-round to best utilize facilities. It would require an appropriation of $1.2 million to open in the fall, $200,000 less than they previously estimated.

As expected, the trustees told the committee they favored the Old Security Life Building at 14th and Stout as a temporary location. Shelby Harper, Denver Chamber of Commerce chairman and member of the task group, was vice-president of Security Life. Perhaps they thought selecting the Old Security Life building was good politics. If they rented that space, the trustees said, the utilization of space would be about 80 percent as opposed to a state-wide average of 50 percent.

Legislative leaders did not want MSC opening in 1964, and neither did the governor. So, given those realities, in March the trustees asked the legislature to allow them open the college in 1965, saying they still needed an appropriation of $165,000 in 1964 just to continue planning.

So MSC did not open in 1964 after all. MSC's opponents celebrated. The power of the University of Colorado regents and alumni won the battle, but the war was not over.

Gerry and the Pacemakers had some good advice for the disappointed visionaries in their 1964 hit song: *"The nighttime shadows disappear and with them go all your tears. For the morning will bring joy for every girl and boy. So.......Don't let the sun catch you crying."*[80]

On March 3, the trustees wiped their tears and told Dr. H. Grant Vest to press forward making plans for Metro State College, saying that HB349 obligated them to continue moving forward to open MSC—the legislative rebuke notwithstanding. This was immediately criticized by the editorial board of *The Rocky Mountain News*. On March 4 they said the legislature was "wise not to fund Metropolitan State College."[81]

The legislative fight over MSC wasn't the only fight that caught the attention of Denverites that winter. A Denver resident named Sonny Liston took on a new boxer named Cassius Clay for the heavyweight title. In the seventh round, Liston threw in the towel saying his shoulder was hurt thus giving the title to Clay (who later changed his name to Muhammad Ali.)

While the visionaries were licking their wounds, Ford made headlines. The first Mustang rolled off the assembly line on March 9. A month later, it made its world debut at the World's Fair in New York City. Millions watched James Bond driving a Mustang in the movie "Goldfinger" shortly thereafter. Soon it was the must-have car for many baby boomers.

As summer arrived, many were curious about what the future would hold for MSC. In July, Walt Lindeman wrote in *The Denver Post* that John Love was still cool to the idea of establishing Metro State College as a four-year college. He was reporting on Love's meeting with his nine-member advisory committee on junior colleges. Committee members said after the meeting they found "a complete change on the part of the governor toward establishment of junior colleges." This was the fourth time the governor changed positions on this issue.[82]

In the fall of 1964, the first wave of baby boomers graduated. Enrollments were up at CU as the Boulder campus grew to 10,900 students. The number of students at the CU Denver Center was up and enrollment increased at CSU as well. Also up was the number of high school graduates in Denver that did not enroll in a college due to the absence of an affordable local college.

The school that was supposed to give Denver-area graduates an affordable option for college, did not open on schedule. It was not there to give students a second chance because the legislature did not fund it in large part to organized opposition from the CU regents and the strong CU lobby. The regents lost the 1963 battle over HB349 but they fixed that during the 1964 legislative session.

The nation was experiencing turmoil and events would continue to change the political and cultural climate in the United States. That spring, Byron De la Beckwith was tried and acquitted twice by all-white juries for murdering Medgar Evers. On June 21, three civil rights workers, James Chaney, Andrew Goodman, and Michael Schwerner, were murdered in Mississippi by conspirators who turned out to be local members of the Klan—some of them members of the Neshoba County Sheriff's Department.

On July 2, President Johnson signed the Civil Rights Act of 1964, first proposed by President Kennedy. It banned discrimination based on "race, color, religion, sex or national origin" in employment practices and public accommodations. The law was a victory for Dr. King and thousands who had been engaged in the struggle for the rights of African Americans, particularly in the South.

Nevertheless, in Denver that fall, the trustees and the advocates for Metropolitan State College were working behind the scenes in secret to lay the ground work for getting money appropriated in 1965 so the school could open. After all, there would be new faces in the General Assembly as a result of the fall elections. Maybe they could win some of those new legislators over.

When word of these secret meetings leaked out, the trustees were immediately blasted by W.L. McDivitt, president of Otero Junior College in La Junta. He said that "petty politics, not sound educational thinking, is at the root of a number of plans being offered for higher education in Colorado," referring to Metro State College. His beef was combining academic education with vocational education. McDivitt was fearful that if MSC opened it would take students away from existing junior colleges in small rural communities like La Junta.[83]

While McDivitt was blasting the trustees over Metro, the presidents of Colorado's senior colleges had a secret meeting to garner support for a state-wide system of junior colleges to be created under a new state board. The presidents voted unanimously that Metro should open in 1965, initially as a two-year institution until 1970 or thereabouts, and it should remain under the trustees, not the new board of junior colleges.

Interestingly, the unanimous vote meant that CU's President Smiley either voted for the resolution, or abstained. The regents, however, contradicted Smiley by issuing a statement to make it clear that they were still against Metropolitan State College, or any college that would threaten the CU Denver Center. They said they supported the rest of the blueprint the college presidents came up with, just not the section about Metro.[84]

Senator Roy McVicker, meanwhile, continued his campaign for a two-year college in Denver in place of MSC. He proposed that the state take the planning money allocated to Metro and use it to plan for a different two-year college.[85]

While the Regents were fighting MSC and the trustees were preparing for a hoped-for opening, Republicans chose Senator Barry Goldwater from Arizona as their nominee for president. Democrats nominated Lyndon Johnson who won by one of the largest landslides in history and his coat tails extended deep down the ballot. Democrats took back control of the House of Representatives in Colorado, and Allen Dines replaced John Vanderhoof as Speaker. This was pivotal in MSC's history.

In Colorado that November, a Republican candidate for state representative in northwest Denver's district 1 blasted Governor Love and legislature for their support of a four-year college in Denver. He said the top priority should be establishing a voc-tech school. "We are pouring millions of dollars annually into institutions for liberal arts and professional training while youngsters who desperately need vocational training get little or no aid whatsoever."[86]

Fortunately for MSC, Greg Pearson did not win that House seat. No one knew it at the time, but just one more "no" vote the following year would have prevented Metro from opening. It is ironic, however, because after Metropolitan State College finally opened, Mr. Pearson became Professor Pearson, one of the most outstanding English and Journalism professors at the college—a college he vehemently opposed. (Years later, the same seat Pearson lost was held by a Metropolitan State College graduate—Representative Bob Bowen.)

In December, the trustees appeared before the legislature's Joint Budget Committee and asked for an appropriation of $859,721 to open the college in the fall of 1965. They said that $179,000 was to rent space in the old May Company Building at 16th and Curtis, not the Security Life Building as previously stated. In addition, they wanted a $65,000 supplemental appropriation to hire a new president to gear up for the fall opening.

The May Company building was available because two major downtown department stores—the May Company and Daniels & Fischer—had recently merged into May D & F.

This left both former store buildings empty as May D & F opened their new store at 16th and Court Place. The new store was connected to the Hilton hotel by a second-floor walkway and included an ice skating rink on the corner. There was no explanation why the Security Life Building was dropped in favor of the May Company building.

On New Years' Eve, Governor Love announced he would ask the legislature to create a super board to control all state colleges and universities. This super board would become the Colorado Commission on Higher Education, and it would play a major role in the history of MSC. That new board was first proposed by Love's consultant, Dr. Russell.[87]

The year 1964 is remembered for several reasons. Timothy Leary published *The Psychedelic Experience*, a book many boomers would read. The Beatles "invaded" America and appeared on the Ed Sullivan Show in February. Their music was nearly drowned out by 700 screaming young girls, whipped into a frenzy, thereby launching "Beatlemania." The Beatles topped the charts that year with several hits including "I Wanna Hold Your Hand" and "She Loves You," along with five others. The Dave Clark Five were feeling "Glad All Over." The Kingsmen released "Louie Louie."

In 1964, the USS Maddox was allegedly fired upon while on an intelligence-gathering mission along the coast of North Vietnam in the Gulf of Tonkin. A second attack on the Maddox and the USS Turner Joy was reported two days later. We now know now that no attacks actually occurred. Before that truth came out, Congress approved the Gulf of Tonkin Resolution, which gave the president power to conduct military operations in Southeast Asia without declaring war.

After a 0-4 start, the Broncos fired Coach Jack Faulkner and replaced him with Mac Speedie. The move paid off right away as the Broncos won the new coach's debut. Nonetheless, the Broncos would win only one more game and finish with a 2-11-1 record for the second season in a row. The CU Buffaloes ended 2-8 for the third season in a row. The Broncos and Buffaloes gave credence to the adage that insanity is doing the same thing over and over expecting a different result.

Another year ended, however, and Denver still did not have a college. Winston Churchill once said, "When you are going through hell, just keep going."

CHAPTER 3

MSC is Finally Born

It takes a worried man to sing a worried song
It takes a worried man to sing a worried song
It takes a worried man to sing a worried song
I'm worried now but I won't be worried long
"A Worried Man" Kingston Trio[88]

'65 AND BARELY ALIVE

The year 1965 was one of those watershed years where events changed society. President Lyndon Johnson delivered his "Great Society" State of the Union Address to Congress, which led to adoption of policies and legislation that produced an unprecedented growth in American social programs. Joe Namath became the Jets quarterback. Winston Churchill died, making Dwight Eisenhower and Charles DeGaul the last WWII leaders who were still alive.

In the spring, Dr. Martin Luther King, John Lewis and other civil rights leaders went to Alabama to attempt to march from Selma to the capital, Montgomery. When the peaceful marchers reached a bridge, Selma police, state troopers, and vigilante thugs savagely beat the men, women, and children, killing one and nearly killing John Lewis, a future Congressman.

The event was seen on nationwide TV. It so shocked the nation that Congress, under the prodding of President Johnson, passed the Voting Rights Act.

In 1965, the U.S. began a bombing campaign in North Vietnam that would eventually result in a Navy officer named John McCain being shot down. He was held prisoner in Hanoi until the end of the war in 1973. In 1965, President Johnson began sending U.S. troops to Vietnam to fight a ground war.

Also in 1965, NASA began launching crews into space in the Gemini program, the precursor to the Apollo program, which would eventually land a man on the moon. The Russians sent the first woman into space that year. It would be 18 years before Sally Ride would break the gender barrier in the U.S. space program.

"The Sound of Music" began one of the longest runs in Hollywood history. Boomers more than likely went to a Drive-In to take in that perfect date-flick: "Dr. Zhivago." Teen pregnancies were significantly up in Denver that year.

Later in June, up to 14 inches of rain fell in a short time near Franktown, flooding Plum Creek, Cherry Creek, and the Platte River. When the three streams came together, it created the worst flood in Denver in 100 years. Nearly every bridge across the Platte was gone, rail cars were tossed about like toys, and entire neighborhoods were under water. Centennial Race Track was destroyed, as were large sections of a neighborhood known as Auraria.

As the 1965 legislative session got underway, Denver legislators wanted to get funding to the trustees so they could keep moving towards a fall opening for MSC. The legislature gave the trustees $65,000 less than they asked for in 1964, so Denver Representatives Frank Kemp, Mark Hogan, and Palmer Burch, along with Star Caywood of Walsenburg, and J.D. McFarlane of Pueblo, introduced HB1101 to appropriate $65,830 to the trustees to open Metro.

Kemp said that if the appropriation was approved, a president would be hired immediately, and a dean of faculty and a dean of technical education would be hired in February. Work could begin on remodeling the temporary facilities to allow for opening in the fall.[89]

A week later, Senator Joe Shoemaker (R-Denver) introduced an alternative bill with eight co-sponsors, including Republican Senators Ed "Sheriff Scotty" Scott of Englewood, Ruth Stockton of Lakewood, Bill Armstrong of Aurora, James Perrill of Denver, David Hahn of Aurora, and Democrats Andy Lucas of Westminster, Anthony Vollock of Lakewood, and Allen Williams of Commerce City.

This bill would require Metro to use existing publically-owned facilities like high schools to save the money needed for constructing a new campus. Shoemaker said there were millions of dollars invested in Denver buildings that could be better utilized. They could be devoted to college programs in the afternoons and evenings after high school students went home. They must not have read Dr. Russell's report either. Fortunately, the bill was never heard.[90]

The legislative process was skillfully used by supporters of Metropolitan State College. The political skills and tenacity of the MSC coalition in the legislature played a major role. Denver legislators like Allen Dines, Mark Hogan, and Roy Romer worked hard to secure votes.

HB1101 came up before the House Appropriations Committee on February 5. The committee chairman, Rep. Star Caywood of Walsenburg, said he would not allow anyone to move to re-open basic discussions about the proposed school in that committee, saying "The proper forum is the floor of the House." Nevertheless, at the hearing CU Regent Bernick said the entire Board of Regents opposed the bill. Rep. Betty Kirk West of Pueblo made a motion to kill the bill, but her motion lost.[91]

During the hearing, Democratic Representative Rich Gephardt of Boulder objected saying the trustees' plans designated 75 percent of the course offerings for Metropolitan State College as academic offerings and only 25 percent were voc-ed. Gephardt argued that it should be reversed—75 percent voc-ed and 25 percent academic courses. He said the needs of the Denver area and the plans for Metro State were in "complete imbalance."

After much discussion, Chairman Caywood moved for passage of the bill. It passed and moved to the floor. Rep. John Mackie, also from Boulder County, said he would surely offer amendments to the bill on the floor.[92]

The argument made by *The Denver Post* and others (including Gephardt), that Metro should de-emphasize academic programs, was ripe with undercurrents of both classism and racism. Inherent in that argument was a belief that privileged (usually white) kids deserve to go to college or a university, but poor and minority kids should just go to a trade school and become a mechanic or some other tradesman.

The editorial board of *The Denver Post* probably took its position for two reasons: first, they were influenced by false arguments from the CU regents and the Denver Chamber of Commerce. Secondly, they were generally conservative and felt if it cost money or necessitated a tax increase, it should be avoided.

Junior colleges were seen as a low-cost alternative to a four-year college because they were thought to be cheaper. Even though Dr. Russell's study disproved that notion, old ideas tend to take a long time to die, especially when powerful interests are pushing them.[93]

On February 8, Representatives Mackie and Gephardt introduced House Bill 1171, a bill that would specifically turn Metropolitan State College into a two-year junior college. The lawmakers said that the CU Denver Extension could handle all the needs for a four-year school in Denver. The CU regents were said to be fully backing their bill.[94]

Oddly, Rep. Mackie had voted to create Metropolitan State as a four-year school in 1963, but now that CU was against it, so was he. In essence, his bill would make Metro a "weeder/feeder" school for the CU Denver Center. It would just weed out poor and undesirable students, and feed the good ones to CU. The CU Alumni Association Board immediately passed a resolution of support for Mackie's Bill.[95]

The Denver Post wasted no time endorsing the Mackie "weeder/feeder" bill in an editorial. *The paper* continued to push for converting Metro to a junior college. They wrote that enough studies had been done and the legislature should immediately expand the junior college system into Denver. Their editorial said that the Mackie bill should have been passed two years prior.

They opposed any academic course offerings whatsoever at Metro, saying what Denver needed was, in effect, a trade school.[96]

What *The Post* did not say is that students who transferred to the CU Denver Center or the University of Colorado at Boulder dropped out at much higher rates than students admitted in their first year.[97]

Then in a surprise move, Representative J.D. MacFarlane of Pueblo, who had co-sponsored Frank Kemp's bill to appropriate money for MSC, flip-flopped and introduced a bill limiting Metropolitan State College to a two-year voc-tech school. So now there were two measures before the legislature that would prevent MSC from ever becoming a four-year college, as well as an appropriation bill to allow it to open as it was designed in law.[98]

Much of the opposition to Metropolitan State College was rooted in the fact that a college is expensive and things that cost money are difficult for short-sighted politicians to support. But the debate over MSC had all the undertones of a greater debate going on in society regarding education of the masses. The notion of higher education for all was new and not universally accepted.

No one would admit it at the time, but MSC, as proposed, was hard for many to swallow simply because taxpayer money would be going to help underprivileged and minority kids at the perceived expense of more affluent kids. If the state funded the CU Denver Center instead of MSC, poor and minority students would be kept out because of the high admission standards and tuition. They would go to a trade school or junior college and learn a trade instead.

The view that elitism, classism and racism played a role in the fight over Metro is not without factual basis. During the debate over funding for MSC, more than one legislator used terms like "hub cap thieves and hoodlums" in legislative hearings to describe MSC students that he had never met, nor wanted to meet.[99]

Miracles do happen! The legislature dealt a surprising blow to CU. Rep. Lenox's HCR 1003 died on a vote of 32-28 on the floor of the House despite having 20 co-sponsors. He introduced the measure to allow the CU branches in Denver and Colorado Springs to offer degrees. House members expressed fear that the measure would give the regents of the University of Colorado too much power. Opponents of the measure said it would also threaten Metropolitan State College (which was the regents' intent).[100]

About a week later, the House Education Committee took up the Kemp/Hogan bill. At the hearing, Dr. Vest (from the Board of Trustees) told the committee that there was a sense of urgency for opening Metro State. He said MSC could open as a two-year school but long-range planning indicated it should eventually be a four-year institution. Vest said the school must open in the fall.[101]

"Metropolitan State College will attract high school students who are not going to college now because access is difficult," Vest said. "This includes those students who are now blocked by geography and family finances from attending college." In other words, the kids that some elitists wanted kept out. He reiterated that the institution would be urban-oriented and designed to provide students with an education and, if desired, a trade. He said that activities such as intercollegiate athletics, a marching band, fraternities and sororities would not be part of the college.

Dr. Kenneth Oberholtzer, Superintendent of the Denver Public Schools, told the committee, "Metro State is not the answer to all our needs but it answers some of them. And we cannot meet metropolitan needs without it." CSU President Stanley Ahman spoke in favor. He had supported Metro State College earlier as a member of the Association of State Institutions of Higher Education, which endorsed Metro.[102]

The CU regents and president spoke against funding MSC. CU president Smiley told the committee that the CU Denver Extension was the only four-year school needed in Denver. He reminded them 7,000 students were currently enrolled. He said the legislature had a dilemma: should it do away with MSC or merge it? If Metro went away or became a junior college, kids with a 3.0 or better could transfer to the CU Denver Center.

Regent Dan Lynch said to create a four-year college would be to "respond to a need that does not exist." He stressed that a junior college was badly needed in Denver, but the CU Denver Center was adequate to handle the needs for a four-year college. Nevertheless, the committee passed the bill. [103]

On March 11, HB1101 came to the floor for second reading. This was a crucial day in the history of Metropolitan State College. However, problems popped up the night before when the Rules Committee met to consider whether to schedule HB1101 for a vote the next morning.

The Rules Committee was tied—three for the bill and three against. However, Representative Conklin, a likely "no" vote was late for the meeting. Representative Dines, the Speaker, allowed the committee to take up his bill before Rep. Conklin arrived. As a result, the bill passed because Speaker Dines, Mark Hogan, and Joe Calabrese voted yes and with Conklin gone, there were just two no votes. Conklin was not happy when he arrived and found the bill was scheduled for second reading.[104]

Had Republican John Vanderhoof still been Speaker, the outcome would have been much different. Vanderhoof had wanted to delay MSC's opening for a decade. So by virtue of the 1964 elections, the bill advanced.

When debate on HB1101 began the next day, Representative Hogan knew it would be tight because he had been "whipping" it (counting votes). During the debate, Representatives Frank Kemp, Palmer Burch, Allen Dines and Mark Hogan spoke for the bill. Representative Forrest Burns spoke out in opposition.

Then Rep. John Mackie offered an amendment which would place governance of Metropolitan State College under the Colorado Board of Junior Colleges. Rep. Mackie said the state should not set up an institution that is "second rate at the outset." He said MSC would be better as two-year school under the junior college board.

The Mackie amendment would more than likely have sealed the fate of Metropolitan State College had it passed. MSC would have been converted to a two-year junior college. There was a lot of support for Mackie's amendment CU and the Board of Junior Colleges were lobbying hard for it. Furthermore, the newspapers had written editorials in support.

After a long debate, it came time to vote on the Mackie amendment. Hogan knew if supporters could get past that vote, then the MSC bill should pass. In a 2013 interview, Mark Hogan said he knew that Rep. Massari of Pueblo might be a yes vote on the Mackie amendment. For reasons no one remembers, Representative Massari did not show up on time.[105]

A division of the House was called for, meaning there would be a standing vote rather than a voice vote. With Massari absent, the Mackie Amendment failed on a 32-32 tie—it takes 33 votes to pass a bill in the House. Whew!

Things appeared to be looking up for MSC, but that did not last long. Since Mackie's other bill, HB1131, had cleared the Education Committee and was sitting in the Rules Committee, Rep. Mackie and others wanted to postpone a vote on the MSC bill (HB1101) until Mackie's other bill cleared Rules and came up in the full House for a vote. The argument was that if both bills passed, there would be a conflict.

Rep. Forrest Burns (D-Lamar) came to the floor and argued for postponing the vote. He said, "There are too many things dangling on a limb I am not satisfied with. I am not opposed to Metro College, but I think we should know where we are going." The Burns motion failed on a voice vote.[106]

So, HB1101 finally came up for a vote. One of the supporters Hogan had lined up for the MSC bill was Rep. John Behr of Grand Junction. A recorded vote was called for and the vote on the bill was the same as the vote on the Mackie amendment: a 32-32 tie. So it failed to pass.

Shock riddled through the Chamber.

Mark Hogan realized that Rep. Behr had voted no after promising to vote yes. While the House was taking up other matters, Hogan dashed over to Behr and told him that it was not a good idea to go back on a commitment. "If you go back on your word," Hogan told him, "no one will ever take your word again." Behr said he would change his vote. Hogan put his hand on Behr's shoulder to signal to Rep. Kemp that it was safe to make a motion to reconsider the vote.[107]

Speaker Dines had appointed a friendly representative to chair second reading that day. At the end of the docket, Rep. Kemp went to the podium and made a motion to amend the Committee of the Whole Report to read that HB1101 actually did pass on second reading. That is a parliamentary procedure that allows the House to take a new vote which, in essence, says that what happened actually didn't happen. In other words, the minutes would read HB1101 actually passed when it hadn't.[108]

There was a vote on Kemp's amendment, and a roll call vote was requested. The motion to adopt the amendment passed 33-32. Behr apparently saw the error of his ways and voted for MSC. The absent Representative Massari had returned, possibly thinking HB1101 was settled, or perhaps by coincidence. Had he not returned, the vote would likely have been 33-31, but it would still have passed, due to Rep. Behr's "conversion." The MSC appropriation bill advanced to third and final reading.

The next morning, HB1101 came up for third reading. Representative Charles Conklin was still angry because Speaker Dines and Rep. Hogan advanced HB1101 out of Rules before he got to the meeting. He made a motion to refer HB1101 to the House Education Committee, saying "the die is not cast." He argued that the legislature didn't know what form Metropolitan State College should take.

Rep. Ruth Clark, Chairwoman of the Education committee, said if the bill was sent to her committee, "I am equally sure you will never see this bill again." There was discussion on the motion followed by a vote. Conklin's motion failed with only 26 aye votes.[109]

Six of the anti-MSC representatives (who had voted no on HB1101 the day before) defected on Conklin's motion. Conklin lost Representatives Everett Cook (Custer), Joseph Gollop (Pueblo), Bill Gossard (Moffat), Betty Miller (Jefferson), Pat O'Brien (La Plata), Tom Wailes (Adams), and Jerry Yost (Adams). Who knows the reason, but Chuck DeMoulin (D-Denver), who had voted for the Kemp/Hogan bill the day before, voted for the Conklin amendment. A no vote the day before would have spelled death. It didn't matter on the Conklin amendment, however, due to the new converts.

It was still not over. Representative John Carroll of Adams County made a motion requesting permission to offer a third reading amendment. Rep. Carroll was likely planning something to hurt MSC since he had voted no on the MSC bill the day before. The anti-Metro coalition was beginning to wear down and Carroll only received 16 votes on his motion to get permission for a third-reading amendment. Ten Representatives who had just voted with Conklin defected.

Hogan urged a yes vote on the MSC bill "before the students who need Metropolitan State College need Medicare." With the last-minute drama out of the way, HB1101 was passed on a 49-15 vote and advanced to the Senate. Representatives Joe Calabrese, Dominick Coloroso, Chuck DeMoulin, Archie Lisco, Frank Anaya, Ken Monfort, John Wheeler, Harold Adcock, Don Strait, Dan Grove, Jean Bain, Ralph Cole, Floyd Haskell, George Fentress, Ben Klein, Isaac Moore, and Hub Safran all signed on as co-sponsors.[110]

Nothing begets victory like victory. Had Representative Massari not been absent on second reading, it is not clear what would have happened to the Mackie amendment. On that day, it seemed like fate was on Metro's side—along with a skilled legislative support team.

The CU coalition against Metro was not done fighting. They would continue to kill the bill in the Senate. The CU regents held at an unprecedented meeting April 17 in Grand Junction—the first ever held outside Boulder, Denver, or Colorado Springs. Did they choose Grand Junction for the historic meeting to embarrass Representative Behr, a Democrat from Grand Junction, who changed his vote from no to yes? The regents said they had planned to hold the meeting there all along.

Either way, they made use of the opportunity. At the meeting, six regents told the audience and the local media that the proposed Denver college would damage the junior college movement in Colorado. Grand Junction just happened to be home of Mesa Junior College, so it created fear among residents there.

CU Regent Bromley said, "Our board has taken the position Metropolitan State College is a mistake." Regent Bernick said, "It is discouraging to think that the junior college need will be answered by a state college." Regent Dan Lynch said, "Metro College will have $1 million in the coming fiscal year, but no faculty, no classrooms. An educational survey has shown we need junior colleges. We should determine our needs so that all institutions won't be starved into mediocrity."[111]

The unfounded assertion that MSC was taking all the money and starving their local institutions got people riled up. The regents did not point out, however, that CU always got more than its fair share of l funding from the legislature to the detriment of schools like Mesa.

On April 20, the Gephardt bill, which would make Metropolitan State College a junior college, came up for a vote in the House. The battle-weary house voted it down on a 45-18 vote. During the floor debate Rep. W.E. "Bill" Foster, Republican of Grand Junction, said "CU has reared its ugly head again to do anything to block Metro." Apparently, he was not swayed by the regents' meeting in his home county three days earlier.[112]

Rep. Gephardt expressed shock at Foster's comment, saying all he wanted "was to ensure orderly growth in Denver." The following day, *The Denver Post* headline stated "CU Drive Against 4-Year School in Denver Set Back." Finally there was a public acknowledgement that CU was behind the efforts to derail Metropolitan State College.[113]

In that same issue of *The Post*, Senator Don E. Kelley wrote a guest editorial blasting Regent Fred Betz for writing a letter to the editor which was "replete with misstatements of fact as well as logic." He said President Smiley and the University of Colorado regents "left no stone unturned to kill Metropolitan State College." Kelley said that when MSC was fully operational it might mean phasing out lower division courses at the CU Denver Center. He suggested that Regent Betz read the law that established Metropolitan State College and "it might temper his prejudice."[114]

The following day, *The Post* editorial board responded to Kelley, saying that Metropolitan State College, regardless of what it was called, should be a two-year vocational educational institution of the junior college type. They said that such a school would "play a major part in the world of the future [with] programs the federal government is supporting strongly." They offered no explanation why a four-year school with an applied sciences program could not play just as major of a role in the world of the future as a junior college.[115]

In the Senate, HB1101 was assigned to the Finance Committee which heard the bill on April 22. Senator Ruth Stockton, Republican from Lakewood, led the opposition and moved to postpone the bill indefinitely. She said that she was just reflecting the lack of sentiment for the proposed four-year school in Denver. Given the vote in the House, she must have been referring to the lack of sentiment among the CU regents. Nonetheless, the committee killed the bill. Both sadness and glee filled the room.[116]

A LONG TIME COMING

> *There's been times that I thought*
> *I couldn't last for long*
> *But now I think I'm able to carry on*
> *It's been a long, long time coming*
> *But I know a change gonna come*
> *Oh, yes it will*
> Sam Cooke, "A Change is Gonna Come," RCA 1964

The Senate defeat of 1101 did not matter, however. Pro-MSC legislators had been pursuing a separate track. The Kemp/Hogan appropriation bill would have made a supplemental appropriation so that the trustees could immediately rent space and hire staff to be ready to open MSC in the fall. Clearly, they would still need an appropriation later on in the session to fund the college's operations for the year. That would need to come from the Long Bill.

Senators Harry Locke and Joe Shoemaker, members of the Joint Budget Committee (JBC), had been working on the Long Bill during all the drama over the supplemental appropriation. Senator Shoemaker was a supporter of Metropolitan State College. The JBC had held hearings on Metro during the previous summer and earlier in the session. The anti-Metro coalition—orchestrated by CU—was at the hearings to object, but they were not persuasive.

They introduced the Long Bill—Senate Bill 344—on March 19. A week later, it cleared the Joint Budget Committee and went to the floor. On April 3, the bill came up for second reading. Senator Shoemaker knew that if he could get the money for Metro via the Long Bill through the Senate, the House would follow suit since Frank Kemp and Mark Hogan had managed to pass HB1101 earlier in the House.

In a very skillful manner, Senator Shoemaker managed to get the supplemental funds added into the Long Bill in case HB1101 ran into trouble in the Senate. In addition, he also added the funds required to open and operate the college the first year¬—without many legislators or MSC opponents noticing. The bill included $1,023,709 for Metropolitan State College. Of that, $750,000 came from the General Fund, $273,709 from tuition, and $4,000 from the Defense Education Fund. There was an additional $97,331 for capital outlay.

The Long Bill passed second reading. Senator Shoemaker did not want to take a chance on waiting a day for third reading, which would have given the opponents time to discover the MSC money was in the bill. So, he requested that the Long Bill be considered on the same day with what is called Special Orders. It passed third reading on Special Orders before many of the Metro opponents even knew what was in it.

The Long Bill then went to the House. On April 9, it passed on a vote of 54-9. For the moment, the anti-Metro coalition was resigned to retreat and fight another day. Governor Love signed the Long Bill on May 17, 1965.

It was now official: Metropolitan State College would finally open on October 4, 1965 and students would attend their first class.[117]

"Metro was born after a long gestation period, the birthing was tortuous. But often the little guys who come into the world under these circumstances and who are reared in adversity develop into big guys who can't be whipped. Let's not give up those visions." Those words were written by an anonymous faculty member in 1967, reflecting back on the birth of MSC.[118]

Since the battle seemed to be over, *The Denver Post* wrote an editorial saying that now that the decision has been made, it was time to bring the argument over the college to an end, that those who supported and those that opposed ought now to join forces to make the college the best institution of its kind that could be developed.[119]

Senator Romer recalled in 2012 that the battle for Metro was the hardest in his career. He indicated that the legislation to create Metro was a "Democratic bill." Indeed most of the early proponents were Democrats, and many opponents were Republicans. It must be noted, however, that without the efforts of Republican legislators like Frank Kemp, Palmer Burch, Ruth Clark, and Joe Shoemaker, and the votes of Republicans in both houses, Metropolitan State College would not exist.

The Rocky Mountain News, however, may have been foreshadowing the future when it said in an editorial following the passage of the Long Bill that the "effort to start a Metro College in Denver seems to us merely to complicate an already complicated situation."[120]

It is never over until it is over; but was it really over?

Along with Allen Dines, Palmer Burch and Roy Romer, Rep. Mark Hogan was very instrumental in passing the legislation that created and funded MSC.

Photo Courtesy of Metropolitan State University of Denver.

CHAPTER 4

MSC is Funded: Now What?

I see skies of blue, and clouds of white,
The bright blessed day, the dark sacred night
And I think to myself
What a wonderful world.
Yes, I think to myself
What a wonderful world
"It's a Wonderful World" Louis Armstrong[121]

In 1965, it was a wonderful world for the visionaries who fought for Metropolitan State College. In the late spring, after a seven-year struggle, the Colorado legislature finally appropriated the money to open the school. Opportunity finally beckoned for tens of thousands of young people—and some not-so-young—who now had the possibility of a college education and the empowerment that brings.

Metropolitan State College was a clean slate—a blank canvas on which something fresh, bold, new and unique could be designed. The founders did not want just any college built; they wanted one that would radically change higher education in Colorado as it existed at the time. That was their vision.

HOW WOULD THE VISION BE ACTUALIZED?

The trustees knew they had the task of actualizing that vision for which many had fought for since 1958. This task was made more difficult by the rough battle the supporters of Metropolitan State College had to wage just to open the school, and the need to still watch their backs. CU only retreated; they had not surrendered. They were still actively plotting the school's demise—even as it prepared to open.

To understand how the trustees went about actualizing that vision, we need to understand the context in which their decisions were being made. One cannot understand 1965 looking through the prism of the world as we know it today. Denver and the nation in 1965 were far different then.

In 1965, Denver was much smaller than today. The population of *the metropolitan* area was only about 850,000—half the population of the state. The City and County of Denver had more influence then because it accounted for 53 percent of *the metropolitan* area's population. By contrast, in 2012 *the metropolitan* area's population was 2.7 million—more than three times what it was in 1965. And in 2012, Denver accounted for less than a third of *the metropolitan* area's people.[122]

Ethnic populations in 1965 were concentrated in just a few areas and not dispersed as widely as today. African-Americans primarily lived in Five Points, Curtis Park, and the City Park West neighborhood. They were just beginning to move into North Park Hill following the fair housing ordinance voters approved in 1957.

Chicanos lived in Auraria, West Denver and Globeville; they were beginning to move into North Denver. The rest of the city was predominantly white, as were the suburbs, except for small sections of Aurora and Adams County. Only two of eight Denver high schools had a majority of minority student populations.

When the legislature created MSC, *the metropolitan* area included only Denver, Adams, Arapahoe, and Jefferson counties. Douglas County was a small rural county; Highlands Ranch was still a ranch; Northglenn was a development called Pearl Mack, and Centennial did not exist. Boulder was separated from the city by farms; the airport was located near Park Hill, just 17 minutes from the state Capitol.

Most of MSC's first students would be baby boomers. Their parents were born during the Great Depression, lived through World War II, and many were veterans of that war. Their life experiences shaped how they would raise their children and how they would react to them. Most of MSC's deciders—the trustees, legislators, college administrators, and many faculty—were born in that pre-World War II period, and many had the same values the parents of future students had.

The economic hardships of the Depression created a generation that was content to focus on their own prosperity, rather than on politics or society as a whole. The boomer-parent generation was determined that their children would have a better life than they did, and part of that meant giving their children the college education they had never received.

The boomer-parents were concerned with having a home in the suburbs, buying the material things they were denied in their childhood. They were working hard to save for their children's college education—at least those in the white middle class. Lower-income whites and minorities were still struggling with the notion that college was out of reach for their children.

The 1950s provided a respite from the social struggles of the Depression and war. With those behind them, boomer-parents could relax and enjoy the ride. Their generation chose Dwight Eisenhower as president, in part because he represented a grandfatherly stability. Political apathy became an antidote to fear. Many found comfort in the changing world of the 1950s by burying their heads in the sand.

In the home, family dinners at the dining room table gave way to TV trays; home cooked meals were sometimes replaced by frozen TV dinners; walking and taking busses were replaced by driving. Listening to Roosevelt's highly anticipated fire-side chats on the radio was replaced by watching Perry Mason and Lucille Ball on TV. Americans became more materialistic, sedentary, and socially disconnected.

While white Americans grew complacent, black and brown Americans became more agitated. Their time for equality was at hand—or at least the struggle for equality was. The peaceful, prosperous complacency of the 1950s soon gave way to a decade of struggle and turbulence that would forever change American culture and society.

In 1960 Eisenhower could not run again so the choice was between his vice-president, Richard Nixon, and a youthful senator, John F. Kennedy. The nation was split down the middle however, and Kennedy edged out Nixon, in large part to Nixon's sweaty-browed performance in the first televised debate in history.

The cultural changes that had begun with the quest for equality by southern blacks in the late 1950s continued into the 1960s. The escalation of violence against peaceful black marchers in the South and Martin Luther King's "I Have a Dream" speech compelled the cautious Kennedy to take action. He told Dr. King, the speech "changed his heart." Kennedy went on to propose the Civil Rights Act, but did not live to see it passed.[123]

The 1960s also saw the beginnings of *El Movimiento*—the struggle of Latinos for their rights, respect, and identity in society—things they had lacked for decades. Their movement gained inspiration and momentum from the struggle of African Americans.

At the same time, women began to demand equality as well. The feminist movement, known also as *women's lib*, was born in the 1960s.

Gays and lesbians enjoying a drink at the Stonewall Inn in Greenwich Village began wondering "What if?" Could they finally come out of the shadows without fearing repression? The NYPD had an answer for them. The police raided the openly gay bar with intent to close it, which led to spontaneous demonstrations and allegations of police brutality. In another time the LGBT community might have accepted that bloody answer, but not in the 1960s. The Stonewall incident began the gay liberation movement in America.[124]

The nation became impatient as a new phenomenon began to emerge—the generation gap. Baby boomers began to distrust their parents' generation. Boomer-parents began to disapprove of their children's generation—and in some cases, even their own children. This may have been an unintended consequence of the 1950s, when boomer-parents and their kids cocooned in front of the TV set every night rather than talking and interacting with each other.

Television began to shape values. To the boomer-parents, ideal values were cast in the mold of the Cleavers and Ozzie and Harriett. Real family life was often much different than the television depiction of the ideal family. This added stress when families realized they weren't as perfect as the Cleavers.

The boomers, thanks to TV, could witness the world from their couch. Their values were being shaped images on the nightly news of racial strife in the South and a war in Indochina. Many boomers heard Kennedy's call to action: "Ask what you can do for your country." They grew impatient with their parents' apathy toward what was going on. In some ways, pressure from their parents to go to college resulted in resentment. Those who were denied the opportunity for college grew resentful as well. Then there was the war in Vietnam.

Why is this relevant to the history of Metropolitan State College? The decisions made about what kind of school it would be, who it would serve, what it would teach and how that teaching would be done were influenced by—if not driven by—these evolving social changes and events. By understanding the times, we can better understand the actions of the deciders, the dissenters, and those who just sat on the sidelines.

THE VISIONARIES WANTED AN URBAN-ORIENTED COLLEGE

The founders had a vision for the new college, but political wrangling meant little of that vision made it into statutes. The legislation creating Metropolitan State College was HB349. It is codified in *Article 20 Chapter 124 Colorado Revised Statutes 1953 as amended.* That statute spelled out the four things Metropolitan State College was supposed to do:

1. To provide undergraduate instruction in the liberal arts and sciences as determined by the trustees, in the manner hereinafter specified;
2. To provide and offer programs of instruction in semi-professional technical education in science and engineering technology on a terminal basis, either on its own campus or through contracts with public school districts in the city and county of Denver and in the counties of Adams, Arapahoe, and Jefferson;
3. To encourage other state institutions of higher learning to offer at the college, by extension, such credit courses as are beyond its scope and function, and to cooperate with such other state institutions of higher learning in the offering of such courses;
4. To serve the needs for higher education in the Denver metropolitan area as well as serve the needs of higher education in the state of Colorado generally.

Essentially, the legislation only stated that MSC was to be a liberal arts and sciences college, which would also provide "terminal" courses in applied sciences and technology, commonly called voc-tech. The word "terminal," by the way, meant resulting in a degree, not a life threatening experience—even if later some students saw that as a distinction without a difference.

So how was Metropolitan State College supposed to fulfill the legislature's wishes and still be true to the vision? That question was debated long after the doors of the college opened. Much of that debate was purely a matter of interpretation, or politics.

To learn what the visionaries thought MSC was supposed to be, we need to look in two places the Legislative Committee for Education Beyond High School's Task Group on the Denver Area and the *Trustees Report on the Operation of Metropolitan State College*, also called the "Green Report." This report was mandated by HB349, and was developed by the trustees for the legislature in December 1963.

The legislative committee and the "Green Report" both said Metro State College should be a state-run, four-year *liberal arts* college with an equal *vocational-technical education program* as well. That double mission was different than other colleges in Colorado at the time, but it was not without national precedence.[125]

In the 1960s, traditional liberal arts colleges were changing to match the needs and realities of their time. Four-year colleges began seeking a new balance between educating for an occupation and educating for the broader aspects of life. Many liberal arts colleges were adding programs with specific occupational objectives to their liberal arts curriculum. This mix of pre-professional, professional, and technical, together with conventional liberal arts courses, helped colleges achieve the new educational objectives of the times.[126]

Faculties and governing boards began to insist that *all* students be broadly educated, regardless of their vocational goals. Hence, each student should be required to pursue general courses to prepare them for the responsibilities of citizenship, as well as to achieve a satisfying personal life. MSC's double mission was just an extension of that.

The trustees determined that MSC was going to provide all students with the courses they needed to live in society, particularly in the city, even if their field of study was purely science or vocational and technical. In other words, it would provide education for citizenship *and* education for work. Legislators and policy makers often forgot this as we will see later.

The "Green Report" explained that Metropolitan State College would be different than universities, which provided a full range of undergraduate programs geared to the professions, graduate studies, and research. MSC would also be different from the junior colleges, which provided many programs that were not of collegiate grade.

Instead, Metropolitan State College would provide a range of programs which were not only geared to the occupational needs and opportunities presented by the economy of the area, but programs to enrich all undergraduates—two-year and four year, liberal arts or voc-ed.

Even though the legislative committee said it wanted the new college to be an urban-oriented institution, the legislation that created MSC only established a college in an urban location, which is much different than an *urban-oriented* college.

In the early years, hardly anyone mentioned MSC without using the words "urban-oriented college." That term was an identifier, a moniker that set it apart from other colleges. Being an urban-oriented college was the raison d'être of Metropolitan State College when it was founded. To understand the visionaries' concept of the urban college is to understand Metropolitan State College.

So, what was an urban college in 1965? There weren't any role models in the region for an urban college back then. The University of Colorado—the state's oldest state-run institution of higher education—was not urban oriented. Colorado State University was originally called Colorado A&M (Agriculture and Mining), and it was not a model for urban orientation either. The exact definition of an urban-oriented college was developed over time and evolved under changing circumstances.

The "Green Report" began defining the urban college by saying what it *wasn't*. Specifically, MSC would not have dormitories, social fraternities or sororities, marching bands, varsity intercollegiate athletics, cheerleaders, stadiums or baton twirlers.

Five years after the college opened a Metro English Professor, Dr. William Tillson, wrote an article on the urban college in MSC's student newspaper. Like the "Green Report," he explained what he thought an urban-oriented college *is not*:

> *It is not monolithic, with administration handing down decisions to faculty who in turn order the students. In fact, it seems to work the other way around... The faculty plays a strong part in policy making...students, in turn, express viewpoints and reinforce those with demands oftentimes. The College is not suburban, not cloistered, not class-ridden: There will never be dormitories, sororities, fraternities, faculty clubs, or other secret societies to perpetuate class, race, or social distinctions... This campus is not ivy, never can be, even in Auraria....There can be no cloister because the sidewalk leads away into social action, political involvement, idea exchange... Metro may be something <u>new</u> in education.* [127]

If that is what an urban college isn't, then, what is it?

The "Green Report" defined the urban college as one that provides opportunities for students to learn while they work. It said MSC would share its students with the office and factory, going one step farther than traditional work study or programs for on-the-job instruction. The "Green Report" said all employers in *the metropolitan* area would be potential partners in work study programs.[128]

An urban college would provide an entirely different experience for the student as well. The report pointed out that for the student of a traditional college, the campus *is* his or her life. For the student at an urban-oriented college, the institution is only a *part* of his or her life. The task of the urban-oriented college would be to provide the students with an education and ease their way in enjoying the rich experience of the huge laboratory of living in the city.

MSC's first president, Ken Phillips, was the one who initially determined what this particular urban-oriented college would look like. Dr. Phillips often called MSC an "extroverted urban-oriented college." What did he mean?

In an interview for *Empire Magazine*, which was a major feature magazine inserted in the Sunday *Denver Post*, Phillips explained the essence of Metropolitan State College saying, "For the first time, an urban college had been created, not just to teach city people, but to teach people for the benefit of their city."[129]

To Dr. Phillips, "extroverted" meant students and faculty would come from the community, work in the community, serve the community, and solve the problems of the community. The community would be much like a "living laboratory" where students could work and have actual experience dealing with business, industry, government, and human problems. Being part of the community meant involvement and activism. That last point is significant.

Furthermore, an urban-oriented college must provide successful outcomes for its students. It must offer special assistance to students, such as counseling and guidance and provide the opportunity for involvement in the community and also be responsible to the individual needs of students. In order to do that, Phillips suggested, the school would need to set up liaison committees to keep up to date with constant changes.

In speeches to community groups, Phillips often described the urban-college as one with no ivy on its walls and no gates separating it from the community. He said that MSC was seamless in its relationship with the community. Business and community leaders would come to the college on a regular basis and be involved in the education there. Likewise, students must be encouraged to get involved in the community.

Phillips pointed out that some "so-called urban colleges—schools physically located in cities—tend to shut themselves away from town's problems and wrap their students in a cocoon." Metro, on the other hand, he asserted, was a real urban college, not just geographically, but practically. "We are teaching city kids to live in the city and solve its problems."

An urban college also makes it possible for some city dwellers to get a college education that might otherwise never get one. Phillips pointed out that the traditional ivy-covered college scares off some minority students. They were not sure they'd be welcome in that traditional upper-middle class white atmosphere.

The urban college must approach voc-tech programs differently as well. At MSC, the approach was to teach how as well as why. Many schools offed vocational technology courses, but their intent was to produce theory engineers. Metro would produce the technicians that make the theory work. This was a fresh approach to train people in city the skills the city needed.

The same approach was applied in MSC's education instruction program. Phillips explained to *Empire* the way education was traditionally taught in Colorado: "They put the urban student in a rural school, fill him with theory, give him a diploma, and throw him back into a city school with minority groups and city problems." MSC's approach, he said, was to train the prospective teachers right in the schools and with the children they'll be teaching.

The history department in the early days of MSC embodied that urban college concept. The first chair of the history department, Dr. Peggy Walsh, was a Goldwater Republican. Yet, she firmly believed that in an urban institution of higher education, there must be diversity— diversity in courses, diversity in faculty, diversity in points of view.

One of her early hires was Charles Angeletti, a self-described socialist. In addition to teaching American Civilization, a course that he created, professor Angeletti taught MSC's first Afro-American history course (as it was known then). He and MSC professor Gwen Thomas put together the ethnic studies program, which became a model for the nation. In addition, Dr. Angeletti taught a course in Urban Survival, which taught students how to survive on the streets with nothing, so they could then go into the communities and fix the problems of the city.[130]

Angeletti's courses, and those of Gwen Thomas, were exactly what an urban-grant institution was supposed to teach. In 2012, Gwen Thomas recalled that the wonderful thing about Metro is that it was new, and the faculty was allowed to try new things to see what worked.[131]

An MSC graduate, Larry Steele, said in 2013 that the engagement of students with the community, as a part of curriculum, was what made Metro what it was in its early years. The opportunity to interact was invaluable in the work place. Students learned what a work ethic is, and how to present themselves when they went on job interviews. They got first-hand knowledge out of their collegiate experience, Steel said.[132]

As Dr. Tillson said a college is urbanized when the boundary lines between the college and the community have been erased. Students participate willingly and generously in the activities of the community, he said, and members of the community feel welcome at the college and programs are devised which add to their lives.

Others in the academic community were saying the same thing. The president of the University of Pennsylvania, Gaylord P. Harnwell, wrote an article in April 1967 which made the point that an urban college had to do more than just teach—it needed to help rejuvenate the city. He wrote that an urban university can become the most effective participant in the amelioration of the city dweller's life.[133]

The U.S. Commissioner of Education, Harold Howe said in a 1967 article that those teaching in the new urban colleges have a unique advantage not being restrained by tradition.

They are free to attack the problems of cities with no deep-set traditions holding them back. A large reason for their existence of an urban college is to focus on the problems of urban society, he wrote.[134]

At about that same time Dr. Clark Kerr wrote an article saying that urban universities would help run and re-build cities. They should admit as many young people who are committed to urban service careers as possible, many of them from urban slum backgrounds, and they should send out faculty members and researchers to act as urban agents to show how to run better urban schools, hospitals, welfare and social aid, police departments and so forth. They would become the chief planners of the structural, cultural and human architecture of cities. The urban-grant college could become a cure for urban slums.[135]

Kerr said later, urban grant colleges need to remove as many academic barriers to admission as possible. They must broaden and intensify the search for talent, especially among minority groups. Further, they must adapt their calendar and curriculum to the particular needs of urban students, with flexible schedules, work study programs, and students learning at their own pace with whatever time they have available. And they would solve the many difficult and complex problems that beset our cities, with particular emphasis on aiding the urban public school system.[136]

These concepts for an urban-oriented college defined the vision many had for Metropolitan State College. The urban college was debated throughout the early years of Metropolitan State College. Not everyone agreed on what an urban college was supposed to be. Everyone knew, however, it was something unique.

SO, WHO WAS MSC SUPPOSED TO SERVE?

The trustees had to decide who Metropolitan State College was going to serve before it could figure out how it would get them to enroll.

Studies conducted by the Committee on Education Beyond High School determined that 80 percent of the high school graduates in Denver had the ability to pursue some type of specialized higher education. And, by national standards, 55 percent of metropolitan high school students had the potential to succeed at two-year level studies, 29 percent at four-year level studies and 11 percent at professional-level studies.

So, theoretically, 84 percent of the high school graduates in Denver were a potential market, but the target market was not all graduates. For one thing, in 1963, only 35.5 percent of Denver high school graduates went to college. This figure was disproportionately much lower in poor and minority neighborhoods.[137]

In a 2012 interview, Roy Romer stated who he thought the new college was supposed to serve: "…those kids who got behind in their K-12 school, or didn't excel…and giving them a new opportunity to develop their skills and their knowledge." Romer said with the open door, the institution gives opportunity to the guy who's working and wants to come back, to traditional high school students who don't fit somewhere else, and to somebody who's still employed but just wants an education.[138]

The legislative committee and many legislators at the time said they wanted the new Metro State College to increase the number of college graduates in the Denver area. To do that, the new school had to reach out to the "non-college-going groups" even if some legislators and others did not think those groups actually deserved a college education. Who were these "non-college-goers?" They were:

1. White students whose families lacked the money to send them to college;
2. Black students who were traditionally under-represented in colleges;
3. Latino students who also were traditionally under-represented in college;
4. Women students who did not attend college in the same percentage as men;
5. Older boomers who joined the military or went to work after high school.[139]

If MSC wanted members of these groups to enroll when they previously hadn't, it first needed to determine why they weren't going to college. There were many reasons why they weren't enrolling.

For many, there was no family tradition of college attendance. Often there were no trusted role models. The way to attract these kids was not only to convince them that they *should* do it; but to make the more difficult case that they *could* do it.

Higher education, as an American institution, was ill-prepared to attract that underserved demographic because so few administrators and faculty members came from poor or minority households themselves. Not all, but most, came from families where at least one parent had a degree or some college education. Many educators in the 1960s lacked a first-hand understanding of the difficulties facing that un-served demographic.

As more and more students entered college in the 1960s, in part to avoid the draft, and in part because that was what their parents wished for, the standards for admission to the "club" had to be loosened. Traditionally, American colleges were designed for upper and upper-middle-class white kids. The rest went to trade schools, union apprentice programs, the college of hard knocks, or if they were female, simply stayed home and raised a family.

In one sense, the problems of white high school graduates who came from poor families were similar to the problems faced by black and Chicano graduates living in the same situation. All three groups shared the financial barriers. All three groups shared the lack of role models in the immediate family because most of their parents, grandparents, aunts and uncles never attended college.

In 1965, most African-American kids who were fortunate enough to go to college attended a traditionally black college or university, which were called "Negro" colleges back then. Denver did not have a Negro college.

There were institutional barriers that kept African-American kids out of college. Almost all public colleges in the South in the early 1960's were segregated, so African-American students could not attend. Northern colleges technically accepted them, but black students were often not admitted due to high entrance standards, a lack of achievable scholarships, and by a lack of preparation by the under-funded inner-city high schools they attended. This often resulted in African-American kids doing poorly on SAT tests geared overwhelmingly to white students.

Money was a huge barrier as well. Due to decades of discrimination, most African-American families did not have incomes high enough to pay for tuition, books, dorms, and food. On top of that, many black families depended on money their children earned just to get by. Those families could ill afford to lose the income their children contributed.

Chicanos had the same educational barriers as blacks. In some cases, Chicano kids had trouble on SAT tests because English was not their first language, or of it was, their vocabulary was different than found on tests. Although they did not suffer legal segregation to the degree African-Americans did, Chicanos were victims of de-facto segregation in housing, employment, education, and in a lack of stature afforded them by white society.

And there is something else to consider. The high school graduation rate among African-Americans was much lower than whites. Chicanos had an even lower graduation rate than blacks, in part because of language difficulties, and even lower family incomes. These individuals were barred admission from most colleges in the nation by circumstance, not law.

For African-American and Chicano students, as well as white kids who graduated from schools in poor neighborhoods, the quality of the education they received in grades one through twelve was not equal to the education that white kids in affluent neighborhoods received.

The schools in poor and minority neighborhoods were funded at per-pupil rates that were a fraction of rates at white schools. Often, the best teachers taught at the white schools. This was due to many factors, including teachers' pay that was often times much higher in affluent schools. Also, many teachers were afraid to teach in schools located in poor neighborhoods, fearing attacks from students or non-students.

Teachers in schools with a majority of black, brown and poor white students often did not expect their students would ever go to college, so they did not encourage them in that direction, let alone prepare them.

Another barrier that kept African-American, Chicanos, poor whites and women from going to college was the lack of encouraging peer pressure. Peer pressure is a stronger factor in adolescent behavior than the example set by parents. If a kid lacks a parental role model for college attendance and pressure from his or her peers, they are not likely to even consider college. If a student's classmates are not talking about going to college, that student is not likely to either.

Lastly, in the mid-1960s, many minority youths had lost hope. On TV they watched people who looked like them struggle for equality and justice, but they did not feel that justice was coming fast enough. Commercials made every kid want material belongings. Poor and minority youths were becoming more aware of the disparity between the things white kids had versus what they had, and they were resentful they could not have them. They did not see education as the way to correct that disparity.

The parents of poor and minority baby boomers were not confronted with that disparity when they were growing up to the same degree as their children. They were not as aware how the other half actually lived before the advent of TV. Self-esteem among minority and poor kids was dropping at an alarming rate, and modern technology was partly to blame, although blame is an inappropriate word for exposing the reality of two Americas.

Furthermore, in the '60s most policy makers still believed that college wasn't for everyone and since state-run colleges were expensive, a college education should be reserved for the well off. Other kids should just learn a trade.

The fourth under-served demographic Metro had to attract was women. American colleges and universities were predominately male. In the boomer-parent generation, that began to change. World War II proved that "Rosie the Riveter" was just as proficient as "Walt the Welder" and the WAC nurse could save just as many lives as the traditional male medic. In wartime many traditional biases and barriers break down.

Girls were generally better students than boys. They matured earlier and learned at a faster pace than young boys. As a result, the number of female graduates receiving scholarships was steadily increasing once the institutional barriers were broken down.[140]

The "Green Report" revealed studies that showed the ratio of male and female students who qualified for two-year studies was nearly equal, but more males than females would be expected to qualify for four-year and professional college training. This raised an interesting question: Were the studies skewed, or were high schools failing to prepare young women for college? Perhaps young women were being conditioned to believe they were not meant for a college or a graduate degree.

In the boomer-grandparent generation, a woman's place was in the home. There was no need for girls to go to college to learn those skills—they learned them from their mothers or Better Homes and Gardens. The major exceptions were teachers and nurses. Prior to the 1960s, most women who went to college became teachers or nurses—a few became doctors and even fewer, lawyers. Once in a while, a woman could become an architect or engineer.[141]

Women who wanted to teach generally went to a woman's college, a teacher's college or university, because a post-graduate degree was often required. Scholarships were readily available for girls who wanted to become educators. As for the others, unless they won a pageant, their parents usually had to pay. The majority of co-eds, as women students were called back then, came from upper middle class or wealthy families and many of their mothers were members of college sororities.

As boomer-parents got married, bought homes and had children they took on debt. At the same time, the influx of new material goods on the market grew. Television was invented; all kinds of fancy new appliances were in stores. Advertising and TV commercials made owning these things a necessity, not an option. Keeping up with the Joneses required a second income. More and more families required two breadwinners after World War II.[142]

Women realized they needed to go to college to increase their earning power—in part to help their spouses pay higher mortgages on bigger suburban homes and make payments on that second car. Businesses began encouraging women to get a degree. This cultural shift not only led to more women with degrees in the work place, but also to more women college professors. These women, in turn, became role models for young girls, sending a message that they, too, could and should go to college.

Metropolitan State College needed to serve this rising female demographic whether it realized it or not. And it took a while before MSC was able to enroll nearly equal numbers of male and female students.

The final group of un-served potential students was the early baby boomers who did not go to college after high school. This group included the high school graduates and drop-outs who went straight into the work force. Included in this demographic were those who went into the military after high school, and who became veterans eligible for benefits under the Cold War GI Bill.

Many of these individuals were married and could not afford to quit their jobs to attend school. It was thought that most of these "older" students would want to enroll in voc-tech classes. As it turned out, many did, but many others wanted a general college education instead. To serve this demographic, the school needed to have both a day and night school. It would also need day care. (It took a future MSC student, King Harris to realize that and do something about it.)

In some ways it was easier for Metropolitan State College to attract potential students who were older and working than the large underserved group of poor and minority high school graduates and women. The reason was that in the workplace or the military, the likelihood of pro-college peer pressure is greater than in high school. Maturity was also a factor.

MSC was ideal for veterans who could take advantage of the Cold War GI Bill, which paid their tuition and some of their living expenses while in college. Because the college was located in Denver, where many vets lived, and tuition was low, the money barrier for veterans was somewhat diminished.

Attracting and serving the un-served groups Metropolitan State College was supposed to and needed to serve would prove to be a challenge. After all, society had not yet figured out how to serve these groups. Whether legislators, the trustees or the administration wanted to serve all these groups or not, the times dictated that not serving them was no longer an option

THE OPEN DOOR

A college can't serve poor students if they can't pay the tuition. Further, a college cannot accommodate underserved, at-risk students if it won't let them in the door, and make it possible for them to stay once in.

The open-door admissions policy was essential if Metropolitan State College had any hope of serving its target demographic market. From the very beginning, the trustees dictated that admissions to MSC were to be open to any person who either graduated from high school or had a GED. It did not matter how low the student ranked in school, so long as they had papers—a diploma or GED.

Enrollment was also going to be open to any student who transferred from another institution of higher education, regardless of their academic standing. There were occasions, however, in which a transferring student who was on academic suspension from another college might encounter difficulty with that open door, but generally speaking, anyone could get in. (Although not everyone could stay if they did not apply themselves.)

Roy Romer called MSC the college of second (or perhaps third) chances. It was intended to provide educational *opportunity* to the masses, not guaranteed education to the masses. If a student received a second or third chance, he or she had to take advantage of it, make it work—and that involved effort.

Metro's open-door policy was first put forth by the legislature's Metropolitan Denver Task Group and it was explained and affirmed in the "Green Report." The open door was seen as a means of widening educational opportunities for high school graduates and drop-outs in the Denver area. The trustees stipulated that MSC would have an open door that was "modified by reality."[143]

The term open door can be misleading, and is really a misnomer. It has various meanings, as the "Green Report" stated. Perhaps the most extreme interpretation is that an institution is expected to take almost every student who applies.

Denver's Opportunity School had an open door. Its motto was: "For all who wish to learn." Under that version, the institution has no set of prerequisites—it doesn't care how far one has gone in school, how old one is, or how one earns a living. It cares only that the potential student intends to profit from the offerings.

In collegiate institutions, open door was always qualified by limiting conditions, such as a high school diploma (or demonstrating the ability of a high school graduate). In addition, it pre-supposes other evidence of ability, interest and performance to give some indication as to whether the student will succeed.

In Metro's case, the open door would stand in contrast with institutions having selective admissions policies. It would recognize that many students may not have demonstrated in high school their real ability due to maturity, or different background levels. The trustees suggested the appropriate motto for MSC might be, "For all who wish to learn and are capable of completing the courses which are offered."

Unlike most four-year colleges, MSC did not use ACT or SAT tests for admission, but they did use them to determine whether a student would be subject to probation or be required to take remedial courses.

The reality about tests like the ACT and SAT is that they are an imperfect and highly subjective measurement of ability, and not a good measure of intelligence. Standardized multiple-choice tests often measure how good a student is at memorization. Sometimes the outcome is determined by a student's luck. Sometimes, choosing A, B, or C on a test is not much different than choosing numbers on a Powerball ticket.

Standardized tests are a poor indicator of a student's comprehension of subject matter, or his or her ability to think and reason. Studies show that standardized tests are also a poor predictor of a student's success in college. Standardized tests are one reason the college population is still made up of a disproportionate number of affluent students. Many well-off parents spend large sums of money on tutors and tutorial programs to help their children pass college entrance tests.

A recent study done by William Bliss looked at 33 public and private colleges and universities and examined the records of 123,000 students from more than 20 states. It found that test scores didn't correlate with how well a student did in college, based on grades or graduation rates.

Bliss said that the people often excluded by ACT and SAT scores are just the people society needs in college. This includes those who are in the first generation to attend college, minority students, students with learning disabilities (like dyslexia), somewhat more women than men and low-income Pell Grant recipients. Bliss said the danger of relying on ACT scores is they truncate the pool of the people colleges really need to have enrolled.[144]

College admission requirements determined who fought the wars that the nation's ruling class elected to fight. In 1965, if young males, especially males of color, did not go to college they likely would be shipped off to Vietnam. Along with money, GPA often determined who went off to fight and die, and who avoided service by enrolling in college. Students in poor and minority schools generally had lower GPA than kids in better schools. This is a major reason that the names on the wall of the Vietnam Memorial in Washington are predominantly African Americans, Latinos, and poor whites.

The reason so many politicians opposed Metro's open door is that it would reduce the number of men who could be drafted to fight in Vietnam. If poor whites and blacks were allowed to go to college and receive a deferment, then by necessity, the college deferment would need to be eliminated thus putting young well-off white men at risk of being drafted. That could not be allowed to happen. Rich men wage wars for poor men to fight, not their sons and daughters.

That is why an open door was and is still important—to give poor test-takers, kids who went to bad schools or had bad teachers, the creative problem solvers, and the great thinkers a chance for a college education. It gave late starters, as Romer called them, a chance to go to college.

The open door did not mean the college only catered to students who didn't do well in high school; its doors were open to all students, including those who simply had obstacles to overcome. These included older individuals who went to work after high school and now wanted to get a college education.

An open door swung both ways. In many cases, it was easier to turn the open door into a revolving door. If, after a great deal of persuasion, a high-risk student enrolls in college and then fails, it is almost worse than if he or she never enrolled in the first place. Failure wrecks self-esteem. It kills hope. It reinforces the individual's notion that he or she cannot achieve. So the college had a responsibility to makes sure that failure happened rarely.

The concept of the open door was not new for American colleges and universities in the mid-1960s, but it was somewhat rare. Critics of MSC, including legislators and the CU regents, used open enrollment against the college before it even opened, calling it second-rate. They charged that because Metropolitan State College was going to provide an opportunity to everyone, the quality of that education had to be inferior.

Had they read it, critics would have seen that the "Green Report" pointed out that the open door did not mean the college would provide a low quality education. The commitment of MSC to the principle of admitting anyone with a desire and capacity to learn meant that it could not permit the student to fail indefinitely.

The "Green Report" said that MSC would protect its standards in both technical and baccalaureate programs by giving weight and credence to past performance and to the recommendations of high school principals. It would provide placement testing and guidance to identify prospective students' areas of weakness and strength for their desired programs. Students who were clearly unlikely to do collegiate level work would be encouraged by counselors to take programs below the collegiate level at other institutions, rather than fail at MSC.

The bottom line at MSC was this: The student who wants to try would be permitted to try. Probationary status would be explicit and clear. And counseling and guidance would be available and encouraged for all those who attended MSC.

In the '60s, attitudes in society were changing, but they were not fully changed. Not everyone agreed that the greatest feature of Metropolitan State College was that it offered a first chance to minorities and the poor and a second chance to late bloomers. To many it was still "one strike and you're out." Of course, money created an exception—even a class ditching, coke-sniffing booze hound could get into an Ivy League school and stay there if his dad was rich and well-connected.

Many academicians at the time debunked charges made by the CU regents and others that Metro would be inferior because of the open door. In an April 1965 article in the *Phi Delta Kappan Magazine*, KU's George Waggoner, Dean of Arts and Sciences, said, "Kansas University is one of few universities with an open door. An open-door policy guarantees nothing except an opportunity of a student who wishes to enter the university to enroll."[145]

He went on to say that despite their open door, in the last eight years KU students won more Rhodes scholarships than any other public university, and all but three private universities; and in proportion to number of graduates, and more Woodrow Wilson fellowships than any other public university.

George Smith, vice-chancellor for institutional planning at KU, made a big point when he said, "If the University of Kansas had turned aside bottom-half students in one five year period, the loss would have been 202 teachers, 176 engineers, 43 pharmacists, 31 lawyers, 25 medical doctors, 22 journalists, and 119 others from the College of Liberal Arts and Sciences and School of Business." He added, "Late bloomers zoom ahead of others who hit the top in their pre-college years." As KU's George Waggoner said, the open door guarantees nothing but an opportunity.

Many of the early MSC students who went on to Ivy League graduate schools only received their baccalaureate degree because of Metro's open door. Those graduates have gone on to make a huge difference in Denver and the nation. For example, in the first few years after it opened, MSC's accounting program had developed a reputation in the industry for having an equal percentage of graduates as CU or DU who pass the CPA exam, which is required to be licensed as a certified public accountant.

One of these students was Milroy Alexander, an immigrant from the Caribbean nation of Grenada, who was admitted to MSC because of its open door. He became a CPA and went on to a job at Touche Ross after graduation, then after eleven years there, he became the Chief Financial Officer for the Colorado Housing Finance Authority, from which he retired after 22 years. He made a difference to countless individuals who were able to find affordable housing, thanks to his work.

Courtney Cowgill, another MSC graduate, spent her freshman year at CU Boulder. Although she was working hard, she was not doing well so she transferred to Metro to study accounting. There were five women in the accounting department when she started, but today the accounting department has over 50 percent women students.

Ms. Cowgill graduated and went on to become the President of the American Society of Women Accountants because MSC taught her how to learn and how to succeed. She credits the faculty and her fellow students for her success. She said she landed her first job at a Big Three accounting firm—not because of her less-than 4.0 GPA, but because two faculty members recommended her.[146]

Another example of the importance of the open door is that of a married foundry worker, King Harris. He was admitted in 1968 following a troubled youth, having only completed eighth grade and getting a GED. He attended MSC from 1968-1972 but did not finish his degree. He took a job as a loan officer at United Bank of Denver, and then went back in 1992 to get his degree.

Before he left MSC the first time, Harris started the school's first day care in the basement of a nearby church. Later, he was appointed by the governor to the Colorado Highway Commission, and is now a Methodist Minister. He is still making a difference in the community. Without the opportunity MSC and its open door provided, perhaps Harris would have continued working at the foundry, which, he said, "would have killed him."[147]

Larry Steele was told by his high school counselor that if he wanted to go to college, he better try Metro because it was probably the only school that would take him. He applied, was accepted, and became another validation of the open door. While a student, Steele worked on the Auraria campaign, helped lobby the legislature, and served on the first planning committee for Auraria after the bond issue passed.[148]

There are hundreds of stories like these. More of them will be told in this book. Many of these stories are not known to anyone, however, except the grateful students themselves, who benefited from the "College of Opportunity," as MSU Denver Human Services professor, Dr. Antonio Ledesma, calls his alma mater.

Virginia Mennenga, who worked with the MSU Denver Alumni Association, said in 2014, "Without exception, all of the alumni interviewed by the Institutional History Committee brought up the fact that the open door and the assistance and inspiration they received from the faculty were the main, if not the only reasons, they were able to succeed in college and in their careers afterwards."

The college's first president, Dr. Phillips, said in the *Empire* interview that "the notion of an open door must coincide with special assistance to students, such as counseling and guidance and opportunity for involvement in the community. He realized that an at-risk student entering college with a questionable support system would do better if that student were involved in his or her community, surrounded by familiar faces, people like him or her. Without those elements, it would only be *a college in an urban location.*

HOW MSC DEFINED ITSELF

After it opened, what did Metropolitan State College itself believe it was supposed to be?

Early on, the faculty and administration began looking at that issue. The president formed a committee to take the legislative mandate, such as it was, and extrapolate that into a policy statement and objectives for the college.

In May 1966, the faculty/administration Sub–Committee on Curriculum developed a policy statement on the nature and functions of MSC, which became the operational policy of the college. This was adopted before the school became a real four-year institution. Dr. Keats McKinney, MSC's first dean, played a major role in development of this policy. He had previously authored the "Green Report" while he was still at Adams State.[149]

To paraphrase that policy, MSC was supposed to be an *urban type* institution dedicated to excellence in teaching by faculty selected primarily on the basis of interest and effectiveness in teaching as well as on academic preparation and special qualifications. Research at MSC was not required and not necessary for promotion. Co-curricular activities were to be developed jointly by staff and students. And, they said, MSC was to serve the community and the State of Colorado.

Metro was to open the door to all who have the will and ability to benefit from the instruction offered. Specifically that included the recent high school graduate; the graduate who has worked several years; the person working full-time who wishes to pursue college studies after working hours; the mature adult facing the necessity of re-training for a challenging economy; and the person of any age who is seeking pleasure and stimulation in the development of his intellectual and artistic interests.

The college was to provide an education that would allow the graduate to function as a reasonable citizen in society. It was to help graduates find work, and it was supposed to "maintain close contact with students, upon whom all efforts are focused."

It wasn't the words written in that policy, but the words not written that would be the basis for both discourse and the discord at Metropolitan State College in the years to come. The school's policy would not be in step with its rhetoric, as we will see in the pages that follow.

Missing entirely from that policy statement, however, was a specific mention of any mission to reach out to minorities, the poor, and women. Perhaps those groups were intended to be incorporated by the use of the words "open to *all* who have the will and ability to benefit from the instruction offered."

This was sort of like the Founding Fathers saying, "All men are created equal," but then forming a government that excluded the majority of the men and women alive at the time the benefits of equality.

There was also no reference in the Green Report for the college to be responsive to the needs of the community—to teach students how to live in the city, or to solve the problems of the city. These missing statements were at the core of what many, including the school's first president, believed Metro State College was supposed to be, but there was no mention of them in official policy, just as there was no mention of them in legislation.

Sadly, the "Green Report" was actually anti-climactic because the decision to postpone MSC was made before legislators even saw it. Almost no one read it. When MSC was finally funded, it happened not by a separate bill, but by a line-item in the Long Bill, with no additional guidance from the legislature. All the trustees had to go on was the "Green Report" and HB349—except for the stipulation MSC could not offer upper-division courses without further legislative approval.

Perhaps if the legislature had the guts to stand up to the CU lobby and passed an enabling bill that stipulated its vision for Metropolitan State College, many battles down the road would have been avoided. All the trustees had to go on was the "Green Report" and the vision of the founders, still simmering below the surface.

In the words of the Essex, "It's easier, easier said than done."[150]

Dr. Keats McKinney was the first administrator hired as Dean of the College. Dr. McKinney recruited the first faculty in record time.

Photo Courtesy of Metropolitan State University of Denver.

CHAPTER 5

It Finally Opens...

And you may find somebody kind to help and understand you
Someone who is just like you and needs a gentle hand
To guide them along so maybe I'll see you there
We can forget all our troubles, forget all our cares
So go Downtown, things will be great
when you're Downtown
"Downtown" Petula Clark[151]

Metropolitan State was going to open in fall of 1965. Finally, there would be an institution to help those who previously could not even imagine getting a college education.

There were scarcely five months to prepare before the doors would open for students. More than likely, no one in history ever attempted to open a new four-year state-supported college in just five months¬—no one. There were more questions than answers, and there wasn't even a physical location in which to set up shop.

Even before the legislature funded the college, the Board of Trustees was planning for the day it would actually open. Nevertheless, planning in the abstract is far easier than planning in reality—particularly the reality of dealing with a skimpy budget and the very little time they had to work with. The legislature gave the trustees less money than they needed, and less time to open the school than common sense dictated it would take.

SO MUCH TO DO, SO LITTLE TIME

The trustees needed an interim president to set up the college up while they finalized their search for a permanent president. They asked Dr. Harlan Bryant, president of Western State College in Gunnison, to assume that role.[152]

They hired Dr. Keats McKinney away from Adams State College to serve as dean. He started work on May 15. Dean McKinney immediately began to develop a catalogue and appoint faculty. He hired Dr. Harold Benn and assigned him the task of developing the course catalogue for students, who would be arriving in less than five months.[153]

Registration was opened and the school began receiving about 12 applications a day. By June 8, a total of 81 students had applied.[154]

Since the college had no facilities, it was given temporary use of room 227 of the State Capitol. It was not in use then because the legislature was not in session. This was MSC's first office where faculty could drop off resumes and prospective students could apply. Metro State was the only, state college or university to begin operations in the Capitol. (At the time this book was written, room 227 was the office of the Deputy Majority Leader of the House, Rep. Dan Pabon.)

The very first non-faculty employee of Metro State College was Ferne Bentley. She was hired as a secretary on May 24, 1965. Later, Ferne would become MSC business manager Curtis Wright's secretary. The second staff member hired was Sandi Jones. She started on July 1, 1965 as secretary to Dean McKinney. She also came from Adams State College where she had worked for Dr. McKinney and helped him prepare the "Green Report."[155]

Dr. Bryant had a small room in the trustees offices in the nearby State Services Building, but Ms. Bentley and Dr. McKinney worked in that small room at the Capitol.[156] When they needed office equipment like a mimeograph or a copier, they used the facilities of the Joint Budget Committee which was located next door.[157]

(For those unfamiliar, the mimeograph was the 1965 version of the laser printer—without the laser or printer. One typed a document on a blue sheet, placed it on the drum of a machine, flipped the switch, and as the drum turned, blue–inked copies came out.)

When Sandi Jones started, Metro was moved to the Capitol's basement because the legislature needed Room 227

Room 227 of the State Capitol was MSC's the first office in May and June of 1965

Photo Credit: Angela L. Schnaubelt

for the special session. Dr. Bryant did not like his room at the trustees' office, so Roy Romer arranged for him to move into an office used by the Senate at the Capitol.[158]

Jones said in an interview that she spent a great deal of time typing and mailing out contracts to faculty members during those first few months. Dr. McKinney was on the road interviewing prospective faculty members around the country. When he found one he liked, she said, he'd call in and say, "Send them a contract."

Dorita Crosby was the first payroll clerk, hired on June 8, 1965. She managed payroll for six employees that first month. By March 1966, the school's payroll would grow to 115. Pat Q. Kiley came on as the college's first data processing supervisor. Kay Elwell was brought in as the first psychometric counselor on Aug 1, 1965. She had been working at CU Denver Center. Faye Louks was hired as the cashier for the business office, and she worked the first registration in October 1965. Betty Reeves was hired for the admissions office in October.[159]

While Metro State was staffing up for its debut, *The Denver Post*, resigning itself to the fact that MSC was going to open, targeted the proposed Community College of Denver. They editorialized that the community college was no longer needed. "Metro State, as laid out by the legislature, appears to come very close to meeting the needs for technical and two-year liberal arts curricula for young people who for various reasons...cannot go away for school," *The Post* wrote. They seemed to still be inferring that Metro was only a two-year college.[160]

In another editorial, *The Post* said that the CU Denver Center should raise its academic standards to differentiate itself from Metro State. They said CU should abandon the "mass education" philosophy and leave that job to Metro. On May 30, the CU Denver Center took that advice and raised their admission standards to conform to the Boulder campus.[161]

This gave the new Metropolitan State College access to the students that graduated below the top third of their high school, since they were no longer eligible to get into the CU Denver Center.

Meanwhile, scarcely a month after the funds were appropriated, leaders of the hotel and restaurant industry in Denver were urging the new Metro State to include a cooking school in its

The Forum Building was still under construction when MSC leased it.

Photo Courtesy of Metropolitan State University of Denver.

69

curriculum, saying it was urgently needed. Dr. Bryant told the industry group, "We will build the technical programs (of Metro) on the needs of the community. A culinary arts program was added to the curriculum the next year.[162]

With students signing up, the pressure was on Dr. Bryant to rent facilities for offices, labs, and classrooms. He needed to make arrangements for a library keeping in mind the legislature gave MSC only sixty percent of the funds that the trustee's planning had determined were required.

The trustees asked a member of the Board of Trustees, Betty Naugle, to work with Dr. Bryant to find facilities to rent. Ms. Naugle was from Denver and had only been on the Board of Trustees for one year. Her husband was a judge, her father a prominent and politically-connected attorney. She became a key person in the early decisions involving the college.

Naugle would prove to be a champion of MSC and higher education in Denver. She was front and center in all the skirmishes the college would encounter over the next decade. She was extremely persuasive and not afraid to state her mind. Things might have turned out much differently for MSC were it not for her service and dedication.

While Dr. Bryant and Naugle were looking at office space, Dean McKinney was busy interviewing potential faculty members and staff. He announced the first six faculty members of Metropolitan State College on June 13. They were: Forrest D. Lillie, Dean of Students; Tom Cook, assistant professor of speech; Milliard D. McLallen, assistant professor of English; Wayne Rollins, assistant professor of English; Keith Rogers, assistant professor of chemistry; and Raymond G. Wilims, assistant professor of sociology.[163]

Dr. Bryant and Betty Naugle were deluged by landlords who were pitching their buildings. One of those pitchmen was Shelby Harper, vice president of Security Life Insurance Co. He had served on the advisory board of the task group that recommended that MSC be created. He had also served as president of the Denver Chamber of Commerce, and was the chairman of the new Colorado Commission on Higher Education (CCHE) when the college opened, having been appointed by Governor Love earlier in the year.

Harper pushed the trustees to lease his company's downtown building as the "Green Report" had stated. Security Life had vacated that facility when it moved into a new skyscraper, which was Denver's tallest building at the time. The new Security Life Building was home to the exclusive Top of the Rockies restaurant on the top floor, where many a business and political deal would be cut, many anniversaries celebrated, and many questions popped to future brides.

The Denver Chamber of Commerce had different advice for Metro though. On June 10, they passed a resolution strongly suggesting that MSC be located in either the old Daniels & Fisher Tower at 16th and Arapahoe, or the old May Company Building at 16th and Champa, which the trustees had also hinted they would rent.[164]

In early June, to the dismay of both the Denver Chamber and Shelby Harper, Bryant and Naugle recommended that the trustees lease space in several buildings, none of which was the Security Life Building, the May Company, or Daniels and Fisher—although it would have been cool to attend classes in a replica of San Marco's tower in Venice and hear the bells tolling at the end of class.

Instead, they chose a yellow office building at 333 West Colfax, in the triangle between Colfax, 13th Street, and Court Place., across from the Denver Mint. It was known as the Kentucky Central Insurance Building, but would be called the TTT Building, short for Three Thirty Three (W. Colfax). The college initially leased just the top floor (for a science lab) and the basement, which would house four classrooms and storage space.

In addition, Metro leased office space for $3 per square foot in the Denver University Administration Building at 1445 Cleveland St., across Colfax from the campus green. Classes were held there day one. It was anticipated that DU would move out to its south Denver campus in 18 months and Metro would get more space.[165]

Dr. Bryant was also interested in a new building under construction at 14th and Cherokee, across the street from the City and County Building, a block from the 333 Building. The building was called the Forum. It was originally intended to be offices for attorneys and bail bondsmen who wanted to be near the city and county courts. There were two problems, though: first, it was relatively expensive, and second, it would require a variance from the Denver Board of Zoning before the college could move in.

The building was designed for general office space, with four-foot wide hallways. Metropolitan State was a college and the city ordinance required five-foot wide hallways. Regardless, on June 15 the trustees signed a lease for space in the Forum, contingent upon getting the variance. They leased floors three through nine, half of the tenth floor, and part of the second. These would be used for offices and fifteen classrooms.

In addition, the trustees entered into an agreement with Denver Public Schools to share facilities at the Emily Griffith Opportunity School on Glenarm for voc-tech classes.[166]

The decision to lease these spaces instead of the Security Life Building came as a surprise to many. In the Operational Plan for Metropolitan State College, (the "Green Report,") the trustees not only indicated the college would be located in the old Security Life Building, but many pages were dedicated to detailed breakdowns of the costs for leasing and renovating that building in phases over a ten-year period as enrollment grew.

It seemed like leasing the Security Life Building was a done deal according to the "Green Report." Costs for no other buildings were detailed in the document. The decision not to lease the Security Life Building would bite Metropolitan State College more than once.

Surprisingly, *The Denver Post* editorial board agreed with Metro's decision to lease the Forum Building, noting the Chamber and others (Shelby Harper) wanted the college to lease space downtown, especially the old Security Life Building.[167]

The college needed a library, but the legislature did not appropriate sufficient funds for even a token collection. Time was running out so Dr. Bryant and the trustees entered into an agreement with the Denver Public Library at 14th and Broadway to allow students to use their facilities. MSC paid $30,000 for those services for the first year. The funds would be used to hire additional library staff to assist Metro State students.[168]

The interim library overlooked the beautiful campus commons—also known as the campus green—complete with fountains, statues, an outdoor Greek-columned amphitheater, and lots of grass for touch football, tossing a Frisbee, catching rays, and conducting the occasional love-in or protest. Some people, though, preferred to call it Civic Center Park.

Later that summer, MSC opened its own library in the Forum to supplement the facilities at the DPL. Charlene Alexis was hired to be in charge of that first library. She saw an ad on Channel 7 and went down to the Capitol to apply. She told Dr. McKinney, "If there is a germ of a library, I want to catch it." That line worked, and she was hired. In November, she hired Joan Meier as the first clerk of the skeleton library, which had about ten books.[169]

Much more space was needed, and facilities were still required for faculty and administrative offices as well as additional classrooms. Once MSC committed to using rented space near the Mint rather than a building in LODO, landlords downtown were quick to present their space for consideration. Shelby Harper, however, had not given up on leasing Metro the old Security Life Building.

Leasing the Forum and the 333 Building were not without controversy. A downtown property owner, Jay Gould, told the press that Metropolitan State College was wasting taxpayer money. He owned the Kittridge Building at 16th and Glenarm, on what is now the 16th Street Mall. He said MSC was paying $ 225,000 a year for only 30,000 square feet of space when they could rent his building, which was 40,000 square feet, for only $60,000 a year, saving taxpayers $165,000.[170]

The trustees argued that the Kittridge Building would require extensive modifications, and the location was not ideal, given the distance from the Denver Public Library.

On June 21, the hearing on the variance request for the Forum Building was held. The Denver Planning Office came out strongly against the variance, saying it would set a bad precedent. They said it would create unsafe conditions for students exiting in case of a fire, and there were many other buildings available for rent. But they were not persuasive, and the variance was granted.[171]

The Forum Building was still under construction when MSC leased the space. The contractor was completing work one floor at a time. MSC first occupied temporary space on the first floor. Sandi Jones recalled that when a floor would get finished, her offices would move up one story. Eventually, they were able to move into the seventh floor, which was the deans' floor.

Nothing seemed to go smoothly for the new college, however. Shortly after the lease for the

Forum Building was signed, lawsuits started flying. It seems that the owners of the Forum had leased the basement to a woman, Margaret Santangelo, who planned on opening a bar called the Jury Room. When Metro State leased space in the building for classrooms, she claimed it violated her lease. City ordinances prohibited a new liquor license that close to a school.

Dr. Bryant said that Metro would still open on schedule despite the lawsuit. He said the bar was not illegal because her liquor license been issued before the college leased space and thus she was grandfathered in. Students, of course, would undoubtedly have outnumbered lawyers and jurors in that convenient bar, had it opened. Santangelo elected not to open it and limited her suit to requesting damages from the owner. The owners of the White Mule, a local bar on Colfax down the street, were delighted she walked away.[172]

The announcement everyone was waiting for came on July 8 when the trustees announced the selection of Metropolitan State College's first president. They chose Dr. Kenneth Phillips from San Diego, California. They said that Dr. Bryant would stay on and assist President Phillips prepare a budget for the first year.

Ken Phillips was born in Buffalo, New York and received his bachelors at the State University of New York. He then enrolled at Ohio State University where he received his masters and doctorate in education. He spent 13 years as chairman of the industrial arts department at San Diego State. Prior to being hired by MSC, Phillips had been at Cal-State San Bernardino where he coordinated site selection, master planning and so forth for the expanding institution.[173]

Dr. Phillips passed away on February 23, 2013, but in an interview taped three years earlier, He recalled how he came to be MSC's first president. In the early summer of 1965, he said that he received a surprise phone call from someone who said that he understood Phillips was interested in the president's job at Metro State College. [174]

He had previously met the president of Colorado State College, Dr. Darrell Holmes, at a college fair and they became friends. Apparently, Dr. Holmes told someone on the Board of Trustees' search committee that Ken Phillips was interested in the president's position. Whether Phillips had indicated that to Dr. Holmes is not clear.

Dr. Phillips told the caller that he knew nothing about the college, and asked if they could send him something to read. The trustees sent him the "Green Report" After reading it Phillips was intrigued about the mission and character of the new school. He understood MSC was to be a standard college "and at the same time, it was to emphasize community-related programs—programs that would support the needs of the community, whatever they might be." He thought that was an intriguing concept.

On the Fourth of July, while Denverites were celebrating the nation's 190th birthday, Dr. Phillips was in Denver being interviewed along with several other applicants. Before the day was over, the trustees asked him to accept the position of president of Metropolitan State

College. Phillips said he had to discuss it with his wife and his current employer, Cal-State San Bernardino. He did not say how those conversations went, but the fact that he accepted indicates they went well.

In the news conference in which the trustees introduced him, Dr. Phillips said he would adhere to the legislative plan for the college which he understood to be a liberal arts college with an equal division for technical and vocational education. There was no mention of an urban-oriented college.[175]

Phillips was what the trustees believed MSC needed: a man with experience in industrial arts, since that is what many legislators and the Denver business community wanted MSC to emphasize. He also had experience in site selection, planning, and other facets of building a new campus. Best of all, he had no scars from doing battle in higher education in Colorado.

He was a short, balding man who was younger than he appeared. He was affable, highly energetic, and he took great interest in students. As Doug Holcombe recalls, "When someone got into an elevator with Dr. Phillips on the ground floor, by the time you got to the tenth floor, he knew your entire life story."[176]

(As a student in 1969, I had the great fortune to travel to Washington DC with Dr. Phillips. We had been invited to the White House by President Nixon to discuss campus unrest and the Vietnam War. My opinion of Dr. Phillips was formed on that plane. I learned that he was a man who cared about MSC and students. He was often criticized, but that was part of the no-win job of running a college in such a tumultuous era.)

The same day Dr. Phillips was chosen, Dr. Lester Thonssen was hired as a professor of speech. In addition, Forest D. Lillie (who went by Dean) was named the first Dean of Student Services. Ironically, he had been on the staff at Otero Junior College, where he worked under MSC's opponent, Dr. James McDivitt, the school's president. McDivitt had sided with the CU regents in their attempt to block MSC earlier in the year.[177]

Shortly after he was hired, Dean Lillie told his neighbor about the exciting new college in Denver. The neighbor had never heard of Metropolitan State College. Lillie suggested that he should go down to the state Capitol and apply. He took Lillie's advice, went to the Capitol, met with Keats McKinney and was hired on the spot. The new professor was Dr. Jerry Wilson, who taught physics and became department chairman in 1969. He was greatly responsible for developing the physics major at MSC.[178]

While everyone was working overtime to get ready to open the doors, storm clouds appeared in the western sky. In July it became apparent that the opponents of Metropolitan State College had not surrendered. A scant two months after the governor signed the Long Bill, and three months before Metro's doors would open, the newly constituted Colorado Commission on Higher Education (CCHE) was making ominous noises.

The Colorado legislature had created the CCHE earlier that year. Governor Love appointed businessman Shelby Harper as chairman; Pat Griffin of Fort Collins was vice-chairman. The first commissioners were Brown Cannon and Richard Schmidt of Denver, Frank Hoag of Pueblo, Phillip Cole of Colorado Springs, and William Stevens of Gypsum. They had oversight over all Colorado higher education institutions and made funding recommendations to the legislature. Clearly, this body could make trouble for MSC if it chose to do so; and it chose to.

Shortly after the new commission opened for business, Jack Gaskie wrote in *the Rocky Mountain News*, "The CCHE gave clear indications...that it considers its teeth sharp, and it intends to bite with them." They grilled Dean Lillie about the school's policy of assigning freshmen to classes according to their ability, as indicated by ACT scores or GPA, and not randomly. Dean Lillie assured them this occurred only in English classes to assist those who needed remedial work.[179]

Members of the commission also asserted that some of Metro's applicants were qualified to go to the CU Denver Extension instead of MSC. They claimed this amounted to a duplication of courses, and they were going to examine the situation. How the CCHE arrived at this conclusion is not known.

The big issue, however, was the commission's displeasure with the site selection procedures specifically leasing the Forum Building. Shelby Harper asked Betty Naugle why she did not consult him before signing the lease. She answered that time was the paramount consideration. Commissioner Cole suggested the lease was invalid since Naugle did not consult with the commission and obtain approval first, but he did not indicate he would take any action.

This was an interesting development. CCHE chairman Shelby Harper had been trying to get MSC to lease the old Security Life Building for some time. Harper was vice-president of Security Life Insurance as well as chairman of CCHE. The trustees had said they planned on leasing that building initially, but then they rejected it twice. The "Green Report" contained a detailed analysis of the building, so Harper had every reason to believe the trustees were going to lease it. Did Harper feel he had been double crossed?

(We don't know if there a connection between that building's rejection and these new accusations? Did Harper have a conflict of interest? All we can do is conjecture. No proof has ever surfaced that there was any impropriety; but there certainly was an appearance of impropriety. It would have looked bad if a state official pushed the state into leasing a building in which he had an economic interest.)

The interesting thing about this is that no one in the news media ever questioned whether there was a connection between Harper's disappointment that MSC did not lease his company's building and his objecting to the leasing of the Forum building. This is normally the stuff an investigative journalist jumps on, so why did they overlook this?

(Some people alleged at the time that political or other considerations played a role in the selection of buildings the college leased. Many buildings were presented, certain ones were chosen, some benefited. That charge has neither been affirmed nor disproven.) This particular skirmish, however, would prove to be the first of many conflicts between the CCHE and MSC.

The day after Harper questioned Betty Naugle, the CCHE met with Governor Love over the matter. He told them that the pressure to open Metropolitan State College caused its officials to bypass the commission. Love said it would have been better if Metro officials had cleared their actions first.

Shelby Harper told the governor he wasn't trying to reverse any of Metro's decisions, he just wanted to emphasize that under the rules they had to ask first. Then the governor and several other commissioners complimented Metro on leasing the Forum Building. Harper was not among them. Were they distancing themselves from the Security Life situation because Harper might have had a conflict? [180]

While the CCHE, to the delight of CU, investigated the alleged duplication and procurement wrongdoing, the administrators of Metro State were busy getting ready to educate students. Every week or so, announcements on new faculty hires were being made. By July, Metro already had 300 student applicants, and many applications from prospective faculty. One of those applications was from a recent Regis graduate, Steve Leonard, who went to the Capitol to meet Dr. McKinney in July.

To the shock of many, Dean Lillie told the CCHE in July that the open doors of MSC might swing shut for some applicants. He said the school would only admit only students with a high school diploma or a GED. Applicants without one or the other could not enroll. Many people assumed that an adult who had been working for some time but had never finished high school could just enroll at MSC. Lillie said they must first get a GED. [181]

This news disappointed many supporters who saw Metro as a second-chance school for those who missed an education earlier because they had to work. To them, the requirement for a GED was an unnecessary barrier.

Rocky Mountain News columnist Robert Chase commented on Dean Lillie's report, writing that reports indicated there were plenty of applicants for Metro State, but those reports were a little unnerving. Chase was unnerved because only 10 percent of the initial applicants were interested in voc-tech classes. The remaining 90 percent were signing up for liberal arts. [182]

Shortly after the drama at the CCHE, Metro's new president, Dr. Ken Phillips, gave his first interview. He said he had every confidence that the new college would become a great one. He said Metro would compete with first-rate colleges and he saw its role as one of making young people successful. Phillips had been in town trying to rent a house before he flew back to San Bernardino to wrap things up. He said he would be on the job full time September 1, before the doors opened. [183]

In July, Dean McKinney hired more faculty members. Dr. Vernie Iazzetta was appointed professor of psychology. Dr. Jon Plachy was named assistant professor of math. Walker Edwards was hired as an associate professor of political science. Gwen Thomas was retained as assistant professor of English. Ms. Thomas previously taught at Tuskegee and Denver Pubic Schools and she was a fellow at DU while working on a doctorate. Charlene Alexis was named MSC's first librarian.

In early August, *The Denver Post* columnist Greg Pinney published a feature about Metro State entitled, "The Rise of Metro College for the Fall Semester." Pinney wrote: "On September 30, a little more than a month from now, Bryant's college will be open for business. Its name: Metropolitan State College."

He began saying that on May 4, Dr. Harlan Bryant, president of Western State College, was packing the car for a trip to Monument Valley, but learned that car would be going east to Denver instead. The trustees had assigned him the job of opening up a new college in just a few months with only $750,000 to spend. The legislature had just turned that money over to the trustees two days before.[184]

Pinney laid out the history of Metro State up to that time, indicating that the trustees chose Dr. Bryant as interim president because he knew the objectives of the college—and the objections to the college. Bryant responded saying, "This could be one of the most dynamic situations in higher education in the whole nation, and I think it will be." Bryant only agreed to serve as acting president, however. He knew that dynamic situations came at a price.

Bryant and his wife moved from the college president's house—the most prestigious house in Gunnison—to a one-bedroom apartment in Denver. Bryant said the only similarity between Gunnison and Denver was loneliness. "In Denver it is the anonymity of the crowd. In Gunnison it is loneliness of the position that city has carved out for the chief of its biggest business," he said.

The first office of Metro was a single room in the Capitol, Bryant told Pinney. Next he moved in with the trustees in the State Services Building. Outgrowing that, they moved back into the Capitol, taking a room (arranged by Roy Romer) in the State Senate Offices. The space was vacant because the legislature was out of session. By August, there were so many staff members Dr. Bryant had to move back to the State Services Building.

Bryant got the college employees out of the state senate quarters just in time to avoid eviction by the special legislative session. "Metro's office space was nothing to the turmoil renting space for the college," Dr. Bryant said. Everyone with office space in downtown Denver contacted him with a pitch. He rented the Forum the TTT Building, the DU Business Administration Building, and Denver Opportunity School. Those buildings, plus the Denver Public Library, were the campus.

Looking back, Dr. Bryant said the "grassy Civic Center Park" gave the college more of a collegiate atmosphere than if the trustees had rented space in one of the buildings downtown (like the old Security Life Building).

Little things are big things when they are done for the first time, and everything at Metro was being done for the first time. For instance, there had to be a salary and benefits schedule as well as an 18-page personnel policy manual before they could interview prospective professors. They had to guess how many students would take a particular course and then apply a complicated formula to determine how many professors would be needed for each course—with no hard data for a school with a new concept to go by.

Staff also needed to calculate how many seats were required for each class. For instance, they estimated that in the first quarter, 1,025 student hours would be spent in English classes each week. That would require 85 class meetings, 24 in a class. So they needed 108 seats, 1,652 square feet of space and seven faculty members—just for English. This had to be done for each course before they could recruit and hire faculty members. It also had to be done to know how much furniture and equipment to buy.

Dr. Phillips said that MSC used the statistical information for the other state colleges under the trustees' jurisdiction to calculate the number of students in each class and the space needed, but in many ways they were guessing, since this was the first commuter college in the system.[185]

Phillips noted that one of the big challenges was printing all the forms and information that potential students needed. He said the biggest problem was getting the furniture and equipment required to fill all the rooms. Phillips noted that it generally took colleges and universities between one and two years to get furniture and lab equipment. Procuring those items in a couple of months was a serious task.

They solved that problem by convincing the furniture companies to let Metro jump to the head of the line and take furniture that was manufactured for other schools. He did not say which other schools' furniture MSC got. It would be poetic justice if some furniture intended for CU were included given their efforts to stop MSC.

At the time, pundits were saying that there was a shortage of college professors around the nation. That was not the case with Dr. McKinney's recruiting efforts. More than 300 persons applied for 37 posted positions. Metro was able to grab faculty members from other colleges. A high percentage of those hires had their doctorates, and many were doctoral graduates. The reason MSC was able to recruit so many was they found the new program attractive and exciting.[186]

As Dr. Phillips recalled, the primary reason MSC was able to attract such a good faculty was that this was a new college with a unique mission. The faculty was able to plan the courses they would be teaching, which was rare. He said many applicants thought that was exciting. Many others were happy for the chance to live in Denver.

Curtis Wright signed on as business manager in August and he hired Bruce Woodward away from the legislature's Joint Budget Committee as MSC's first accountant. Together they set up the business and procurement offices. All the while, students were applying for admission. By the time Dean Lillie arrived he had 200 applications on his desk.

A challenge for the new staff at Metro was keeping the two "halves" of the college equal, meaning the academic and the vocational. Betty Naugle said that, "if the two halves of the college aren't integrated, one begins to take a back seat—usually the vocational technical side." Another challenge was building a "college spirit." That was going to be hard since there were no athletics, no band, no baton twirlers, and no cheerleaders

Dr. Harlan Bryant told Pinney he enjoyed his assignment, but it was frantic. "Starting a college in a reasonable time is one thing, but doing it in four months is something else," Bryant said.

Yes, it was something else, and not many would have been up to the task.

As opening day drew closer, the pace of enrollment began to pick up. On August 22, Dean Lillie reported that 698 students had applied. He predicted that the FTE (full-time equivalent) number would likely be closer to 950 than the 750 the Legislature appropriated for. To make matters worse, the legislature had previously cut the appropriation for the underestimated 750 FTE by 25 percent.

By Labor Day weekend, the first 600 MSC students were accepted. Many of these individuals were working full- or part-time. *The Rocky Mountain News* reported that although there were more students than expected, the college was not offering the voc-tech classes that the proponents had authorized. Dr. Phillips responded saying that those courses were coming later.[187]

As the public scrutiny of Metro grew, *The Denver Post* took a glass-half-full approach. The headline of a Greg Pinney article in September was entitled, "New Denver College to Offer Training in 4 Technical Fields." Pinney quoted Dr. Phares, the Dean of Applied Sciences, who said that career fields would be offered in data processing, engineering design, instrumentation, and electronics.[188]

That week Barbara Schempp of Denver became the 1,000th student to enroll at MSC. She was pictured in *The Denver Post* next to Dr. Phillips.[189]

Students were required to take placement tests to determine if they required remedial classes, unless they already had ACT scores. Those first placement tests were held in the DU Law Center Auditorium. Testing took place over three days at the end of September, 1965, followed by registration. The newspapers published pictures of prospective students taking those exams.[190]

One of those students was a young farmer from Norton, Kansas who had wanted to go to the CU Denver Center but had applied too late. They sent him over to Metro. Roger Braun passed the tests and registered for classes. After graduation, he became the first Student Center Director of the Auraria Higher Education Center and namesake of the Roger Braun lounge in the Tivoli.

Four days before the doors opened, *The Rocky Mountain News* published a picture of MSC librarian Charlene Alexis sitting in an empty room reading a book. The article was entitled "Metro Library in Quite a State." The article pointed out that this was a temporary situation since MSC would have an "instant library," also known as the Denver Public Library.[191]

Ms. Alexis, who had no staff in the beginning, said that the empty library was used to sign up students, leaving her little time to convert it into an actual library until after registration. While students used the DPL, Alexis began to build Metro's own collection. Ten years later, that collection contained 40,000 copies. She said that was her most satisfying achievement

Ken Phillips, hired as MSC's first permanent president
on July 4, 1965. He resigned in 1971.

Photo Courtesy of Dr. Kenneth Phillips Family

OCTOBER 4, 1965: IT BEGINS

After what was probably the fastest rollout of a new state college in the history of the United States, Metropolitan State College opened its doors to students for the first time on the October 4, 1965—*five months* after it was funded. Powerful and well-connected forces had spent the better part of two years trying to stop it, but now they watched helplessly as a faculty of 36—half of whom had doctorates—began teaching over 1,189 students, 774 of whom were full-time. Nearly all these students were from Colorado, and most lived in *the metropolitan* area.

This is how Carson Reed, a 1983 graduate of Metropolitan State College and English major, described the opening of the college in a piece he wrote for *Metrospective* on the school's 25th anniversary in 1991:

> *It was the summer of 1965 and there were more of us than you can possibly imagine. The first couple of crops from the post-war baby-boom had just been harvested out of high school… A problem. In Denver, a big problem. More than 60 percent of the state's newest high school graduates lived in Denver…*
>
> *Those were dangerous times…But those were the times fraught with possibility. In times like those, you might have thought anything was possible, even creating a great college for Denver's Lost Boys and Lost Girls, out of nothing but thin air…*
>
> *Open a college in rented buildings in the heart of downtown Denver and throw the doors open and see what happens next… Minorities. Women-hell let anybody in. Base it on the idea that Freedom means the right to try, even if you might fail. Some college! There was no campus, no library, no student union, and no faculty lounge. There were no dorm rooms, no fraternity houses, no athletic fields, and no ivy-covered towers. But on October first, 1965 the 35 recently-hired faculty and staff of Metropolitan State College threw open the doors of the Forum Building and waited to see what might happen next. By the time the dust had settled, 1,100 students had enrolled at a college that didn't even have a football team.*

Yes, the first state-run college in Denver was finally open, and it did not have a campus; it operated on what many called the "invisible" campus. Metropolitan State College consisted of some rented space in the Forum Building, space in the 333 Building, rented space in the DU Administration Building, access to the Denver Public Library, shared classrooms in Denver's Opportunity School, and use of the YWCA gym and pool.

More importantly, a very large percentage of the students sitting in desks at Metropolitan State College that October day would not have been able to go to college were it not for the long-suffering efforts of so many who worked tirelessly to make it happen.

Among the students who started school that day was Doug Holcombe. He had flunked out of Colorado State College the previous year—for poor spelling, of all things. Even with the open door, it took the intervention of State Representative Wayne Knox to get Holcombe accepted—albeit on a year-long probational status. Thank goodness for Metro State spell check had not been invented yet.

Holcombe went on to play a major role in shaping his new college's future. CSC's loss was clearly MSC's gain. He was *the post*er-boy for the second chance that MSC provided for so many students over the years.

Tony Ledesma also started classes on MSC's opening day. He called Metro "the college of opportunity." Ledesma, a first-generation Mexican born in this country, grew up on Denver's west side and graduated from St. Joseph's High School at 6th and Fox—just a half a mile from the Cherokee Building. Dr. Ledesma, whose name is actually Antonio, came to Metro five different times—twice as a student, and three times as a faculty member.[192]

He was one of the many students who, because of their financial situations, could not have gone to college if it were not for Metro. As the first in his family to go to college, he was not successful on the first try, but after working two years, in 1972 he came back and got his degree in English with two minors: psychology and speech. He went on to get three graduate degrees including his doctorate.

Joseph Fuentes, Sherman Hamilton, Barbara Montano Vialpando, Doug Schuck, Heather Cowan Sheets and scores of others also started classes that month as well. They would later graduate from MSC and go on to make major contributions in Denver—Joe Fuentes as a journalist, Sherman Hamilton as a lion in the public relations industry, Barbara Montano as a filmmaker, Dough Shuck as a businessman, and Heather Cowan as an educator.

From the start, MSC proved that it takes more than a beautiful campus to make a great college. Students, faculty, and administration—all dedicated to knowledge—are what make a college. Charlene Alexis recalled it this way, "Everyone had a glimmer of stars in their eyes [Everyone] was, in their own way, pioneering."[193]

When Metropolitan State College opened its doors in October of '65, there were 163 courses offered to those student pioneers: 44 English classes, of which 15 were remedial; 11 math courses, four of which were remedial; one anthropology class; eight art classes; five biology classes; two chemistry classes; five economics courses; two French; three geology; one German; nine history; two philosophy classes; four physics courses; three political science classes; six psychology; three sociology; three Spanish, and seven speech classes.[194]

MSC had three divisions offering nine different associate degrees since the upper division had not been authorized. They were:

Division of Arts and Sciences
    Associate in Arts
    Associate in Science
Division of Business
    Associate in Business,
    Business Administration
    Office Administration
    Executive Secretary
Division of Technologies
    Associate in Applied Sciences
    Data Processing
    Engineering Technology

Years earlier, Colorado's Blueprint for Higher Education predicted that Metropolitan State College would enroll 318 students in its first year and 821 its second year. Instead, 1,189 students enrolled that first quarter, more than triple, and 774 of them were full-time students, 415 part-time. Dr. Ken Phillips said that the college had to stop taking students that first quarter because they ran out of room and money for supplies. Maybe the one-year delay in opening helped boost enrollment, or maybe it demonstrated the pent-up demand for a Denver college.

Who enrolled that first quarter? Only 10 percent of the initial student body came from the top one-third of their high school class; 19 percent came from the middle third; and 61.5 percent from the lower third. The remaining 9.5 percent either transferred in from another college or came in with a GED. Sixty one percent of the student body came in through the open door.[195]

As anticipated, 93.1 percent of students lived in Denver or the one of the other three metropolitan counties. Of those, 637 were residents of Denver; 199 were residents of Jefferson County; 46 came from Arapahoe County; and 27 lived in Adams County. Most students registered for a full load. Not all who signed up were true freshmen: 135 had taken courses at another college or junior college, but only 32 came in as sophomores.

Of the initial students, 72.3 percent graduated from a high school in Denver or one of the other three metropolitan counties. The other 27.7 percent came from 95 different high schools in 30 different Colorado counties, substantiating the studies that predicted rural kids would come to Denver after graduating from high school.

In what was somewhat of a surprise, the average age of the first group of registrants was 19 years—only slightly higher than other colleges in Colorado. The number of single students outnumbered those who were married 5-1. Not surprisingly, however, males outnumbered females 4-1. The college had its work cut out to attract more older, married, and female students.

In terms of the new students, 20 percent were interested in business while only 6.4 percent were interested in pursuing voc-tech programs. The remaining 73.6 percent wanted to pursue liberal arts and sciences. This was a major deviation from what the state's blueprint had predicted. It predicted that only 321 would enroll at all, and of those 17 percent would register for voc-tech and only 10 percent in business programs.

Despite predictions from earlier critics that the quality of education at Metro State would be inferior, Metro's faculty was actually one of the most qualified to be found in any state-run college in the state of Colorado. Over half of the initial faculty had their doctorates; still more were pursuing their PhD. By the end of the first year there were 36 faculty members, with two positions to fill.

See Table I for a list of the first faculty and first administrators of MSC.

The initial year of operation meant that there were a lot of firsts—events that would not be noteworthy if they had not occurred for the first time. For instance, the first social event at

MSC was a dance held November 11 at the Hellenic Center on East Alameda Ave. The music was provided by the band Soul Survivors. The event was free and from all reports, a good time was had by all.[196]

Dr. Lester Thonssen, a speech professor, has the distinction of being the first faculty member from Metropolitan State College to publish a book which listed him as being a teacher at MSC. His book, "Representative American Speeches," came out the same day the college opened.[197]

Another first that quarter was the inauguration of MSC's first official student center. It was a small facility in the Forum Building where students could grab a beverage or stale snack from a vending machine. But the real student center was the White Mule. Today's student center in the Tivoli is great, but it does not hold a candle to the Mule. Nothing could duplicate the spirit at the White Mule.

The Mule was a nondescript neighborhood bar on the south side of Colfax at Elati Street. It had catered to a mostly blue-collar crowd that stopped by for a few cool ones after work. Some of the patrons lived in the adjacent West-Side neighborhood, others worked at the nearby *Rocky Mountain News* and *The Denver Post* plants, or the Denver Mint.

It took about a minute and a half for students to adopt the White Mule as their student center, study hall and home away from home. It was the campus meeting place—a place where students could get to know each other, try and get lucky (in pool of course), and share a couple three cool ones—sometimes with their instructors and an occasional administrator who was brave enough to venture in.

Whites, African Americans, Chicanos, Asians, Native Americans, hippies and jocks all mingled at the Mule where beer was the great equalizer. Battles and several revolutions were plotted there. Lady luck often shined her countenance on student patrons of the White Mule at closing time—it was the '60s after all. Some professors even held classes in the back room adorned by a collage of photos clipped from magazines artistically arranged by MSC student Waller Theopolis "Junior" Potter IV (real name).

An MSC student named Larry Strutton worked in the production room at *The Rocky Mountain News* in the 1960's. He stopped in the Mule one night for a beer and the owner told him he could have whatever he wanted on-the-house, but not to come back. The owner said that whenever Larry walked in and the guys that worked at the *Rocky* saw him, they gulped down their beers and left. "I can't afford you," the owner told him.[198]

OPEN A MONTH AND ALREADY A CONTROVERSY

The doors of the college had hardly been open a month before critics re-started their negative propaganda campaign. *The Rocky Mountain News* published an article on November 14 under the headline "Metro State's Blueprint Changes."

Roger Braun was one of the first to register at MSC. The lounge in the Tivoli bears his name to honor his years of accomplishments at MSC before and after graduation. *Photo Courtesy of Metropolitan State University of Denver.*

The first Dean of Students at MSC was F. Dean Lillie, shown dancing in the student center.
Photo Courtesy of Metropolitan State University of Denver.

The White Mule became the unofficial student center and campus meeting place.
Photo Courtesy of Metropolitan State University of Denver.

The *Rocky* was questioning whether Metropolitan State College was following its blueprint and the intention of the legislature. The concern was that even though MSC enrolled more students than estimated, fewer were enrolled in voc-tech classes than predicted.[199]

One would think that legislators, the CCHE, and the press would be falling all over themselves to compliment and praise the trustees and administrators of Metro State College for a job well done. Not only did they open the college in less than five months, but the school beat enrollment expectations the first quarter. Furthermore, enrollment looked good for the second quarter as well. One would think that deserved something besides criticism! Dr. Ken Phillips shed some light on this in his interview, saying:

> *"When I arrived in Denver and started to get acquainted with the situation of higher education in the Denver and Colorado area, I was surprised to discover that there was a lot of contention about Metro. There was one group of people who thought it shouldn't be established at all, that it was a waste of money. There was another group that wanted to make it just a community college. And then there was another group that was supportive but really didn't comprehend what an amazing impact this was going to have on the community of Denver both economically and socially."*

Perhaps he was right. Many people did not understand what an amazing impact MSC would have on metropolitan Denver, and they missed the forest for the trees. Perhaps MSC's second quarter pre-registration numbers threatened the CU establishment. For whatever reason, a new round of criticism began in the press and at the CCHE in early December.

Some legislators began to question whether the trustees and the college administrators were in compliance with the legislature's wishes for the college. Representative John Mackie and Senator L.T. Skiffington, who were on the Advisory Board of the CCHE, said in a December commission meeting that Metropolitan State College was "not filling its intended role." Representative Mackie had been the sponsor of a failed amendment earlier in the year to convert MSC to a junior college.[200]

CCHE Chairman Shelby Harper declined to comment in the meeting but later he told a *Denver Post* reporter that Metropolitan State College was indeed not concentrating enough on voc-tech courses. Was that Security Life Building kerfuffle rearing its ugly head again?

Trustee Betty Naugle defended the role of Metro State. She said the trustees' position was based on the statute the state legislature passed when it created the college. She quoted the law, which states: "Metro is to offer programs of undergraduate instruction in the liberal arts and sciences as well as programs in the semi-professional technical education and science and engineering technology on a terminal basis."

Ms. Naugle boldly put them in their place, adding, "If there is any confusion on Metro's role, Mr. Harper, Representative Mackie, and Senator Skiffington should look at the law again." She pointed out that 27.5 percent of present Metro enrollment was now in applied sciences such as business, electronics, computers training, manufacturing processes, panel wiring and data processing. [201]

Nevertheless, the power structure was not backing down. Charlie Roos wrote an editorial in *The Denver Post* saying that CCHE chairman Shelby Harper needed to play referee because both the CU Denver Center and MSC were exceeding enrollment expectations. He asserted again that Metro was not living up to its obligations in voc-tech. "Even though Metro couldn't have athletics and dorms," he wrote, "it wouldn't be long until someone said Metro can't be a first-rate school without them.[202]

In saying a referee was needed because enrollment at both Metro and CU Denver were exceeding expectations, Charlie Roos must have felt that it was a bad thing that more Denver residents were finally getting an education than people expected. Perhaps he was just reflecting someone else's point of view. His prediction about athletics would end up being correct.

This exchange was not an insignificant event. It was the manifestation of a philosophical struggle that would go on for years over what kind of institution Metropolitan College was going to be. Was it a true urban college offering a quality education to urban students? Or should it be a junior college or trade school? Or, should it be swallowed up by the CU Denver Center?

This struggle for Metro's identity went beyond a debate over what the college's role should be. It was a conversation about whether inner-city kids, from low income or minority families, deserved the same educational opportunities as those from more affluent white neighborhoods.

Should high school graduates in poor areas go to a trade school or to no school at all? Could those young people study liberal arts or sciences, or did they only qualify for voc-tech courses because of their parents' station in life? Furthermore, were voc-tech students entitled to take general college courses as well as occupational courses, to expand their horizons?

This debate was just beginning.

Unfortunately, but not coincidentally, this controversy over MSC's role occurred just before Dr. Phillips was scheduled to appear at the legislature's Joint Budget Committee to justify the school's budget request for the second year. A few students and faculty members attended the hearing to show support for their college.

Dr. Phillips requested $1.6 million to run the college for the next year—a 110 percent increase over the $750,000 he was given for the first year. Phillips said he anticipated a 142 percent increase in instructional costs due to increased enrollment. He told the JBC that the school also needed $50,000 to search for a permanent site. "Wheels should begin turning without delay."

Representative Frank Kemp of Denver, who had sponsored the supplemental appropriation bill for Metro in the previous session, and Rep. J.D. McFarlane of Pueblo said the "program of the college must be decided first"—a reference to the ruckus raised earlier in the month by Shelby Harper, Rep. Mackie and Senator Skiffington. Phillips was asked if any sites outside Denver would be considered for the school's permanent campus. He said he would look at all options.[203]

President Phillips believed that one of his most important roles was to educate the community about the new college in order to garner support. Two months into the first quarter, Phillips spoke at a luncheon meeting of the City Club in downtown Denver. After reporting that enrollment exceeded expectations, Dr. Phillips was asked when the school would have a campus. He said the process for choosing a site for the permanent campus had already begun.

He estimated the college would need a 350 acre campus to allow for the 17,000 students expected by 1980. Phillips said it would require 2.5 million square feet of space in three and four story buildings, which would take up to 80 acres. The rest would be parking for 10,000 cars, athletic fields, and open space. He said if only 40 aces were available for buildings, they would need to be eight stories. If the campus were located downtown, as many wanted it to be, the buildings would have to be 16 stories high.

When asked about inter-collegiate athletics, Phillips said he had not thought about it but, he added, MSC had already been asked to join inter-collegiate athletic organizations even though it had no teams. He was asked about dorms and replied they would consume an additional 40 acres of land, but the legislature and trustees did not want Metro State to build them. Phillips said his staff wanted the college to become a four-year school as soon as possible by adding a class each year in 1966, 1967, and 1968.[204]

Dr. Phillip's answer to the question about whether he would consider sites outside Denver stirred up a minor brush fire. Denver Mayor Tom Currigan responded by directing the Denver Planning Board to initiate a study to determine where in Denver a permanent campus for MSC should be sited. Currigan asked the board to complete the study by that July 31.[205]

Meanwhile, suburban officials were heartened by Phillip's comments that he would look at sites outside Denver. Delegations from Adams, Arapahoe, and Douglas counties began pushing locations in their counties for the school's permanent home. The Arvada City Council passed a resolution stating it wanted to land the school and would be presenting a site to Dr. Phillips and the trustees.[206]

Phillips recalled in a later interview, "We had a lot of people coming in and suggesting that we ought to be in this community or that community. And really, it would be just ideal if we could be in the city of Denver." Soon a new round of controversy would engulf the fledgling institution as the first quarter ended.

What did students think about their new college after the first quarter? They liked it and proof came from an unlikely source. An article written by Pat Evans appeared in the CU Denver Center's student newspaper *The Sentry*. Its headline: "What is Metro Really Like?" Interviews were conducted with students at MSC to get the story from the horse's mouth. The reporter asked, "Why are you attending Metro? What are your general opinions of Metro?"

Here are some of the anonymous answers from MSC students after their first quarter:

- *"Metro is a new school with very few students and therefore small classes, I have two classes with 10 students each and for $62 a quarter, it is inexpensive for almost individual instruction."*
- *"Metro has a good idea in letting anyone in who wants to get in, yet keeping the standards high."*
- *"It's ok now but it's going to be great in the future, In fact better than CU."*
- *"At the beginning of fall quarter my feelings were indifferent, but particularly watching the school progress, I have grown proud of the school and am pleased to call it my school."*
- *"I feel the teaching staff is one of the finest qualities. I have enjoyed my classes, and I feel I am getting really more than can be expected."*
- *"MSC is not an easy school in terms of grading; I sincerely believe MSC will become a major college."*
- *"This school is good for all who want a good college education plus it is a lot more economical."*
- *"Speaking from experience this school has finer instruction than CU because of the desire of the staff to make our students work for their degree."*
- *"I feel that given enough time, money, and chance metro will far surpass CU and DU because the students take an active interest."*

The response was probably a surprise to the readers at the CU Denver Center. The author said that girls would like Metro because 50 percent of boys complained there weren't enough young women there. The article was signed: Caveat Populi—*People Beware.*[207]

This was a good report card for a school cobbled together in less than five months. It was probably not what the CU regents had hoped for, but it was the first written confirmation of the "Metro spirit."

At the end of the first quarter, the trustees held a banquet to honor Dr. Keats McKinney, dean of the college; Mr. F.D. Lillie, dean of students; Mr. Curtis Wright, business manager; and faculty member Dr. Harold Benn for the outstanding work they did getting the college ready for operation in a span of just five months.[208]

As 1965 drew to a close, the Denver Broncos were the laughingstock of the AFL, finishing the season with a 4-10 record. Denver fans were becoming Broncomaniacs anyway. They bought 20,000 season tickets that year. The Broncos got help from an Adams County restaurant owner and Democratic leader, Frank Ciancio, who bought most of those 20,000 season tickets at the behest of the Bronco's owners. He then re-sold them on a per game basis and often treated politicians and business leaders to a complimentary Bronco game.

Coach Eddie Crowder was finally beginning to bring some respectability to the CU Buffalos. They finished the season 6-2-2, tripling their previous year's wins.

The top movie of 1965 was "the Sound of Music" starring Julie Andrews and Christopher Plummer. It barely beat out "Dr. Zhivago" and "Cat Ballou." The top songs of 1965 were "Wooly Bully" by Sam the Sham and the Pharaohs, "I can't help myself (Sugar Pie Honey Bunch)" by the Four Tops, and "(I can't get no) Satisfaction" by the Rolling Stones.

In 1965, 230,991 young men were drafted and many ended up in Vietnam. Even though many people were not yet focused on it, 1,928 Americans lost their lives in Vietnam in 1965, a big increase over the 216 that died the year before. The war was still in its infancy.

CHAPTER 6

The College Fights to Advance

Here they come again, mmm
Time to get a move on, mmm
Catch us if you can
Catch us if you can
"Catch Us If You Can",
Dave Clark Five[209]

As the second quarter began, the number of students enrolled dropped to 1,059. This included 320 new students and 739 returnees. Of the 320 new students, 157 enrolled in college for the first time and 163 transferred from another school. Dean Lillie announced that 300 new students were accepted for the winter quarter. Two-thirds of those were freshmen, he said, and the remainder transferred from other colleges around the state.[210]

RETENTION PRESENTS A CHALLENGE

The Rocky Mountain News reported that Metropolitan State College had lost 38 percent of the students who enrolled in first quarter. According to the article, half of those students were suspended for academic performance, and the other half quit voluntarily. Of course, many of those were replaced by new students.[211]

The article stated that 56 percent of all first quarter students got grades so low they were suspended. According to the college, 515 students received grades of C or better, however 453

Registration doubled in MSC's second year. Students line up in front of AA
Building to register. *Photo Courtesy of Metropolitan State University of Denver.*

students, who received grades between C- and F+, were placed on probation. Sadly, 221 students got Fs and were suspended.

Since Metropolitan State College had an open enrollment policy, the failure rate was projected to be high because only 10 percent of the students came from the top third of their class. Hardly anyone expected the failure rate to be quite this high, however. What was worse, many of these students failed remedial courses or high school level courses, not college level classes.

Critics were quick to suggest that MSC was a failure. Many saw this as a reason to close the open door, if not the front door. Actually, the Metro drop-out/failure rate was higher than at other colleges, including junior colleges, because MSC gave marginal students a chance. This situation presented the college with a challenge: how to keep the door open and help marginal students succeed in college.

On January 13, Robert L. Chase wrote an article in *The Rocky Mountain News* entitled "Metro State's Purpose," in which he said MSC should be congratulated for holding academic standards at a high level, since 56 percent of the students were suspended. He was cheering their failure and holding failure up for accolades.

Chase said that the failure rate raised questions about whether Metropolitan State College was properly planned and whether it could fit into the state's education picture. He also raised a question about high schools, saying "Should high school students be handed a diploma if they are not ready for college level work?" Chase recommended that high school students on the edge not get a diploma but rather a "completion certificate." He added that remedial work should be done in high school, not a state college.[212]

Legislators faced students in MSC's first legislative forum sponsored by PROSPECTUS. Organizer Vivian Bartel is on far right. *Photo Courtesy of Metropolitan State University of Denver.*

Perhaps he was right about that last statement. High schools were not preparing these at-risk students for college because there was no expectation that they would ever get an opportunity to go to college.

This was just a preface for things to come.

ANOTHER ATTEMPT TO MAKE MSC A JUNIOR COLLEGE

On January 15, top House Republicans introduced a resolution that would clarify Metro's role by re-emphasizing voc-tech courses on a two-year basis at MSC. Naturally, the resolution was introduced by Republican Representatives John Mackie and the former speaker, John Vanderhoof, who was now minority leader, Democrats had regained control of the House.

The resolution directed Metropolitan State College to proceed with dispatch to develop vocational and technical education courses on a two-year basis. Further, it mandated that MSC function as the junior college for the Denver metropolitan area. And, it ordered the college to discontinue its search for a site outside downtown Denver and instead concentrate on locations in or near the state capitol complex. They didn't want Metro close by be neighborly.

Mackie and Vanderhoof thought that by ordering MSC to stop looking at sites outside of downtown Denver, the size of the school would be constrained because of high land costs. By suggesting that MSC acquire the DU building across the alley from the Forum Building, they were in effect making a back-door effort to put an enrollment cap on the school. Meanwhile, the CU Denver Center was gleefully ready to take over the liberal arts role from the redefined Metropolitan State College. Betty Naugle suggested again that they should re-read the law that created MSC.[213]

The trustees were having none of that, however. On the day after the Mackie/Vanderhoof resolution was introduced, the board reaffirmed its plan for Metropolitan State College. They defied the two legislators by passing a resolution on a unanimous vote that affirmed their plans to make Metro State a four-year college as soon as possible. The board instructed President Phillips to add the junior year in 1968 and senior year in 1969. This, of course, would require legislative approval. The stage was set for a confrontation.

Phillips told the trustees, that as of the second quarter, "27 percent of MSC students were taking voc-tech courses and the percentage will rise once the college determines what skills Denver businesses need for the school to teach."[214]

In order to diffuse criticism, the day after the board meeting Phillips announced that MSC would begin offering aerospace courses. He invited representatives of airlines, airports, Martin Co, Kensair, Hughes Tool, Stanley Aviation, Combs Aircraft and the FAA to meet with him and Dr. Gail Phares, Dean of Applied Sciences, to discuss the program.[215]

The following day, Robert L. Chase commented about Mackie's bill, writing, "Enough confusion has been spread [by Metro] it seems to me...The administration of this institution interprets the legislative authorization as establishing the first two years of a college." What did Chase think the legislature established if it didn't establish a college? Apparently, he also needed to also read the legislation.[216]

There was a brief respite. Colorado resident Peggy Fleming won the U.S. skating championship in January and was honored on the floor of the state legislature. This took lawmakers' minds off of MSC for a few minutes while they lined up to get their mugs in a photo with the attractive Olympic-bound athlete.

Meanwhile at the White Mule, students were talking basketball. Wilt Chamberlain had just broken the NBA career record, scoring 20,884 points.

Denver's TV stations were quite interested in Metro State in those early days. Several times, camera crews from KOA (NBC channel 4 back then) and KBTV (ABC channel 9) televised shots of students taking placement tests and enrolling. There were more articles in the Denver daily newspapers about Metro than CU. Even if many were not exactly positive, the fact they spelled the name right was all that mattered.

While the enemies of MSC were trying to make life difficult, planning was still moving ahead for a permanent campus. Denver Mayor Tom Currigan asked the Denver Planning Board and the Denver Metropolitan Planning Commission to do a detailed study on the feasibility of locating the permanent campus of Metropolitan State College in downtown Denver. Ray Jenkins, planning director, said the study would be done by July 1966.

There was some discussion at the Planning Board meeting about locating the college in the Skyline Urban Renewal project in lower downtown if the new buildings could be built as high-rises. The Skyline project would clear a large number of blocks in that the city determined were blighted. The area roughly went from Curtis Street to Market, and 14th to 20th streets. It encompassed the southeast part of what is today called LoDo.[217]

Back at the Capitol, Denver Representative Wayne Knox had become the new chairman of the House Education Committee. Knox had voted against the appropriation to allow the college to open in 1965, and he voted for the Mackie bill which would have converted MSC to a junior college. Knox invited Dr. Phillips and representatives of the Board of Trustees to appear before his committee to address the Mackie/Vanderhoof resolution.[218]

On January 26, Dr. Phillips appeared before the committee and told skeptical legislators that there would be no competition for students between Metropolitan State College and the new junior college opening in September. He said the course offerings would be different and there would be no duplication of voc-tech courses either. If necessary, Dr. Phillips said, Metro would give up its two-year voc-tech courses and concentrate on educating those students in their third and fourth years.[219]

Meanwhile, on Jan. 29, two hundred students from nine colleges and universities in Colorado, including six students from Metropolitan State College, met with Governor Love to protest the under-funding of higher education by his administration and the state legislature. One student asked Love about the per capita drop in educational funding, "Is this the way we achieve excellence?" The question went unanswered.[220]

On February 2, it was Representative Mackie's turn to appear before Knox's committee. He denied that his resolution was trying to limit Metro to a two-year college. (Perhaps he hadn't read his own resolution). Mackie said that Metropolitan State College was not fulfilling its role as spelled out in the legislation that created it so therefore he was just trying to make MSC comply. (Perhaps he hadn't read that legislation either.)

Shelby Harper, chairman of the CCHE, raised the old argument that MSC was an inferior college because of the nature of the students it was attempting to attract. He told the committee that the legislature needed to decide whether it wanted a quality college in Denver or not. "It is difficult to have a top quality institution that admits all applicants," he said.

Harper went on to say, "We have been talking out of both sides of our mouths in reference to quality." He said the CCHE decided Denver needed all three levels of institutions: a junior college, a four-year college, and a university. Yet, by allowing MSC to exist, let alone with an open door, the commission was destroying the educational quality they advocated. He believed that education of the masses precluded excellence. Harper seemed to be endorsing the traditional view that only the elite deserved a college education.

Herrick Roth, a former state senator who served on the Education Task Force and a strong supporter of MSC, testified that the Colorado AFL-CIO favored making MSC a four-year institution. Roth's testimony was important because Rep. Knox received strong backing from organized labor and he was not likely to go against their wishes.[221]

Two Denver senators who were also MSC supporters, Democrat George Brown and Republican Joe Shoemaker, issued a statement saying Metro's original plan was to be a two-year voc-ed institution, but now the mission changed because students themselves asked for liberal arts courses. Shoemaker's endorsement carried a great deal of weight, and it was a blow to those who were attacking MSC on the grounds that it was not adhering to the legislature's wishes.

Meanwhile, MSC took more wind out of the opposition's sails. Dr. Phares, dean of applied sciences, reported there was a growing interest in applied science programs from professional organizations, business and industrial training programs, including Cherry Creek High School business teachers, American Society of Tool and Manufacturing Engineers, IBS, FAA, United, Marathon Oil, and the Colorado Nurseryman's Association. This helped silence some of the critics who said MSC was not doing enough in the applied sciences.

The CU Denver Center announced figures for the winter trimester and enrollment was down to 5,695 students. The decrease in head count was blamed on Metro. However, students signed up for more credit hours than in past. The increase in hours was attributed to the fact that the Denver Center started offering degree programs.[222]

That month, the MSC Bombers finished in second place in the YMCA Men's Basketball League. The Bombers team included: Dave Bowers, Wayne Vigil, Ali Pouraghabagher, Dick Frisbie, Joe Fuentes, George Vince, and James Van Howe. Back on campus, the publications board announced the creation of a new student magazine called *The New Campus Review*.[223]

While the Joint Budget Committee was considering the appropriation for MSC's second year, a new controversy arose. Representative J.D. McFarlane of Pueblo, a member of the JBC, criticized Metro State for misusing a $12,000 supplemental appropriation. It was part of a $40,000 appropriation to help students stay in school. The high suspension and dropout figures from MSC's first quarter brought the issue to light.

Rep. Marvin Wolf of Boulder tried to cut MSC's appropriation due to the large number of dropouts. His argument was that the legislature appropriated money based on anticipated enrollment for the fiscal year. Since so many dropped out or failed, he argued, MSC did not need the full appropriation. He seemed unconcerned that Metro's appropriation had been cut by 40 percent to begin with.[224]

Despite the controversy, Metro's supporters on the JBC, including Joe Shoemaker, gave the new college a Valentine's Day gift. The Long Bill, passed by the committee, recommended an appropriation for MSC that was $21,000 more than Governor Love requested in his budget on top of the disputed $40,000 supplemental.[225]

(Perhaps the surprise appropriation was a result of the good impression MSC students made on the JBC. Several students, including Doug Holcombe and Roger Braun, testified before the JBC earlier that session.)

Shortly after the JBC hearing, a report came out that gave opponents of MSC new ammunition. The Colorado Department of Education declared that the era of increased high school graduation rates due to the baby boom was over. The 1966 graduating class in Colorado was estimated to be 29,079 students, only 483 more than the class of 1965, or an increase of 1.7 percent. By contrast, the 1965 class was 21.3 percent larger than the year before.

Even though the baby boom would continue nationally for a few more years, the department said that the marked slowdown of people with families migrating into Colorado was affecting the numbers. They predicted that enrollment would level off in 1966 and increase at a smaller rate for years to come. Some argued that the need for increasing MSC's funding was going away.[226]

The world was shocked on March 4 when John Lennon announced that the Beatles were more popular than Jesus. This issue was hotly debated in classrooms and at the White Mule. Soon, the Lennon controversy took a back seat to the riots that broke out in Watts. Scenes of violence on TV once again focused the nation's attention to racial relations in the U.S.

That spring, the Soviet's Luna 10 became the first craft to orbit the moon, putting more pressure on the U.S. space program to beat the Soviets to the moon. Also, the Cultural Revolution movement began a purge in China, and caused deeper isolation of the nation from the world community.

As the winter quarter of 1966 drew to a close, the MSC faculty celebrated with a cocktail party at the American Legion across the street from the Denver Public Library. The notice made it clear that spouses were *expected*. This was no low-class affair. Well drinks cost a whopping 50 cents, and high rollers shelled out 55 cents for call brands. The hors d' oeuvres, however, were free.[227]

At the end of the quarter, the faculty had a fancy dinner at the Pinehurst Country Club. This cost $6.00 a person. There was dancing and the room was replete with flowers. It was a cash bar, however. According to accounts, a good time was had by all.

THE SPRING OF '66

In the school's first spring quarter, enrollment was 933 students—down from 1,189 in the fall. Some of this was due to natural attrition—students who decided college was not for them. Others may have run short of funds. According to President Phillips, this attrition was less than average for colleges and less than anyone expected for a college with an open door.

In March, the US Air Force approved tuition assistance for military personnel to enroll at Metro. Coupled with the Cold War GI Bill, this would increase the number of active members of the military and veterans at MSC. Meanwhile, the presidents of the state's colleges, including Metro, told the trustees that the GI Bill was likely to flood the schools with new students. They thought there might be an additional 2,000 to 2,500 more students in the five colleges than they were budgeted for.

Phillips said the largest number of those new veterans would enroll at MSC because of its low tuition and location in Colorado's largest city. Darrell Holmes, president of Colorado State College, said there were two solutions: cap enrollment, or get the legislature to increase the appropriations. MSC's business manager, Curt Wright, told the trustees that Metro should not accept additional students without having the supplemental appropriation first.[228]

Frank Abbott, executive director of the CCHE, threw ice water on the college presidents when he said that the enrollment increase from the GI Bill would not be anywhere as great as they claimed. Abbott predicted it would be about half as many, citing information he claimed he obtained from the VA. Abbott would be proven wrong by future enrollments, however.[229]

Despite Abbott's statement, the trustees passed a resolution that dealt with many issues of importance to MSC. The resolution stated that when the MSC budget was prepared, it was based on an expected 1,755 FTE (full time equivalents) but unless enrollment is limited, 2,800 students were expected. The resolution also approved hiring 32 new faculty members including Dr. Merle Milligan, dean of arts and sciences; Jean Bulger, assistant professor of nursing; Vern Moody, music professor, and Dr. Duane Mehn, professor of physical education.

The trustees also approved a five-year contract with a company called Bargain Bookstore to operate Metro's bookstore. And they approved leasing an additional 3,200 square feet on first floor of the TTT building.

In April, at the request of Dr. Phares, the curriculum committee forwarded a proposal to the trustees for the applied sciences division. It was approved and sent to the CCHE. Included in that was a proposal to initiate a police sciences program. Here were the proposed degree offerings for the coming year that were submitted to the CCHE:

Associate Degree

    Aerospace Engineering Technology

    Culinary Arts

    Ornamental Agriculture

    Police Science

    Registered Nurse

    X-ray Technology

Baccalaureate Degree

    Business Management

        Accounting

        Business Data Processing

    Engineering Technology

        Electronics

        Mechanical

        Police Science

Dr. Phares told the CCHE the school had sufficient staff for the first year, but he needed to add ten new positions for the second year.[230]

Almost immediately there was pushback over the police sciences program. Trinidad State Junior College filed a formal protest with the CCHE, saying if the Metro State police science program were approved it would take students away from Trinidad Junior College.

A month later Shelby Harper dealt another blow to MSC when he recommended that the CCHE refuse to approve the culinary arts and horticulture programs. Harper said the commission needed to determine if they were duplicative, and the commissioners agreed. President Phillips strongly objected, but to no avail. The commission did not even take up the police science program.[231]

Was that Security Life Building at play again?

At the end of the first spring quarter there was a student assembly in the Wyer Auditorium, located in the basement of the Denver Public Library. It was held there because there was no student center. There was a great deal of dissatisfaction among the male students because men outnumbered women more than three-to-one on campus. Women students, however, seemed to be ok with the ratio.

Nevertheless, the issue of gender imbalance at Metro had to be addressed. President Phillips and a few outstanding bachelor students including, Doug Holcombe, Lynn 'Spike" Davis, and Roger Braun, collaborated to create a machine that they claimed would increase female enrollment. They said their machine was able to turn men into women.

The inventors brought their machine to the assembly and the three bachelors climbed inside. Dr. Phillips turned the knobs, smoke appeared, and when it cleared the three bachelors had indeed been turned into women. The crowd went wild. Unbeknownst to the audience, the men exited through a hole, went backstage and changed into dresses and wigs.[232]

By the time the spring quarter ended and students went on summer break, the college released information that showed that after the first three quarters, one third of the students at Metro were failing, and 583 were suspended.

President Phillips reiterated to the press that the number of failing students was actually *lower* than he expected. He said that faculty's efforts to stimulate students were producing positive results. He said that it took a quarter for students to know the faculty meant what they said about going to the library and completing their homework.[233]

Phillips pointed out that the typical school with an open-door policy experiences a 50 percent failure rate. At Metro, 59.1 percent of all students had grades above C that quarter. This was up from 43 percent in the fall quarter. MSC was figuring out how to retain the at-risk students.

MSC got a plug from the wife of an evening student that helped counter the bad press over the failure rate. Patricia Gilmore took exception to an article written by the editor of the CU

Denver Center newspaper degrading MSC because of its open door. She wrote a letter to the editor of *The Post* entitled, "Metro State Meets Needs of Denver Area Student," saying in part:

> "...Metro was never intended to become a 'status school.' It was intended to provide a college education for those students who must live at home and attend college and those who must work and go to school at night. This does not mean watered-down courses...It does mean a school whose administration and faculty are concerned primarily with the needs of the metropolitan student...my husband does go to Metro State in the evening, not because they have an open door or because he could not make it anywhere else, but because the Denver Center could not or would not meet our needs and this is what Metro State is trying to do."[234]

In June, MSC's first summer session was about to begin. One of the commitments made to the legislature during the struggle to get Metropolitan State College funded was that it would achieve a high degree of utilization of its facilities by operating year-round. The summer session was important to the college's credibility and it would allow students to get their degrees in less time.

The North Central Association held a conference on summer schools and issued a report advising colleges and universities not to turn the summer sessions into a "junkyard for marginal students." They urged colleges and universities to adopt a policy to get gifted students to enroll in summer sessions to enhance the prestige of the summer term.[235]

Unfortunately, that first summer session was underwhelming. Only 476 students enrolled for classes. As a result, the administration and the curriculum committee made changes to the course offerings and the structure of the schedule for summer sessions to attract more students going forward.[236]

Also in June, the CCHE reversed its earlier decision and granted conditional approval for six additional programs at MSC, including culinary arts, aerospace technology, ornamental landscaping, X-ray technology, and registered nursing. It was still contemplating the police science program. Ultimately the commission ruled out a four-year police science program and four-year engineering studies. They said Metro needed to prove these courses did not constitute a duplication of courses offered elsewhere before students could enroll

President Phillips was angered over the ruling. "You leave us in a very difficult position. Under the circumstances, it would be easier for us to stop doing anything," Phillips said "The same duplicating yardstick they applied to Metro should apply to all colleges equally, but it doesn't." [237]

Phillips was angry because from the beginning, many in the legislature and the CCHE, particularly Shelby Harper, repeatedly said that Metro was not doing enough in the voc-tech area, which the legislature wanted MSC to emphasize. But every time MSC tried to add applied science courses, the commission blocked them. It was a no-win situation. Was Metro deliberately being set up for failure by Harper and Abbott? Or did it just look that way?

News columnist Robert L. Chase took Dr. Phillips to task for daring to object to the CCHE ruling, but he agreed that the CCHE should be able to tackle duplication that happened before the commission was created. That was what Dr. Phillips was referring to when he said the standard should be applied equally. Many of the programs the commission criticized were already duplicated before MSC was born.[238]

While the administration was fighting with the CCHE over curriculum, the Denver Planning Board, at Mayor Currigan's request, was busy reviewing the site study for MSC's campus. The initial sites identified were:

1. A site off the Valley Highway between 6th and Broadway;
2. A site adjacent to Ft. Logan;
3. A site in College View near Loreto Heights College;
4. Bears Stadium (which became Mile High Stadium);
5. Lowery Air Force Base;
6. Park Hill Golf Course;
7. Civic Center area near the current leased buildings;
8. The Auraria neighborhood;
9. The Skyline Urban Renewal area between Larimer and Union Station;
10. A site near the Federal Building on the east edge of Skyline.

Based on recommendations from MSC, the planning board increased the projected enrollment that the new site would need to accommodate to 20,000 students—up 3,000 from a previous projection of 17,000.[239]

In the summer of 1966, there was a major breakthrough that clarified MSC's new campus situation. On July 6 the Denver Planning Board released the 200-page report that evaluated sites for the MSC campus. To the surprise of many, the Planning Board and the mayor's Platte River Committee preferred the Auraria site. The report stated that locating the college at Auraria would "strengthen the central core of Denver as focal point of economic, social and cultural activity in the region."

Auraria was the oldest neighborhood in Denver. It was located across Cherry Creek from downtown Denver, and a few blocks west on Colfax from the 333 Building and the Mule. Despite its historical significance and proximity to downtown, parts of Auraria had become blighted and damaged in the '65 flood. However, about 200 families and several historical structures occupied the site.

The report concluded that locating the new college in Auraria would both eliminate blight and prevent new blight. Auraria would strengthen the city's urban renewal program by providing a desirable customer for the cleared land, the report stated, and generate economic and environmental support for additional private development in the surrounding community.

Auraria would provide "balanced access" to the college from all parts of *the metropolitan* area, it reported, and it emphasized the site's proximity to recreational, cultural, and entertainment facilities. The report also suggested Auraria would provide a broad range of employment opportunities for students in nearby downtown Denver. In addition, Auraria had good access to public transit and proximity to the Denver Public Library.

The report projected that it would cost $17 million to buy and clear the land at Auraria. In comparison, the Civic Center site would cost $34 million and the Skyline site $30 million. The Union Station site was less at $13 million, but rejected because of traffic problems and environmental issues related to clearing the land.[240] The report also favored Auraria because there were possibilities for joint utilization of parking for a future Bronco stadium and a new convention center.[241]

The State Historical Society, however, informed the planning board that there were several historical markers in Auraria commemorating the neighborhood's historical significance that had to be dealt with.

In August, Mayor Currigan urged the trustees to select Auraria as the location of the college. The mayor told them that MSC would do a great deal for its students, but also for the community, economically, socially and culturally. "Auraria is an ideal location. If you can serve both objectives at once—the value to the student and the value to the community—this approach deserves the most serious consideration." [242]

Currigan assured the trustees that the city would not thrust Auraria upon them, but it stood by to help. Denver Planning Director James D. Braman Jr. told the Board: "The urban college hasn't been done quite right anywhere in the country. The Trustees have the chance to produce the ideal urban college on the Auraria site."

President Phillips told the board his staff would make careful studies of the proposed sites. He indicated he would hire a technical consultant but it would take two years to complete such a study.

In late July, the CCHE finally approved the police science program for MSC, as well as one at Arapahoe Junior College. Dr. Frank Abbott, executive director of the CCHE, said that the MSC program needed to be kept flexible to best serve the needs of the Denver police department and others in the area, and MSC's program should not duplicate programs at Trinidad College and Arapahoe JC.

Abbott told *The Post*, "The Arapahoe and Metro programs should provide opportunities for police officers to extend their qualifications at the same time that they should help attract qualified young people into this important field." He said programs would cooperate with the Colorado State Patrol Academy at Camp George West and with the newly proposed Colorado Bureau of Investigation. Shortly thereafter, Carleton "Pat" Reed was hired as the first chairman of the police science department.[243]

Professor Joseph G. Sandoval wrote in his history of MSU Denver's Criminal Justice and Criminology Department that "Metropolitan State College would soon become the premier center of criminal justice undergraduate education in Colorado and the region." When MSC initiated the first four-year criminal justice or police science program in Colorado, law enforcement had hit a low period in Denver, and around the nation.[244]

Recently, there had been a scandal in the Denver police department. Police officers were operating an organized burglary ring. Officers in Denver and around the nation were constantly being accused of using excessive force and even brutality in dealing with suspects. After the Miranda decision, many suspects were released because officers were not properly reading them their rights.

"By the middle of the 1960's there were questions about the racial composition of the Denver Police Department and of the relations between the police and minorities in the city," Sandoval wrote. There were various deadly incidents in which police shot and killed members of both the Negro and Mexican-American communities, as both were known at that time."

There was also discrimination within police departments, as documented by a *Denver Post* feature entitled, "The Color Line." It highlighted discrimination in various cities throughout the United States against Negroes and other minorities in their assignments as police officers.

Within the first two years after the MSC police science program started, more than 200 students were enrolled, and 50 percent of them were professionals in the field. There were about 16 women in the program at the time.[245] Soon, all the command officers in the Denver Police Department would have a BA from Metropolitan State College compared to none with degrees when MSC began police sciences in 1966.[246]

(Professor Sandoval began as a student majoring in history and political science in the early days of the college. While a student, he worked as an Arvada police officer— and would become the only member of the force at that time with a college degree. Sandoval came back to MSC as a professor and ended up as chairman of the Criminal Justice and Criminology department.)

One thing that Professor Sandoval remembers about his student days is that there was a sense of camaraderie at MSC that permeated through the faculty as well as the student body. There seemed to be a sense that both were involved in an experiment that neither wanted to see fail.[247]

In August, MSC recruited Donald Wolfe from Adams State College to produce the first *Viewbook*. The book was co-sponsored by the Associated Students of MSC. It was published September 23. It was used to recruit future students.

Since so few students were enrolled in summer classes, what were they doing that summer? Married and older students were most likely working at the jobs they had during the school year, but probably working more hours. Younger students were likely working at a summer job to earn money for the upcoming school year.

The summer of '66 provided a great opportunity for students (and some faculty) to begin doing the research required to cast an informed vote on the 2012 Colorado Marijuana initiative. (It is never too early to commence research.) Some of that scholarly activity may have taken place at local drive-in theaters while they were watching "Batman" or "Who's Afraid of Virginia Woolf?" Chances are that not much time was spent watching the news. In late August, the Beatles performed their last public concert at Candlestick Park in San Francisco.

Chicanos in Colorado were beginning to get restive about a political system that seemed to be unresponsive to their needs. The Hispano Party was formed to run a slate of candidates for public office. The Hispano Party nominated Levi Martinez for to run for governor. Denver's Corky Gonzales, former MSC student and founder of the Crusade for Justice, tried to throw water on it. He said it would be better to get the existing political parties to nominate Spanish-surnamed candidates, and get them elected, rather than go the third party route.

In 1966 MSC was listed for the first time in the official Hotel-Motel Denver Greeters Guide under the column "While in Denver." They must have thought that MSC was something someone might want to check out after visiting the mint or catching a show at Sid King's.

As September drew near, MSC was preparing for fall registration and the beginning of its second year. That fall, Richard Castro dropped out of St. Thomas Seminary and enrolled in Trinidad Junior College, a move that would lead him to Metro State College. Joe Sandoval had left St. Thomas the year before Rich Castro enrolled, and he was preparing to register at MSC in the fall. Robert Bowen graduated from Machebeuf High School and entered St. Thomas Seminary beginning a journey that would unexpectedly bring him to MSC as well.

It seemed like St. Thomas Seminary was a recruiting ground for future activist students at MSC.

YEAR 2: ENROLLMENT DOUBLES

On September 25, 1966, Denverites saw a two-page photo in *The Denver Post* which showed Metro State's newly acquired classroom facility, the AA Building. Wrapped around it was a block-long line of students waiting to register for classes. The caption read, "If you think Metro College isn't popular just take a look at this" [248]

When classes began in October, 2,434 students had enrolled—an increase of 105 percent over the first year's enrollment. Over half of those students were baby boomers from the class of 1966, enrolling in college for the first time. An additional 731 students returned from the previous year. One of the new students was Richard Castro, who transferred from Trinidad Junior College.[249]

Jim Saccamano, who had graduated from high school in the spring, enrolled at MSC that quarter. He said that he came to Metro because it was the only school he and his parents could afford.

Unfortunately, men still outnumbered women, but the margin was reduced. It was now only 3 to 1, down from 4 to 1 the previous year.

As projected, 91 percent of all students came from the four-county metropolitan area. A shocking 91 percent of all students signed up for liberal arts courses. The number who signed up for voc-ed was up to 74 percent, although many of those also registered for liberal arts classes, too—much to the dismay of those who wanted MSC to be a trade school.

Metropolitan State College had the highest percentage of in-state students in the state of Colorado, over 96.4 percent. Colorado State University in Ft. Collins had the lowest proportion with only 76.5 percent. So it appeared the demographics of the student body were beginning to conform to the founders' expectations.

As the second year began, the number of faculty increased to 80, including administrators, who at that time were required to teach one class a year. A total of 43 out of the 80 had doctorates—the highest percentage in the state. This must have been a disappointment to those who had asserted that the education at MSC would be second-class.

MSC's invisible campus expanded to seven locations. In addition to the new AA Building at 1300 Glenarm, the campus included the Forum building, the Student Center/Bookstore on Bannock, the TTT Building, rented space in the DU Administration Building, shared space in the Opportunity School, rights to use the Denver Public Library, and multiple locations for PE classes. These were in addition to the campus green, also known as Civic Center Park.

In the 1966-67 academic year, several new divisions were added, including humanities, math and sciences, social sciences, and public services. The number of courses offered jumped to 252.

There was some angst, however, among second-year students who had enrolled a year earlier. If the legislature did not approve the upper division in the next session, they would have to transfer at the end of the academic year and take their junior classes elsewhere. Nevertheless, students were hopeful, although the faculty was somewhat nervous. Many had come to MSC counting on upper division classes being offered.

That fall, thanks to an agreement with Denver General Hospital (DGH), women and men in the nursing program would train at the hospital. The applied sciences division also began developing courses in quality control.

Student government was born in the fall of '66. Two students, Doug Holcombe and Lynn Davis, thought it was time to organize a student government. They met with Dean Lillie and made their case. The dean agreed it was a good idea, so he set up a meeting to further discuss the matter.

Much to the surprise of Holcombe and Davis, when they showed up at the meeting, they found a room full of about 20 students. It seems that Lillie had invited other students, who showed up with supporters, knowing the officers would be chosen on the spot. Holcombe and

Davis came alone since no one had told had them that the dean planned on setting the government up right then.

At the meeting, the assembled group selected the MSC's first student government. The person with the most supporters in the room was Brian Lininger, so he was chosen the school's first student body president. Roger Braun was picked to be vice president. Roger said in a 2013 interview that he came to the meeting because he saw a posted notice, and he thought it would be interesting to hear what was going on.[250]

Essentially, everyone else who showed up was designated as a senator. The first senate included: Lynn Davis, Doug Holcombe, Shannon Quinn, and Lauren Watson. Holcombe said that had he known what was going to happen, he would have brought fans and the outcome would have been different.

One of the first things the new student government did was co-sponsor two forums for students and faculty members to meet and question candidates running for office that fall. Since there was no auditorium, the forums were held on the tenth floor of the Forum Building. On October 18 and 19, candidates for various offices including the United States Senate, House of Representatives, Governor, Lt. Governor, State Senate and State Representative were invited and given a tour of the campus. About 50 students attended.[251]

The forums served two purposes. First, students and faculty had an opportunity to meet and learn something about the candidates. More importantly, they gave the candidates, some of whom were incumbents, their first opportunity to see Metropolitan State College and learn first-hand that the students were receiving a good education in the new college, and that students were involved in their school.

That second fall quarter, students in the fledgling music program were busy rehearsing for their first-ever public performance. In November they presented the "Three Penny Opera" at the Loreto Heights College Theater, since Metro had none. Tickets for the opera sold for much more than three pennies, however. Adults paid $1.50, but kids got in for 50 cents.

This performance, and many which followed, including concerts and debates, not only helped the students who participated, but they helped improve the reputation of the college in the community.

MSC's speech department was making its mark. Professor Coulson, the department head, said in a newspaper interview that the goal of the speech department was to create a unique program and not just follow the long-established patterns seen at other institutions. In addition to communication theory, Coulson said, practical applications would be taught, which combined public address with conference leadership and group dynamics. These were skills students could use throughout their careers and everyday lives.[252]

In November, Reverend Hardegree, the campus chaplain, and MSC sophomore Vivian Bartel formed a group called PROSPECTUS to discuss the topics of the day, particularly those outside the campus. On November 15, the group began with what it called the "Images of Man" series. Dr. Ohlson, MSC professor of economics, spoke on the topic of a planned economy.

The first woman's organization on campus, the Associated Women Students (AWS) was formed in the fall of 1966 to assist women students with the challenges of college life. Heather Cowan, temporary chairwoman of the group, announced the activities planned for the winter quarter, including a style show at which the now extinct department store, Montgomery Ward, presented new fashions for men and women, modeled by Metro students.[253]

MSC's first student newspaper began that fall—*The Metropolitan*. It helped connect the students and kept them informed on what was going on at their school. The editor was Richard R. Rios, the associate editor was Joseph Fuentes, Kathy Fox was copy editor, Nancy Bills worked on the editorial page, and Jim Saccamano served as the feature editor. Saccamano graduated in 1970 and went on to become the long-serving public relations director for the Denver Broncos, and after he retired, host of his own sports TV show.

Joe Fuentes, as did so many active students, worked full time while he was the associate editor, and later the editor. He was the police reporter for *The Rocky Mountain News* and was later promoted to news writer.

The second issue of *The Metropolitan* reported that a new student constitution had been approved. Student senator Lauren Watson described the new constitution as one that could not be changed. Another senator, Shannon Quinn, said the new charter was slanted toward students. Student government met at the Wyer Auditorium in 1966 since it had no offices.

The Metropolitan reported that the MSC College Republican club, organized in 1965 by Wanda Graham, was alive and well for the second year. In addition to starting the CRs, Graham served as president pro temp of student senate. The College Republican club was the largest student organization on campus during the first few years. That may have had more to do with Wanda's persuasive personality than the popularity of Republicans. The Young Democrats were "still in the process of organizing" in 1966, according to *The Metropolitan*.

Rae Bernaman, a member of the finance committee, said Dean Lillie would help her get the budget properly established. The flag committee announced it would raise a flag at the Forum Building. Student government chartered several clubs: the Spanish Club, the Mountain Climbing Club and Phi Beta Lambda.

The student center advisory board (SCAB) was formed that week because of alleged problems with the student center. It would govern the student center henceforth. Student members included Clarence Arnold, Heather Cowan, Judee Grout and Jim Kangiesser. Faculty members included Chuck Allbee and James Parker. Staff representatives were Ray Ogle and Rosemary Woods. Their first order of business was to establish a cleanup committee for the student center. The second order was to find a better acronym for the committee.[254]

Early December brought good news. There was a breakthrough regarding whether MSC would get its upper division approved in time. The CCHE recommended to the governor and the legislature that Metro should become a four-year institution. Their statement said Metro should offer undergraduate programs in the arts and sciences and in designated technical and professional fields appropriate to an urban undergraduate college. The commission added that the entire program of the college should "reflect and take full advantage of its urban setting."

The collective sigh of relief was heard as far away as the summit of Pikes Peak.

The commission indicated that third-year classes could begin in 1967-68, and the fourth year in 1968-69. They also said that as the two-year colleges planned for Denver progressed, MSC should phase out its two-year programs in technology and focus its efforts on baccalaureate degrees and occupational programs of more than two-year duration. The commission also said the CU Denver Center should phase out freshman and sophomore classes.[255]

The next part of that announcement, however, foreshadowed future events. The commission said that Metro should "establish standards of admission that will provide reasonable assurance that admitted students can succeed in its program." What the CCHE really wanted to do was close Metro's open door. That would come to light before long.

There were more firsts for the college that quarter. The first Christmas party was held on December 5 at the just-completed student center, scheduled to be dedicated in January. The Christmas dance was held at the Villa Italia Forum. Men's attire ranged from tuxedos to coats and ties. The women wore cocktail dresses. Music was provided by the Stewart Jackson Big Band, and at intermission, Jon Adams, a top-rated folk singer, entertained. The chair of the dance committee was Mary McBride, assisted by Rae Bernaman, Shannon Quinn, and Rosemary Woods.

This was Metro's first Christmas dance and it was the last time a Big Band orchestra would play for a college dance anywhere in the nation.

Rae Bernaman presented Governor Love with a ticket to the dance. He failed to show up, however. Perhaps he had a better offer, or maybe he just hated the Big Band sound.

The highlight of the evening, according to accounts, was the crowning of the king and queen of Christmas festivities. There were 30 candidates in the first round of voting, but that was pared down to ten finalists. The candidates that made the cut for king were: Roger Braun, Jim Ello, Doug Holcombe, Kirk Hunter and Dave Karins. Queen finalists included: Chris Gude, Judee Grout, Jeannette Hull, Judi Jones, and Shannon Quinn. Most of the queen candidates planned to teach when they graduated, however, Jeanette Hull and Shannon Quinn planned on becoming airline stewardesses (as they were called then). [256]

The elections for king and queen were controlled by a crack committee, consisting of Lynn "Spike" Davis, Jim Kangiesser, Chuck Brock, Kirk Hunter and Judee Grout. After votes were tabulated and verified to ensure there were no ballot irregularities, the announcement was made. The King and Queen of Christmas were Doug Holcombe and Judi Jones. In addition, students chose "*The Columbine*" as the name for the college's first (and only) Annual. That big announcement was made at the Christmas Dance.

These activities helped create camaraderie for the students in the new school. That was very important because MSC was a commuter college; there were no athletics or other traditions to bring students together to interact socially.

In addition to the coronation of Doug Holcombe and Judi Jones, 1966 was remembered for other events. In October, the Baltimore Orioles swept the LA Dodgers to win the World Series. Joan Baez and 125 anti-war protestors were arrested in Oakland. The National Organization for Women (NOW) was founded.

Congress passed a law that gave 125,000 Cuban refugees the right to become American citizens. Any Cuban who managed to get to the shores of the United States automatically received legal status with an easy path to citizenship. This would change national politics and U.S. foreign policy for decades to come.

Fishmongers got a kick in the gut in 1966. American Catholics found out they would no longer go to hell for eating meat on Friday. It was not clear, however, what would happen to the unfortunate souls who were already in hell for eating meat. And Catholic women could now go to mass without covering their heads—just like men.

In 1966, the U.S. military intensified its "Rolling Thunder" campaign of carpet bombing North Vietnam. The U.S. also began wide-spread use of Agent Orange and napalm on suspected Viet Cong positions and villages in South Vietnam as our military presence continued to grow. Desertion rates were increasing.[257]

To replenish the ranks thinned by desertion and to allow for escalation of the war, 382,010 young men were drafted in 1966. Most of them received a ticket to Vietnam, and for many, it was a one-way ticket. Nothing did more to promote college attendance in the mid and late 1960's than the draft board and the college deferment.

A guy named Hafiz Al Assad led a coup that toppled the government in Syria. He, and later his son, Bashar, would rule Syria for decades.

In California that November, a soap pitchman and actor named Ronald Reagan was elected governor. Soon, under Reagan's leadership, California became one of the first states in the nation to make abortion legal—years before Roe v Wade. This is not a typo. A Republican actually legalized abortion and still became a saint. California was also the first state to make LSD illegal. That did little to diminish LSD's popularity, however.

The Colorado Buffaloes were finally back. They ended the football season with a 7-3 record. After the Broncos lost their first two games, coach Mac Speedie was fired and replaced by Ray Malavasi. Under Malavasi the Broncos would win only four games, finishing with a 4-10 record for the second year in a row. Following the season, the Broncos hired Lou Saban from the Bills as both general manager and coach.

Beatle John Lennon met Yoko Ono and moved into The Dakota building in New York City, overlooking Central Park. Their marriage was blamed for the breakup of the Beatles, although Paul McCartney has recently said it was really creative differences, which happened at the same time that led to the group disbanding.

The top song on the 1966 Billboard chart was Barry Sadler's "The Ballad of the Green Beret," beating out the number two song "Cherish" by the Association. Third place went to "(You're my) Soul and Inspiration" by the Righteous Brothers. As for movies, "The Good, the Bad and The Ugly" took top honors.

On New Year's Eve, Dick Clark rocked in the New Year as usual. Metro was still open, and it had come a long way in a little over a year.

The largest student organization on campus in the beginning was the MSC College Republicans. Wanda Graham, club president, is second from left. *Photo Courtesy of Metropolitan State University of Denver.*

CHAPTER 7

They Didn't Think We'd Make It

Purple haze all in my brain
Lately things just don't seem the same
Actin' funny, but I don't know why
Excuse me while I kiss the sky...
Is it tomorrow, or just the end of time?
"Purple Haze"
Jimi Hendricks[258]

WINTER 1967: A STUDENT CENTER, A YEAR BOOK, AND STUDENT LOBBYISTS

1967 was a bellwether year, even at MSC. The winter quarter began and 2,173 students were enrolled at MSC. That was double the 1,102 from the previous year's winter quarter. Of the 2,173 students, 1,554 were men and only 524 were women. The majority (1,484) signed up for arts and sciences and 594 enrolled in applied sciences. Clearly, MSC had to do more to attract and retain women.[259]

Before the quarter even began, the CCHE took a meat axe to MSC's operating budget request for the next fiscal year. The trustees and the college had requested an appropriation of $3.4 million, but the commission slashed it to $2.9 million, while capping costs at $929 per student. The commission also whacked the budgets of all the other colleges and universities in the state.

Shelby Harper, CCHE chairman, asked the institutional representatives to take up their criticisms with the commission staff rather than directly with the legislature. In other words, he did not want the institutions lobbying against the budget cuts.[260]

As a result of the budget cuts and Harper's directive, MSC had nobody to turn to for assistance except its own student body. Students were the only ones with standing to speak with the legislature about funding, since they were not paid by state-appropriated funds like administrators, faculty, and the trustees. Harper's ban on lobbying had to be honored by administrators, but it was not binding on students.

Doug Holcombe was now in his second year and working on his associate degree. Like many students, he had a work-study job to help with the cost of tuition and books. Holcombe's job was to deliver mail to the various offices around the campus. One day, he rode the elevator with Dr. Phillips and by the time they reached the tenth floor, Doug had an assignment.

Holcombe was asked to go up to the Capitol every day between classes, sit in the gallery and take notes about what was going on. He picked up a Pink Book, which had the names of all legislators, and a Blue Book which listed the bills that were coming up each week. If any bills affected Metro, he would alert the president. This assignment allowed him to get to know many of the legislators.

In February, the legislature considered the Long Bill. Unfortunately, the bill cut Metro's already sparse budget by $700,000. The *MSC Faculty-Staff Newsletter* reported the story, saying, "The budget is falling short of what is needed for Metro. We need to either limit admissions or raise the budget. Why aren't Denver newspapers and Denver legislators moving vigorously to support MSC? Most editorials focus on CU becoming high quality, not on MSC." The newsletter added, "Students needed to help!"[261]

When the MSC budget was cut, Holcombe decided it was indeed time for students to help. He formed a group of what he called "the smartest students he could find," including Roger Braun, Becky Imatami, Barbara Adair, Dave Daniels, Shannon Quinn, Rae Bernaman and Judi Jones.

These students went to the Capitol every day and met with as many senators and representatives they could corner. Often times they took them across the street to the Quorum, where the student-lobbyists had a regular table. Other times they met in the cafeteria in the Capitol basement.

Their purpose was to educate the legislators about Metro and show them that the student body was not a bunch of derelicts, drop outs, drug dealers and hub cap thieves, which was the impression many legislators had of Metro students. (One day, on the floor of the House in debate over Metropolitan State College, a senator from Arapahoe County, Hugh Fowler, had said something to the effect of "Metro students were a bunch of hubcap thieves.") Those impressions were widely shared by Metro's nemeses—the supporters of the University of Colorado.[262]

Many people at that time confused Metropolitan State College with a high school located in northwest Denver called Metropolitan High School. It was an alternative school, set up to educate at-risk students, many of whom had been in juvenile hall.

These unpaid student-lobbyists wanted to convey that the state was getting its money's worth by investing in Metro. Their message was that MSC students were older, many were working, many were veterans and they could not get an education without MSC. Furthermore, these students studied hard, held full or part time jobs, and many had families.

This effort had a huge impact by changing the impression legislators had of Metropolitan State College. Only students could have done this. Faculty members would be seen as self-serving. Administrators were prohibited from lobbying. There was no alumni association and no boosters. Metro had its students, and that was all it needed!

Although students from the CU Denver Center and occasionally other colleges came to the Capitol, no students in the second half of the 20th century had ever put on such an organized, consistent and professional lobbying effort like the one Doug Holcombe put together in 1967. That effort was continued by student leaders into the 1970s.

Holcombe did not know that this student lobbying program would end up playing such a huge role in the success of the young college. There is more about student lobbyists in this book.

The other big news in the winter of 1967 was the grand opening of MSC's new college center. It was located in a remodeled two-story paint store at 1345 Bannock Street, across the alley from the Forum Building. The lack of a student center was one of the biggest pet peeves about the college at that time.

Roger Braun said, in a 2013 interview, that in Metro's first year, students discovered the cafeteria in the basement of the City and County Building, across the street from the Forum building. Soon it was filled with Metro students at lunchtime. The very next year, Metro got a student center. Was it more than a coincidence?[263]

Colorado Lieutenant Governor Mark Hogan helped Dean Lillie and Marjorie Woods, director of student activities, cut the ribbon. The Metro State Choir and the Madrigal Choir performed. Claire Thompson, a freshman member of the choir exclaimed, "It's fabulous," as *The Rocky Mountain News* reported.

The new center had food service and a bookstore in the basement. The main floor had a seating area that was also able to serve as an assembly facility. There was a study lounge upstairs and offices for student government and the student activities staff.[264]

Still, there were a new set of challenges facing the young college—challenges that perhaps few envisioned. MSC was an urban college, an institution designed without walls separating it from the city. In 1967, it became apparent that things happening in the city ended up happening in the college as well.

The passage of the Civil Rights Act and the Voting Rights Act did not quench the thirst of African-Americans for justice and equality. Stokely Carmichael, a militant activist, continued to recruit blacks, particularly young blacks, into his effort to use "black power" to gain equality. His message found fertile ground with many Metro students in 1967, especially a student senator named Lauren Watson, who later joined the Black Panther Party.

The rise of black power, however, caused reactionary whites to begin demanding "white power." Racial tensions were on the rise in the Denver community and that meant tensions were rising on campus as well even if the black student population was still small.

Community leaders began to worry about black militants and the reaction from whites. City leaders were growing fearful that Denver might see race riots like other American cities had experienced.

A symposium was held at Loreto Heights College to discuss white power, but the organizers also invited black power advocates, including Lauren Watson, to serve on the panel. This is how *The Denver Post* reported on the event:

> *"Three Negroes agreed Saturday that the only way Negroes are going to get power is to take it-and if that means black power, so be it. Though all declared Negro demands are legitimate, none said the races were hopelessly and completely separate."*[265]

The three "Negroes" *The Post* was referring to were Joe Brown, editor and publisher of *The Denver Blade* and a member of the Congress for Racial Equality (CORE); James Reynolds, Director of the Colorado Civil Rights Commission; and Lauren Watson, a student at Metro State College.

Lauren Watson made the strongest case for black power, saying he did not think that "asking is going to accomplish anything for the black man in the United States. If their demands can be met through the ballot box, I think this is the right approach, but I don't think they can. I think white power must be met with black power."

Watson, like many young blacks at the time, was growing impatient with the rate of progress, or lack of it, in America. He was intending to send a signal that blacks would not roll over under the threat of any white power movement. Not everyone on campus found comfort in Watson's growing acceptance of black power, however. Tensions would continue to rise and future events would change and shape MSC.

Despite the social undercurrents, life at Metro went on. The student magazine, *The New Campus Review*, released its second issue in January, and it was on sale in bookstores around town. Immediately, the publication was criticized. A New York publisher wrote a letter to the editor saying, the NCR was "too good looking." He said critics prefer mimeographed publications that are produced off-campus, independent of deans and faculty.

Professor Robert Rhodes, NCR's faculty advisor, and Duke Hill, the student editor, disagreed, saying the magazine was a "forum for creative expression and doesn't need to appear poverty stricken." This is another case where Metro just couldn't win. It was called second class and at the same time, blasted for looking too high class.[266]

Since there was finally a place to hold assemblies, MSC student lobbyists wasted no time inviting state legislators to the campus to discuss issues. Five state legislators and a member of the CCHE faced a packed student center on January 27 to answers questions about proposed legislation that affected the school.[267]

Senators Roger Cisneros and Anthony Vollock and Representatives Dan Grove, John Mackie, and Wayne Knox showed up, along with Dr. Norman Dodge, assistant director of the CCHE. The session was chaired by MSC student Vivian Bartel, the executive secretary of PROSPECTUS, the campus organization that sponsored the forum. The student lobbyists were operating sub rosa.

The two big issues students pressed the legislators on were whether Metro would be allowed to continue with a voc-tech program and whether the legislature would allow MSC to become a four-year institution next year.

Representative Mackie got the first question because he was the one who continually proposed turning Metro into a two-year school. Mackie said Metro State College should remain what it was (a two-year school) until a system of community colleges was established. After that, he suggested, Metro *could* become a four year school. That answer did not go over very well with the students.

Wayne Knox, who had voted against funding MSC, said the question was not a matter of competition between schools, but a question of state and community needs. He said the biggest need in Denver was for "service-type" jobs. Translation: poor and minority kids should go to trade schools because Denver needs service-type workers. Many students may not have understood the representative's code words.

Although no commitments were made, legislators were impressed with the professionalism of the students, even if they did not like the questions.

Dean Lillie released some interesting demographic information on the makeup of the MSC's student body. He said that 9.2 percent, or 229 of 2,443 students enrolled at MSC, had a Spanish surname. He said that was higher than the 8.7 percent of Spanish-surnamed citizens in Denver as a whole.

Lillie also indicated that there were only 75 blacks at MSC, or 3 percent of the student body, compared to the 6 percent in Denver as a whole. President Phillips said the college was making an effort to reach out to minorities.

The previous year, Phillips said, the percentage of students with a Spanish surname was only 6.3 percent, showing a 50 percent increase in one year. In MSC's first year, blacks accounted for fewer than 2 percent of the student body so there was some progress there as well.[268]

Lillie said that 51 percent of MSC students came from Denver, 17 percent were from Jefferson County, 15 percent came from Adams County and 9.5 percent were from Arapahoe County. A total of 3.9 percent came from elsewhere in Colorado and the remaining 3.6 percent were non-residents. The average age rose from 19 to 22.8 years.

Lillie attributed the age increase to students enrolling because of the Cold War GI Bill. He said that the number of students majoring in applied science rose 37 percent over the first year. He added that 312 of 2,162 students attending MSC were doing so under the GI Bill; 9 attended as war orphans and 12 were disabled vets.

A letter to the editor in the second issue of *The Metropolitan* gave insight into what was on students' minds that quarter. The unidentified student complained about the college bookstore, saying, "Only at [Metro] can a true student of business see a one-in-a-million phenomenon—a corrupt, over-priced, monopolistic, hawk shop with the front of an innocent, truthful Bargain Book Store. Three cheers for the Metro Bookstore!"

In its next issue, *The Metropolitan* published an editorial claiming that student did not have his or her facts straight. It claimed the student was "just blowing off steam." This was the beginning of what would become commonplace at MSC—dueling point and counter-point editorials in subsequent issues of the student newspaper. Free speech and academic expression are at their best when there is no interference from the administration. At MSC, there wasn't any interference—at least at first.

Carmel Smilanic wrote an editorial that expressed frustration with the public image of the college. "Why can't Metro get more and better publicity? Most people get quizzical expressions on their faces and react as if you just said a dirty word when you tell them your school is Metro State," she wrote. "Most of the hard work and efforts of the planners and professors goes unnoticed by the general public. This teamwork is what should make us all proud of our college. So why can't it be acclaimed for all to hear.[269]

One way to understand Metropolitan State College in its early days is to look at what people in the college had to say about it. Who were the thought leaders, the achievers, or simply the most popular people on campus at the time? One can get a feel for that by looking at the student publications from that era including the new yearbook called *The Columbine*.

Don Park was the editor of *The Columbine*, Karen Kammerzell was associate editor, Jackie Green business manager, Bill Hester photography editor, and Marcia Des Jardins was art editor. The book featured pictures of the administration, faculty, and ninety of the 2,100 students at MSC.

Interestingly, a two page photo spread in *The Columbine* proposed the following: *The problem has three possible solutions, choose one of the following:*

1. *fight the system*, with a picture of the State Capitol;
2. *conform to the system*, with a photo of a row of 1967 cars;
3. *or jump*, with a photo looking down from the roof of the Forum Building.

The yearbook also contained a photo of an unidentified MSC co-ed (as women were called back in the day) who was seemingly smoking a bowl. The caption beneath the photo, written by the poet J. Keats, read, "Tis very sweet to look into the fair and open face of heaven." There was no explanation of what was in that bowl, or what message was being conveyed other than the obvious. Was this foreshadowing 2012?

In addition, there was a photo of President Phillips with his President's Circle. Each month the president met with the heads of all the campus organizations, including student government and the various clubs, to discuss whatever was on their minds.[270]

The Columbine featured the organization PROSPECTUS, which was essentially a one-woman show led by Vivian Bartel. Nevertheless, it was very active in bringing in outside speakers, including legislators and others, to discuss the issues of the day.

It featured Lamplighters, a service organization, and the Philosophy Club, whose president that year was Mildred Myneeder. Also Mu Sigma, a woman's social organization which the caption said was formed "just for fun." The yearbook gave a shout out to another service organization—Circle K, as in Kiwanis.

The Spanish Club and its president Dave Simmons were featured. Another active club was the Drama Club which offered all students "an opportunity to participate in any facet of the Thespian Art," as their caption said. The Publicity Club celebrated its first anniversary in 1967. And Phi Beta Lambda, the first professional organization on campus, was pictured with members engaged in "thoughtful moments." What they were actually contemplating was a ski trip.

Betsy Choppock, 1966 May Fest Queen, was given a two-page spread, whereas the King, Lynn Davis, got only half a page. Also with a two-page spread was MSC's Winter Festival Queen, Judi Jones whereas the King, Doug Holcombe, only merited a single page spread. Holcombe and Davis should have filed gender discrimination complaints with the Student Publications Board.

Change was everywhere in '67. Student Health Services moved into new digs in the TTT building on Colfax at the beginning of the quarter. Congressman Rogers notified the college by telegram that it was approved for a federal grant in the amount of $24,092 to be used for language labs. He would have sent an e-mail, but it hadn't been invented.

The Metropolitan changed its staff. Richard Rios remained the editor but the new associate editor was Roger Braun. There was a new editorial page guru, Richard Peterie. Jim Saccamano was still the feature editor, but Mike Brigman took over advertising. The faculty advisors were

Dr. Henry Bagley and Joy Yunker, both English professors. Before the year was out, the student publication would go through more changes—just like the times.

In February, nine women competed for the title of Metro College Sweetheart of 1967. They were featured in a photo in *The Rocky Mountain News*, described as "girls." The contestants were: Barbara Taylor, Judee Grout, Jackie Green, Judi Jones, Cindy Tomhave, Deanne Cox, Penny Wilson, and Gaye Toren. An additional contestant, Mary Manning, was not pictured. According to the News, judging would take place in the new Grange building on West 26th Ave.[271]

The competition took place at the Grange as planned. *The Metropolitan* announced the 1967 Metro Sweetheart this way:

> *"It looked like a Republican year for MSC when radiant Gaye Toren stepped forward to be crowned Metro Sweetheart of 1967...wearing an emerald green dress of chiffon crepe with silver accessories...Miss Toren graciously thanked those students assembled..."*

Gaye was sponsored by the College Republicans club, but it is not certain if she really was a Republican. Jackie Green and Deanne Cox were her attendants. The women met their unnamed escorts on the dance floor according to *The Metropolitan*.[272]

(Looking at events like the Metro Sweetheart contest through today's eyes might give one a skewed impression. The students who competed in all these campus king, queen, and sweetheart contests—men and women—in the 1960's were also good students. Most have graduated and have gone on to successful careers. Most of them contributed to their school through activities in various clubs and organizations, and some were student lobbyists.)

That same week, Professor Vern Moody presented a lecture recital on the history, background, and moods of the Negro spiritual and American folk songs. He followed the lecture with examples of songs from American history, including "Deep River," Land of Degradation," and "Sweet Little Jesus Boy."[273]

Fifty students made the winter honor roll. Among them were students involved in both student government and *The Metropolitan*, including James Saccamano, Kathy Howard, Jerry Cronk and Roger Braun. And a new student government constitution—written by Roger Braun—came up for a vote and passed.

Clarence Arnold coined the most-used attack line future Republicans would use against the future Affordable Care Act when he protested the fact that students were forced to buy insurance that he said "they don't want, don't need, and can't afford." Arnold said that when he asked Dean Lillie why he was forced to buy insurance, he was told that, "No one is forced to go to this school.[274]

John Horton wrote in *The Metropolitan* that students and faculty were concerned about Metro's image, but he would settle for any image at all. He said the most far-reaching activities

Doug Holcombe was one of the first to enroll in MSC,
and one of its most distinguished alums.
He organized MSC's student lobbyists.
Photo Courtesy of Metropolitan State University of Denver.

Interior sot of MSC's first official Student Center, located
on Bannock Street across the alley from
the Forum Building
Photo Courtesy of Metropolitan State University of Denver.

at MSC were found in the intramural club-based sports programs. When teams from outside Denver came to play, they wondered if there even was a Metro because of the lack of fans cheering the team on. He said the fact no one seems to care was the worst possible impression that could be made about MSC, noting the players outnumbered the fans.[275]

While students were at the Capitol trying to reverse Metro's fortunes, dissent began rearing its head—not among students, but the faculty. English Professor Robert Rhodes wrote the very first letter to the editor in the *MSC Faculty-Staff Newsletter,* on February 20, 1967. He was expressing concerns that the vision of Metro's urban college was being sold out by capitulation. He entitled it, "A Call to Vision."

Professor Rhodes wrote that a college is designed to a great extent by its vision of itself. He said the vision at MSC was in great danger of becoming too short-sighted to play the large role required by its location and the school's great responsibility to Denver and Colorado. He posited that this short-sightedness would become myopic "if we educators continue to react to outside political and institutional pressures rather than provide our own leadership—our own vision of the kind of school we want to create."

He said the faculty was "running scared" and they should have more confidence in themselves. "It seems we are overly defensive in our willingness to cut back programs and budget requests before we are required to do so," he asserted. Rhodes noted that the students, however, had not yet caught this legislative virus and as yet did not share the negative attitude of the faculty. He concluded "Metro State College was beginning to go underground, and only moles seem to do well in such an absence of light."[276]

Immediately, there was institutional pushback against Rhodes—some from his fellow faculty members. They said that programs must conform to Metro's Plan of Operation, passed by the curriculum committee the year before. They said that limitations on programs were imposed by availability of funds, not lack of innovation. New programs must be approved by the division chairman, the section dean, the dean of the college, the curriculum committee, the academic affairs committee, the trustees, and finally, the CCHE.[277]

Robert Rhodes might have been the first faculty member to question whether MSC was following the vision of its founders, but he would not be the last. Increasingly, many students began questioning the school's commitment to the vision as well.

MSC BECOMES A FOUR-YEAR COLLEGE

The time had come to authorize Metropolitan State College to become a legitimate four-year institution. The legislature had only authorized the freshman and sophomore years when it funded the college. The 1963 statute that created the college required legislative approval to activate MSC's third and fourth years. Unless MSC got that authorization in the 1967 session, students then in their second year of studies would need to transfer.

The Denver Chamber of Commerce had a new president, Rollin D. Bernard, who was the president of Midland Savings and Loan. He replaced the previous president, Shelby Harper. Bernard was able to get the Chamber to pass a resolution endorsing a bill to activate the upper division. He said, "Metro State College needs to be a four-year institution with emphasis on general college training." Previously under Harper, the Chamber had recommended MSC become a two-year trade school.[278]

Since the CCHE had passed a resolution in support of the third year at MSC in 1967-68 and the fourth year in 1968-69, it forwarded that recommendation to the governor and the legislature. In a move to appease the CU regents, the CCHE reversed its position on the CU Denver Center. Previously the CCHE said that the Denver Center should eliminate its first two years and let MSC handle those students. That was no longer going to be the case. The commission restored funding to the Denver Center for freshman and sophomore years.[279]

In yet another flip-flop, *The Denver Post* wrote an editorial on March 8 saying it was time to move ahead on Metro State. They acknowledged that the demand was growing because Metro's enrollment had doubled. They advocated adding the third and fourth years, which they had previously written editorials against.[280]

Ahead of the legislature's vote, Mayor Tom Currigan urged passage of the bill. Also, Dr. George Becker, MSC biology professor, wrote a letter to *The Post*, encouraging the legislature to add the third and fourth years "for the sake of many of my students who simply cannot afford to go away to college."[281]

Then, Governor John Love gave an address on education to the General Assembly in March. Since he had flip-flopped on issues concerning Metropolitan State College so many times in the past, no one knew what he might say. To the relief of Metro supporters, the governor endorsed the concept of MSC finally being a four-year college.

"The commission has endorsed, as do I, the recommendations of the Trustees of our State Colleges that Metropolitan State College offer the third year of instruction in 1967-68 and the fourth year in 1968-69," Love told the lawmakers. He added that the commission was completing agreements with the CU regents relating to the Denver Center, which would provide for a complementary rather than a contesting role for the Center.[282]

With the governor on board, Senator Frank Kemp introduced Senate Bill 314 to activate the upper division at MSC. The bill was co-sponsored by senators Fay DeBerard, Ted Gill, Will Nicholson, Joe Scheifflein, Allen Dines, Allegra Saunders, and Bill Garnsey. The House sponsor was Representative Palmer Burch, and it was co-sponsored by representatives Floyd Haskell, Clarence Quinlan, Jean Bain, Ralph Porter, Star Caywood, Ken Monfort, J.D. Mac-Farlane, Forrest Burns, Wayne Knox, and Ben Klein. It was sent to the Finance Committee.

It was somewhat surprising that Representative Wayne Knox co-sponsored the bill. In the past, he had not been a big supporter of MSC. At the PROSPECTUS forum earlier, he said that the need in Denver was for service-type jobs. Perhaps speaking with MSC students gave the representative a different perspective.

Lt. Governor Mark Hogan said he was pleased Governor Love had strongly endorsed the funding of the third year at Metro State College. Hogan urged minority Democrats to respond to the governor's recommendations.[283]

As was always the case, when legislation affecting MSC was introduced in the legislature, some lawmaker introduced a separate bill to do the opposite. Shortly after Senator Kemp introduced SB314, Representative George Fentress introduced HB1509, which would restrict MSC to two-year status. It was assigned to the House Education Committee. This was just one more attempt by allies of CU to make Metro into a two-year school.

The student-lobbyists were at the Capitol every day (and often not in class) lobbying to support SB314. The faculty got involved as well, writing letters to their legislators. The MSC

Faculty- Staff Newsletter listed the names and addresses of all senators and representatives and asked the faculty to write them all, and to contact as many as they could in person and urge support of the bill.

When the bill came up in the Finance Committee, students, some faculty and a few administrators were at the hearing. President Phillips addressed the Fentress bill indirectly saying that there was no point in forcing Metro, which already offered two-year vocational courses, to mark time until more junior colleges were established in the area. He said that Metro would offer those two-year vocational courses until it was told to phase them out.

Phillips indicated that 79 percent of the students enrolled at MSC wanted a bachelor's degree. He told the committee that many MSC faculty members with doctorates would leave Metro if the expansion was delayed.

Doug Holcombe, representing MSC students, spoke for the bill. He pointed out that many students, like him, were completing their second year and if the bill was not approved, their college education would be interrupted. By this time, the student lobbyists had met with most members of the committee, made their case, and established rapport.

Meanwhile, students had written letters to legislators and sent letters urging the legislature to support the bill to the editors of the two Denver newspapers. In addition, 2,000 MSC students and faculty—nearly every student and professor at the college—signed a petition urging the legislature to allow the third and fourth years.[284]

The effort paid off. The Kemp bill passed the committee and went to the floor for second reading. On March 25, it passed on a voice vote with no opposition and was scheduled for third reading. On March 27, the Senate approved SB314 on a vote of 34 ayes, zero noes, and 1 absent. It was then sent to the House.[285]

In the House, SB314 was assigned to the Education Committee, chaired by Rep. Wayne Knox of Denver, who co-sponsored the bill. It came up for a hearing at which President Phillips and Doug Holcombe testified again. The bill was approved and sent to the Rules Committee.

The only opposition to the bill came from Republicans George Fentress of Jefferson County and John Fuhr of Arapahoe County. Fentress said that after voting no, he really was for MSC becoming a four-year college in the fall, but he voted no to call attention to education funding (whatever that meant.) Was he just downplaying his efforts since his side lost? [286]

When the Rules Committee took up the bill, they referred it to the Finance Committee since it had monetary implications. The Finance Committee heard the bill, passed it, and sent it back to the Rules Committee, which scheduled the bill for second reading.

The bill finally came up in the House for second reading. On Tuesday April 18, the House of Representatives passed SB314 on third and final reading with a vote of 54-7, with four not voting. The only dissenting votes were: James Braden (R-El Paso), Bill Gossard (R-Clear Creek), C.P.Doc Lamb (R-Morgan), Ted Schubert (R-El Paso), Lowell Sonnenberg (R-Logan),

This is how the Metropolitan reported the news that MSC was now a 4-year college

Photo Courtesy of Metropolitan State University of Denver.

R.E. Wilder (R-El Paso), and John Vanderhoof (R-Garfield), the Speaker. The bill went to the governor who signed it and MSC was finally a four- year college.[287]

In the next issue of *The Metropolitan*, in an article entitled, "Students Make a Difference," President Phillips wrote about the passage of SB314. "After months of toil, sweat, blood, and tears Metro came of age. At about 10:00 am on Tuesday April 18, 1967, the House of Representatives passed SB314 on third reading by a resoundingly overwhelming vote of confidence in Metro's future."

President Phillips wrote a letter to the "Friends of Metropolitan State College," stating that students, friends, faculty, and administration should be gratified with the action of the House and Senate. Phillips expressed his particular gratitude to the legislature and also to the students.

"Many legislators indicated their positive reaction to the approach that our students took as they worked in support of the passage of SB314," he wrote. "Our students made an extremely significant contribution, and must be commended for a job well done!"[288]

Imagine what would happen if nearly every one of the 23,000 students enrolled at MSU Denver in 2015 signed a petition for or against any issue. It would certainly send shock waves through the system.

Dr. Harold Benn, who put together Metro's first catalogue, said that now that the legislature had acted, work needed to be done to get the new catalogue including the junior level classes printed. Once again, he met the challenge.

ADDRESSING THE PROBLEMS OF THE CITY

An urban college is supposed to address the problems of the city, and in the beginning, MSC did just that. While the legislature was deciding Metro's fate, PROSPECTUS was doing more to promote the college's image, both internally and to the larger community, than any other organization on campus, according to *The Metropolitan*.[289]

PROSPECTUS sponsored a forum in late February to discuss "Black Power and Civil Rights in Denver." Vivian Bartel chaired the discussion in the Student Center and Gwen Thomas was the moderator. Participants included James Reynolds, Director of the Colorado Civil Rights Commission; Dorothy Davidson, Executive Director of the Colorado Branch of the ACLU; David Butler, head of the Park Hill branch of the NAACP; and MSC students Manny Martinez, with the Crusade for Justice; and Lauren Watson. Thirty-five students attended.

The forum was held because of the increasing tensions in the community between black power and white power. Several of the participants, including Lauren Watson, had spoken at the Loreto Heights forum a couple of months earlier.

There are two significant things about this event. The first is that students, in a new school with no traditions, sponsored a forum on black power and civil rights. Secondly, it is remarkable that these MSC students were able to get a ranking state official, as well as high-ups in the ACLU and NAACP to show up to the smallest college in the state to discuss civil rights.

It is instructive to look at what was said at that Forum to get a perspective on the times. Ms. Davidson said that the civil rights issues in Denver were the same as in the rest of the country, including police brutality. But, she said, Denver was better than some other areas, particularly in legislation and there were agencies established to deal with civil rights.

James Reynolds said, "White people both psychologically and emotionally feel a need to keep Negroes where they are—on the deck." He said that Denver needed to desegregate the schools, break up ghettos, and open up employment opportunities for blacks and Chicanos.

Both David Butler and Metro's Manny Martinez said that some civil rights organizations were being directed by Anglos behind the scenes. This was being done through financial influence. Butler criticized white people who, he said, often supported civil rights because of a guilt complex and then withdrew their support when their conscience had been satisfied. "A person must be willing to go all the way," he said.

Student Lauren Watson said, "Talking about human rights is like going to the man with your hat in your hand and saying give me something that is already mine." He said that a civil rights commission was even needed was an insult. He told the students that disunity is not a sign of weakness. He reminded them that our revolution was won by a small band of determined men.

Butler added, "Negroes need to know where they have been in order to know where they are going." What must be done, he said, is to educate the Negro about himself in order to provide more self-respect. He told the group he did not like the term civil rights and preferred "human rights" instead adding laws shouldn't be required to get people to treat Negroes like human beings.[290]

Although Denver escaped the riots that had occurred in many big cities, not everything was rosy when it came to civil rights. It is very encouraging that at an early date, it seemed like there were no walls between MSC and the community. The issues discussed at that PROSPEC-TUS forum were the same issues being discussed in minority communities.

Segregation in housing had not been legally allowed in Denver since the 1950s, but de-fac-to segregation still existed in 1967. Blacks and Chicanos primarily lived in their own neighbor-hoods, which many considered to be ghettos. There were economic and psychological barriers to integrating neighborhoods.

There were many more cases of excessive force or downright police brutality in minority neighborhoods than in white neighborhoods. The incarceration rate for blacks and Chicanos was far greater than for whites, then as now. Whites who were accused of crimes almost always had private counsel. Blacks and Chicanos more often than not had to rely on public defenders. The results were evident.

City and state services were not equally distributed between affluent and minority neigh-borhoods. Zoning laws were not enforced in minority areas. Trash was not picked up as dili-gently, pot holes were not fixed as quickly, snow was not plowed with the same dispatch as in southeast Denver. Blight and decay were allowed to creep into residential neighborhoods, including one called Auraria.

There was not equal opportunity for employment. Even if employers did not blatantly discriminate, whites got the best jobs—especially if the shop was not unionized. Whites got the promotions, and they made more than minorities who were doing the same jobs. The same was true with women, then as now.

Schools in minority neighborhoods were hardly equal to schools in white, more affluent neighborhoods. The graduation rate for white high school students was much higher than for black or Chicano students. And, contrary to what some would like to have us believe, it had nothing to do with genes—it had everything to do with the lack of resources available for mi-nority schools, and for their communities at large.

The first step to solving a city's problem is to admit there is one. The students who orga-nized that forum at MSC, with faculty help, and the students who attended must be com-mended for seeing and facing up to the problem. MSC was helping address the social problems in the city, like it was intended, but the pace was too slow for many who had grown impatient. As the MSC visionaries hoped, students like Manny Martinez and Lauren Watson were in-volved in the struggles in their communities as well as at their school.

A promising political science student, Joe Sandoval, was becoming concerned about brutality in the Denver Police Department, and insensitivity towards minority groups. Years later as a MSC professor, he did something about it—through education. That was and is the essential element of the urban-grant college.

In 1967, entertainers like Bobby Gentry were trying to get society to come to grips with racial issues. White folks made her song, "Ode to Billy Joe," the number three hit in the nation. Few probably understood that it was about the murder of a young black boy in Mississippi by the KKK.

As important as civil rights and racism were, students were still concerned with campus issues. Parking was a problem from day one and getting worse. Revenue from student parking tickets was probably balancing the city's budget. One day Doug Holcombe and Lauren Watson were talking about the problem. They decided to stage a protest at City Hall.

They quickly organized some students and staged a sit-in at the mayor's office to protest the parking tickets. After a while, the mayor's assistant told them to go visit with the deputy mayor, who managed public works. They had the meeting and the upshot was that parking referees began waiving half of the amount of the fines—but students had to take the ticket to the referee. This was probably the first of many peaceful protests that MSC students would organize.[291]

THE SPRING OF '67: FIRST STUDENT ELECTION; FIRST GRADUATION

Spring quarter began and 2,106 students were enrolled. At spring quarter registration, Ray Ogle, a member of the student center staff, conducted an informal and non-scientific survey of students. He was assisted by students from the psychology department. The survey's findings were:

- Students viewed social life most favorably—higher than academic achievement.
- High achievers viewed social life more favorably than low achievers, suggesting to Ray Ogle that they had more time to participate in social life.
- Females regarded academic achievement more favorably than males.
- Students polled seemed to feel the education quality at Metro was not as high as at with other colleges, but their concern seemed to be more with the quality of the *student body*, not the institution or faculty.
- Low academic achievers rated Metro more favorably than average or high achievers. This might indicate that MSC was serving the needs of this group more than the high achievers, Ogle suggested.

This was an unscientific poll, but it is interesting to note the difference in these responses compared to the responses to questions asked a year earlier by a reporter for the CU Denver Center newspaper. Students had a high impression of the school back then. In Ogle's survey, there seemed to be a feeling among students that MSC's student body was not "high quality."

One could posit that the attitudes about the MSC student body that CU and others were spreading around might have created a false self-image. Articles regularly appeared in the newspapers in which some leader accused Metro of being a "low quality school." Were students buying into that? Or was the survey just flawed?

Another possibility was that the students who answered the survey may have equated minorities, hippies, and students from poorer neighborhoods with low quality. There was prejudice in Denver at that time, and there was a growing rift between traditional students and those in the counterculture. Students reflect the values of their communities. Perhaps that is the reason for the change in attitudes. Or again, maybe it was just a flawed poll.

In spring of '67, the counterculture was just building up steam and the rift between the counterculture and traditional students on campus began to rear its head. One example was a letter to the editor, written by MSC student Paul Cusimano. He compared hippies to barbarians—at least their fashion.

"If we look back into history, we notice the types of apparel worn by different groups of people," he wrote. "Particularly, I would like to draw attention to the similarity of dress of the barbaric tribes and present day *mod* dressing...It is my conviction that the participants of the present day mod style of dressing are regressing back to forms of our preceding barbaric tribes."

He went on to say that he felt that these followers of modern change were afraid of the world as they saw it and thus were looking for a way to change it. He hoped that in time, this unrest would pass under the bridge and we could all return to the civilization and culture to which we belong.[292]

Nothing relives that kind of campus tension like the "Silly Season." In April, a group of students took Professor Vern Moody's car and deposited it inside the student center. After a good laugh, the students had to figure out how to get the car out. The solution was for a group to lift the car through the doorway. *The Post* published photos of the small car inside the student center, and a picture of students carrying it out.[293]

In late April, the Associated Students of Metropolitan State College (ASMSC) held its first actual election for student government. The previous student body president and other officers had been "selected," not elected, because it was the first government and there was no constitution under which to conduct an election

Chuck Brock, a member of the interim government, was elected student body president. Chuck was pursuing a career in radio and television and said his goal was to make student government more accountable in spending student money. Roger Braun, the current vice-president, was elected as the new vice-president. Roger was an education major who said his goal was to increase awareness of the student government to the student body. Richard Hildreth was elected to the student court and Walter Gibbs, Clarence Arnold and Doug Holcombe were elected to the senate.[294]

The MSC board of publications and public information (BOPPI) held its inaugural meeting on April 17, 1967. The new board would oversee student publications and handle disciplinary action, including removing newspaper staff from office—a power that would be exercised a few times at MSC. BOPPI indicated there were openings at the student newspaper.[295]

The Metropolitan filled those vacancies with new staff. Bonnie Pasco was the new editor; Barbara Spencer, associate editor; David Hawley, page one editor; Vic Avram, editorial page; Judee Grout, feature editor; John Horton, sports; Bill Hester, photographer; Duke Hill, advertising; Marcia Des Jardins, business manager; Bob Paslay, circulation. Dr Bagley and Joy Yunker remained the faculty advisors.

The men's basketball club, the MSC Mustangs (the ancestors of the Roadrunners) finished their basketball season with a .500 record. John Horton noted that interest and support picked up in the last few games, after he wrote an article blasting students for not supporting the team. He said that was most encouraging. The most valuable player on the Mustangs was Wayne Vigil, whose ball-handling and passing kept the team alive according to Horton.[296]

In May, the Colorado Collegiate Association (CCA) sponsored its annual academic College Bowl in which teams competed against students from other colleges and universities in various academic categories. Metropolitan State College fielded its first team and won first place in the junior college division, taking home its first trophy. The team had to compete in the junior college division because the school only had freshmen and sophomores. Apparently not everyone at MSC was a low academic achiever, as some had predicted.[297]

That same week, KOA TV news ran a documentary on the growing problem of LSD in Colorado. As the counterculture grew, LSD was rapidly becoming the drug of choice for the many baby boomers influenced by Dr. Timothy Leary and the growing "hippie culture." The substance, despite being called a "psychedelic drug," was still legal, whereas possession of marijuana was a felony in Colorado and much of the nation. This documentary followed the forum on LSD that PROSPECTUS previously sponsored.[298]

Greg Pearson joined the MSC faculty in the spring quarter to teach communication courses. Pearson was working on his Ph.D. in political science at the University of Colorado. He was a decorated member of the Marine Corps, having served in the Korean War. He had been an unsuccessful Republican candidate for Congress in 1966 and served on the Denver and Colorado GOP central committees. In 1964, Pearson had run for state representative on an anti-Metro platform. Perhaps his motto was, "If you can't beat 'em, join 'em."[299]

The spring honor roll was announced and Roger Braun was once again enshrined.

On May 24, Betty Naugle asked the CCHE to approve Metro's request for funds to plan for a new campus. The commission's executive director, Frank Abbott, said no funds would be released until the roles for Metro, the CU Denver Center, and the Community College of Denver were determined. Chairman Shelby Harper agreed, stating that everything should be put aside until the question of "who does what in Denver is answered."

In May, PROSPECTUS held another forum in the student center. This time students could ask administrators whatever questions they wanted. This later evolved into a regular event that would be called a "Bitch-In."[300]

There was more front page news that week. Judi Jones, the former Queen of Christmas and Winter Festival Queen, was pictured in *The Metropolitan* wearing a swim suit. She had just won the Miss Metro contest. The runners-up, pictured on page 3, were Judi Brown, who did a comedy skit, and Sally Thee, who sang "Man of Constant Sorrow." For her talent Judi Jones sang, "You're Going to Hear from Me." That was just a warm-up for Judi as she went on to compete in the Miss Colorado pageant in July.[301]

Also in May, Professor Carleton Reed had received a telegram from Congressman Byron Rogers announcing that MSC received a grant from the Department of Justice for development of a police science degree program.[302]

Shortly thereafter, the City and County of Denver announced that if police officers enrolled in MSC's program, it would reimburse them for 90 percent of the cost of tuition, up to six quarter hours, if they earned a C or better. Denver's Chief of Police, George Seaton, said that it was his "express policy to encourage officers of this department to avail themselves of formal education by enrolling...The complex responsibilities and duties of police work require that officers understand their community, their government and its functions and conditions which breed criminal and delinquent conduct."

The Denver Post published two editorials within two weeks, praising the new program and the police departments who encouraged officers to attend college classes. *The Post* pointed out that one of the major goals of the city's offer was to assist officers to advance within the department. It also suggested that a special benefit was for members of minority groups who would "use these college courses as a springboard for promotion to command positions."

Denver's Manager of Safety suggested that minority recruits take a "cram course" at MSC before they took the civil service exam, which would increase their likelihood of passing the test and being accepted into the mostly white police force.[303]

Given the complaints that many minority students expressed about police brutality at the PROSPECTUS forum held earlier in the year, it seemed like the program at MSC might do something to increase the sensitivity of future police officers towards minority groups, and to increase the numbers of minority officers in the force as well as in positions of authority. This was an example of an urban college solving urban problems, or at least providing an opportunity to do so.

The very first commencement in the history of Metropolitan State College happened in June. Twenty-eight students received Associate of Arts or Associate of Arts and Sciences degrees.

For a list of the very first graduates of Metropolitan State College see Table II.

President Phillips wrote an open letter to the college, saying that Metropolitan State College had come of age during those past months, due to the ambitious and hard-working students, a dedicated faculty and the college administration, all working together. They had combined to produce the ingredients of a highly successful academic year.

Phillips cited many firsts, including winning the College Bowl, the first Miss Metro competition, the first student constitution, first debate competition, first intra-mural baseball game, the police science grant from Washington and all the honors given to MSC by various organizations.

"We have travelled a great distance in a very short time. So now to our fine students, faculty, and administration let me extend words of personal appreciation for all of our achievements, and for turning 'growing pains' into 'gains,'" he wrote.[304]

There was another shake-up in June at *The Metropolitan*. There was a new staff composed of Richard Rios, editor; Barbara Spencer, associate editor; Dave Hawley, page one editor; Bonnie Pasco, page two editor; Doug Holcombe, sports editor; Bill Hester, photographer; Marcia Des Jardins, art editor; Duke Hill, business manager; and Bob Paslay, circulation manager. Judee Grout remained as feature editor and Dr. Bagley and Joy Yunker remained the faculty advisors.

The recipients of the first President's Award were listed. Student body president Chuck Brock was selected for his work as chairman of the CCA College Comment TV show and his work at the legislature, as well as other things. Charles (Chick) Todd was also selected for his work in student government, on the Concert Choir, and other achievements.[305]

As the quarter ended, the college rented another building at 11th and Cherokee and began remodeling what would become the Cherokee Building. The Metro library was preparing to move from the third floor of the Forum Building into its new digs in the Cherokee Building. The library would be part of a learning center, and there was room for 21,000 books. Students could still use the Denver Library, however. Back then, there were no e-books, so college libraries required space for lots of books.[306]

John Tumler won the Intramural Golf Tournament at Fitzsimons and Overland golf courses. Marc Kessel and Nancy Sheehan won the badminton title. Joe Taylor beat several players to win Metro's intramural tennis title. Joe was ranked number three in Colorado according to Duane Mehn, chairman of Metro's health, physical education and recreation department.[307]

The war in Vietnam was escalating rapidly. A national poll, however, found that more students considered themselves to be hawks than doves, by a large 49 to 35 percent margin. The rest had no opinion. That position would change over the next two years, as more and more students' friends came home in body bags or joined the growing number of MIAs.[308]

"To Sir with Love," by Lulu was a hit that summer. Also hot that summer was "The Letter" by the Box Tops, the Association's "Wendy," and the Monkees "I'm a Believer." However, many boomers preferred the new sound of the era, like "Light My Fire" by The Doors, or Jefferson Airplane's "Somebody to Love" and "White Rabbit." Those would become anthems of a new counterculture that was just getting its wings in the summer of 1967—the Summer of Love.

MSC's first library was small, but used.

Photo Courtesy of Metropolitan State University of Denver.

CHAPTER 8

The Times
They Are A-Changin'...

Come senators, congressmen, please heed the call
Don't stand in the doorway, don't block up the hall
For he that gets hurt will be he who has stalled
The battle outside ragin'
Will soon shake your windows and rattle your walls
For the times they are a-changin'
"The Times They Are A Changin'"
Bob Dylan[309]

THE WINDS OF CHANGE

During the first two or three years, MSC students were not much different than college students had been since the end of WWII. Metro students were somewhat atypical in that they were older, had jobs and were more focused on getting an education than many students at residential campuses. Generally speaking, however, they were mostly white, mostly male, and wanted an education to have a better life, except more were from the middle class.

Events in the summer of '67, however, shaped society and MSC for more than a decade. Social changes led to dissent, protests, civil disobedience and a general questioning of authority. Course material as well as how certain classes were taught at Metro changed along with society. So did the intensity of the debate about course material and how it was taught.

This makes more sense if we understand the context of the times. For those born after the late 1960s, (or those too stoned at the time to remember), it helps to widen the lens a little and examine what was happening in the nation.

Baby boomers grew up during the Cold War and their school days were punctuated by atom bomb drills. School kids were taught to take cover under their desks to save them from the nuclear bomb. This was frightening for a young generation helpless to do anything about it.

The Cuban missile crisis marked a turning point. President Kennedy had stared down Khrushchev, the missiles were gone from Cuba and nuclear war was avoided forever, or so everyone thought. Boomer kids, who for so many years had been fearful, suddenly felt safe. They had a new hero: the president who saved America from nuclear annihilation.

The assassination of President Kennedy changed things. It was inconceivable that our president could be murdered. Many boomers were angry, depressed and confused. Everything they had been taught about their country seemed like a lie. What could they believe in? There was growing dissatisfaction with the war and the materialistic society in general.

Against this backdrop, youths known as "flower children" massed in San Francisco in the summer of 1967. Soon, that spirit spread across the nation and became the counterculture. The counterculture and the resistance to it would play out at MSC for a decade, starting with the Summer of Love. The counterculture was a phenomenon that must be understood to understand MSC's history in this period. So, let's take a closer look.

THE SUMMER OF LOVE AND THE COUNTERCULTURE

> *When the truth is found to be lies*
> *An' all the joy within you dies*
> *Don't you want somebody to love?*
> *Don't you need somebody to love?*
> *Wouldn't you love somebody to love?*
> *You better find somebody to love.*
>
> -"White Rabbit: Grace Slick, Jefferson Airplane[310]

To understand the '60 without examining the counterculture is like studying the 1920s without discussing prohibition, the flappers and the Charleston.

The Summer of Love was the name given, not to a period, but rather a happening—a happening that jump-started the social phenomenon known as the counterculture or the hippie movement. This cultural and political shift changed the way many in the boomer generation thought, and how they interacted with authority figures—at least for time. It led to a reactionary movement that divided families, the generations, and the nation to this day.

This counterculture phenomenon had its roots as far back as the 1950s with the beatniks and bohemians in places like Greenwich Village in New York City and North Beach in San Francisco. However, it morphed into a massive social movement when, 100,000 young people converged on San Francisco, and took over the Haight-Ashbury neighborhood in 1967.

It began when artist Michael Bowen organized a "Human Be-In" in Golden Gate Park in

January. More than 30,000 current and future hippies came to that "gathering of tribes," as he called it. The Human Be-In led to hundreds of smaller be-ins around the country in multiple cities including Denver.[311]

What set this event apart was the ubiquitous presence of LSD specially-produced for the gathering by chemist Owsley Stanley. Open smoking of marijuana was commonplace at counterculture gatherings, but after publication of Timothy Leary's book *The Psychedelic Experience*, LSD became the drug of choice because, for one reason, it was legal then.

The event was co-organized by Timothy Leary, who authored the counterculture movement's slogan: "Turn on; Tune in; Drop out; and Always question authority." Leary compared the movement to great religions of the past saying that the participants "seek to find the divinity within and to express this revelation in a life of glorification and the worship of God."[312]

Turn on, he said, meant to go within one's self to activate their neural and genetic equipment¬—to become sensitive to the many and various levels of consciousness and the specific triggers that engage them. Tune in meant interacting harmoniously with the world around one's self—to externalize, materialize, express their new internal perspectives. Drop out, Leary said, suggested an active, selective, graceful process of detachment from involuntary or unconscious commitments. It meant self-reliance, a discovery of one's singularity, a commitment to mobility, choice and change. Drugs, he thought, were one way to accomplish this end.

Unhappily, Leary's explanations of this sequence of personal development were often misinterpreted by many to mean, "Let's get stoned."[313]

The "Human Be-In" served to proselytize the crowd, and those watching via the media, about the key philosophies of the 1960s counterculture or hippie movement. The hippies, sometimes called flower children, were an eclectic group. Some were interested in issues and politics as a means of bringing about change. Others were into art, music and poetry as the vehicle for self-enlightenment, which would then result in social change. Many were into eastern religions and meditation. All were eager to integrate new ideas and insights into their lives.

Many hippies rejected consumerism and the materialistic values of their parents' generation. They rejected American uptightness and prudishness. They rejected things they were being taught as song "Itchycoo Park" demonstrates: *I'd like to go there now with you. You can miss out school, won't that be cool. Why go to learn the words of fools?*[314]

The flower children embraced sexual freedom and nudity (free love), which many outsiders called promiscuity. Free love was a means of spiritual connection with their fellow human beings. Almost all hippies opposed the escalating Vietnam War, so the peace movement found fertile ground in the counterculture. The two fingered V-shaped the peace sign and peace symbol were popularized by the flower children and soon spread across the entire society. Even Nixon flashed it, usually with both hands.

Hippies adopted many ways of achieving their cultural and political individuality including communal living, colorful and unconventional dress, long hair, beards, and the practice of not shaving. They were ecologically aware and believed in achieving a higher consciousness through the use of psychedelic mind-expanding drugs like acid (LSD), mushrooms, mescaline, pot, hashish and for some, popping Quaaludes.

Later that spring, anti-war activists formed the Spring Mobilization to End the War in Vietnam. Its chairman was James Bevel, a civil rights activist and member of the Southern Christian Leadership Council (SCLC). They put together a massive demonstration in New York City on April 15, 1967, marching from Central Park to the United Nations. Dr. Martin Luther King Jr., Harry Belafonte, James Bevel, and Dr. Benjamin Spock all marched and spoke at the demonstration.[315]

They met for a two-day conference in Washington DC in May and the National Mobilization Committee to End the War in Vietnam was formed. The conference featured speeches by Jerry Rubin, Abbie Hoffman, and Allen Ginsburg. New Mobe, as it was called, staged many protests in Washington DC against the war that spring.

MSC became the center of Colorado's student anti-war effort.

Shortly after the Human Be-In, John Phillips of the Mamas & the Papas wrote the song "San Francisco (Be Sure to Wear Flowers in Your Hair)" for his friend, Scott McKenzie. The song was released on May 13 and became a hit. San Francisco soon became a magnet for hippies and would-be flower children from around the country. By spring, local authorities were alarmed over the 100,000 counterculture types who were moving into the city, especially the Haight-Ashbury district.[316]

The young people who came to San Francisco found free food, free drugs and free love in Golden Gate Park. A free clinic was established to treat whatever maladies they came down with, which were many. There was also a free store that gave away the basic necessities to anyone in need of them. In short, Haight-Ashbury became a giant commune—a hippie utopia.[317]

A wide range of people showed up in San Francisco: teenagers, college students, middle-class curiosity seekers, and even partying military personnel from bases within driving distance. Some came to participate, others as voyeurs. As the crowds grew, so did the number of reporters, correspondents and photographers capturing the scene and disseminating the photos and video worldwide. The music complimented and completed the scene.

When a generation of baby boomers saw this on television, it changed many of them. It popularized LSD and marijuana. These drugs were elevated from the status of forbidden drugs to an instrument of enlightenment. Mind-expanding drugs like acid and mescaline were almost like sacraments for the counterculture and were shared by and among fellow believers—hippies, flower children, and of course, the wannabes just along for the ride. The lyrics of *Itchycoo Park* said it all, *"What will we do there? We'll get high. What will we touch there? We'll touch the sky."*

During the Summer of Love, copy-cat events were held in many cities, including Denver. The first Denver Be-In occurred on the campus green of Metropolitan State College (Civic Center Park.) A dozen or so hippies camped out and sang songs while many more curiosity seekers just observed.

With the aroma of marijuana wafting from their circle, some engaged in nudity, which the authorities called outrageous behavior. The Denver police moved in and many of the flower children—flowered headbands and all—were given a ride down to the police building.

Later that summer, Timothy Leary came to town and spoke. Individual hippies began having "love-ins" in their homes or communes where they were less likely to be hassled by law enforcement than when camped out on the campus green. For at least four years, several duplexes and row houses on MSC's invisible campus were the scenes of psychedelic love-ins.

(There was a mini-baby boom across the nation the following spring as tens of thousands of children were born. A whole generation of kids would enter kindergarten in 1973 with names like Earth, Cloud, Moon-Unit, Echo, Jupiter, Dharma, Flower, Summer and Peace. Coincidentally, many of their parents had participated in the Summer of Love. Many students interrupted their college education due to pregnancy.)

The heavy use of LSD and other drugs, along with the new music, served to unify the hippies and wannabes. They were universally against the war in part because of the draft. It was cool to be against racism, intolerance, bullying and violence because people were connected. There was great peer pressure to "make love, not war."

Despite all the jokes, flower children really did have deep discussions about the meaning of life. Discussions probed the hypocrisies of society, the false gods of materialism and wealth, and our crimes against humanity and social injustice. They really believed, at least at some level, in their slogans of love. Young people began to look at things differently than their parents and many of their professors and college administrators. And that would often lead to conflict, but less so at Metro than at other colleges.

This political and cultural shift was profound, but not long-lasting. Flower children came from all rungs of society. Many came from upper or upper middle class families. A majority were white kids. They came into the movement with biases attitudes learned early in life. Many changed their childhood outlook during the movement because they were enlightened, others because it was cool.

Unfortunately, when the euphoria of the sex and drugs wore off, and babies came along, many of the newly-adopted attitudes of the hippies gave way to the attitudes they learned as children. That is why many former flower children are one-per centers and hedge fund managers today.

The book *Children in Politics*, by Fred Greenstein, was required reading in several political science classes at MSC in '68 and '69. Greenstein makes the case that children form their

Flower children offer flower to police at a demonstration in Summer of Love 1967. *Photo Credit; U.S. Government Photo, Department of Defense 1967, National Archives.*

political and social opinions at a very early age—as early as age 7. Some argued that the book was incorrect because so many students had flower-child political leanings while their parents were conservative. MSC professor Bob Clifton suggested those students were an exception, not the rule.

Good things came out of the counterculture movement. For one thing, the anti-pollution laws of the 1970's were enacted in large part because the hippies raised awareness of the issue among the boomer generation and society in general.

Women's equality advanced greatly because of different attitudes held by the baby boom generation and in particular the flower children, who supported the cause of the feminist movement.

The Vietnam War ended in large part because the movement against it had become mainstream. This was mostly due to the hippie opposition to the war, and the anti-war protests led by militant students and former students. Eventually, they changed America's position on the war.

The counterculture was much more tolerant of different races and sexual orientations than their parents' generation. African-Americans and Latinos made strides in the late 1960s and '70s, due mostly to their own initiative. However, many young white people, especially college students, joined the marches and demonstrations to support civil rights for blacks and Chicanos.

Counterculture youths supported striking farm workers and advocated boycotts of grapes, California lettuce, and Coors beer, which helped the United Farm Workers led by Caesar

In the Summer of Love, it was common to see Love Busses like this one.

Photo Credits: Photo Liftarn, Wikimedia Commons.

Chavez to secure better wages and working conditions for mostly Latino farm workers. These causes drew widespread support from students at MSC.

Lastly, the softening of attitudes toward the LGBT community began with the hippie generation. The children of boomers, especially the flower children, were certainly more tolerant than their parents and grandparents. Eventually, this tolerance spread, particularly among the children and grandchildren of boomers.

BLAME IT ON THE MUSIC

Perhaps the biggest thing to come from this era was how music influenced the counterculture. Before the Summer of Love, groups like Jefferson Airplane, Buffalo Springfield, the Grateful Dead, The Doors and Santana were just local bands. The exposure they enjoyed that summer catapulted them to the forefront of the music world. Other artists like Pete Seeger, Bob Dylan, Joan Baez, and Peter Paul and Mary also found a niche in protest songs.

Even the Beatles adopted a new sound with lyrics containing double meanings. Popular music shifted away from seemingly trivial things and focused on the issues of the day like war, drugs, and social injustice. Lyrics like "Lucy in the Sky with Diamonds" (LSD) addressed the drug cultural in a subtle way, while others hit it head-on.

Most of the new popular music glamorized the drug culture with lyrics like "feed your head" by Jefferson Airplane, which referred to psychedelic drugs. Songs also rebuked things boomers had been taught about the values of society like Jefferson Airplane's song "White Rabbit" asserting that: *"One pill makes you larger And one pill makes you small And the ones that mother gives you Don't do anything at all."*[318]

Many of the musicians of this era embraced antinomian ideas in their work. As a result, the youth in the counterculture came to dislike authority and its ability to set boundaries around them.

Antinomianism, in a religious context, is the term used to describe the belief that man is saved by faith alone and therefore does not need to perform good works to achieve salvation. Antinomianism was an exaggeration of the doctrine of justification and thus became controversial even within Protestantism. In a secular context, antinomianism invalidated traditional institutions, laws, and rules in general.

In very simple terms, music came to assert that the laws and rules of society are arbitrary and often imposed by the powerful to oppress the weak, and as such, man has no obligation to follow them. It meant, for example, that students had no moral obligation to follow rules.

Jimmy Hendrix was one of the most popular musicians of the time, and arguably one of the most influential of the era. Hendrix had an "antinomian personality," which was evident in the evolution of his music, particularly the songs "Fire," "Foxy Lady," and his re-recording of Bob Dylan's "All Along the Watchtower." Lawrence Chenoweth wrote, "Hendrix went from defeat to self-loathing to empowering the self through unorthodox means," adding that he perfectly illustrated the psychological path of the antinomian.[319]

Jefferson Airplane also advocated those ideals in their music. They believed love was too fallible to be construed as a source for happiness. Instead, joy would come from a sense of individuality that would obliterate the pain of aloneness. Their song, "White Rabbit" rejects the reason and teachings of an older generation so that truth and transcendence could be found. Drugs, other than the ones your mother gives you, are a viable way to find "truth."

Baby Boomers needed to escape more than just the pain of aloneness; they needed to escape the horrors of the war, fear of nuclear attack and fear of the draft. They needed a refuge from what they came to realize as the excesses of materialism and capitalism that would eventually destroy the middle class many of them came from. They could see that the earth itself was being destroyed, and that was too painful to deal with.

A new genre of protest songs, building on the foundation of folk singers like Peter Paul and Mary, Joan Baez, and Bob Dylan, became popular. While those singers focused on a better world, peace and a new consciousness, the new protest songs were more explicit about the absurdity of war. An example was John Lennon's "Give Peace a Chance"[320]

Let me tell you now
Everybody's talking about, revolution
Evolution, masturbation, flagellation
Regulation, integrations, meditations
United Nations, congratulations
All we are saying is give peace a chance
All we are saying is give peace a chance

And Edwin Starr asked about war, and answered his own question:

War.
What is it good for? Absolutely nothing!
Listen to me...
War means tears to thousands of mothers' eyes
When their sons go to fight and lose their lives...
It's an enemy to all mankind
The point of war blows my mind
War has caused unrest
Within the younger generation
Induction then destruction
Who wants to die?

The Internet, Twitter and Facebook were not even fantasized about in 1967. Music was the medium. It had as much or more influence on the views and attitudes of many students in colleges and universities than anything they learned from their parents or teachers. And, when the listener was high, the message seemed more profound. If people weren't turned on, they had little idea how tuned-in people viewed things around them.

In the 1960s, many blamed popular music for the deviance and rebellion of the younger generation. Music wasn't the cause, but it certainly played a role in challenging baby boomers to question everything including authority. That questioning opened the door to new movements like the SDS, Black Power, La Raza Unida, and women's liberation.

THE COUNTERCULTURE AND GENERATION GAP AT MSC

In the middle of 1967, there were probably three categories of students at MSC. First, there were students who were caught up, in varying degrees, in the counterculture, and/or the social revolution going on at the time. This included the peace movement and the various battles for equality being waged by blacks, browns, and women.

Second, there were students who opposed the counterculture, the hippies and their drug-using free-love lifestyle. These students viewed the counterculture as nothing more than an excuse to party. They rejected many of the political positions of the counterculture group.

Many in this group were veterans who had seen the war up close and personal. They were leery of those who criticized the war since they had risked their lives fighting in it. These students felt like their sacrifice was not appreciated, and some viewed as cowards those who protested without serving.

Lastly, there were students who were too involved with their own education, their families and their jobs to get involved in either group. They had worked too hard to have an opportunity for education (or a second chance) and they wanted to stay focused and above the fray.

Many students at MSC were married and had to work because they had families to support. They resented the free-love lifestyle depicted on TV. Students who could barely afford to go to college did not empathize with students whose parents were rich enough to send them to college just so they could party.

Nearly half a century later, almost all the faculty and alumni interviewed by the MSU Denver Institutional History Committee recalled that most Metro students in that era, even those inclined toward the counterculture, were there first and foremost to get an education. They knew that this was their best, or in some cases, last opportunity for a college education.

Things began to change in late 1967, however. By design, Metropolitan State College was an urban college. That meant that things going on in the community would influence things on campus. Students came from the city, returned home to the city after classes, and brought what was going on in their community to campus. The counterculture set the stage for a decade of dissent, protest and confrontations at Metropolitan State College.

As these cultural clashes popped up at Metropolitan State College, they presented both a challenge and an opportunity for the faculty, administrators, and student leaders. Over the next few years, they were confronted with new issues like drug use on campus, city streets or the adjacent Civic Center Park. How should they deal with students who came to class high?

President Phillips faced pressure from legislators and the business community to crack down on drug-using students. How leaders at MSC dealt with all this determined the course of the college. Many administrators and faculty members—especially the older ones—saw a different reality than many of the students they had to deal with.

There was a huge generation gap that had to be bridged if the institution was going to succeed. And it had to be bridged in a way that did not alienate older, married and veteran students who were not tuned in to the counterculture. Faculty members had to be skilled and adept to succeed with this new challenge.

President Phillips often said that it was critical that faculty make an attempt to communicate with the students on their level. Some did that well, others not so much. As a whole, the faculty at Metropolitan State College did a better job than their counterparts in other institutions of higher education, and it bore fruit.

Other administrators and faculty members like Keats McKinney were traditional and did not have a great deal of tolerance for faculty members who embraced counterculture ideas. He was much less sympathetic to student protests and dissent than Phillips. McKinney used tenure as a lever to insure faculty members did not go too far, in his opinion.

Many students in the late 1960s questioned authority. They were not likely to take anything a teacher or administrator said at face value, and they were less likely to follow orders than their parents were. This challenge to authority led to confrontation. The doctrine of *in loco parentis* clashed with the perceived rights of students. College administrators often became obstacles to dissent. Students who came to class high were more questioning and occasionally more confrontational.

As the Vietnam War dragged on, young people became more resentful and distrusting of government and authority figures. On the other side of the fence, particularly after the election of Richard Nixon, the older generation became less tolerant of their own children and their children's generation. They pushed back on drug use, dissent, demonstrations, perceived promiscuity and every manifestation of the cultural divide. This in turn put pressures on administrators and faculty to clamp down.

The very notion of clamping down is the opposite of academic freedom, and it goes against the very intent of what a college or university is supposed to be. Since Metropolitan State College was striving to be an urban college, the cultural changes in the 1960s had a dramatic impact on the direction the institution would take. This affected the lives of everyone involved.

As the decade-long civil rights struggle spilled out of the South into northern cities, many young African-Americans, including those at Metro, grew tired of discrimination and police brutality and they began demanding justice and opportunity. Nationally, a new generation of black leaders—Bobby Seale, Angela Davis, and Huey Newton—formed the Black Panther Party. The group had a presence at Metropolitan State College, and a student, Lauren Watson, became a key leader of the Denver group.

Latinos intensified their demands for justice and civil rights as well. Caesar Chavez organized hundreds of thousands of farm workers—many children—demanding humane working conditions and some semblance of a living wage for the people who harvested Americans' food. Resentment over losing their land grants at the hands of the U.S. Cavalry in the 1800s gave a cause for many Latino leaders, like Ries Lopez Tijerina, to organize around. This struggle was called *El Movimiento*.

A national leader of *El Movimiento* was Corky Gonzales, who formed the Crusade for Justice. He and many other MSC students, including Richard Castro, Ed Lucero, Virginia Lucero Castro and Joe Sandoval became involved in that struggle.

National feminist leaders like Betty Freidan, Gloria Steinem and Bella Abzug began demanding equality for women and an end to paternalism. The women's liberation movement was just beginning in 1967. Although many associate "women's lib" with young women burning their bras and not shaving, the movement's issues were far deeper than that. The women's movement changed American society. Metropolitan State College became be a battleground in that movement as well.

Inspired by the black voting rights movement, young Americans, upset with the fact they could be drafted at 18, but could not vote, began demanding the right to vote. Students at Metropolitan State College were front and center in that effort in Colorado and nationally.

Student leaders at Ivy League institutions like Tom Hayden and Mark Rudd began organizing sit-ins and protests. Organizations like the Weather Underground, the New Mobe and SDS were formed. Soon large student protests sprang up around the nation, often violent.

Even though Metropolitan State College was in the front line of the protests of the '60s, and had its share of so-called radical groups like the Black Panthers, the Mau Mau Underground and the SDS, it escaped violence and bloodshed. The nature of the student body, the openness of faculty and administrators, and the efforts of student leaders are the main reasons.

In a 2014 interview, history professor Charles Angeletti reflected on why Metro students were not as radical as those at DU or other schools. He said that kids whose parents had money could get bailed out and they had lawyers. That was not true with Metro students. They came to get an education and they could not afford to lose their jobs. "Metro," Dr. Angeletti added, "did not have rich kids living in tents pretending to be radical."

In the late 1960s, student leaders at Metro were taking a different approach. They were lobbying and persuading in lieu of picketing. Roger Braun called that "Metro's version of dissent." There were demonstrations, particularly against the Vietnam War and racism, but most of the students who supported those efforts, were also working in the community for change within the system.[321]

FALL OF '67: MSC AFTER THE SUMMER OF LOVE

When students came back to campus in September, at the beginning of Metro's third year, there was a noticeable change in the appearance of many of them. Many had been to San Francisco to participate in the Summer of Love. Others watched it on TV.

Many men had longer hair; some had ponytails. They often wore colorful head bands, tie-dyed clothes and bell bottoms. The admonishments from their parents to get a haircut had the opposite effect. It only served to make long hair a symbol of rebellion.

Many women hair replaced the big hair of the early 1960s with long straight hair. Long skirts were common, and so were necklaces and earrings adorned with peace signs. Wire-rimmed glasses began replacing the previously popular, Goldwater-style plastic rims.

The faint smell of pot was more commonplace, particularly in the alleys behind classroom buildings and the Mule. Students and faculty were dividing into camps. The counterculture had arrived at MSC.

When students returned that fall, *The Metropolitan* was gone. It had been replaced by a new student newspaper named *Your Choice*. There was a new editorial staff. Sallyann Ulrich was editor-in chief; Clarence Arnold, managing editor; Karen Barbour, feature editor, and Chick Todd, business manager. Kathy Howard covered clubs and Vivian Bartel was the correspondent for student government. The new sports editor was Liz Crowley, replacing Doug Holcombe.

The editorial staff launched a "'name *the paper*" contest, asking students to submit names more creative than *Your Choice*. The lucky winner received dinner for two at the Plainview Inn on west 38th Avenue, a half a mile east of Elitch Gardens.[322]

President Phillips welcomed the new students with an open letter in *Your Choice* at the beginning of the quarter. In addition to the usual, Dr. Phillips said that although academic work "should be your first concern, there are many out-of-class opportunities for broadening your education. I believe that to become well balanced every student should join an organization which interests him or engage in some other kind of worthwhile student activity." Did that include protests?

Phillips said in his letter that there was some doubt during the summer whether the new student newspaper would get it together, but he was delighted that it had.[323]

Metro began its third year with 3,591 new and former students and an FTE of 2,659. MSC had the largest increase in enrollment among the nine state supported colleges—up 47%. *The Rocky Mountain News* ran a picture of kids lining up to register. Enrollment was slightly lower than the 3,600 the trustees anticipated, however.[324]

One of those enrollees was a transfer student from Trinidad Junior College named Richard Castro. Another student that enrolled that fall was Larry Strutton. Like so many MSC students, Larry went to school full time and worked nights in the composing room at the nearby *Rocky Mountain News*. After two years, Larry was promoted to system production manager, a position he held during his last two years at MSC. After he graduated, Larry was promoted to production manager. Eventually, Larry became the CEO, president, and publisher of *the Rocky Mountain News*.

Strutton was one more example of what Metropolitan State College meant to the individual students who attended, but also to the Denver community. He came to Metro because it was the only place where he could work nights and go to school in the day. Had MSC not opened, Larry does not know how his career would have ended up.[325]

Another notable MSC student and alumnus also began his college career in the fall of 1967. Rick Reeser was a veteran who chose to settle in Denver after his tour of duty ended that year. In an interview in 2012, Reeser said that his roommate told him about a new state college downtown. He went down applied and was accepted. Thanks to the open door, Reeser said, he did not need to dig up a bunch of paperwork just to enroll. There will be more about Reeser in subsequent chapters.[326]

In the fall of 1967, Dr. Irv Forkner, head of the business department, hired Ken Shaw to be coordinator of the data processing program. Metro State had one of the first data processing programs in the nation, certainly one of the first at a four-year college.

According to MSC Professor Joe Megeath in *History of the Computer Information Systems (CIS) Department,* written in 2014, Dr. Forkner described the establishment of the computer program by saying, "It was like a baby left on a doorstep. No one wanted it so I picked it up and brought it in."

Dr. Forkner likened the computer industry to the automobile industry, Megeath wrote, in that it would come to affect businesses and individuals in ways unforeseen at the time. How true!

"It would have been hard in 1967 to find another Business Division/School housing a study of computers," Megeath wrote. "A decade later it would be fairly common, and by the end of two decades it would be difficult to find a school of business that did not include a Management of Information Systems program. Bringing the computer baby into the division of business at that time was a remarkable move."[327]

Charles Angeletti joined the faculty of Metropolitan State College that fall as well. He was hired as an assistant professor in the history department. Later, he taught the first Afro-American history courses at MSC. At the time of this writing, Dr. Angeletti is still teaching at MSC—one of the longest-serving faculty members at the college.

The Metro student House and Senate met at the student center. Roger Braun introduced an amendment to the constitution to eliminate the House and have a unicameral student government consisting of 16 members. Representative Mary McBride briefed members about the upcoming dance.[328]

The first official dance held on campus happened on Friday, October 13, in the student center. Admission was 50 cents for stag, and 75 cents for a couple, entitling the revelers to free Cokes. There were only full-test Cokes since Diet Coke had not been invented. The student newspaper did not report on how many students had flasks of rum or Jack to dilute their cokes with, or sugar cubes to set the mood.

In those days people who were 18 or who had a fake ID could drink at 3.2 joints in Denver. The law provided for two types of beer: 3.2 percent alcohol and the so-called 6 percent. Everyone really believed 6 percent was nearly twice as potent as 3.2, but in reality the difference was minimal. Nevertheless, 18-year-olds could legally drink 3.2, and there were separate bars that sold only that.

The student newspaper ran an ad for a local 3.2 watering hole—La Pichet. They held drown nights on Wednesdays and Sundays from 8-11. Partiers could drink all the pitchers of 3.2 Coors they could get down for a $3 admission. Holding it down was another matter. For $3, a student could drink enough to exceed the legal blood alcohol limit. But who stopped there?

An enterprising student could find either a drown night or a ladies' night every night of the week. And for those over 21, there were plenty of hangouts as well. Right on campus students had the White Mule and Sullivan's to grab a beer between classes. Vets could drink at the American Legion or the VFW both of which were adjacent to the campus. One bar, the Sands Lounge at 1523 Glenarm, added the Sands Study Hall which had nightly dancing and served 3.2 beer and pizza.

The trustees accepted a report from the consulting firm A.C. Martin narrowing the potential sites for the new campus to three: Auraria, 14 acres assessed at $18.2M; Civic Center, 201 acres assessed at $20M; and North Stadium, 188 acres assessed at $11.3M.[329]

On October 11, PROSPECTUS hosted another bitch-in in the student center. Unfortunately, it was hampered by bad acoustics and a poor PA system. Most students were watching the World Series on TV instead of participating. Some students did voice complaints, however. Some faculty members expressed their views also. The main complaints were student apathy, hassles at registration, lack of parking, a need for bike racks, academic standards and student evaluations.

An editorial in *Your Choice* stated that the bitch-in was not a success. "Where does responsibility lie for what we learn? Do we as students have the right or need to criticize the manner in which we are exposed to knowledge set before us by persons we call 'Doctor or Professor'...I believe we are entitled to evaluate how we are taught, what we are taught, and by whom." This was the first shot across the bow for student dissent.[330]

Dr. Jack Yuthas invited Kenneth Goff, a Baptist minister, to speak in one of his psychology classes. Goff told the students "communism was a real threat to the existence of the present establishment throughout the world." He said communists seemed to be assimilated in all areas, explaining why the police could not control anti-war demonstrations. He advocated rigid racial classifications and stemming communist aggression throughout the world by "ballots or bullets." Goff was foretelling the religious right's support of bullets as a foreign policy.[331]

The Mayor of Arvada offered the trustees a site in Arvada for a fraction of the cost of Auraria. Economically, that would have been great for the trustees to accept. However, a suburban site was not conducive to the goals of an urban college.

On October 16, *The Denver Post* wrote an editorial saying they supported Auraria for three reasons. First, it was good for the city of Denver and re-development of Platte Valley. Second, it afforded the best opportunity for federal participation in land acquisition for urban renewal, which would reduce land costs by 50 percent. Third, it was the best site for higher education and technical education in Denver. *The Post* said MSC should continue to be accessible to the greatest number of students. [332]

The opponents of the Auraria site like Arvada began to surface once it looked like MSC might actually locate there. In mid-October, *Cervi's Journal*, a weekly business publication, reported that the proponents of MSC were putting too much emphasis on minority student enrollment. Minority groups were 7 percent of MSC's current student enrollment, the Arvada backers said, and it could be as high as 20 percent. "Should this 20 percent dictate the future course for Metro?" they asked.[333]

Just before Halloween, the trustees recommended Auraria as the site for Metropolitan State College's campus. Stuart McLaughlin, chairman of the trustees, made the announcement and appealed to the downtown business community to assist in financing the facilities on the grounds that MSC would provide educational, cultural and social values there.

McLaughlin also wrote a letter to Mayor Currigan saying that in the case of all other colleges in the trustee's system, the cities or communities donated the land for the college. He warned property owners there would be a potential loss in property values if MSC was forced to move to the suburbs. He urged Mayor Currigan to contact large property owners and get them to commit to funds.[334]

The reason the trustees were asking for funds from the business community is that the Auraria site was appraised for $18 million whereas the cost for a suburban site would be $500,000. The site Arvada's mayor was pitching would be even less.

President Phillips weighed in on the matter, saying that the decaying area of Auraria would have to be declared an urban renewal project before it would be possible to put the college there. He added that even with urban renewal, the cost of the site would be very difficult to get through the legislature, particularly if the state were asked for a dime. He noted Pueblo had given money for SCSC's campus, thus setting a precedent.

He identified some problems with the Auraria site that were noted by the consulting firm A.C. Martin: A) Where would Denver put the Skyline Freeway that currently was proposed to go through the site? B) How would utilities be provided? C) What would be done with the traffic on Lawrence and Larimer? D) What would be done with St. Elizabeth's Church, a national historical landmark?[335]

On Halloween, *The Denver Post* wrote an editorial entitled "Auraria is right for Metro." They acknowledged that the land cost would be a problem for the legislature. *The Post* said it was up to Denver to do something about the economic obstacle.[336]

In early November, things began heating up over the trustee's pick of Auraria as site for the new campus. In early November, the South Platte Area Redevelopment Council (SPARC) endorsed Auraria, saying it would be the best possible step for redevelopment of the Platte Valley. "Denver could be a national leader in the development of a truly urban institution responsive to the needs of the community and the individual student," the group's spokesman said.[337]

Shortly after that, CCHE Chairman Shelby Harper, the guy who pushed the Security Life Building, told Trustee Betty Naugle to study the Park Hill Golf Course as an alternate site. He said that the city-owned course near City Park would be just as good as downtown for an urban college. Harper managed to convince six members of the commission to agree with him on Park Hill, but they took no formal vote.[338]

The Denver Post came out in an editorial against the Park Hill Golf course idea. They said building on the course would deprive the city of a needed green belt and it was not as functional as Auraria, which had better transportation access. They urged downtown interests to wake up and find out what they would miss if MSC located away from Auraria.[339]

Harper did not get much support for his Park Hill idea, but he managed to stir up some members of Denver City Council. Councilman Hoot Gibson suggested that College View in his southwest Denver district would be a better site than Auraria. He wrote a letter pushing the site to CCHE Executive Director Frank Abbott even though the planning department study had looked at it and passed on it.[340]

Meanwhile that fall, the humanities division launched the Cultural Caravan. The program gave MSC students free tickets, on a first-come basis, to cultural events in Denver. Funds for the tickets came from a grant received from the Colorado Council of Arts and Humanities and from student fees.

The program was designed to involve students intimately with the cultural affairs of the urban community, to support cultural events in Denver, to educate Metro students more intensely in the arts by their actual participation, to provide supervised discussion of each event and to make it possible for persons who never attended such events to go. Students participated in a Q & A with actors at the end of each session.[341]

Metro State got a second student newspaper. Joe Fuentes, who had been on the staff of *The Metropolitan*, started another newspaper called *The Neoteric Puff*. The first issue came out on October 30, 1967. In addition to editor Joe Fuentes, Gregory Caldwell served as the associate editor; Bonnie Pasco, managing editor; and Don Park, business manager.

The Neoteric Puff was not an official newspaper of Metro State College, but the administration knew who they were, Editor Fuentes wrote. The purpose was to establish a new and more adequate news medium for Metro State. "We hope it will be recognized by the college someday," he added.

Fuentes addressed the reason for the new paper, writing that, "Representation of the majority of students should be the primary function of any student publication. When it fails to consider the welfare of the majority, then it becomes necessary for the interested students to take some action...Editors of the newspapers must work toward the goal that the publications are a workshop for the future and not only for personal use...The success will be for the benefit of the school—administration, faculty, and students"[342]

The other officially sanctioned newspaper, known unimaginatively as *Your Choice*, picked a winner in its name-the-paper contest. Dr. Barbara Blansett and student Don Morreale were the twin winners, each suggesting *Metro Gadfly*. That name was chosen because of its relation to Plato's Apology, in which he referred to Socrates as a gadfly for the Greek state of Athens, according to a spokesman for the newly-named paper. MSC's newspaper promised that it intended to play gadfly to the state of MSC.

Metro Gadfly beat out other entries such as The Certiorari, Proculator, Interpreter, Mirror Confusion, The New Breed, The Forum, Urbanite, The Megopolin, Prospective, Metrometer, The Denver Omnibus and Cab Co., and Free Love and Nickel Beer—a crowd favorite. The first issue of the *Gadfly* was a collector's item because it had the wrong date—Oct. 23 instead of the actual publication date of Nov. 6.[343]

Student body vice president Roger Braun reported that student government was investigating problems with the campus quarterly magazine, *The New Campus Review*. Vivian Bartel was appointed executive secretary of student government, and also appointed to the college center board, formerly known as SCAB, which oversaw the student center. She had been active in student government since it started in 1966. Her real accomplishment was being the force behind PROSPECTUS. Carol Salter was selected for the college center board. Clarence Arnold, a math and science major and managing editor of the *Gadfly*, was appointed chief justice.[344]

October 1967 was a key month. Daniel Martinez, an MSC student, using funds from student government, attended the National Mexican-American hearings in El Paso. President Lyndon Johnson addressed group, as did the president of Mexico, Gustavo Diaz Ordaz. These hearings came at the height of the War on Poverty, before the Vietnam War would do President Johnson in. They also came just as *El Movimiento* was getting going.[345]

Martinez wrote a guest editorial in the *Gadfly* when he returned sharing his thoughts on how MSC fit into that developing Chicano struggle His article helped spark Chicano activism on campus. "Perhaps at no other time in American history have human interest problems been as magnified as they have been in the last ten years," he wrote. "Never have so many of the Spanish-American leaders stood their ground so firmly, with the conviction to overcome the many conflicts that are now arising from poverty and social oppression."

Martinez expressed the importance of the War on Poverty and the importance of the Spanish-American War on Poverty. "For the first time in our history," he wrote, "we the Spanish-Americans have been confronted with an opportunity to verbalize our needs, and to express our desires and convictions to our government. Although many, if not all, of these opportunities have always been at our fingertips, we have either lacked the courage or the education to pursue them and to make them a part of our everyday lives."

"This is where colleges like Metro, as part of a community, can help to step-up educational advantages for all who care to better themselves," Martinez declared. "Metro can help to overcome many problems with the community it represents. Metro can become a leader in creating awareness in its students and in its faculty. Metro can, through this awareness, put in its members, a new surge of life, and a desire to instill its students with the skills that are pertinent to survival in our society."

He concluded by expressing regrets that leaders such as Caesar Chavez, Reis Lopez Tijerina, and Rodolfo (Corky) Gonzales were not invited to address the hearings. "They are great men with good ideas," Martinez wrote. "We should not acknowledge some leaders and ignore others."

The following week student elections were held for class president and other posts but only 2.8 percent of students bothered to vote. Incoming freshmen cast more votes than sophomores and juniors combined. John G. Mosley was elected junior class president, Jess Martinez was the sophomore president, Gary Young was elected freshman president, Joe Weber was elected vice-president and Janet Wilson won secretary/treasurer.[346]

Freshman senators were Gary Pickett, Ed Lucero, and Penny Wilson. Students also selected the name "Prophets" for the school mascot.[347] (No worries, the name wouldn't stick.) The student Senate killed Roger Braun's bill to combine the two houses of student government into one.[348]

The Summer of Love had an immediate impact on what was being discussed on campus in the fall of 1967. PROSPECTUS began focusing its forums on issues that arose from the new and growing counterculture. The first was a forum held in the student center in November in which Denver Manager of Safety Hugh McLearn debated hippie leader, Walter Gerash, over unequal enforcement of the law. Police officers were also on the panel.

A Denver policeman identified only as Officer Gray said that police officers make split-second decisions and therefore hippies might be subject to search and seizure more readily than others because police officers felt hippies were more likely than other citizens to be engaged in unlawful activities. Manager McLearn defended the police, saying that to regulate the social arena in which this society performs, the police often select whom they arrest by methods other than those prescribed by law, and non-conformists would be watched more closely than others.

The safety manager's statement shows the police were profiling hippies, minorities and other non-conformists. They were the ones the police selected for arrest by "methods other than those prescribed by law," McLearn admitted. This shows the deep societal gap that resulted after the counterculture arrived on the scene. This led to violent clashes between the police and hippies, protestors and other groups, which became more frequent over the next four years. Sometimes the clashes were bloody.

Vivian Bartel and PROSPECTUS deserve kudos for bringing these issues out into the open. That is what an urban college is supposed to do. (Eventually, the so-called hippie leader, Walter Gerash, grew up to become one of the most prominent criminal attorneys in Colorado, specializing in high-profile cases.)[349]

PROSPECTUS addressed another counterculture issue in a forum—LSD, which had become tremendously popular during the Summer of Love. MSC chief justice of the student court, Clarence Arnold, said that the public was afraid of LSD, yet no one had proven any lasting harm to the user from the psychedelic, mind-enhancing drug. He said LSD, which was still legal in Colorado (although not for long), should be left up to individual choice.

Shirley Harmon of MSC Student Health said LSD caused chromosomal damage, anxiety, and psychotic behavior. Ms. Harmon was asked if she had any personal experience with LSD and indicated she did not. Arnold rebutted her, saying, "Any damage done by LSD was done to the establishment, not to the individual using it."[350]

In November, Hispano students were successful in getting many MSC students and faculty members to join the growing boycott of "scab grapes." Twenty-five MSC students demonstrated at Safeway. As a result, Safeway took the non-union grapes off the shelves. According to the *Gadfly*, King Soopers also removed them. The United Farm Workers union, headed by Caesar Chavez, went on strike in California over the inhumane housing and working conditions endured by the migrant farm workers.[351]

Competing marches over the Vietnam War took place on campus in November. A large group of mostly veterans held a "March for Freedom" to show their support for the war. They were met by a group of anti-war protestors carrying signs that read "Stop the War" and "Bring Troops Home."

Soon, one of the anti-war protestors was accosted by a pro-war marcher, and the photo of him lying on the ground made the front page of the *Neoteric Puff*, along with pictures of the pro- and anti-war marchers. This demonstrates how divided the campus was becoming over the war, and how strongly each side felt.[352]

Those marches, and all the protests that sprung up around the country after the "Summer of Love," prompted the *Neoteric Puff* to write an editorial asking whether protestors were doing the rest of the students a favor. The author said that none of the recent things written about protestors pointed out that these "long-haired, unshaven members of society" were doing the rest a favor.

"Only too often do individuals remain passive on matters that concern their welfare," he wrote. "Even though conscience demands definite action, passivity sets in and the burden of expressing the opinion of the minority (if it is a minority) falls on the shoulders of the few. The question then becomes 'Why must the protestor use the means that causes so much controversy?'"

The anonymous writer said that if the common man has a complaint, he will not be heard unless he can attract some attention. With this element of attention, the demonstrator can bring ignorant members of society to the realization that there are problems that must be given ultimate priority. The writer's suggestion was that everyone should look deep into what the protestor is trying to convey and hope that the objections he has are at least heard.[353]

In the fall of 1967, Metro's nursing school opened with 39 students, according to Jean Bulger, coordinator and director of the nursing program. Nursing classes were spread around, with some being taught at MSC, others at Lutheran Hospital, Denver General, Mt. Airy Hospital, the Spaulding House (now Rehabilitation Center), and a nursing home.[354]

David Thomsen made the news for being the only male enrolled in the nursing program. He was pictured in *The Rocky Mountain News* with Linda Winkler, Jo Van Arsdale, Ranaye Cotton, and Helen Turner.[355]

On a lighter note, Metro got cheerleaders in November, to cheer on the athletic club teams as they competed around town. Pam Younkin, Beth Duncan and Pearl Gonzales beat out the competition. They made their first appearance at a basketball game in December. Obviously, this happened in defiance of the "Green Report" which asserted MSC would not have cheerleaders or baton twirlers. It also said there would be no athletics either. [356]

At the end of November, Sallyann Ulrich wrote an editorial in the *Gadfly* putting into perspective what Metro State College had going for it. She had just returned from a meeting of newspaper editors from Colorado and New Mexico where she heard constant complaints that their administration won't do this, or their faculty won't do that. She told them, "MSC does not have those problems." She wrote:

> *"MSC has a lot going for it. We don't have to take our hats off to any other college. When we get our degrees, we'll know we worked for them. Because of the size of our classes we can demand more personal attention and get it (try that with 100 or 200 students in a class). Our professors take interest in students as individuals, for one thing, because of the wise decision by the 'powers that be' not to have a 'publish or perish rule' or a 'research above all' law, our professors have more time for us. The administration is willing to cooperate with us if we take the time to ask them..."*

Her only complaint was that, due to the nature of a commuter college, there was not ample time and opportunity for students to interact with one another and the faculty, partially because there was no place for it, and few activities conducive to such interaction.[357]

At the end of the quarter Dean Lillie and Curt Wright told student government that student fees would have to go up $10 for full-time students and 50 cents an hour for part-time students. They said they needed more money for the student center reserve fund that would someday pay for a future student center on the new campus. This did not sit well with students. They circulated petitions against the fee increase. They also demanded to know where their money was going, but that fell on deaf ears. Wright felt that was none of the students' business.[358]

To celebrate the end of the quarter, student government threw what it called the "biggest and best dance of the year" at the Carpenters Local Union Hall. The band "A Penny's Worth of Now" provided the music.[359]

Eddie Crowder led the CU Buffs to another winning season, finishing 9-2, and won a trip to the Bluebonnet Bowl, which the Buffs won 14-13. The Denver Broncos, sadly, finished the season with a dismal 3-11 record.

"The Graduate," "Cool Hand Luke," and "You Only Live Twice" were among the top movies of the year. The Beatles failed to make the top ten top for the first time in years. The top five songs in 1967 were an eclectic collection of: "To Sir With Love" by Lulu: "Light My Fire" by The Doors; "Windy" by the Association; "Ode to Billy Joe" by Bobby Gentry; and "The Letter" by the Box Tops.

In 1967, 486,600 young men and women were serving in Vietnam and sadly, 11,393 would not come home. Of the brave men and women who died for their country in 1967, 25.8 percent of them were Chicanos; a similar number were black.[360] That year, an additional 228,263 young men were drafted into the Army and thousands went to Canada to avoid the draft.

Competing demonstrations for and against the war were held on campus. Here pro-war students are seen marching. *Photo Courtesy of Metropolitan State University of Denver.*

A group of Veteran students sit in on Colfax to protest the way the state was treating them. *Photo Courtesy of Metropolitan State University of Denver.*

CHAPTER 9

Student Activism Grows

You say you want a revolution
Well, you know
We all want to change the world...
But when you talk about destruction
Don't you know that you can count me out...
You tell me it's the institution
Well, you know
You better free you mind instead
"Revolution" John Lennon/Paul McCartney[361]

It had become a New Year's Day tradition for Denverites to open their newspapers and find a bombshell about Metropolitan State College. That had been the case the previous few years. New Year's Day 1968 was different, however. There were no bombshells—not yet.

WE'VE GOT THOSE LEGISLATIVE BLUES AGAIN

On January 17, however, as the Colorado General Assembly was beginning its session, the all-too-familiar bad news headlines began to appear. *Cervi's Journal* published an article entitled, "Public apathy imperils Metro." The article in Gene Cervi's weekly business newspaper painted a bleak picture for the prospects of MSC obtaining funding to purchase the Auraria site and actually build a campus.[362]

Senator Harrie Hart, Republican from Colorado Springs and chairman of the Joint Budget Committee, said "It will take $90 million to build the campus, and we are nowhere near cutting loose that kind of money." Hart said that George Brown was the "lone voice" on the

JBC supporting funding for Auraria. "Accommodating 20,000 to 30,000 students' leaves me cold" Hart said. "If we get budget request from CCHE we will act on that."

Bill Armstrong (R-Aurora), who had voted against funding for Metro and against adding the upper division, said he was not only concerned about the overall cost but also the nature of the institution itself. "We were told the emphasis was to be on educating kids who wanted to go to college while working. It was to be no frills. Now they want about 180 acres and an expensive building project which exceeds the original concept."

George Fentress, Republican from Lakewood, who previously had tried to make MSC a junior college, said he would prefer that MSC be located in Arvada, where it would cost $500,000, not $18 million. "They are trying to commit us to Auraria and that will strap the legislature into doing something," he said. "How do you treat other universities in relation to something as big as Metro?"

Shelby Harper, chairman of the CCHE said the commission was 100 percent behind Metro (glad he cleared that up), but, Metro State had to win an identity. "It had not got that," (his words), and "Until it gets exciting you cannot get it off the ground," Harper said. Most people were not aware of it as an institution and therefore the dollars did not look promising. (Harper should have been careful what he wished for about Metro becoming exciting.)

Harper warned that even if the legislature put up $6 million, it would come too late for a matching grant. He sounded other death knells: "There are other needs that exceed $200 million for the other campuses throughout the state. With that kind of backlog we could not in good conscience approve $6 million for Metro for land acquisition—particularly when there are alternatives available for that institution to accomplish its objective elsewhere." This looked like 1964 all over again.

WINTER QUARTER 1968: CALM BEFORE THE STORM

As winter quarter 1968 started, enrollment was 3,385, up considerably from the previous year's total of 2,162. The student body included 2,720 freshmen, 505 sophomores, 91 juniors, 6 seniors and 69 classified as other. Of these, 2,608 were continuing students and 777 registered at MSC for the first time.

The percentage of women students increased in the winter quarter. There were now 926 women and 2,459 men. The oldest student, Margaret Haberland, was 64, and the youngest was only 17. More than half of the students, 1,787, came from Denver. Jefferson County was home to 555, Adams County, 438; Arapahoe County, 370; Boulder County, 135; 60 came from 29 other counties of Colorado; 40 were from out of state.

That quarter veterans composed 16 percent of MSC's total enrollment, and 575 of them were Vietnam Vets.[363]

The *Rocky Mountain News* reported that in 1967, a total of 60 percent of Denver's high school graduates went to college, and 37 percent of them (1,787) went to Metro. The national average for graduates going to college was just 40 percent. The previous record, set in 1964, was 58 percent. In the 1967 class, the number of boys and girls going to college was nearly equal. MSC was responsible for increasing the number of graduates who were able to go to college, thus helping Denver beat the national average.

Both student newspapers—*The Neoteric Puff* and *The Gadfly*—had gone out of existence. *The Puff*, an unofficial paper, went broke and student government had reportedly lost interest in *The Gadfly*. The faculty newsletter gave a commendation to *The Gadfly*'s editor, Sallyanne Ulrich and the other students for the six issues they published during the fall. Nothing was said about Joe Fuentes' *Neoteric Puff*.[364]

A newsletter called *The Metropolitan* published one mimeographed issue in February, but it was considered by many to be a joke. Then on March 25, Joe Fuentes, former editor of *The Metropolitan* and *The Neoteric Puff*, started a new publication called *THE PAPER*. This one was officially sanctioned. Joe Fuentes was editor; Ruth Pettit, associate editor; Bernie Donahue, managing editor; Al Kummerlin, sports editor; and Wanda Graham was the feature editor.

Metro student-lobbyists, led by Doug Holcombe, were up at the Capitol every day, meeting with legislators and trying to get them to adequately fund the college. Shelby Harper had said that Metro needed an identity, something exciting for people to get behind. The student-lobbyists were building that identity and generating excitement on the Hill for MSC.

At the Capitol, they were working to get the legislature to approve funding for a permanent campus, despite the statements by many legislators that no funding would be forthcoming. They were also talking to legislators about intercollegiate athletics for Metro.

Holcombe's student-lobbyists were making a good impression on the legislators. They were successful in changing the previously negative image of MSC into a positive one. The fact that well-dressed, knowledgeable and articulate students were up there every day because they cared about their school was exciting. This was unusual especially when protests were popping up all over.

The "Green Report" had prohibited athletics and thus the college could not be seen as lobbying for athletics. The student-lobbyists, however, were not officially speaking for the college. As citizens they were building legislative support in order to provide political cover for the trustees so they could reverse their position. The reason the "Green Report" had prohibited athletics was because the legislature had indicated it did not want to see athletics at Metro when it passed the bill authorizing the school.

MSC did not have fraternities and sororities, but there was no shortage of social life in the duplexes and apartments surrounding the campus or on Capitol Hill. In the winter and spring of 1968, there were different strokes for different folks. A typical weekend might include a love-in, during which participants would drop some sort of psychedelic enhancer and sit around nude in a circle, contemplating the meaning of life and love and often practicing the art of love. After all, as the Beatles hit asserted, "Love is all you need."[365]

Other students might have gone to a Wiccan ritual or a meditation session at another apartment. There were always several keg parties on a given weekend. And there was usually more than one party where the revelers would sit around sharing a few joints, solving all society's problems, laughing hysterically over nothing. Students didn't need frat houses or video games to party. And they did it all without posting a single Instagram.

These parties were generally attended by the younger single students, and an occasional couple. Older married students were generally not interested in parties. Many students worked weekends and could not participate. But following the Summer of Love, these counterculture events were happening at Metro, too.

In March, the trustees and the CCHE granted authorization for Metro to offer majors in behavioral sciences, music education, applied music, and health and recreation, as well as a minor in speech pathology.[366]

It seemed like the first quarter of 1968 was going to be a typical quarter. The legislature was in session and still hoping to under-fund Metro. Parking was getting tighter, buses were not convenient and light rail was still 20 years away. Students dashed like Roadrunners down the streets of downtown Denver to get to their next class. The White Mule was the center of campus life, with help from the Burger Chef next door. But the winter of 1968 was not going to be typical.

ACTIVISM HITS MSC

Come and sing a simple song of freedom
Sing it like you've never sung before
Let it fill the air, tell the people everywhere
We, the people here, don't want a war
- "Simple Song of Freedom" Bobby Darin[367]

In the winter of 1968, things were changing on the American political scene. The Vietnam War was escalating. Close to half a million troops were deployed and casualties were mounting. The draft was digging deep into the ranks of the male baby boom generation, falling disproportionately on blacks, Hispanics, and poor whites since the sons of more affluent families were in college.

A photo of a young naked Vietnamese girl fleeing an American napalm attack made the evening news and newspapers across the nation. The image shocked many, and it began to sink in how horrible that far-away war was. The news reported that Agent Orange had killed more innocent civilians than the Viet Cong. It was making American soldiers ill, but it was making the chemical companies rich.

Earlier, on New Year's Eve, the Youth International Party (Yippies) had been founded by a group of anti-war, counterculture activists including Abbie Hoffman, Anita Hoffman, Jerry Rubin, Nancy Kurshan, and Paul Krassner. They had been involved in the Summer of Love. Poets Allen Ginsberg and John Sinclair were members, as was William Kunstler.

The group was really named "Yippies." Its formal name "Youth International Party" came later, according to Paul Krassner, the group's co-founder. They wanted a name that conveyed the radicalization of the hippies. He said they had come to share awareness that there was a linear connection between putting kids in prison for smoking pot in this country and burning them to death with napalm on the other side of the planet.[368]

In the summer of '68, the Yippies became a household word and their influence would be felt at MSC.

Lyndon Johnson, who became president after President Kennedy was assassinated, won election in 1964 by the largest landslide in history. However, the war was beginning to erode his popularity. In 1968, a majority of Americans still supported the Vietnam War, but those numbers were beginning to fall.

A little known Democratic Senator from Minnesota, Eugene McCarthy, decided to challenge President Johnson for the Democratic presidential nomination over the issue of the Vietnam War. McCarthy was one of the few senators who opposed the Gulf of Tonkin Resolution, which was passed in response to trumped-up charges that the North Vietnamese attacked two American ships in the Gulf of Tonkin.

Under the leadership of his youth coordinator, Sam Brown (of the famous Buster Brown shoe family and future Colorado State Treasurer), McCarthy was attracting a strong youth following around the country. Tens of thousands of college kids were "getting clean for Gene." McCarthy was working especially hard in Iowa, the site of the first caucus, and New Hampshire, where the first-in-the-nation primary would be held.

Meanwhile, many Democrats who were either dissatisfied with Johnson or simply yearning for a return to Camelot (the name given to the administration of John Kennedy) were pushing Senator Robert F. Kennedy to get into the race. Among them was Caesar Chavez, the head of the striking Farm Workers Union, and who was on a hunger strike.

Kennedy did not like Johnson and he was also opposed to the war, but he did not believe a successful challenge could be made to the sitting president. So he eluded the calls to get into the race. When the New Hampshire primary was held on March 12, Senator McCarthy came very close to beating President Johnson. This led Kennedy to believe he could win, so on March 16, he announced his candidacy for president in the same room his brother did in 1960. Two anti-war Democrats were challenging the sitting president.

While Johnson was being challenged from the left, former vice-president Richard Nixon was making a strong push for the Republican nomination. Nixon lost the presidency to John Kennedy, and then in 1962, lost his bid for California Governor. After that loss, Nixon told reporters, "You won't have Dick Nixon to kick around anymore."[369]

But in 1968, there was Nixon, hoping to form a coalition of Goldwater Republicans, southern Democrats and blue-collar union members, all of whom were not happy with the social programs of the Johnson Administration, especially those regarding race and affirmative action.

Nixon put together a "southern strategy" to convert segregationist whites and bigots in the South away from the Democratic Party to the Republican Party. These whites felt the Democrats had abandoned them with the civil rights legislation and affirmative action. Nixon's coalition also included many boomer-parents, who were dissatisfied with the free-love drug culture taking hold in their children's generation.

When the anti-war wave hit Denver in 1968, the largest club on MSC's campus was still the College Republicans, who had just re-elected their founder, Wanda Graham, for another term. Graham worked on the student newspaper and was a good organizer. The average Metro student was older, many were married, and it had one of the highest percentages of veteran students in Colorado. So the student body was more conservative than most campuses. The Young Democrats had still not yet set up shop at MSC.

Despite the demographics, there was a growing radicalization of many Metro students following the Summer of Love. Opposition to the Vietnam War was growing. Lingering issues of racial inequality caused young African-American students to become more impatient and militant. African-American leaders from Dr. Martin Luther King Jr. to Malcolm X were speaking out vehemently against the war. It was being portrayed as a white man's war that poor blacks, browns, and whites were forced to fight.

As a result of this impatience, the Black Panther Party was taking hold in Denver and on the campus of MSC. Metro student senator Lauren Watson joined the Panthers and gradually became more militant.

The Chicano struggle for justice was also gaining steam nationwide. At MSC, Chicano students were organizing and winning the support of some white students as well. One issue that united blacks and Chicanos was their opposition to the war in which their people were disproportionately being killed. Chicano student organizations like UMAS and the Hispano Youth Congress were gaining membership and enthusiasm, and were becoming more militant, but in a non-violent way.

Some white students were also becoming more militant. A chapter of the fledgling Students for a Democratic Society (SDS) was started at MSC to oppose the war and racism. Another student senator, Wayne Talmage, was actively involved in the SDS movement.

Against the backdrop of discontent, another MSC student, Bob Bowen, was angry that his peers were being drafted and sent off to die in a war that they had no say in. In 1968, the voting age in all but four states was 21, yet 18-year-olds were being drafted. They could get married and go into debt, but they had no say in selecting the politicians who made the policies that directly affected their lives.

During a discussion over the fact 18-year-olds could not vote, Bowen's dad told him, "If you feel that strongly, quit griping and do something about it." That night, Bowen decided to form an organization to get the voting age in Colorado lowered to 18. He called it the Y.E.S. Committee (Youth for the Extension of Suffrage) because he wanted an easy slogan: "Vote YES."

Bowen contacted newspapers, radio stations and the TV channels to announce a press conference for the following day. One call he made was to The *Rocky Mountain News*. Since it was a Sunday night, the call went to a reporter who normally worked the police beat but was filling in at the city desk. His name was Joe Fuentes, the editor of the student newspaper at MSC. Fuentes put the notice of the news conference on the wire.

The following morning when he came home from class for the news conference, the front lawn of his parent's duplex in Northwest Denver was full of TV cameras and reporters, anxious to hear about this movement, not knowing it was still a movement of one.

The nervous student told the reporters that the Y.E.S. Committee would be circulating petitions to put the 18 year old vote issue on the ballot that fall. Joe Calderon, vice-president of the student body at Northeastern Junior College in Sterling, CO, immediately joined the effort. Soon, he was getting calls from student leaders around the state, union leaders, and others wanting to know where to get the petitions. Of course, they did not yet exist.[370]

Fuentes had told Bowen that he should go to the student government office at MSC and look up Doug Holcombe. Bowen met Holcombe the next day and this began a life-long friendship and mutual participation in countless causes.

At that time, Holcombe was a junior, a member of the senate, and organizer of the student lobbying efforts at the State Capitol. He was also preparing to run for student body president with Joe Fuentes as his running mate. With their support, the student government voted to endorse the Y.E.S. committee.[371]

The nation was jolted on March 31, 1968, when President Lyndon Johnson went on national television and announced that he was not going to seek the nomination of his party for re-election in 1968. This was seen as a huge boost to the candidacy of Senator Kennedy.

That same week, Bobby Kennedy came to Denver. The rally was mainly attended by enthusiastic students, many from MSC. Kennedy was introduced to the overflow crowd at the Denver Auditorium, just outside MSC's campus, by Robert McNichols, son of the former governor and nephew of the deputy mayor. McNichols was also student body president at

Regis and president of the Colorado Collegiate Association. Bowen had worked with Bob McNichols at the Mile High Kennel Club during the summers.

Kennedy pleased the crowd when he endorsed the notion of lowering the voting age. There were so many MSC students at the rally that when student body president Chuck Brock was introduced, he got a louder ovation than Mayor McNichols. Brock, by the way, was a member of the MSC College Republicans. Bowen introduced Holcombe to Senator Kennedy. According to newspaper accounts, the hippie crowd was noticeably absent.[372]

Senator McCarthy came to Denver three weeks later, appearing at the University of Denver. Senator McCarthy was more popular at DU than at MSC, perhaps because MSC students tended to be from families with lower incomes. McCarthy appealed more to upper-class students, intellectuals and the "hippie crowd." Kennedy was more popular with minorities and working-class students.

In the following weeks, MSC students began dividing into camps. Despite the fact that the College Republicans were organized on campus and the Young Democrats were not, students were more interested in issues than political parties—particularly the issue of the war in Vietnam. On one side, there were supporters of Gene McCarthy and Bobby Kennedy who opposed the war. On the other side, pro-war students were divided between the supporters of Lyndon Johnson and the Republican candidates.

In Denver, the Kennedy and McCarthy camps decided to work together at the precinct caucuses to insure that a majority of anti-war delegates would be elected. The "Kennedy-McCarthy Coalition," as it was called, decided to run slates at the caucuses who pledged to vote for either McCarthy or Kennedy at Convention, whoever was leading.

In April, while representatives of both Gene McCarthy and Bobby Kennedy were on campus setting up organizations, outside events changed everything.

MARTIN LUTHER KING'S ASSASSINATION SHOCKS MSC

On the evening of April 4, 1968, Dr. Martin Luther King Jr. was murdered as he stood on the balcony of his hotel in Memphis, Tennessee. That shot, like the one that killed President Kennedy four and a half years earlier, was heard around the world. The nation was stunned and stood in disbelief.

Senator Kennedy had been campaigning at Notre Dame in Indiana that day and flew to Indianapolis for a speech. He was given word about the assassination as he stood on the platform. He had the task of telling the crowd, many of whom were African Americans, the tragic news. As expected, there were screams and wailing. Many feared a riot would break out.

Senator Kennedy gave one of the best ad lib speeches of his career when he told the grieving and angry crowd

"For those of you who are black and are tempted to fill with—be filled with hatred and mistrust of the injustice of such an act, against all white people, I would only say that I can also feel in my own heart the same kind of feeling. I had a member of my family killed, but he was killed by a white man."

He quoted a line from the ancient Greek playwright Aeschylus, "Even in our sleep, pain which cannot forget falls drop by drop upon the heart until, in our own despair, against our will, comes wisdom through the awful grace of God." He then delivered one of his most well-remembered remarks:

"What we need in the United States is not division; what we need in the United States is not hatred; what we need in the United States is not violence or lawlessness, but love and wisdom, and compassion toward one another, and a feeling of justice towards those who still suffer within our country, whether they be white or whether they be black...we must dedicate ourselves to what the Greeks wrote so many years ago: to tame the savageness of man and to make gentle the life of this world."

That speech was deemed by many to be one of the greatest in American history, ranked 17th by communications scholars in a survey of 20th century American speeches. Joe Scarborough, former Republican Congressman and the host of "Morning Joe," said that speech was what prompted him to enter public service.[373]

The crowd dispersed quietly, but that was not the case everywhere. Riots erupted in more than a hundred U.S. cities, including Chicago, New York, Boston, Detroit, Oakland, Pittsburgh, and Baltimore. During the riots, 35 were killed and more than 2,500 were injured. The property damage was astronomical particularly in poor urban neighborhoods. Across the country, approximately seventy thousand Army and National Guard troops were called out to restore order.[374]

The news hit MSC hard. There was a mixture of tears and rage among most of the students and faculty members. Although, just as in the nation as a whole, many white students could be heard making disparaging remarks. To them, Dr. King was a disruptive force in America—the America they preferred. They were, however, in the minority. Most mourned in disbelief. This was the second assassination of a beloved leader in less than five years.

MSC students held a memorial a couple of days after the murder. James Kirtland, student activities coordinator, helped organize it. The student body president, Chuck Brock, said, "Today we must begin a search, not only for an assassin but a personal search of the mind."

The *Rocky Mountain News* covered the service, writing, "It was not the kind of memorial service where your dress was important. There were no barriers to those clad in blue jeans and sandals, turtle necks and short sleeved shirts. The openness of the appearance was symbolic of Dr. Martin Luther King, the man the students had come to hear eulogized."[375]

At the service, Reverend Acen Phillips from Mt. Gilead Baptist Church said:

"The death of Dr. King was the greatest loss since assassination of JFK—a loss not just to Negros but a loss to America. Dr King brought us a long way and now we must move from protest to production. I challenge Denver to become a unique community. Negroes and whites must stand together. For the first time flags are at half-mast for a Negro; for the first time there is mourning in every corner of the world for a Negro."

Sherman Hamilton, president of the MSC Afro-American student union, thanked the 500 students and guests who attended. The Metro Concert Choir under Vern Moody sang hymns. Other speakers included MSC President Ken Phillips, Reverend Washington and Reverend Lewis.[376]

A week later, Martin Bronstein, published an editorial in *THE PAPER*, "All Denver Mourns Dr. King." He said, "Dr. Martin Luther King has been dead for over a week; he has been buried and the whole world had mourned him. Now it is time to turn to the living and their problems... Weeks of action lie ahead."[377]

King's murder may have increased the already-existing focus on the lack of black history being taught in American institutions of higher education. Shortly after the assassination, Dorothy King addressed the Afro-American student union about Negro history having been deleted from American history books during the last few years. She mentioned the *Negro Fact Book*, which featured facts about the Negro race. It would not be long until MSC's curriculum addressed black history and culture.[378]

It takes time after an event like that before the impact is completely known. It goes without saying that Dr. King's death made many African-Americans, and some whites, more militant. He was the voice and face of non-violence. When this peacemaker's life was prematurely snuffed out by an act of violence, many felt justified in turning to violent retribution.

King's murder led many young African-Americans to join more militant groups like the Black Panther Party. They believed what Malcolm X had said, that freedom would be gained by any means necessary. MSC's Lauren Watson left school at the end of the quarter to work full time with the Panthers.

There were no riots on the MSC campus, but King's murder made many African-American students impatient for change, and less willing to accept anything that had the perception of racism. Sometimes, protests took place over a blatantly racist statement made by an administrator or faculty member. Sometimes they occurred over things that were construed as racist, but really weren't intended to be. Often African-American students protested policies that they felt were unfair. These protests were usually peaceful and did not require intervention by the police.

Two weeks after Dr. King's memorial service, 200 protestors from MSC marched to the State Capitol. The march was organized by a group called the Black-Brown Coalition, but it included black, brown, and white protestors. The purpose was to demand that the legislature improve job opportunities, job training and education for minorities.[379]

Legislators took notice, and some called Betty Naugle and President Phillips to complain and encourage MSC to crack down before things got out of hand. Cooler heads prevailed on campus, fortunately.

In the years following Dr. King's murder, however, many black MSC students got involved in protests off-campus where police did intervene. This almost always made things worse. The boundaries between the urban college and the community were often indistinguishable. That was the intent of the founders and perhaps this led to some unpredictable consequences.

Memorial for Dr. Martin Luther King on campus 1968.

Photo Courtesy of Metropolitan State University of Denver.

SPRING QUARTER 1968: RACE, ATHLETICS AND WAR

The college's third spring quarter enrollment was 3,201 which was above the estimate of 2,919. The FTE was 2,229— higher than the 2,130 estimated when the budget was approved. This would require a supplemental appropriation, but there was no guarantee it would be forthcoming.[380]

The inaugural issue of *THE PAPER* published photos on the front page showing long lines of students registering at MSC with the caption "Lambs Led to Slaughter." The back page had a picture of "Mighty Mount Metro" also known as the rather large pile of dirt from the excavation for the new Denver Art Museum being built on campus across the street from the student center on Bannock.[381]

On the last Saturday in March, it was Metro's turn to host the CCA College Bowl, this time as defending champions, since they won the previous year. It was held at the Cherokee Building.

There were 22 sanctioned organizations at MSC in the spring of 1968. These clubs and their heads or faculty advisors included: the Afro-American Student Union, Bernard Robinson; the Administrative Management Society, Gary Austin; the Chess Club, Mike Todorovick; Circle K, John Paul Jones; College Republicans, Wanda Graham; Drama Club, Chuck Coulson; Flying Club, Andy Esparza.

In addition, there was the Forensics Club, Chuck Coulson; French Club, Rich Hildreth; Judo Club, Sidney Johnson; Math and Science Club, Mike Brigman; Mano, Alex Delgado; MSC Nursing Club, Linda Winkler; PEMM, John Mendenhall; Pep Club, Dr. Bieber; PROSPECTUS, Vivian Bartel; Readers Theater, Mark Olson; Spanish Club, Dr. Jean Fair; Student Government, Chuck Brock; Twelfth Nighters, Jo Ann Goldhan; Veterans Club, Mr. Charles Angus.[382]

The trustees realized racial tensions were on the rise and could erupt into violence. The board met and directed the presidents of the five colleges, including MSC, to take immediate action to improve race relations on their campuses. The board's executive director, Grant Vest, said the presidents should consider insuring that the various social organizations on campus include all ethnic groups to increase communication and reduce tension.[383]

At that same board meeting, Doug Holcombe, Roger Braun and student body president Chuck Brock were allowed to address the board to urge them to permit intercollegiate athletics at Metro. Chuck Brock said "Metro students want to participate like any other students." Doug Holcombe told the trustees that 1,800 students—half of the entire student body—had signed a petition for varsity sports. Roger Braun, the student vice president said, "We need a unifying agent here at Metro, something to identify with. And so far we haven't gotten it"

At the beginning of spring quarter, Bernie Donahue had written an editorial in *THE PAPER* saying MSC was half a college because it did not have intercollegiate athletics not knowing Doug Holcombe, Chuck Brock and Roger Braun were preparing to go to the Board of Trustees to get intercollegiate athletics approved.[384]

President Phillips weighed in saying that Metro students hadn't fit the mold envisioned by the legislature. For one thing, he said, there were not as many part time students with full-time jobs. He stated that even older students at Metro were enthusiastic about sports. Phillips cited a student/faculty report that said that athletics would provide a cultural contribution, a unifying influence, and a standard of excellence for the college to follow calling athletics "the last stronghold of the rugged life."

Dr. Mehn, head of MSC's health, physical education and recreation department was blunt. "Metro is looked down on academically," he said. "Our students come here with their heads down. Sports can create not only school spirit and pride but also acceptance among the public." He pointed out that when Metro whipped Regis, it generated more school pride than anything in the two years he had been at the school.

The chairman of the board of trustees, Stuart McLaughlin said he found those arguments persuasive, but said the commitment was made to the legislature for no athletics, and it was difficult to get out of. He had no idea Doug Holcombe and other students had been at the legislature all year quietly drumming up support for intercollegiate athletics. They would just double down on their efforts.[385]

During the spring of 1968, student dissent against the war was on the rise, and MSC was no exception. In 1968, 550,000 U.S. men and women were deployed in Vietnam, and there was no end in sight despite the attention the war was getting in the presidential campaign.

MSC students watched as fellow students protested recruitment by Dow Chemical at New York University. The University of California at Berkley, scene of protests for the last three years, saw more protests in 1968. Demonstrations and sit-ins occurred on dozens of other campuses, including the University of Colorado, Denver University and even in Paris, France.

At Columbia University, an SDS activist found documents in the International Law Library that connected the university with the IDA (Institute for Defense Analysis) a weapons research think tank supported by the Department of Defense. Columbia had kept this affiliation secret.

In a different era, that would have been seen as a feather in Columbia's cap, but not in 1968, and not in the middle of the Vietnam War. The SDS began a protest that lasted for months and six SDS leaders known as the "IDA Six" were put on probation for violating the university's anti-demonstration policy.

Later that spring, Columbia announced it was going to proceed with its plan to displace African-American residents of adjoining Harlem in order to build a new gymnasium in Morningside Park. The Student Afro Society (SAS) began protesting. They were soon supported by white SDS members, led by Mark Rudd. Eventually the SDS occupied the Low Library and three other buildings to mobilize students against the war and Columbia's involvement.

Celebrities like Jane Fonda and Tom Hayden (who had led takeovers at University of California Berkley), and street people joined students in the takeover. They took the university's dean and others hostage. The New York City police put an end to the protest on April 30 when they stormed the buildings. Over 132 students and faculty members were injured in the melee.[386]

The Columbia protests stirred up a big controversy at MSC. While administrators nervously watched the events around the nation, including Columbia, Metro students took sides.

In addition to debating the issue in sociology, political science and history classes, the debate played out in the student newspaper.

In early May, dueling editorials by Bernie Donahue and Martin Bronstein appeared in *THE PAPER*. On the right, Donahue blasted the Columbia protestors for idolizing Castro and Lenin. "The rights of the minority must be protected but the will of the majority must prevail," he wrote.

On the left, Marty Bronstein applauded the Columbia protest and also a recent sit-in at Denver University. He said he hoped that if a protest happened at MSC non-apathetic students would sit in. This would not be the only editorial written about the Columbia protests in the MSC newspaper. Students wrote letters to the editor for the next few issues, weighing in on Columbia and the larger issue of student protests.[387]

Legislators and trustees were taking note of the student newspaper's handling of this issue, and they were voicing their concerns regularly to Dr. Phillips, as were Denver businessmen.

Other things were happening on campus. *THE PAPER* started another effort to change the name of the college. The attempt the year before had gone nowhere. They said that the college could be in metropolitan Moscow with its current name. They suggested Central Colorado State College as a new name. Associate editor Bernie Donahue wrote an editorial suggesting other names for the college: Auraria State College, Denver State College, Central Colorado State College and South Platte State College. Needless to say, nothing came of it.

Jim Kirtland, the student activities director, announced that the college center would expand, adding an outdoor French-style cafe. He indicated there would be a food bar that served actual food. As it turned out, both of those statements would prove to be optimistic. Hardly anyone would mistake the outdoor tables for a French cafe, and many debated whether what the snack bar served was really food. It was an improvement to vending machines, however.[388]

Student government sponsored a book drive for the under-funded library. Kathy Howard, a member of the student senate, was chairman of the drive. There were awards for the person, club, organization and class that donated the most books.[389] The drama department announced the cast for their presentation of the play "Madera." The cast included Louise Gold, Jim Cavoto, Dick Ricketts, Kathy Roberto and Joy Dorenbach.

Mid-term exams had to be postponed when the AA Building was evacuated due to a bomb threat. Police told MSC to evacuate at 9:00 am after an unidentified male called and said he had placed a bomb on campus. Nothing was found and police had no suspect. Perhaps it was a student who forgot to study. This was the first of many such incidents, and they became more frequent each year.[390]

As spring set in, some members of *THE PAPER's* staff noticed that the number of women students at MSC was on the rise. They ran a full page with pictures of women with the caption, "In 1965 student body basically all male; in 1968 situation has changed—pictures say more than words." The students pictured were Bini Droll, Elene Dubman, Bobbi Richard, and Ginger Petersen.[391]

The following week the front page of *THE PAPER* featured Annette Schnitker, wearing a bikini and catching some rays between classes on the campus green. They were pushing the upcoming election of the May Fest Queen. In addition to the contest for queen, May Fest featured stud poker, a dunk-the-girl-attraction and a slippery pig contest.

That issue had multiple large pictures of queen candidates, including several of *THE PAPER's* candidate, Nancy Jo Dazey, a photo of Belle Greenwell, a former queen, and several female students who were not candidates including Donna Dowell and Glenda Greenfield. It must have been a slow news week. With that publicity, she won and Tom Taylor rode her blouse tails in as king. Sherman Hamilton and Frankie Heggar and the team of Roger Braun and Becky Imatami were runners-up.[392]

There were grumblings, however, that the newspaper was objectifying those women by publishing pictures in the manner they did.

Your Father's Mustache, a local pizza joint, ran an ad in *THE PAPER* with their new FAC (Friday after Class) prices for all the beer one could can drink: Guys $3 Girls $1. Prices were good between 4:30 and 7:30.

Student elections were held in May and only 232 students voted—7 percent of the student body. Doug Holcombe was easily elected president and his running mate, newspaper editor Joe Fuentes, was elected vice president. They beat Wayne Tallmadge and Sherman Hamilton.

Other officers elected were: Al Kummerlin, Athletic Board; Andy Esparza, Student Center Board; Dee Clark, Curriculum Board; and Gary Pickett, Publications Board. Class officers were: Mike Brigman, senior class president; Jerry Cronk, junior president; Maurice Brown, sophomore president. Class representatives were: Margaret Haberland, senior class; Kathy Howard, junior class; Rick Reeser, sophomore class representative.[393]

At the election, a straw poll asked all students (including those not old enough to vote) their preferences for president of the United States. The results were: Robert Kennedy, 34 percent; Gene McCarthy, 21 percent; Nelson Rockefeller, 26 percent; Hubert Humphrey, 9 percent; Richard Millhouse Nixon, 9 percent; Lyndon Johnson, Ronald Reagan and George Wallace each received 1 percent; George Romney garnered zero percent of the vote. Rockefeller, Nixon, Reagan, and Romney were Republicans. Wallace, a former Democrat, was running as a States' Rights Party candidate.

Among students who were old enough to vote (over 21) the results were: Nelson Rockefeller, 35 percent; Gene McCarthy, 23 percent, Robert Kennedy, 18 percent, Hubert Humphrey, 14 percent, Richard Nixon, 10 percent; Reagan, Johnson, Wallace, and Romney got zip. This straw poll showed how popular Bobby Kennedy was among students who were between 18 and 21. When they were factored out of the poll, his popularity dropped by nearly half.

While students around the nation were demonstrating about the Vietnam War, at Metro, Chicano students were beginning to get organized to redress grievances their people had had for decades. Two MSC clubs, the Hispano Club and Mano of MSC, held a conference on the problems of Spanish-surnamed people.[394]

Speakers at the conference included Dr. Daniel Valdes, MSC professor of sociology; Tom Pino, editor of *La Voz*; Corky Gonzales, MSC student and leader of Crusade for Justice; Fred Romero from the U.S. Department of Labor in San Antonio; Father Canjar, Pastor Holy Rosary Church; and Ms. Maryann Rhoades, Colorado Department of Education.

Dr. Valdes gave the keynote in which he addressed brown power and his hopes for the conference:

> *"I hope the conference will produce men and women who can forcefully and dramatically give voice to the anguish cry of the poor sick, lame, and oppressed. Many are found in the horns of a dilemma caught between the group they belong to and the aspiration of the middle class America. Some have broken the chains strapped on them by semi-colonialism...Brown power challenges both the authority of the ruling classes and the legitimacy of traditional values. It is not simply a vision or cultural pluralism but fulfils the need for psychological equality."*

At the conference, Tom Pino said neither political party offered the programs a changing society needs or wants, therefore, he suggested that Chicanos start a third party. Father Canjar said the Catholic Church had taken Hispano Catholics for granted for many years. He said the church has to take an active role in pragmatic social action, and it must do it immediately.

Maryanne Rhoades said schools were controlled by a "white Protestant" value system and schools would not be acceptable until they allowed Hispanos' values to be reflected in the school system. She pointed out that schools in the U.S. did not prepare people to live in a heterogeneous society. They must teach us *how* to think, not *what* to think, she said.

Dan Martinez, an MSC student, spoke up and said the Church must give scholarships. He said Metro needed to revise textbooks to give proper consideration to the contributions of Spanish-surnamed persons in the U.S. and Colorado.

Suggestions that came from the conference were:

1. Establish committees of students to develop programs to improve educational opportunities.
2. Create industrial and business opportunities for the disadvantaged Spanish- surnamed individuals.
3. Design proposals for positive comprehensive self-help programs.
4. Generate the Spanish-surnamed movement in Colorado.
5. Create greater appreciation for Spanish and Mexican history and heritage.
6. Create an increased involvement and responsibility of the Catholic Church.
7. Generate overall statewide student participation in various community matters.

In early May, the political parties held precinct caucuses. In keeping true to what an urban college is supposed to be, Professor Bob Clifton urged his students to at least participate by going to their caucus, no matter which party, and support whoever they wanted. If the student was too young to vote, he told them to at least go and observe. One student, Bob Bowen, took the challenge.

He was not old enough to vote, but wanted to speak at his Democratic caucus to encourage passage of a resolution in favor of the 18-year-old vote. He went to see the long-time party boss of Northwest Denver, Mike Pomponio, at his DX restaurant. Pomponio ran all the precincts in that section of town. He gave Bowen the address for the caucus in his precinct and told him he could attend but not vote.

On the day of the caucus, Bowen went to that location only to discover there was no such address. By the time he found the correct address, the doors were locked and he was not allowed entry. This infuriated him and he vowed to organize a movement before the next election to end the rule of bosses like Pomponio. (That eventually happened, thanks to the help of many Metro students including Doug Holcombe, Dave Ball, Sonja Eldeen, Dan Beck and Larry Steele, to name just a few.)

After the caucuses, political science professor Bob Clifton wrote a guest editorial in *THE PAPER* entitled, "There is more democracy in the Soviet Union." He decried the apathy in society, particularly, among young voters like the students at MSC. His message is still very relevant today.[395]

Clifton stated that less than 1 percent of Americans attend assemblies where delegates are selected who determine the candidates for all levels of government. In the election, he noted, we are free to choose between Tweedle Dum and Tweedle Dee, but few involve themselves in determining who Tweedle Dee and Tweedle Dum are.

The problem with that, he wrote, lies in who makes up the 1 percent who decides. They were members of the John Birch Society [the '60s equivalent to the Tea Party], the League of Woman voters, conservative idealists who nominated Barry Goldwater [the '60s equivalent to Ted Cruz] and the liberal idealists who were attempting to nominate Gene McCarthy.

"We have perpetuated too many myths in this nation about democracy, and it borders on apostasy to criticize it," Clifton wrote. "After all, did we not fight a world war in order to make the world safe for it? Is it not still our most enabling rationale for our existence in Southeast Asia?" The difference between this nation's democracy and Russia's, he posited, is that we have the opportunity to change the one percent to 100 percent, but we probably never will. We will continue to sleep with an illusion because it is more comfortable that way, he added.

For this reason, he was determined that his students participated in the process called government, particularly since a good number of them had a proclivity for complaining about it. He realized that good government would not inspire them to leave the TV set. Therefore he threatened them with a poor grade if they did not attend a precinct caucus, either as an observer or participant.

"Attend they did," he wrote. Many were elected delegates, some were elected precinct committeemen and nearly all were disillusioned. "How disillusioned? Hopefully enough so they get off their cans and do something about what they saw." Many of Clifton's students (and later on, Jett Conner's and Wally Weston's students) actually did something about it, or at least tried to.

An article in *THE PAPER* explained that the Colorado Collegiate Association (CCA) was an association of student governments from institutions of higher education in Colorado. They joined together to establish better communication between colleges, junior colleges, students and the outside world. It gave students an official unified voice, and it made that voice heard by the state government through its legislative commission, which worked to pass legislation favorable to college students.[396]

The CCA had been around for a while, but not every college participated. Doug Holcombe helped change the CCA into a viable and powerful organization over the next year. On May 25, MSC hosted a CCA meeting. Dr. Phillips and Dean Lillie addressed the group about forming a liaison board for CCA, which would be composed of college presidents, deans, and faculty who would serve in an advisory capacity to CCA.[397]

The Colorado Commission on Higher Education had been lobbied by Doug Holcombe and CCA earlier in the spring to allow a student to sit on its advisory board. At the Metro meeting, Bob Bowen was approved as the first student ex-officio member of the CCHE Advisory Board. Also at that meeting, it decided that MSC would be the nerve center of CCA.[398]

Towards the end of the quarter, the publications board announced that *THE PAPER* would be back in fall, bigger and better. The new staff would be: Joe Fuentes, editor; Marty Bronstein, managing editor; Bernie Donahue associate editor; Don Park, business manager; Frank O'Neil, advertising manager; Peter Hertlein, photographer; and Wanda Graham, feature editor.[399]

At MSC's second commencement, 53 students received Associate Degrees in Applied Science and Arts and Science. Among them were Jerry Cronk, Rondie Keith, Richard Hildreth, Dieter Keifer, Sally Ann Ulrich, Bernardo Valdez and Marvia Valdez—all of whom were either involved in student government, a club or a campus publication.

Joe Fuentes wrote an editorial supporting tenure for sociology professor Ray Wilims. Fuentes said that discussions in Willms' classes were pertinent to present social conditions. He said that the atmosphere in his class was conducive to learning. Nevertheless, he was denied tenure and booted from the college.[400]

This was a blow to urban orientation. Professor Willms, in his short time at MSC, was very successful in getting students from diverse backgrounds to listen to each other. In one class, his students included Lauren Watson, a member of the Black Panthers, along with members of the Chicano organization, Crusade for Justice, as well as some members of the College Republicans.

Willms provoked students into getting their pent-up anger and frustration out into the open. Tempers flared and there was angry name-calling including some racial epithets. At the end of the quarter, though, each group at least had an understanding of where the others were coming from. Understanding one another and communicating with each other are essential to living harmoniously together in the city.

That was exactly that kind of education an urban college was supposed to provide. An urban college was supposed to teach people from the city how to live in the city. Willms did that. It seemed, however, that Dr. McKinney and others were not ready for quite that much urban orientation.

The effort to lower the voting age got a boost. President Lyndon Johnson endorsed it. The Y.E.S. Committee, with support from Metro's student government and the CCA, had chapters on most campuses in the state by late spring of 1968. Both political parties took up resolutions to support the 18-year-old vote. The Democrats passed them, but the Republicans did not. There was support, however, from many Republicans, including both of Colorado's senators, Gordon Allot and Peter Dominick, and some state legislators.[401]

Initially, the plan was to circulate petitions to place the measure on the November ballot. The drive only started work on this at the end of March, and with limited funds, it was determined in June that it was not practical to get enough signatures in time. Therefore, the focus switched to asking the 1969 legislature to place it on the 1970 ballot.

Martin Moran published a story in the *Rocky Mountain News* about President Phillips, entitled the "Atypical President." He wrote that MSC was unlike any other school in the country and the same can be said for its president Ken Phillips, who he described as short, stubby and looking older than he was at age 48. He said Phillips was dedicated to the philosophy of MSC and hoped it would gain the reputation of a place that is a teaching-institution concerned with the success of each student.

In the article, Phillips reiterated the mission of Metro as an urban institution. "I hope we can be the kind of place that has the reputation of welcoming people into it," calling it a living laboratory. "Historically, colleges and universities are remote from their communities and the walls have remained un-breached. They don't want students distracted by realities of life outside their ivy covered walls and communities tolerated them for their economic gains," Phillips said adding Metro was on the threshold of breaching that tradition.

He went on to say that as an urban college, Metro should dedicate itself to total involvement in the community's social, cultural, and economic affairs. Students and faculty must be engaged in the mainstream of urban life and they must be the solution to urban problems. "No walls, visible or invisible; be extroverted, not introverted. College and community should live together intimately. We have a contract with humanity. The reason for our existence is to focus on the urban problems and needs of metro Denver," Phillips asserted.

Phillips explained why he was convinced the college needs to be downtown. "Have you ever watched a Spanish-American kid who never thought he'd have a chance for college? He's scared," Phillips said. "He works up his nerve and comes in then leaves. He may go through this several times; finally he talks with others of his race in the school and eventually applies for admission. It is incidents such as this that convinced me the college should be downtown."[402]

Spring quarter ended and students took final exams the first week of June. In the middle of finals, an event happened that would rock the nation for the second time in two months. As we will see, summer would bring more change to society, and changes to Metropolitan State College.

The student newspaper called student registration in the spring of 1969
'Lambs Led to Slaughter
Photo Courtesy of Metropolitan State University of Denver.

CHAPTER 10

Protest, Dissent and Diversity

There's something happening here
What it is ain't exactly clear
There's a man with a gun over there
Telling me I got to beware
"For What It's Worth" Buffalo Springfield[403]

SOMETHING WAS HAPPENING

During finals week of spring quarter in 1968, something happened that would change things at MSC. Senator Kennedy's presidential campaign had gained steam. He challenged Senator McCarthy and Vice-President Humphrey in the primaries, and he won them all, except Oregon, where McCarthy had an early advantage. The big prize was California. When the votes were counted, Senator Kennedy had won it too. He gave a victory speech to screaming supporters at the Ambassador Hotel in Los Angeles ending by saying "It's now off to Chicago and the Democratic Convention to win there."

For reasons still not explained, after his entourage left the stage, they were directed through the kitchen of the hotel. Shots rang out, and Senator Kennedy lay on the floor, shot in the head. He died two days later, never re-gaining consciousness. A Palestinian named Sirhan Sirhan was arrested and convicted. As was the case with his brother's assassination and Dr. King's, the investigation concluded the assassin acted alone. Few believed it then or now.

This was the second assassination in two months, and the third in less than four years. Buffalo Springfield was correct. Something was definitely happening in America. This was the third time that a bullet took down not only an American political leader, but a leader that a majority of baby boomers and African-American students looked up to and believed in. Without anyone to believe in and rally around, many youths, black and white, would find ways other than the ballot to express their growing discontent and disillusionment. This hit MSC hard.

In the aftermath of the Kennedy murder, a student named Byron Anderson wrote a letter to the editor. His letter could very well have been written in 2015. It proves that if we don't learn from history, we will repeat it. Here is some of what he wrote:

> *"It seems our society is very unoriginal. We wait for a tragedy to happen before we do anything about it. The necessity for law and order is long overdue, and has now been exemplified by the death of Senator Robert F. Kennedy. Such deaths cannot be tolerated. The government must provide for a meaningful and safe existence for all its citizens. It is not that I should have the right to go out and shoot someone, but rather that I should have the right to go out and not get shot at.... This means that such senseless violence, as we are experiencing, must be attacked, I think on three fronts. First... to create equal and just laws...Second, We must not only discourage would-be lawbreakers, but discourage their means... The right to bear arms needs a new interpretation. This country is too sophisticated to retain its frontier image... Thirdly, attack the problems which cause the violence... We cannot teach nonviolence unless we are non-violent ourselves."[404]*

Just as it would today, Anderson's article met with opposition. The following week, *THE PAPER* published an article by Rodney Wolford saying that gun control laws are not the answer to violence. He wrote:

> *"Just remember, if you support gun legislation or any legislation that limits your freedoms you are giving back for government controls the very rights and freedoms on which the American form of government and way of life is based. Your freedoms, your children's freedoms and the future freedoms of Americans rest on just such issues as gun legislation...Supreme Court Justice Mosk tells us 'It will be a sorry day for America if demagogic politicians or hysterical commentators...persuade our courts to be any less concerned over individual constitutional rights.'"[405]*

The article was accompanied by a photo of the barrel of a gun pointed at the readers. The caption read, "Avoid the red tape...buy your guns now. Support the candidate of your choice. Make your vote really count, Campaign '68."

That summer, following the murders of Dr. King and Robert Kennedy, the generation gap was getting wider, alienating families and separating the generations. Marty Bronstein, the new editor of Metro's student newspaper, wrote an article in *THE PAPER* that addressed that issue. His piece was entitled, "Parents, Are You Hypocrites? Or, Rather, Are Your Children?"

Bronstein said that parents look at their children and no longer comprehend them. "You try to put the blame on drugs, bad schools, undesirable friends, bad moral climate, and even as a last resort, insanity. Unfortunately, the main stimuli for your children's reactions is YOU! He posited that the first thing a child notices was the parent's hypocrisy. "When you see an article about a kid being arrested, look at the name. It might be your son or daughter," he added.

Perhaps Bronstein was on to something. Much of the rebellion among the younger generation was in fact caused by resentment of the hypocrisy of their elders, including their parents, politicians, and in some cases, teachers.[406]

When the summer quarter began most students were off to jobs, but some enrolled in the summer session. Enrollment that summer was 1,071, a dramatic increase over the 73 students in 1967. Half of them were enrolled for the full ten-week session. The rest enrolled in one of the two five-week sessions. Some took the ten-week and one five-week session along with it. One of those courses was on American Negro Literature taught in first 5-week session by Gwen Thomas.[407]

The *Rocky Mountain News* wrote about Thomas's course stating that the long neglect of Negro poets, authors, and playwrights posed real problems to the teacher initiating the course. It called the class groundbreaking. "The body of white-authored American literature has been critically reviewed and analyzed since this country began," Gwen Thomas said. "However, prior to the last decade, the black man's song has been unsung, unrecorded, and unavailable."

Her course included works by major African-American poets like Lucy Terry and novels by black authors: *Native Son*, by Richard Wright; *The Invisible Man*, by Ralph Ellison; *Nobody Knows My Name*, by James Baldwin. Also, it included the plays *The Dutchman*, by Leroi Jones; and *Raisin in the Sun,* by Lorraine Hansberry. The course was also continued during the academic year.[408]

On a lighter note, Doug Holcombe organized a beach party at Aloha Beach, a popular swimming hole, beach and saloon on North Federal Blvd. An MSC student owned the facility and gave Holcombe a good rate. The student newspaper announced the event with an article that began, "Sun, water, sand, bikinis, boats, and bands all await your appearance Saturday June 29, at Aloha Valley Beach for the MSC Beach Party." The party featured free food and soft drinks, boating and sun. There was a dance at 8 PM. The article mentioned Aloha had a lounge, but their products were not free.

The Beach Party was well attended and fun was had by all. Dean Lillie was rewarded for his attendance by getting tossed into the lake. *THE PAPER* ran a story showing a bikini-clad woman in the foreground with a tiny, out-of-focus image of Gary Picket in the background. The caption of the photo was "Gary Picket flipping burgers at Beach Party."[409]

Maureen Halpin wrote a feature article on a MSC student she called "Sister Ranger." Yes, Metro had a nun as a student. She was studying to be a teacher so she could teach at Marycrest High School after graduation.[410]

PROTESTS TURN VIOLENT

Protest was on the minds of many, especially in light of the widespread protest at Columbia. In June, *THE PAPER* published a two-page spread entitled, "Facts Presented on Takeover at CU (Columbia University)," also written by Marty Bronstein.

In July, the first signs of the battle between some students and Metro's police science program appeared. This just foreshadowed a much bigger battle to come. Marty Bronstein wrote an article attacking Denver Police Lt. Robert Shaughnessy, a teacher in Metro's police science program. Bronstein said that Shaughnessy should never have been allowed at Metro. He warned prospective students to beware of Shaughnessy if they planned on taking courses in law enforcement.

Bronstein wrote that he felt that if he said the wrong thing in class, Shaughnessy would pull out his snub nose .38 and let him have it between the eyes. He went on to enumerate a number of not so flattering revelations the teacher made about the Denver Police Department.[411]

The summer of 1968 ended tragically. In August, the Democratic National Convention was held in Chicago. With Senator Kennedy dead, the prospects for an anti-war candidate winning the nomination were dim. Eugene McCarthy did not have the widespread appeal Robert Kennedy did. As a result, Hubert Humphrey was certain to be the nominee. Humphrey advocated the same policies as President Johnson, and that included a continuation of the Vietnam War.

Anti-war groups planned protests in Chicago for months. New Mobe, the SDS and the Yippies all converged and camped out in Grant Park. Over 10,000 demonstrators came to Chicago. Mayor, Richard Daley, said he would not tolerate protestors taking over his city. He denied permits to the demonstrators in the hope that would stop them from coming. It only made them more determined. After tensions built up for a week, all hell broke loose on August 28.[412]

Daley sent Illinois National Guard troops and thousands of police in riot gear to Grant Park to disperse and arrest the protestors. After a young boy lowered the American flag from the pole in the park, police came in and beat him with clubs. The crowd retaliated by throwing rocks and chunks of concrete at police, chanting "Hell no, we won't go." As the police brought out tear gas, protestors began calling them "pigs."

SDS leader Tom Hayden told the demonstrators to move out of the park and into the streets so the tear gas would affect local residents and more people would be able to witness what was going on.[413] The amount of tear gas used to suppress the protesters was so great that it eventually made its way to the Hilton Hotel, where it disturbed Hubert Humphrey while he was in his shower.[414]

Meanwhile, all of this was being captured by television cameras and shown around the world. Protestors began chanting, "The whole world is watching." Hundreds of police officers and protesters were injured. Dozens of journalists covering the actions were also clubbed by police or had cameras smashed and film confiscated.[415]

Inside the convention, the nominating process was going on. Senator Abraham Ribicoff was giving a nomination speech for George McGovern and he used that opportunity to tell the convention what was going on in the streets outside the hall. Mayor Daley was caught on camera shouting an obscene and anti-Semitic remark. Meanwhile, Senator Hubert Humphrey won the presidential nomination. The TV cameras were focused on the riot outside.

That incident tore the nation and the Democratic Party in two. It radicalized a large number of young people and students, including many at MSC. This event brought the growing generation gap to a head and helped the candidacy of Richard Nixon. By the time classes started in September, tempers had cooled down, but the wounds were still there.

THE FALL OF 1968: BOMBSHELLS DROP

In the fall quarter of 1968 there were 4,629 MSC students—more than the 4,613 the trustees projected and more than the 3,591 who had enrolled the previous year—a 28.9 percent increase. This made the three-year-old Metro State the seventh largest college in Colorado. MSC nudged out Western State by 250 students, but it was 1,700 behind the sixth largest: Southern Colorado State College in Pueblo.[416]

One of the students who started classes at MSC was King Harris. He was typical of many students who enrolled at Metro. He was older, married, and had children. Harris was employed at a foundry, but its workers went on strike. While on strike, he asked himself if that was what he wanted to do for the rest of his life. He decided the foundry wasn't it, so he enrolled in Metro. He said it was about the only college a guy like him could get into because he had not really gone to high school.

In a 2012 interview with Doug Holcombe, Harris recalled his first days at Metro. He was sitting in Elaine Cohen's English class and her assignment was a very simple: write a one page essay about who you are. "I could not write a half a page," Harris said. "I had no idea where to begin. I'd only completed eighth grade." He knew there was nothing wrong with his intellect, but he had no training for completing such an assignment. However, Harris said, Elaine Cohen, Gwen Thomas and other professors began to mold him in a way that taught him how to write.

One of the new faculty members that fall was Jett Conners, who Bob Clifton recruited to teach political science. In a 2012 interview, Conners said that what held Metro together in those early days were the people—students, faculty, and staff, to some extent. Metro didn't have a campus, he said, it was a collection of rented buildings everywhere. He added that it still does not have a campus since it shares Auraria with two other schools.

Conners recalled that when he got to Metro, two or three years after the doors opened, there was already continuity. There was an atmosphere, mostly provided by students, who were non-traditional, and a faculty who were in many ways very traditional, but were working in a completely new environment themselves. Professor Conners went on to become chairman of the political science department, and vice president for academic affairs for the college.[417]

Things seemed to be normal as the quarter kicked off with an "Intro to Metro Week" sponsored by student government. It was led off by the folk singing group Frummox, from the Denver night club Sign of the Zodiac. They performed in the student center, where there was also a reception for new faculty members. The speech department held a "Coffee Frenzy." The group Sugar Bush closed out the week with a concert.[418]

Then, on September 6 the executive director of the CCHE, Dr. Frank Abbott, dropped the first major bombshell at a commission meeting. He proposed taking Metro's Auraria campus site and using it for an "educational center" that would combine Metropolitan State College, the University of Colorado Denver Center, and the new Community College of Denver on one campus. Abbott said that things like parking, recreational spaces, admissions, counseling, library, labs and lecture auditoriums could be shared.[419]

Abbott said he came up with the idea because the CCHE was about to recommend to the legislature that no state money should be used for Metro's Auraria campus. He said, "There is no chance the commission will change its mind." In other words, it was his way or the highway.

Abbott and Shelby Harper, CCHE chairman, were insistent that the city of Denver, not the state, had to buy the Auraria site. Abbott did not explain why putting three schools on one site justified state money, while MSC alone did not.

The new ex-officio student representative, Bob Bowen, was at the meeting and was stunned. After the meeting, he returned to the student center and reported Abbott's "mega campus" proposal to the student senate. As expected, the reaction was not positive.

Gary Pickett, a senator, started a petition drive against it. When Abbott got wind of this petition, he was unhappy that the cat was out of the bag. Abbott claimed he was just brainstorming. It was a well-orchestrated brainstorm.

Marty Bronstein reported that bombshell in *THE PAPER*. "After years of planning and building MSC into what it is today, and then be told we might be losing our separate identity," he wrote, "is disappointing and quite a letdown."

He said that Denver had needed a college of its own for years. He suggested that CU was behind the mega campus plan. "CU has one advantage," he wrote, "It is set up in the state constitution." Dean Lillie and Dean O'Dell both said it was not time to panic yet. They said they were studying the proposal.[420]

Frank Abbot's brainstorm, as it turned out, would change the history of Metropolitan State College and the very nature of the college.

September was a month of bombshells. In addition to the mega campus, the dean of students, F. Dean Lillie, suddenly announced that he was leaving MSC to pursue his doctorate at the University of Colorado. He indicated he would return, however, but as it turned out, that was just a smokescreen.[421]

Lillie told *THE PAPER* that the school and students were great. Then he said "Students are people, and we must be able to communicate with them. When communication is missing, student dissent begins." That struck many students as being a strange statement for a guy who was just going off to work on a doctorate. It also seemed odd to students that Lillie would decide just three weeks into the first quarter that he had to leave to pursue his doctorate immediately. Lillie stuck to that story when asked about it.

A few days later, Dr. Robert Thompson was named dean of students to replace Dean Lillie. Cheryl Baker became the new student activities coordinator.

A third bombshell exploded right after that. Student body vice president Joe Fuentes resigned his post. Joe said he had a conflict of interest being vice president since he was also editor of the student newspaper. Doug Holcombe nominated Jim Waggoner to replace Fuentes.

Nevertheless, life went on. The MSC Players announced they would be performing "Spoon River Anthology" and "Suppressed Desires" in the next couple weeks. The president of the theatrical group was Louise Gold, vice president was Jim Cavoto.

Richard Castro and John Maldonado announced that the Hispano Club was actively recruiting new members. Their goal for the quarter was to implement some of the proposals adopted at the statewide conference on poverty they had sponsored in the spring.

Margaret Haberland organized a club for women over age 25 who were resuming or starting their education on campus. She said that the meetings of the group would be held in both mornings and evenings to allow women enrolled in both day and night classes to discuss common concerns.[422]

The health, physical education and recreation department, led by M. W. Eversole, announced there were 24 activities planned for the coming year. New programs included a mixed archery meet, men's bowling, women's basketball, women's softball, and a track and field day to be held during May Fest.[423]

In the midst of all this, MSC hosted another meeting of the Colorado Collegiate Association in September. CCA president, Don Burchfield, a junior at DU, announced he had appointed Bob Bowen as chairman of the CCA Commission on Legislative Affairs.[424]

Presidential candidate Richard Nixon held a rally downtown, just off campus.
Wayne Talmage (L) and Sherman Hamilton (R) attended.
Photo Courtesy of Metropolitan State University of Denver.

The presidential campaign came to campus in October. Richard Nixon held a rally just off campus downtown, and 5,000 attended, including MSC students Wayne Talmage and Sherman Hamilton. Looking at a photo in *THE PAPER*, they were not impressed.

The MSC chapter of the SDS held a rally at the student center, and then they went to the Nixon rally. Peter Hertlein, photographer for *THE PAPER*, managed to sneak a close-up photo of Nixon. According to the article, the mood of the crowd was full of mixed emotions: some applauded him, others, not so much. *THE PAPER* said while students rallied, the police and CIA were searching downtown buildings.

MSC student Pat Dolan wrote an editorial in *THE PAPER* saying he was "shocked to see so many people support a guy who wanted to continue slaughter of Vietnamese peasants and children." [425]

At the end of September, Professor Bagley said that his office in Cherokee 124 is always open and "both hippies and people were welcome to drop by. More than one person was heard saying, "Hippies *are* people."[426]

While the presidential campaign was being waged, a debate was taking place in classrooms at MSC, particularly, but not exclusively, in political science, sociology and history classes. Many students questioned the direction society was going, but some also questioned the very foundations of the nation. The difference between classroom discussions in 1965 and 1968 was like night and day.

The events in Chicago, the war, the plight of the farm workers, as well as the deaths of Martin Luther King and Bobby Kennedy radicalized many students who had not previously been radicalized. Some were students like Lauren Watson, who affiliated himself with the Black Panther Party, and Wayne Talmage, a political science student and member of the first student government, who was now a member of the MSC chapter of the SDS.

Talmage wrote an essay in October 1968 entitled "Declare Your Position" which summed up what many students felt at the time, and what they were saying in class. Here is a short excerpt:

> "*The foundations on which this country was founded are demonstrably false... We have provided life, liberty and pursuit of happiness based primarily on the antitheses of these concepts. We have been granted political rights which are largely neutralized by our social and economic structure. Bluntly, we have guaranteed every man woman and child the right to starve, to lose his dignity, to find a wretched journey--the quicker the death, the quicker the serenity.... A society which attempts to make commodities or objects of human beings, a society more interested in production and efficiency, a society which refuses to recognize it is inextricably linked by its existence to uphold these rights—this is a society irreparably corrupt. Its existence is not only a violation of humanitarian values, but a direct and unmistakable repudiation of its right to exist.*

Talmage finished by asserting that no man dare remain neutral in the questions and values posed. "Either you affirm this declaration," he wrote, "or you join the ranks of the misanthropes."[427]

He was not alone in this thinking. Many MSC students no longer saw America as a place that bestowed the rights of life, liberty and the pursuit of happiness. These feelings—these beliefs—became the underpinnings of dissent and violence that would tear the nation and the generations apart. Perhaps Dean Lillie understood this growing dissent and felt that his superiors didn't. Perhaps that is why he left abruptly.

Immediately, there was pushback to Talmadge's essay. In the next issue of *THE PAPER*, Steve Barnhill wrote an editorial entitled, "What, Really, is SDS For?" I strongly denounce you, SDSer, and your kind because you are a feeble-minded communist-egotistical disciple of campus insurrection. He added, "Tom Hayden got a tour of Hanoi," referring to the fact Hayden visited North Vietnam. Tom Cadwallader, a staff member of *THE PAPER*, replied, "I don't think they are communists. Wayne Talmage said they'd take money from anyone."

This exchange showed that the student body was divided over the war and the counterculture. For the most part, the faculty was divided as well. The administration was pretty united in opposition to the counterculture, especially any antinomian ideals that challenged authority. This back and forth debate escalated over the next few years.

When the student senate finally had a quorum, several programs that Doug Holcombe had been working on were introduced for approval. The first was a proposal for a book exchange to be operated by MSC student government. He said that the high cost of books was a great concern to the 4,600 students at MSC.

Another proposal was that the senate set up a committee to push the Denver City Council to eliminate parking meters around campus. That committee would also negotiate with parking lot companies to sublease blocks of parking spaces to the Associated Students of MSC, which would then re-rent them to students at reduced rates.

Rick Reeser organized a forum for representatives of the presidential candidates to speak to students and answer questions. Professor Ruth Weiner of Temple Buell spoke for Vice President Humphrey; Rev. James Miller, pastor of Montclair Community Church and leader of the Denver John Birch Society, spoke on behalf of George Wallace; Declan O'Donnell, a member of the Colorado Young Republicans and former Volunteer chairman for Romney, spoke for Richard M. Nixon.

That month, the student senate appointed Dick Ricketts to the student center board; Rick Reeser, Suzanne Holcombe, and Criss York were named to the programming committee. Chuck Brock, former student president, was picked to represent MSC students at the new Model Cities agency.[428]

October was a productive month for student government even if most students were totally unaware it existed. The parking proposal was approved and students began approaching parking lot operators to see if they would agree to sublease their lots. The book exchange was approved, however Martin Bronstein proposed a book co-op suggesting if the book exchange flopped, then a co-op should be established.

Bob Young was approved as vice president after Jim Waggoner declined Holcombe's nomination. Cindy Tomhave was appointed treasurer, Bob Smith was appointed to academic standards, Rick Jones to the campus development committee, and Ed Sadowski was named to the library committee.

CCA held another meeting in October as it became evident that MSC—the third smallest state college in Colorado—had for all practical purposes, taken over CCA under the leadership of Doug Holcombe. It was announced that CCA would present its new TV program on KOA. Metro's Bob Greenwood would be the technical producer.

CCA took up the topic of student unrest and how it varied from campus to campus. It also questioned whether student government was effective or not. The topic if student power consumed much of the meeting and MSC's student lobbying program was of great interest to students from other institutions. It was proposed that CCA locate its state offices on MSC's campus to be close to the Capitol. This, of course, would give MSC even more influence in the CCA.[429]

Things heated up again in October. Succumbing to public pressure, the trustees adopted new rules aimed at student protesters. The rules provided that a student could be suspended or expelled for acts which interfered with others' rights, or disrupted the normal functioning of college. The president of each college was given the right to suspend or expel any student pending final disciplinary action. Minor violations were handled by the dean of students.

Growing dissent on campuses was causing the business community and the state legislature to pressure the trustees to put a tough policy in place. Conventional thinking was that dissent could be silenced by disciplining or expelling a few rotten apples. The administration was divided over this policy. President Phillips, as we will see later on, did not believe that repression was the best answer to growing student dissent.

The math and science departments got six new labs on the third, fourth, and fifth floors of the TTT building in November. Doug Holcombe appointed Wayne Talmage to the budget committee; Carl Isberg to academic standards, Pearl Gonzales and Dave Daniels to the athletic committee.

Jim Kirtland, chairman of the student affairs committee, reported that 15 students made *Who's Who*: Clarence Arnold, Vivian Bartel, Roger Braun, Charles Brock, Delores Clark, Jacob Ello, Joe Fuentes, Wanda Graham, Richard Hildreth, Kathleen Howard, John Jones, David Karins, Alvin Kummerlin, Mary McBride, and Kathleen Roberto.

Robert Thompson was named Dean of Students after F. Dean Lillie suddenly resigned.

Photo Courtesy of Metropolitan State University of Denver.

THE ELECTION OF 1968

In the last week of October student government sponsored a forum for candidates in the upcoming state elections to meet students. A lavish spread of food was provided by a caterer hired by student government. No candidate saw fit to show up, only one candidate's wife.

This angered student body president Doug Holcombe and other student leaders. After much discussion, three students decided to run for state representative as write-in candidates in the November election, which was less than a week away. Jerry Cronk ran in district 29; Rick Reeser in Denver's district 10; and Doug Holcombe Denver's district 2. Holcombe ran as a Democrat, Reeser and Cronk as Republicans.

The students and their campaign manager stayed up all night to hash out a platform they could all agree to run on, as Doug Holcombe recalled in a 2013 interview. They had to agree because all the media outlets had an announcement of a news conference the following morning.

The announcement said, "The action by the students in no way reflects attitudes on part of the administration. This movement is controlled by students. Students want support from student body, interested students needed to canvass."

The next day at the news conference Doug Holcombe said, "If I only get 1 percent the campaign will be a success." Their platform included planks on education, tax reform, voter reform, consumer protection, labor, law enforcement, drug and alcohol addiction and welfare reform.[430]

They knew that they would not win given the fact write-in candidates had almost never won a legislative race. Also, the election was just days away and they had no money. They did get publicity though. The Denver TV stations carried the story, as did the daily newspapers.

Doug Holcombe was so occupied putting together the platform and holding the news conference that he neglected to tell his wife, Suzanne, an MSC student. She got a call from a local union official who saw Doug on TV and called to offer his support. That, of course, is not the best way for a wife to learn her husband was running for office.

The fact that anyone, let alone a labor leader, would take that campaign seriously enough to offer support showed that the students succeeded in showing that students at MSC were not hubcap thieves and drug addicts. They actually had substance, and many of them believed in addressing grievances through the system rather than by blowing things up.

Holcombe said that that campaign paved the way for other MSC students to run for office and win. He noted that a few weeks after the election, student government invited legislators to campus and "the house was packed." He said that this time the legislators were served franks and beans. In fact, at the end of that dinner, legislators stood up and gave a prolonged standing ovation to the students who made presentations. This was student power![431]

Student elections were held and Falk Berger was elected Justice. Tom Cadwallader won as a write-in candidate for the student affairs committee, but he was told he was told he could not take office because write-ins were not allowed. Jim Langendoerfer was elected freshman president; the vice president was Chris East, freshman representative was Pam Konrad.

Hubert Humphrey won MSC's mock election receiving 227 votes to Nixon's 140. Lane received 36 votes and segregationist George Wallace surprisingly got 25 votes. A total of 304 students voted to lower the voting age to 18 and 125 voted against. Most students disapproved of the Electoral College by a 379 to 41 vote. Students preferred a national primary instead of conventions to nominate presidential candidates by 309-114.[432]

CCA held its final meeting of 1968 at Colorado School of Mines and Metro's Bob Bowen was elected executive vice president; Sandy Swanson of CSU was elected first vice chairman meaning she would be the next CCA president. After the vote, delegates adjourned to Bratskeller, which was the only 3.2 pub located in a state college.[433]

The national elections were held in November and voters ended the Great Society by electing Richard Nixon. He had put together a coalition that included former southern Democrats, segregationists and white blue collar workers in big cities who he convinced that the affirmative action programs of the Democratic Party were taking away their rights and jobs. Nixon rallied fundamental Christian and Catholic voters with his "moral majority."

Nixon hoodwinked many anti-war voters into supporting him by saying that he had a secret plan to end the war in Vietnam. He refused to discuss that plan, saying it was top secret. Since President Eisenhower kept his election promise and ended the Korean War, gullible voters believed Nixon. This deception later earned Nixon the moniker, "Tricky Dick."

Had voters taken a history class at MSC from Dr. Walsh, Stephen Leonard, or Charles Angeletti, or one of Bob Clifton's political science classes, they would have known that Nixon had no secret plan.

Marty Bronstein wrote an editorial entitled "Give Nixon Time." He acknowledged that people were unhappy, but he urged students to be patient.[434] The fact that Nixon did not end the war meant that during the next few years there would be an increase in dissent, protest, and violence on the college campuses of America.

Nixon's presidential campaign had focused on what he called the moral majority. Nixon and many others viewed the counterculture as immoral. Congress felt like it had to get into the act of cleansing America by passing a series of morality bills. Tom Cadwallader wrote an editorial in his Polemics column in *THE PAPER* in November on that pending morality legislation.

"The constitution guarantees the right of life, liberty and the pursuit of happiness, but our legislators assured us that this just ain't so. Everywhere we go and everything we do is under scrutiny. We are a nation of sheep, to coin a phrase. Not so? Take a look at the 'Clean Law.' It concerns exposing minors to dangerous materials. It prohibits nudity and near nudity and libraries and bookstores could be shut down for displaying such materials," he cautioned.[435]

Cadwallader also blasted attacks by jackbooted thugs on the SDS, referring to the crackdown by police at an SDS rally held at Denver's Chessman Park. He also brought attention to several morality bills before the legislature, characterizing them as stupid legislation and an insult to the intelligence of any good campus agitator. This legislation attacks a symptom without even a vague awareness of the actual disease—that disease being administrative bureaucracy.

"Representatives wanted to prevent confrontations like Berkeley and Columbia from happening at Metro," Cadwallader wrote, "Yet they do nothing to eliminate the reasons for those confrontations. They simply make showdowns illegal. The next thing you know, the Capitol will be bugging our bathrooms," he predicted.[436]

After this article, things started to get shaky for *THE PAPER*. Certain legislators and the trustees took offense to some of the articles, particularly those critical of the legislature. They were expressing those feelings of displeasure on a daily basis to President Phillips.

In December, Bob Bowen wrote an article for the "Voice of Youth" column in *The Denver Post*, posing the question: "Why is the Image of the Student so Bad?" The article was timely because media coverage of demonstrations had polarized the public's view of students.

"In a day of riots, confusion, and disorder on the campuses of this country...One might think that the college student today has but one aim: to tear down society and all the institutions that make it up. Nothing could be farther from the truth. "Students of a decade or two ago weren't bothered by the fact that Negroes were not allowed in 30 percent of the schools, hotels, or restaurants of this country, or that John Foster Dulles was selling us down the river at Geneva—the Mekong River that is."

Bowen contended that students were generally...the rabble rousers trying to spark the nation's conscience. They were marching and demonstrating alongside African Americans in places like Selma and Mobile. Students were the ones supporting striking farm workers Students, he said, would not conform to the old hallowed ways, especially in politics. They wanted a new approach.[437]

CONTROVERSY STRIKES *THE PAPER*; EDITOR RESIGNS

A major controversy visited the student newspaper and the campus. The entire situation underscored the tensions and divisions that existed just below the surface in 1968 and 69.

Tom Cadwallader interviewed former MSC student and Black Panther head, Lauren Watson. The interview focused on racial trouble at Denver's Cole Junior High School. Watson had been called into the school by the assistant principal to see if he could keep the situation under control because the kids respected him.[438]

The interview demonstrated the journey Watson had taken since his early days at MSC. He was much more radical in 1969. He had left MSC and became active in the Black Panther Party. Police raided the Panther headquarters on Watson's wedding night and allegedly found three guns. Watson told Cadwallader that the Panthers were entitled to as many guns as they wanted. He quoted Watson who said, "F**k McNichols," referring to the mayor.

Watson explained the Panther's perspective on the need for a more radical form of black power. "Black people," he said "have no alternative or choice whether they want to be part of the solution or not. Because of all the values that have been heaped on us mentally and physically for the past 300 years, revolution is necessary to free our minds and our souls...necessary for us to survive as human beings. If we did anything less than actual revolution...we would not be human beings," Watson asserted.

When asked why he referred to cops as "pigs," Watson replied that they have the minds of pigs, the heads of pigs and they lack intelligence and intestinal fortitude. "They root around the community destroying lives and property," he said. "When anyone walks through the community, it is like casting the pearls before swine."

Needless to say, these comments did not go over well in many segments of the MSC community. Students and professors in the police science program were not amused. Legislators also noticed; so did the trustees. But Cadwallader published part two of the interview in the next edition anyway.

There was immediate pushback. *THE PAPER* was flooded with feedback from students. One was from a black student, Craig Bowman, who responded with a simple assertion: "It takes one to know one—a pig that is."

Bowman reminded the "connoisseur of pigs" (his words) that "it is one thing to evaluate the very real indignities and injustices imposed on the black men of this nation's history; it is perfectly valid to deplore the continuation of that colonialism in many facets of our present society. But it is another thing to forget human dignity and still another thing to point out the pigs in our midst by acting, talking, and thinking like one...." He signed it "Craig Martin Bowman, a student black and beautiful" and added the following *nota bene*: "It has occurred to me that I might have to add that I am not a 'Tom.'"

As one would expect, two leaders of Metro's African-American Student Union replied to Craig Bowman. Nancy Gregory wrote, "Anyone who judges Lauren Watson on the basis of hearing one of his speeches or reading *THE PAPER* is being more unfair to himself than Lauren." She asserted that Watson had given his life to the black community. Greg Branum wrote, "It just occurred to me that if anyone has to add that 'I am not a Tom' he had better take another look."

Cadwallader responded to critics, saying that all Watson was doing was holding a mirror to our convoluted, self-congratulatory, quasi-loving oppression of the black people. "The violence will not be Watson's violence," he wrote. "He will only be the club that we, in our ignorance, will use to bash in our own heads."

Then, white students reacted. Doug Anderson wrote: "Dear Mr. Watson: It is too bad that you had to get profane in the Cadwallader interview. It is too bad because it is self-defeating. All you did was give people an excuse to ignore what is important," He went on. "You let them off the hook. Again they can avoid facing a black human being and what a lot of black people really feel."

Another group including Jim Saccamano, Roger Lesser, Fred Estey and Gary Arnold, wrote that MSC was actively involved in an effort to present a favorable image to both state and local governments. "These officials all read our paper and their impressions are based thereon. The article cannot but widen the already extensive communication gap between MSC and those personages."

They were concerned that MSC's image had been unduly slighted due to the fact that the student government was actively involved in its "non-lobby" approach to the state legislators. They said they felt that the manner in which *THE PAPER* presented the Watson article negated those attempts.

An unsigned response came from a Watson supporter who delved into the etymology of the word that had the administration and the trustees the most upset. It pointed out that the use of the word, which finds its origins in old England, is an abbreviation for 'File Under Carnal Knowledge.' "The use of the word by Watson...does not imply any sexual connotation. Rather, the word as used lent emphasis to the summary of his bitterness, his hatred and his thorough disrespect for the establishment...a white racist society," he wrote.

The back and forth did not stop there. Geri Butler replied, "We are not colored people but Black and proud." Then Bowman responded, saying he had never been taught to feel ashamed of being black. "I have the feeling," he wrote, "that there are more 'Toms' that could blow a white ass off the face of this earth faster than you can sing 'Aunt Jemima's pancakes without her syrup is like the spring without the fall.' There is only one thing worse in this universe. That there's no Aunt Jemima at all."

The controversy ended when the student senate passed a resolution demanding Joe Fuentes resign for printing the Watson interviews. Bob Young, vice president; Jerry Cronk, Dee Clark, Jim Langendoerfer, Pam Conrad, Andy Esparza, Rick Reeser, Gary Picket, Margaret Haberland, Maurice Brown, Kathy Howard, Mike Brigman, and Al Kummerlin all voted for the motion.[439]

Joe Fuentes responded to the senators, saying, "It is time for students to start riding the senate in the direction of majority opinion."

Tom Cadwallader blasted the student government for demanding that Fuentes resign. In his "Polemics" column, he accused the student government of being in league with the administration and somehow complicit with destroying the urban concept at MSC. Cadwallader asserted that "student government was totally impotent; the student body is completely subjected to the whims of the school administration; and the student government succeeds only when the administration does not care to make an issue of the point at hand."

"Student power is a farce. Student government is a misnomer," he went on. "The only reality we have to accept concerning our freedom is that we have none. Freedom requires responsibility and responsibility cannot be accepted if it is not delegated," he added.[440]

Joe Fuentes, under pressure from many sources, including the student senate, some faculty and administrators, abruptly resigned as editor. In his final editorial, he said that *THE PAPER* was out of money and the administration might not appoint associate editor Marty Bronstein to take over as editor. Fuentes said the student paper may be "done." As it turned out, its goose was nearly cooked.[441]

The year 1968 ended after the 298,406th young man had been drafted. Most of them went to Vietnam where 16,899 Americans were killed; tens of thousands were maimed and wounded.

"Hey Jude" was the number one song that year. "Love is Blue" by Paul Mauriat was number two. Bobby Goldsboro's "Honey was number three. "Sitting on the dock of the Bay" by Otis Redding was number four. Many students were indeed sitting somewhere that year knowing that people just needed to be free. The top movie by a long shot was "2001: A Space Odyssey," but "Rosemary's Baby" received a lot of analysis in classrooms at MSC.

The Denver Broncos under Lou Saban had another disappointing season with a 5-9 record. Despite the record, the games were sold out. Many students paid $4.50 to watch the Broncos since there were no sanctioned Metro teams to cheer on. The Colorado Buffalos also had a bad year, ending with a 4-6 record—the first losing season in four years, and a harbinger of things to come.

Three MSC students waged a write-in campaign for State Representative three days before
the election. Pictured left to right: Jerry Cronk, Bob Bowen (campaign manager),
Rick Reeser, and Doug Holcombe.

Photo Courtesy of Metropolitan State University of Denver.

CHAPTER 11

Turmoil, Student Power and Athletics

When the moon is in the seventh house
And Jupiter aligns with Mars
And peace will guide the planets
And love will steer the stars
This is the dawning of the age of Aquarius
Harmony and understanding, sympathy and trust abounding
No more falsehoods or derisions, golden living dreams of visions
Mystic crystal revelations, and the mind's true liberations
Aquarius, Aquarius "Aquarius/Let the Sunshine In"
The Fifth Dimension[442]

On January 20, 1969, Richard M. Nixon took the oath of office. The Americans who had voted for him could hardly wait until he restored law and order to America, especially on college campuses. Many Americans, especially those of draft age, were anxiously waiting for the new president to initiate his secret plan and end the Vietnam War. So were the parents. of the men and women who were serving in Viet Nam. Their hearts stopped every time the doorbell rang.

There was an atmosphere of anticipation at MSC as winter quarter began.

THE WINTER OF '69

In the winter quarter, Metro's enrollment was 4,172, down from the 4,629 in the fall, but significantly more than the 3,244 students from the previous year.[443] Things seemed to be off to a good start. Tom Cadwallader landed an exclusive interview with blockbuster producer Otto Preminger for *THE PAPER*. This was a feather in Cadwallader's cap, but also it gave prestige to the student newspaper.[444]

The MSC chapter of American Association of University Professors elected Dr. Daniel Valdes, sociology professor, as its president; Dr. John Spradley was elected vice president and Dr. Elizabeth Wright was chosen as secretary-treasurer. Both were associate professors of English.

Two MSC students, Bob Bowen and Joe Fuentes, were invited to attend the National Student Symposium at Georgetown University in Washington DC. The conference was organized by the Council on International Relations and United Nations Affairs (CIRUNA). The purpose was to put on the record the recommendations of students from all parts of the country with varying political opinions. The chairman of the symposium said we will present the ideas to the new president, cabinet and proper advisors. He was acknowledging that students had power to make the president listen.[445]

In January, Isetta Rawls, an MSC student, gave a talk on "The Negro and Early Colorado" at the Hadley Library. *THE PAPER* commented that Rawls was another example of the immense pool of talent that MSC is acquiring. "We as students are proud to be associated with Ms. Rawls," the article stated.[446]

"The Colorado Collegiate Association had accomplished things at the state legislature through dialogue that even surprised militant students," an article in *THE PAPER* said about the successes of CCA's Legislative Affairs Commission. The CCA had won a seat on the CCHE advisory council; it convinced the narcotics subcommittee of legislature to reclassify pot as a dangerous drug, not a narcotic, changing the penalty from a felony to a misdemeanor.

"Last year proved what can be done by students when they organize and work effectively," the CCA vice president said. "No student likes to give in to the system but when they go through the system responsibly, they can change it, and it needs to be changed. We need changes in this state, and we need a new approach to politics in general. This will come eventually; young people will be responsible and the CCA will be right in the middle."[447]

In addition, CCA persuaded the Board of Trustees of State Colleges to allow a student a seat on its board. Stuart McLaughlin, board chairman, said the trustees would welcome the CCA representative. Jim Blake, a student at Southern Colorado State College, was promptly appointed to represent CCA on the board.[448]

Campus unrest at CU was causing knees to jerk at the state Capitol and legislators decided to get tough. Rep. John Fuhr (R-Aurora) and Sen. Ted Gill introduced a bill to control civil disorders. If a person interfered with the operations of a college or university, they would face a $5,000 fine and a year in the county jail. Senator John Bermingham (R-Denver), judiciary committee chairman, launched a probe on campus disorder. He wanted to determine what laws were needed "to restore peace to the pursuit of education." Governor Love jumped in, saying that student unrest was a matter of concern.[449]

In addition to locking radicals up, Senator Gil wanted to bar any state funds from going to any member of faculty at CU who might be a member of the communist party. He seemed to be channeling the discredited former congressman, Joe McCarthy.[450]

Representative Tom Grimshaw (R-Denver), who had been lobbied by the Metro student lobbyists and the CCA, drafted a bill to deal with disorder without going to the extremes called for in the Fuhr/Gill bill. Grimshaw said, "We believe the vast majority of students are mature law-abiding citizens, and we urge that nothing be done which, undeservedly, reflects upon this responsible majority. We urge the General Assembly not to create a problem by punitive legislation directed at the vast majority of students who are not part of the problem."

The CCA sent a delegation to lobby against the Fuhr/Gill bill at the Colorado legislature. Dr. Darrell Holmes, president of Colorado State College, testified that one of the purposes of any college is to provide for the free interchange of ideas of all types. CSC sophomore T.V. Hagenah said, "Don't pass legislation that could be used or misused to repress legitimate student activity." The committee agreed and killed the bill.[451]

Meanwhile, MSC's Doug Anderson won second place in original oratory in a national speech meet. The MSC faculty team played the KIMN radio DJs in a basketball game for charity. The team included Dean Milligan, Dr. Jon Plachy, Dr. Duane Mehn, Kenneth Tager, Eugene Roon, William Mumma, John Ferguson, Kenneth Thayer, Irving Brown, Wilford Eversole and a few "ringers." Due to their assistance, MSC won.

Student government held a "nasty-in" but most students just played cards, according to *THE PAPER*. The "nasty-in" obviously lacked the special elements that made "love-ins" so popular. Doug Holcombe appointed W.T. "Junior" Potter as CCA representative. Junior had served as chargé d' affaires to CCA President Sandy Swanson of CSU. His first tasks were to head up the CCA Intercollegiate Art Show to be held in April and to plan the 1969 College Bowl.

Holcombe also arranged for Colonel Orbitz of the Selective Service to come to the student center in February of 1969 to answer questions about the changes in draft classifications under President Nixon. Holcombe asked all male students to report to the student center.[452]

It leaked out that MSC had hired campus security which immediately caused concern among some students at the student newspaper. In light of recent crackdowns by the Denver police on the SDS and the Black Panthers, *THE PAPER* reported, many students were nervous especially right after the trustees adopted a policy of expelling students for participating in protests.[453]

In early February, the CCA met at the Air Force Academy. Don McKinley, CCHE chairman, and Frank Abbott, executive director were the guest speakers. Dave Ball, who covered the meeting for *THE PAPER*, wrote that Abbott and McKinley urged greater student participation in education. He said that CCA had set up an advisory committee to study the pros and cons of intercollegiate athletics at MSC and report to CCHE. CCA was also lobbying to lower the voting age to 18 and change the draft and narcotics laws, according to Ball.[454]

197

There was good news for MSC's new Auraria campus in January. Mayor McNichols said that Model Cities approved $12.4 million for planning and construction of the complex in Auraria. "I am very happy about it all," said a surprised Mayor McNichols. He said that the federal government had provided the tools, now it is up to the city and state to do their parts in the development of the Auraria site as campus of Metropolitan State College.

Phillips joined the chorus saying, "I am just thrilled beyond words over the federal grant." We are halfway into the woods." He did not speculate how MSC would get out of the woods, however. *The Denver Post* wrote an editorial saying HUD's approval showed that officials in DC liked the idea of the mega campus. "This is the biggest dream project in higher education around anywhere. Now that it is on the front burner, officials need to make it go," *The Post* wrote.[455]

The CCHE finally reversed its position on Auraria funding. The commission's chairman, Don McKinley, said that the state should now participate with Denver in acquiring the land for MSC. McKinley said the CCHE would submit a report to Governor Love and the legislature with those recommendations.[456]

Denver still needed to come up with its share of the money. Real estate magnate and planning board member Hudson Moore proposed a $5.2 million bond issue to finance Denver's share of acquisition costs. This struck a positive note with the city.[457]

CHICANOS STRUGGLE FOR RESPECT

Ed Lucero, an MSC student and leader of the Hispano Youth Congress, announced that he was a candidate for Denver school board. Lucero called himself a victim of the Denver Public Schools in his announcement.[458]

Meanwhile, Chicano students at MSC were demanding representation on the board of the National Urban Coalition, an organization working to improve inner cities and assist minorities. Two members of MSC's Hispano Youth Congress, Norm Pacheco and Ed Lucero, demanded that students be represented. The Urban Coalition's local branch agreed and named Norm Pacheco to the position since Ed Lucero had decided to run for the school board.

MSC's Hispano Club sponsored Hispanic Culture Week, a week-long cultural exposition in the student center emphasizing Hispanic culture. The event featured art exhibits donated by Centro Cultural of Denver from artists and sculptors in the Denver area.

An innovative feature at that event was the use of a "telelecture," which allowed nationally prominent guest speakers to address the students. They could ask questions of the guest speakers directly through microphones set up in the student center, and be answered, even though the speakers were thousands of miles away. This may not sound significant to readers in an age of live streaming on the Internet, but in 1969, it was pretty high tech.

Speakers addressing students via telelecture included Dr. Fred Romero, director of labor programs for five states in the Department of Labor; Dr Julian Zamora, chairman of the President's Committee on Rural Poverty; Vincent Ximenes Commissioner on the Inter-Agency Committee on Mexican Affairs; Reyes Tijerina, president of Allianza Federal De Mercedes, who took over a courthouse in New Mexico in a dispute over land grants; and Paul Sanchez, National Field Representative of the AFL-CIO.

Local speakers included Father Joseph Torres, the archdiocesan director of Mexican affairs. He explained the difficulties Chicano people face in the modern society, saying, "The alienation has basically resulted from the fact that for three centuries, the Spanish-American people living in the southwestern United States were isolated both technologically and culturally from the rest of the U.S. Their way of life was both simple and adequate, so they had no need for cultural advances. As the family was the basic unit of society, legal systems, police, and governments were unnecessary."

"As it became more difficult to live off the land, they began moving into cities. However, the transition from a simple rural society to a complex, materialistic society was not easy. Their innate shyness hindered communication with others, and lack of education prevented them from obtaining good jobs. Their serene, peaceful way of life was shattered by the confusing, highly-technical pace of city life. To solve these problems the Hispanos will have to work together and help each other," Torres added.

After the conference, an Anglo student, James Meyers, wrote an editorial critical of whites, saying, "For any white man to ignore the grape boycott, the Coors problem, or to buy carnations is insensitive and may be fatal in the end." He said the Hispanic people had asked nicely for the rights and respect God gave them. For the white man to continue to pay lip service to their humanity will be a tragedy. "There have been a few Hispano demonstrations and riots. Perhaps there need to be a lot more," Meyers suggested.[459]

Later that spring, MSC's Hispano Youth Congress hosted a dinner and counseling session for Hispano youth at Denver's North High School. The purpose was to convince

Richard Castro, usually working behind the scenes, was very influential in the Chicano rights movement on and off campus. Photo taken by Dave Neligh in 1990.
Photo Courtesy of Metropolitan
State University of Denver.

students at North that they, too, could go to college. Graduates of North and all schools located in poorer, minority neighborhoods in Denver did not attend college in the same numbers as graduates of schools in wealthier neighborhoods.[460]

PROTESTS GROW

The popular folk singer Joan Baez and her husband, David Harris, spoke at an anti-war rally at the Greek Theater on the campus green in February. After the rally, there was a discussion in the student center which was open only to MSC students. (Doug Holcombe was instrumental in getting the singer/war protestor to the rally. She and her husband were friends with another popular singer, Judi Collins, whose brother went to MSC and was an acquaintance of Doug Holcombe.)

Baez sang three songs and said, "I think we need a revolution. We have to form a brotherhood of man." Dave Harris made it clear that the revolution that his wife and he were advocating was a non-violent one. According to *THE PAPER*, most students at the discussion wanted to hear a message of non-violence. Approximately 400 people, mostly students and a few faculty members, showed up.[461]

Baez was known in the 1960s for her beautiful voice, and for the message in her songs. She recorded renditions of many Pete Seeger songs, generally advocating peace, love and harmony.

Popular folk singer and activist, Joan Baez, spoke and sang at a rally against the Vietnam War organized by MSC students. *Photo Courtesy of Metropolitan State University of Denver.*

She was not popular at 1600 Pennsylvania, however.

College administrators were grappling with the growing number of protests popping up daily on campuses. James Hester, President of NYU, published an article in the winter issue of the *College and University Journal* that advocated dialogue, but only after law and order on the campus is assured. The restoring law and order part resonated with many MSC faculty members and Dean McKinney.

Some faculty members, however, were less uptight about the unrest. There is no absolute rule, but it seemed that the faculty members who taught the courses in which most of the so-called radical students were enrolled—sociology, political science and history—were less concerned about restoring order than faculty members in other disciplines in which fewer activists enrolled. Perhaps interaction and communication was the difference.

The *MSC Faculty-Staff Newsletter* reproduced part of Hester's article in which he wrote that we should accept the fact that the present encounter between generations is *more* severe than any other experience of this kind in recent times. The university must be the focal point of this encounter—not begrudgingly, but welcoming the opportunity to play a central role in the creation of the society of the future.[462]

"For the university to be effective in achieving accord between the generations," Hester stated, "we must instill in ourselves...a tough, clearheaded commitment to the rule of reason. We must be determined to *prevent* any irrational faction from abusing the freedoms we had won so the university can continue to be the forum in which constructive discourse can take place."

The growing discord on college campuses was subject of a national survey of student attitudes toward dissent. The survey of 243,156 freshmen on 358 campuses found that 4.1 percent thought chances were good they'd take part in demonstrations; 54.4 percent thought colleges and universities had been too lax with student disorder; 56.4 percent thought student publications should be subject to censorship by colleges; and 31.7 percent thought a college had the right to ban outside speakers.

The previous year, before the violence in Chicago, 4.8 percent said they would have participated in demonstrations and only 48.3 percent thought colleges should be stricter on demonstrations. Clearly there was a backlash even among students.[463]

Violence was increasing on college campuses weekly and administrators brought the police on campus more frequently to disperse crowds, end sit-ins, and other forms of protest. This compelled Doug Holcombe to write a letter to the editor of the Denver daily newspapers, putting some perspective to the way students were being characterized in the media.

"In this time of turmoil on college campuses across the nation it is time for some of the more responsible students to stand and be counted," Holcombe wrote. "It is time to take a positive leadership role and move the great amount of hither-to misdirected energy of students in a positive and worthwhile direction."

He pointed out that the student riots accomplished one very important thing—they made people in the country sensitive to student opinion. "Before the riots," Holcombe wrote, "student opinion was something to be swept under the carpet and ignored. It is unfortunate that it takes a major disaster to make the American public aware of a problem."

But, he asserted, the time for rebellion was past, and the time was here for the young people to go forth and work through the established structure to bring about needed and reasonable change. Holcombe noted that at Metropolitan State College, student dissent had been minimal because of a progressive administration and faculty who were open to student opinion. Consequently, student energies had been directed in positive directions.

"In the recent election," Holcombe said, "three Metro students ran for the House of Representatives on a write-in campaign, not as a protest, but to show that students do have an interest in the state of Colorado." He said that another MSC student had announced his candidacy for a seat on the Denver Board of Education. "This type of involvement is very important if the students of today are to become the leaders of tomorrow," Holcombe stated.

Lastly, he recognized the work of MSC's student lobbyists, saying that eight interested students decided to go to the legislature to work on solving some of the problems that MSC was experiencing. "Through this type of involvement," Holcombe said, "we are making a definite and positive contribution to modern day society."

The faculty newsletter re-printed Holcombe's letter with this preface: "In a period when newspapers are filled with stories of student violence, it is refreshing and encouraging to be reminded that some student leaders are working for the improvement of society rather than its destruction. A fine letter Doug. Our compliments to Metro students for such endeavors!"

History and ethnic studies professor Charles Angeletti responded to Holcombe's letter with one word: "Ouch!"[464]

STUDENT POWER: THE 18 YEAR-OLD-VOTE, INTERCOLLEGIATE ATHLETICS

Unfortunately, a newspaper poll in January 1969, to which very few students responded, found that most students were unaware of the accomplishments of CCA and student government. It found 67 percent felt student government did nothing.

Some of that was due to apathy. A lot of it was due to the fact that the real action taking place was not in the student senate, it was in the activities that Doug Holcombe and other students were involved in away from campus, namely at the Capitol.

Holcombe downplayed the efforts of the student lobbyists because he did not want business manager Curt Wright to know. Wright had warned against the student lobbying effort. Even though many students were unaware of it, legislators at the Capitol were growing increasingly more impressed with Metro students because of the good impression the lobbyists were making. That is why CCA scored the victories it did.

The legislature was in session and MSC students were at the Capitol. In addition to fighting for a decent appropriation for MSC, the student lobbyists were also promoting the 18-year-old vote. Since there was no time the previous year to get enough signatures to place the measure on the ballot, students were asking the legislature to approve a measure to lower the voting age. The good will that the MSC student lobbyists had earned during the previous session helped.

The bill was hung up in a Senate committee. Frank Kemp knew the measure was one vote short, so he kept laying the bill over to prevent it from being killed—in part because he supported it, and in part because he was impressed with how professional the student lobbyists were, and he wanted to help them. Kemp had been a huge supporter of MSC from the beginning. Seeing students working within the system made him proud.

One afternoon, Doug Holcombe, Bob Bowen and some of the other student lobbyists were trying to figure out a way to get that one last vote. They were looking at the pink book to see if they could find anything that might help them approach committee members. One of the students noticed that a majority of the committee members were Methodists. A light bulb went off. What if they could get the Methodist Church to endorse the measure?

The next day, the student lobbyists showed up at the office of the Methodist bishop for Colorado and with some persistence, got a meeting. He explained why the voting age should be lowered. The bishop said he agreed, and so did his church on a national level. He asked what he could do. The students asked him to call a couple of hold-out members of the committee. In looking at the list, the bishop said he knew one senator and agreed to call him.

The next day the bill came up in committee. That senator had been a no vote, looking a bit tired, he spoke. He said that hell hath no fury like an angry wife. In the interest of domestic tranquility, he was going to vote aye. The bill passed out of committee and on to the floor. It seems when the bishop called, the senator was out, and so the bishop told his wife why he was calling. The senator's wife could not understand why her husband would be opposed to that measure and said she would speak with him. Speak she did.[465]

Student power did not end there. Intercollegiate athletics was the next target.

In 1968, Doug Holcombe had a conversation with Dr. Mehn, one of his professors in the P.E. department. Holcombe told Dr. Mehn he was concerned that there was not as much camaraderie at MSC as there was at CSC, where he had first attended college. Dr. Mehn said that intercollegiate athletics would help build that camaraderie.

When MSC was established, the legislature and consequently the trustees and the CCHE, prohibited intercollegiate athletics at MSC—the only four-year state school with such a prohibition. Dr. Mehn told Holcombe that only the students could lobby to change that. Faculty and administrators would not be able to because it would be seen as insubordination. Holcombe agreed to take it on.

The previous spring, Holcombe, Roger Braun, and the then student body president, Chuck Brock, had asked the trustees to approve athletics. However, the trustees felt like they could not do so because of commitments made to the legislature in 1963. Proponents of Metro had argued from day one—even when it was just a proposal before the Legislative Committee on Higher Education Beyond High School—that there would be no intercollegiate athletics. The "Green Report" specifically excluded athletics.

Roy Romer and other early supporters had often argued that Metro would be an urban college with "no athletics, marching bands, baton twirlers, sororities or fraternities." The other concern was that if the students pushed athletics, it would become an issue that would hurt Metro in the legislative battle to get the new campus at Auraria funded. So it was a delicate situation.

In 1969, as the new student body president, Holcombe decided it was time to act. He put together a group of what he called "the smartest students he could find." His new lobbyist team included: Roger Braun, Dave Daniels, Bob Bowen, Barbara Adair, Pearl Gonzales and Shannon Quinn.

There was a problem. Certain powerful administrators were against intercollegiate athletics, and particularly the timing. They were fearful that the legislature might penalize MSC's budget, or even the new campus. There was also concern about whether student fee money, which supported both student government and the CCA, could be used to lobby.

The students' position was that the money spent on the lobbying effort was student money. It came from student fees and all the college did was collect it. Once appropriated, the students argued, it was no longer under the control of the state, but rather the students who had paid the fees to begin with. They saw the administration's argument as being the same as the college buying a case of paper, then telling *the paper* store that they couldn't use that money to take a legislator to lunch.

Curtis Wright, MSC's business manager, did not buy the students' argument. So Holcombe had two choices: quit, or continue on the down-low. There is not a single quitter chromosome in Doug Holcombe's DNA, so the lobbying effort went ahead albeit sub-rosa.

Holcombe' lobbyists approached the legislature to get a bill allowing athletics passed, or at least provide political cover for the trustees to act themselves. They found a supportive state legislator who had not been in the legislature when MSC was created or funded. Therefore, he had no prior position to defend. The legislator agreed to sponsor a bill if needed.

However, since the legislature had not envisioned intercollegiate athletics, they did not put any prohibition into the law. They relied on the trustees and the CCHE to carry out their intent. The upshot: no bill was needed for the trustees to approve athletics, just political will.

Holcombe knew it would be better for the trustees to act, rather than the legislature. It was dangerous to introduce a bill approving athletics because it would cause CU to fire up its lobbying machine. CU had not wanted Metro opened to begin with, and they would certainly use that as a "we told you so," argument. CU did not want Metro competing for students, and it certainly did not want MSC siphoning off fans for games, especially football. Therefore, with an uncertain likelihood of legislative success, the strategy was to take the battle to the Board of Trustees.

Meanwhile, Roadrunner players and fans generated some bad press while the student- lobbyists were trying to get intercollegiate athletics approved. A brawl erupted at a basketball club game. MSC was trailing Colorado College when a foul was called against MSC. On court, away from the foul, a scuffle broke out between two players. Both benches emptied and a donnybrook ensued. Fans from the stands joined in. The referees could not restore order, so the game was called with 3:45 remaining, giving Colorado College the win. The Denver press gladly covered it.[466]

Holcombe laid the groundwork, speaking to individual trustees like Betty Naugle. It was a tough sell because the trustees feared reprisal from unfriendly legislators. Nevertheless, Ms. Naugle encouraged Holcombe to make another presentation to the board, which he did.

The nervous trustees asked how students felt about their fees going to intercollegiate athletics. Holcombe told them that a survey was taken at spring registration. Of the 2,936 MSC students who responded, 77 percent favored intercollegiate athletics if there was no fee increase, 65 percent said it should be financed by ticket revenue, and 66 percent favored using community facilities rather than building new ones.[467]

Given the legislative support, the trustees reversed themselves. They agreed to allow athletics except football at Metropolitan State College. One catch: they wanted yet another student referendum. Holcombe told them one would be conducted at the fall elections.

Members of the sports committee of the Denver Chamber of Commerce supported the MSC students. Chamber representatives told the trustees that athletics, organized and conducted for educational purposes, would serve as a unifying factor in the college as well as the community. They quoted Plato, "He who is only an athlete is too crude, too vulgar, too much a savage! He who is a scholar only is too soft, too effeminate! The ideal citizen is a scholar-athlete!" They said that athletics develop self-discipline and self-sacrifice because they train a person to think under pressure and under emotional distress.[468]

While Holcombe's group was at the Capitol making the case for athletics, Metro's men's basketball club ended its season 2-14. "Our record is not impressive as far as won-lost records go," the coach said, "but what really counts is the efforts and determination that was put into the program by so many including the team, our coaches and you, the loyal fans who helped make the 68-69 season a success."[469]

Dale Canino published an editorial in the same issue, saying that MSC's sports program had hit an all-time low. He accused the club of taking on the policy of discrimination—not racial but discrimination based on hair style. "If you have long hair you are not allowed to play in any of the teams. This policy is just plain nonsense. *THE PAPER* called for an immediate end to this policy." He added, "Remember, sports department, you don't legally exist, and there are a lot of long hair students paying student fees." He was unaware of what Holcombe was up to.[470]

THE SPRING OF '69: FIRST CLASS GRADUATES

March came in like a lion. Campus telephone operator JoAnne Decker received a bomb threat over the phone. She said a female voice sobbed, "There's a bomb set to go off at 10:44 in the AA building." Administrators called the Denver Police who responded and evacuated the building. The owner of the AA Building, Mr. A.A. Keith, refused to leave his fourth-floor apartment. No explosives were found and the building reopened at 11 a.m.[471]

Gary Holbrook started the first debate program at MSC that spring. Professor Holbrook had been recruited away from CU by Dr. Keats McKinney. They had known each other when they were both at Adams State College. Holbrook said in a 2013 interview that he came to Metro because he liked the program, particularly the fact that Metro had a more mature student body. Early on, Holbrook-coached debate teams began winning. Within ten years, the MSC debate team had the reputation of being one of the best in the nation.[472]

Meanwhile, the bond issue for Denver's share of money to purchase Auraria was moving forward at city hall. Mayor McNichols said that he would like to a see a bigger bond issue put before voters later on, rather than a small one in May. He said the decision on the bond issue depended on whether the Colorado General Assembly passed a bill to put up its matching share.[473]

The CCA had met that same month and elected new officers. Bob Bowen was re-elected executive vice president; Bruce Russell of CSU replaced Sandy Swanson as president. MSC's Junior Potter won a surprising upset victory over CU's Joe Calderon for vice president. Rich Hammond of MSC was elected treasurer. Don Smith was elected vice president of junior colleges. Board members were: Joe Calderon of CU, Bill Bradberry of Colorado Mountain College, Gary Guy of Rangeley, and Pete Kliche of Trinidad.[474]

Back on campus, in what was likely to be the last issue of *THE PAPER* after the Watson interview controversy, Dave Ball interviewed the CCA vice president. Ball prefaced the interview by saying, "After we published our disastrous and fatal (to *THE PAPER*) interview with Lauren Watson, the main student concern was that the interview was not relevant to MSC. Ball, who called Bowen "MSC's all-purpose critic and philosopher-statesman," said this interview was relevant.

In the interview, the VP was critical of the student government with the exception of Doug Holcombe, three senators, and an unelected student who did most of the work. He did not share Cadwallader's indictment of the administration, but he did share the view that the urban-oriented college was an endangered species.

Mary Maestas was chosen as MSC Sweetheart, the first Chicana to win the title at MSC; the first runner up was Phyllis Plastino, second runner-up was Denise Elliott.

On March 6, student government hosted another dinner for state legislators and their spouses. This time, 50 legislators, half of the general assembly, showed up. Unlike the previous fall, this dinner was informal with beans and franks. The invitation said, "In this day of student revolt, we hope you will visit our campus where it is evident that institutional pride is what makes the difference."

President Phillips gave the welcome. Doug Holcombe gave information on the characteristics of the student body and the proposed Auraria site. Circle K presented the Outstanding Faculty Member reward to Dr Lester Thonssen. MSC orator and student, Doug Anderson, gave the concluding speech. At end, the legislators gave the students a standing ovation.[475]

After three weeks without a student newspaper after the Watson interview, the publications committee voted to re-open *THE PAPER*. They installed Marty Bronstein as editor; Tom Cadwallader as managing editor; business manager, Rick Reeser; advertising manager, Frank O'Neil; drama editor was Dave Lewis; and Karl Isberg was named literary editor.

Bronstein wrote an editorial thanking everyone who supported him. In his piece, he asked why no one told the students that Dean Lillie was not returning. It had leaked out that week that Dean Lillie, who said he was working on his doctorate, had actually resigned. At the time, he said he was returning. This confirmed suspicions many students had at the time about Lillie's untimely departure. Lille was forced out—perhaps by Dean McKinney.[476]

In that same issue, despite the earlier controversy, Tom Cadwallader wrote another "Polemics" column, this time about dissent. He wrote, "The right to dissent is inherent in a democracy. The fear of dissent is inherent in a bureaucracy of the status quo." He said students must realize that dissent has to be allowed to exist. Without the perpetration of a physical or moral wrong upon a person or group of people, there would be no dissent, he reasoned.

"When a person who has not been wronged acts in a manner contrary to the social mores of his culture, he becomes a criminal," Cadwallader wrote. "But when a person is not acting but reacting to a moral injustice, he is a dissenter—and the greater the injustice the greater the reaction." He quoted Carl Becker's *Freedom of Speech and Press*: "...even in a republic the natural rights of man need to be safeguarded against another sort of tyranny—the tyranny of the majority..."

The timing of that column was interesting, coming on the heels of the news about Dean Lillie. In his statement announcing his phony leave of absence, the dean commented that if there is not proper communication with students, dissent will occur. Was Cadwallader just commenting on the growing climate of dissent in colleges across the nation?

The CCA began addressing the two-ton elephant in the room: drugs. The CCA announced it was initiating a state-wide drug research information program. It was applying for a grant to establish a state-wide clearinghouse for drug research and information. The clearinghouse would open in May and serve as center for research on drug use and its effects in Colorado. It set up the program because drug use was the number one health problem on campuses in Colorado and it was being completely ignored by college health centers, which were hoping it would go away.[477]

College health centers in 1969 were not addressing the fact that many women were attempting self-abortions and often with disastrous consequences. Roe v Wade had not yet come before a court. CCA began dispensing birth control information and counseling in student health centers across Colorado. It was pressuring health centers to also dispense birth control pills in order to avoid unwanted pregnancies and cut down on self-abortions.

A bill, pushed by the CCA, to make simple possession of marijuana a misdemeanor passed the House and was now in the Senate. This was a major victory for student lobbyists from Metro and other colleges. Denver District Attorney Mike McKevitt, a Republican with eyes on higher office, spoke out in opposition to the bill When asked by reporters what his position was, Governor Love said he would "take a long look at whether to sign it."

In the 1960s and 70s, the police would pull a young person over for a bad headlight or something, smell pot, find a joint, and then arrest the kid who would be charged with a felony. In other cases, police would stop and frisk students who were marching or picketing and arrest them. The fear of police harassment over marijuana put a damper on student demonstrations and led to anger and resentment.

The marijuana laws often resulted in the kids, who could not afford a lawyer, doing serious time for possession, having a felony on their record which damaged their future careers, and took away their right to vote. Poor, black, Hispanic, and Native American kids generally did time whereas kids from affluent white families got a plea bargain. Their parents could afford a good attorney. This double standard was the main argument students used against Colorado's archaic marijuana laws. Furthermore, the law was not reducing marijuana use.

The CCA assembly condemned what it called "the politically motivated refusal of Gov. Love to host a top level conference on higher education to find solutions to the underlying problems behind campus disorders." The resolution said that unless the root cause of disorder was addressed, disorder would continue to escalate.

The MSC student senate approved a referendum to lower the GPA requirement for student government to 2.0 from 2.6. All this work at the legislature was making it tough on some in student government to maintain a 2.6 GPA.[478]

Back at the Capitol, instead of coming up with matching money to buy the Auraria site, some legislators were in the mode of doing everything they could to mess with Metro. Senator Kingston Minster introduced SB368, which would limit enrollment at MSC and every other school in the state except CU, CSU, and CSC. Doug Holcombe asked students to lobby against the bill. If it passed, he said, it would negate the need for the Auraria campus and might lead to renewed efforts to merge MSC with the CU Denver Center.[479]

The college was publishing an Annual featuring the eighty graduating seniors. Holcombe objected to the fact it was being paid for by student fees, rather than by the students themselves.

The following week was a big one at MSC. The 18-year-old vote was up in a committee at the legislature and *Empire Magazine* was doing a big cover-story feature on Metro State. Also, the CCA art show was being held at the student center. Lieutenant Governor Mark Hogan was judging it. Hogan was one of the key legislators who pushed the bill through the House of Representatives that allowed MSC to open. All these happened on the same day.

In the morning, the House State Affairs Committee held a hearing on the 18-year-old vote. It was scheduled in the largest committee room due to the large number of witnesses and observers. Bob Bowen, who began the effort to lower the voting age, testified before the committee. He was joined by Doug Holcombe and several student body presidents from across the state. Other speakers supporting the 18-year-old vote included a representative of the Methodist Church; Herrick Roth, president of the Colorado Labor Council and several other advocates.

There were witnesses in opposition too. The number one argument in opposition was the growing dissent and protests around the nation. They failed to make any coherent or causal connection between the protests and the right of a young man to vote for the policy makers who were sending them to die and taxing them without consent.

Due to prior student lobbying, the bill passed the committee.[480]

The second event that day was the art show held in the student center. In addition to the prestige of having the lieutenant governor on campus and the resulting press coverage, the event will remain memorable for what was happening off camera.

Earlier, at the 18-year-old vote hearing, a freshman reporter for THE PAPER, Dale Debber, wanted to get all the legislators' comments on tape for a story he could peddle to radio stations. He was crawling around on his hands and knees behind the committee members with a microphone causing a mild distraction.[481]

Doug Holcombe, who had spent two years trying to convey a good impression of MSC students to the legislature, saw all that work going down the tubes by that student's inappropriate actions. Unfortunately, he could do nothing about it. Debber got away before Holcombe could confront him.

Later during the art show, Holcombe spotted Debber, chased him up the stairs to the balcony of the student center and grabbed him by the feet. At that moment, Mark Hogan was coming up the stairs to meet student government members in their offices. Debber was hanging over the balcony, held by his feet.

Fortunately, a student warned Holcombe that Hogan was on his way up, so he released the reporter without further incident. Hogan missed the ordeal. Years later, all the participants laughed over the situation. Holcombe never intended to drop him, just scare him. Debber disappeared, possibly out of a window onto the roof.[482]

The third event that day was a series of photo shoots for *Empire Magazine* and its interview with Doug Holcombe. *Empire* asked Holcombe to find students for the photos, and he hand-picked students to represent the diverse student body. In order to put on a good image, the wardrobes were carefully managed and makeup properly applied.

The *Empire* cover showed the students, wearing their best clothes, enjoying the campus green—also known as Civic Center Park. Another photo showed a group of typically-dressed students in a trash-filled alley behind the student center sitting on an early 60s vintage Impala. Yet another photo depicted a group of roadrunners in their Sunday best dashing across Colfax Ave.

The article was entitled, "Metro State: Denver's Invisible Campus." It was the largest spread ever done on Metropolitan State College in the Denver media. Feature writer Olga Curtis did a great job depicting what life was like on campus, and what students were like, even if the photos did not catch students in their everyday garb.[483]

Curtis began saying that the "college of 4,629 students, smack in the middle of Denver, ought to be fairly visible especially when it is the newest, most unusual, and fastest growing four year school in Colorado. But ask Denverites about Metropolitan State College and most of them don't seem to know where it is, what it does, or why." She said Metro State blended so completely into the city, it was difficult to see.

Curtis pointed out that the only gathering place was "an alley-side student center so small it can only accommodate one-twentieth of the student body at one time." She did not know that student fees were going into a fund for a student center those students would never see.

"Compared to those in other Colorado schools," Curtis wrote, "Metro students might seem underprivileged and deprived. But they don't think so. In fact they seem to be the most contented, self-sufficient collegians in Colorado. Their school, they say, gives them what they want—a city education geared to the people." She pointed out that MSC was the only four-year college in Colorado with an open-door policy. "Although this will change in a few years," she predicted, "anyone with a high school diploma can get in." Students reading the article were unaware that the open door was scheduled to close in a few years.

Dr. Phillips told her how the school opened in October 1965. "Usually you plan a school for years before you start taking students. But Metro State was virtually an 'instant college. In just four months we rented space, bought equipment, hired faculty, accepted students, and started teaching." He noted that" The only reason we made it was because of the high morale the school generated. Everyone pitched in—the trustees, the faculty, and the students."

Curtis credited Dr. Phillips for making Metro State work. She noted that he took a big salary cut to take the Metro job, and then worked 16-hour days to get the school organized. She called Phillips "one of the few American experts in the vocational technical side of higher education."

Empire called Metro an experiment, but it was working. "The need for this type of urban-college has already been proven," Phillips asserted "Before we opened only 32 percent of metro Denver's high school graduates went on to college. Now it's 55 percent and Metro State College accounts for most of it. Give city kids a chance to go to college and more of them will go,"

Curtis said the student population "mirrored Denver with almost the same percentages of minority groups, young marrieds, and working people." Metro drew its students from every profession—policemen in uniform; employees from Honeywell, Public Service and RCA. There were also housewives, nurses, and full time young students, aircraft mechanics and salesmen, she noted.

How invisible was the invisible campus in 1969? "There are physical education students taking classes in the YMCA and the YWCA; nursing students in four different hospitals; flight trainees at five airports; and science students getting work experience in machinery manufacture or electronic assembly at firms such as Miner-Denver, Inc. and General Electric. Every Metro State student no matter what his major must take certain liberal arts courses. These are centered in seven downtown buildings," Curtis explained.

Curtis brought home the point that MSC was continually being short-changed at the legislature. "In the 1968-69 budget for state-supported schools, Metro was given less money than any other institution," she wrote. "It received only $925 a year for each full time student compared with $1,310 for CU, $1,028 for SCSC, and $941 for CSC." Perhaps it might be different, she mused, if Metro had a football team where the president could entertain legislators his box, or even a dining room where he could take them to lunch after a tour of the campus.

What she did not say is that to many Metro-area legislators, MSC was a dummy school set up to cater to minorities and lazy white kids. Doug Holcombe hit it on the head when he said, "Some legislators think of us as some kind of 'Flunk-out U' or 'Last Chance college.' Well it's ok and it isn't. I was dumped by CSC for low grades, Holcombe admitted. "I decided I had to study and now I am having no trouble here keeping up my grades even though Metro academic standards are very high."

"What people don't realize is that it is easy to get in Metro but very hard to stay in," Holcombe continued, "Kids who flunked out of other colleges work harder here. We've got something great going at Metro State and it is worth the effort. In less than four years we've built up such a great sense of pride that some of us hope Metro never changes."

Meanwhile, spring quarter enrollment was 3,944, which was 207 more than expected, and over 900 more than the 3,028 from a year earlier. Unfortunately, MSC was not funded for that many students once more.[484]

Things heated up that spring. There had been several peaceful protests on the MSC campus by Chicano and black students who had concerns about what they thought were "racist statements of policies by certain faculty members." Even though these were peaceful, the fact they happened made administrators and legislators nervous. As Cadwallader had pointed out, the legislature was considering several bills to crack down on protests. The trustees had issued a policy on how administrators were to do so.

The police riot at the Democratic National Convention had radicalized many students, even Young Republicans like Tom Cadwallader. The nation was divided over the war although more people were beginning to oppose it more than previously. The nation was also divided over the counterculture and the so-called hippie movement, which many thought was only about drugs and sex. Violent police crackdowns on student protests were polarizing college campuses even more. The students came down on both sides.

Then, campus violence came to Colorado. CU invited the president of San Francisco State University, Dr. S.I. Hayakawa to speak at the Boulder campus. Hayakawa's severe crackdown on protestors in San Francisco made him a darling of the right and a hero of the Nixon Administration. He was hated by the SDS and the left, as well as peaceful students who still believed that in America, citizens had the right to assemble peacefully and express their opinions openly.

During the speech, Hayakawa used inflammatory rhetoric which riled up the protesting SDS students in the audience. Some students began disrupting and throwing chairs, so the police came in. Students were injured and some arrested. The Denver media demonized the SDS and deified Hayakawa. This incident was fresh on the minds of students at MSC and on the nervous minds of faculty and administrators.

Shortly after the incident, the CU regents, led by Joe Coors, voted to disaffiliate SDS. Regent Dan Lynch criticized SDS, but he said they had the right of free speech. Robert Pitler, assistant law professor, defended SDS for 50 minutes. Neither persuaded the board. Regent Joe Coors prevailed in squashing SDS.[485]

Dave Ball, a reporter for *THE PAPER*, interviewed a student about the CU incident. His answer showed the sentiments of many MSC students at the time when he said that the whole Hayakawa incident at CU was one of the biggest "misrepresentations of the truth and snow jobs ever perpetrated on the citizens of Colorado by the press." People did exactly what Dr. Hayakawa wanted them to do—overreact, he said

Hayakawa over-antagonized the black students and the SDS in hopes they would respond negatively, and they did, the student said. "Granted, the actions of the disruptive segment of the audience were irresponsible but so was Dr. Hayakawa, in his remarks and in his actions."

"Even if the few students were irresponsible, so are the demagogues who are saying 'Don't let the 18 year olds vote—look what they did at C.U.' Dr. Hayakawa… has probably irreparably damaged of all the students in Colorado—and that is precisely what he intended to do," the student asserted. [486]

Many students and probably most of the faculty and administrators, sided with Hayakawa. Nevertheless, the incident resulted in swelling membership in SDS chapters across the state and at Metro. In addition, anti-war groups like New Mobe and the Moratorium were growing. The Weather Underground's Denver chapter was getting stronger and more militant. In fact, one of its members from Denver was on the FBI's most wanted list.

The Black Panther Party was also growing in Denver and on campus. The Afro-American Student Union was getting more vocal. Chicano students were getting involved with the Hispanic Youth Congress and UMAS. Students were choosing sides in what was likely to be a battle. Metro's SDS chapter split that spring. Many of the members formed an organization called the Students Democratic Alliance (SDA). Wayne Talmage was one of the leaders.

On the other side of the political spectrum, Metro's Young Republican delegation was not allowed to be seated at the YR state convention. The reason given was that they were not an official club. Kathy Howard, student government secretary, sent a letter to the Young Republicans saying they were indeed a recognized club. The YRs ignored it.

Under protest, the Metro delegation including Wanda Graham, Rick Reeser, Alex Delgado, Jerry Coleman, Maurice Brown, Jane Holmes, Tom Cadwallader and Gary Pickett walked out of the convention hall. Tom Cadwallader wrote an article blasting the Young Republicans for the move accusing them of being elitists. Maybe MSC needed fraternities after all.[487]

Student government elections were approaching. These elections were going to be different than the usual student government contests because student power and student protests were two big issues on students' minds. Some were sympathetic with protestors, or they were protestors themselves; others were opposed to the concept of the counterculture and student protests.

Wayne Talmage and Michael Fitzgerald announced their candidacy on the SDA ticket. Two senators, Gary Pickett and Gary Arnold, ran on the United Action Party ticket after deciding against the name "Gary Party." Two other students, Bruce Berman and Dean Baucus ran on the Prime Party ticket. Blacks and Chicanos did not field candidates for president.

Talmage, who had run against Doug Holcombe the year before, said he and his running mate were committed to peaceful, legitimate change. He asserted that the present student government had proven itself to be ineffective. He and Fitzgerald were both political science majors. Talmage said SDA was organized around student power as a right to act and be treated as though you are a free citizen in a democratic society.

Many student leaders including Doug Holcombe persuaded Bob Bowen to run, primarily to keep the momentum going at the legislature. Bowen announced his candidacy for in late April. His running mate was Jim Cavoto, a drama major.

In an interesting twist, Metro's SDS chapter endorsed Bowen & Cavoto. In a unanimous statement, the group denounced the SDA party as middle-of-the-roaders and sell-outs. They blamed Talmage for the previous failure of the SDS at Metro. "The SDS supports in principle many points of the SDA platform," the statement said, "but we cannot support Talmage." Almost everyone believed the SDS endorsement was actually instigated by Talmage in order to make Bowen look like the radical. *THE PAPER* endorsed Bowen/Cavoto.

Elections were held, and Bowen/Cavoto received 525 votes. The Prime candidates, Bruce Berman and Dean Baucus came in second with 219. The Gary's were third with 202 votes, and the SDA ticket received 143. It takes a majority of the votes to avoid a runoff, so Bowen/Cavoto fell 21 votes short. A runoff with Berman/Baucus was necessary.

THE PAPER published a front page editorial endorsing Bowen/Cavoto in the runoff. They said he was the student power candidate. "Berman wants students to have a *voice*," they wrote, "but Bowen wants them to have the *say*. Bowen and Cavoto won the runoff.[488]

Shortly after the student government election, Mark Boyko, who headed the parking committee, announced that he was successful in getting parking restrictions eased. Boyko convinced the city fathers (they were all men) to increase the parking limits from one hour to two. This meant that students would only have to move their cars after every other class before getting a ticket.

Boyko who enrolled in 1967 became one of the most reliable work horses of student government. Not only did he actually do the things he signed up for, but he was usually successful. In addition to the parking committee, Boyko worked on the book exchange. Later, he became the chief justice of the student court.[489]

While students were taking finals and getting ready for summer, signs were on the horizon that it might be a long, hot summer. Tom Cadwallader wrote about the "Rhetoric of Violence" in his "Polemics" column saying that Lauren Watson had promised Denver "a long hot summer." Corky Gonzales threatened to "change the system with our bodies."

Cadwallader said that militant leftists in Denver would do well to take a lesson from the Czechs. When Russia invaded Czechoslovakia, he asked, did the people go out and burn Prague? No—they painted over the street signs. "The Russians may have been there, but they had no idea where they were at or which way to go," he wrote.

Many students spent more on parking tickets than tuition. Mark Boyko convinced the city to increase parking limits to 2 hours.

Photo Courtesy of Metropolitan State University of Denver.

"Non-violent revolution meant something—it can exist. I doubt it will, but it can," he said. "It's a simple question of making your own rules; being more original. Would you rather be more intelligent than the other guy, or more dead?" [490]

The MSC Players closed their 68/69 season with a production of Arthur Miller's award-winning drama "All My Songs" It was produced by Professor Robert Coulson and featured Jim Cavoto, Kathryn Joy, Kathy Roberto, and David Lewis. [491]

Just as Doug Holcombe was about to hand the student presidency over to Bob Bowen, Joe Fuentes wrote a tribute to Doug in *THE PAPER*. It went like this:

> *History has illustrated that the outstanding accomplishments of any individual often times go unnoticed and unrewarded. For this reason The Paper would like to bestow special accolades on an individual who deserves more praise than mere words could ever possibly hope to convey... This year MSC has been extremely fortunate and privileged to have such a person sacrificing his time for the future of the college. The person is Doug Holcombe, president of the student body.*
>
> *The Paper has often been constructively critical of the activities of student government but not without being aware of the efforts of the president. MSC had several outstanding students this year as in the past but none approached the accomplishments of Doug. Many may not agree with this evaluation because Doug often times was forceful and a bit disruptive and because, at other times, he was too subtle for actions to be noticed. Consider for a few moments the impact Doug had on State legislators while lobbying for the benefits of the college and the students. Consider, too, the effect and impression he made on the Board of Trustees during his many encounters he had with them...*
>
> *Doug was not a straight "A" student, according to the MSC admissions office, but most certainly, he deserves a multiple "A" for his outstanding achievements this year. Doug, the Paper congratulates you; and because we lack more appropriate words, we thank you. Lastly, we envy you and wish you could remain at MSC to help guide and inspire excellent leadership.*

The Awards Committee, consisting of Charles Angeletti, Roger Braun, Dennis Farhar, Dave Karins, Jim Kirtland, Mary McBride, Chuck Norick, Jon Placky, Kathy Roberto, Dr. Harry Temmer and Dean Thompson, selected students for various awards.

Those receiving the Outstanding Student Award included: Barbara Adair, Edmon Adams, Roger Braun, Richard Denny, Joe Fuentes, Louise Gold, Margaret Haberland, Doug Holcombe, Suzanne Holcombe, Becky Imatami, John Jackson, Mary McBride, Mary Elizabeth Peiner, Robert Smith, Phyllis Van Arsdale and Chris York Special awards went to Mark Boyko, Doug Holcombe and Bob Young. [492]

The Roadrunners baseball club team had a winning season but lost to DU on May 12, dropping them to 15-14 for the season.

The quarter ended with *THE PAPER* running a full-page photo of a woman student wearing a quite revealing bikini, catching some rays on the campus green. The caption: "Spring."[493]

In June, forty-one students made history by receiving Metropolitan State College's first Bachelor Degrees. In addition, eighty-one also received their Associate degrees. Governor John A. Love delivered the historic commencement address.[494]

For a list of the first baccalaureate graduates of MSC see Table III.

One of those graduating was Dennis Heap, who was the first graduate of MSC's aviation technology program. Heap had a couple of unsuccessful tries with colleges before getting into Metro. Then when the Aviation Department at Metro started, he enrolled. He worked his way through college and became a good student. He said after he graduated his career kind of took off from there. "Metro was my ticket to get away from unloading grain and doing labor jobs," he said.[495]

One person who should have been on that stage was Doug Holcombe. He had spent so much time lobbying for the college that he did not complete his student teaching in time.

The first baccalaureate class of Metropolitan State College received degrees in 1969.

Photo Courtesy of Metropolitan State University of Denver.

CHAPTER 12

We Haven't Seen This
Vintage Here Since 1969

How can people be so heartless?
How can people be so cruel?
And especially people who care about strangers
Who care about evil and social injustice
Do you only care about the bleeding crowd?
How about a needing friend? I need a friend
"Easy to Be Hard" Three Dog Night[496]

THE SUMMER AND FALL OF '69 AND ALL WAS FINE, MAYBE

The summer quarter of 1969 began with an enrollment of 1,000 FTE, which beat the projections of 885. The head count was 1,770 up from the 1,173 students a year earlier. This indicated that the fall enrollment was likely to beat expectations as well.[497]

Despite the growing enrollment, Metro State continued to get short-changed by the state legislature. MSC's budget request was cut to $4,681,000, or an increase of only $1.1 million, or $51 per FTE. This was the lowest per-student funding level in the entire state.

There was concern whether Denver would experience major disorders during the summer of 1969. Denver's Commission on Community Relations appointed an MSC instructor, Mildred Biddick, to assess the likelihood of violence in Denver. Her conclusion: Denver was ripe for major disorders during the summer.

"Denver is not yet completely polarized but the process is alarmingly apparent," she wrote. "The national communication is so compelling these days that contagion of attitudes is inevitable." She blamed the often unconscious attitudes of Anglos for preventing the fulfillment of the expectations of minority citizens. In Anglo-Negro relationships, change may be possible when both parties have equal status (like in the military), in which an African-American is seen as individual.[498]

The CCHE continued to propose enrollment caps on state colleges. One way to avoid increasing budgets was to decrease the number of students in institutions of higher education. Under Abbott's plan, MSC would be capped at 5,107. Abbott said that the schools were not legally obligated to adhere to the caps, but he made it clear they were expected to do so.[499]

Professor Charles Angeletti, who taught the first Afro-American history course at MSC, spoke at a consortium which aimed to improve the way minority history was taught in the Denver public schools. He said, "The unfair treatment of minorities in our history exists at the public school level because this is the way history teachers are taught to teach in college." In other words, if things were going to change, they had to change in the education departments of colleges.[500]

A group of 49 MSC faculty members sent a letter to the editor of *The Post* letting everyone know they did not agree with those who castigated Nixon for his "condemnation of campus rioters." They said the majority of educators did not agree with those who criticized Nixon. They hoped the silent majority of professors would start supporting the presidents of colleges and universities during these critical days, asserting expulsions were called for—expel the rioting element!

Not all educators agreed with those 49 professors. The president of the University of Iowa, Howard R. Bowen, wrote that no younger generation had ever seen eye to eye with its elders, and this current generation was no exception…Current students, he said, were far ahead of his generation, and to indict the present generation of students and young faculty—as some are inclined to do—was grossly unfair and irresponsible."[501]

Ken Phillips and other college presidents were sued in June. A group of teachers, represented by the ACLU, filed a suit to declare the state's new loyalty oath unconstitutional. The suit alleged that the oath infringed on the right of free speech and violated the equal protection amendment in that it arbitrarily treated teachers differently than other state employees. Further, the suit alleged that the oath infringed on contractual rights and due process. Professor Morton Ohlson was the plaintiff from MSC.[502]

The Colorado Supreme Court eventually ruled that the loyalty oath was constitutional.

New appointments to various student government positions were announced: Gary Arnold was named executive assistant; Dennis Shell, treasurer; Carl Carrillo, cultural affairs director; and Marsha Konrad, social affairs director.

The new student body president asked the student affairs committee to help subsidize the book exchange by buying books. He asked the student affairs committee to set up a scholarship program for needy and talented students. He proposed a committee to evaluate professors and a committee to develop a new student orientation procedure. Marsha Konrad began working on the second annual beach party.

The MSC Hispano Youth Congress met and submitted proposals to insure that the civil rights of students were preserved. They asked for several committees to be set up, including committees to study improvements in grievance procedures; discipline appeals; a committee to seek federal grants; procedures for scholarships, financial aid and loans; and an ethnic studies committee to develop Asian-American, Latin-American, Mexican-American and Afro-American studies and human concerns.[503]

That summer, MSC sponsored a sports program at Denver's Manuel High School, a predominantly African-American school. The program provided instruction for boys and girls in various sports, including basketball, baseball, gymnastics, tennis, Volleyball, wrestling, football, and weightlifting. The instructors probably learned as much as the kids they coached.[504]

Metro's Show Choir and the college got some serious props. Denver's Planning Director, James Braman Jr., sent a letter to Dr. Phillips commending the choir for its performance at the CU Transportation Conference. He said that he truly felt the launching of the college was perhaps the most important single development within Denver in *the post*-war years.

On July 20, 1969, Buzz Aldrin and Neil Armstrong landed their Apollo 11 spacecraft on the moon, fulfilling President Kennedy's promise to land a man on the moon before the end of the decade. There was a watch party in the MSC student center and a few dozen summer session students and faculty members gathered to watch the landing live on TV. America had just won the space race.

That summer, a secretary at Denver's Gates Rubber company told a coworker, Joe Megeath, about a new college in downtown Denver. He decided to drive down and check it out. He went to the business department in the Forum building and put in an application with the chairman, Dr. Irv Forkner. The two men talked for over an hour, and Megeath decided that teaching at Metro was what he wanted to do for the rest of his life. He wanted to teach, and unlike most schools, Metro would allow him to just teach.

He was hired to teach in the new business systems program. Eventually, he became the dean of the business department. MSC was one of only a handful of colleges in America that had an information systems program in 1969. By the1980s, every school in the country had one.[505]

Also that month, Dr. Dan Valdes, head of the behavioral sciences division recruited Sheldon Steinhauser as an affiliate instructor. Steinhauser had been active in the Anti-Defamation League. Two years later, he was offered a contract. Today, he is the second-longest serving professor at MSU Denver.

Immediately, Steinhauser began involving the community in his classes, and his classes in the community. "I came in as a practitioner, not as an academician," Steinhauser said in an interview. He took students to a mental health center, to the welfare department, and on a bus tour of some of the substandard housing in downtown Denver.

The '60s were particularly interesting because of the passion with which so many students were reflecting the feelings that were out in the community and the society generally, Steinhauser said. "What I saw was that students were holding rallies; they were excited about a number of issues. I don't find that same passion today," he noted.

August was an eventful month. A new student assistance program was announced. Student government would begin giving financial aid to disadvantaged students in the fall. This was necessary because the federal and state governments were failing to live up to their responsibilities in helping disadvantaged students stay in school.[506]

The Hispano Youth Congress (HYC) and the United Mexican American Students (UMAS) merged. Ed Lucero, president of the HYC, announced that his group had voted to become affiliated with UMAS and work together for La Raza. On July 31, HYC and UMAS reported what they described as a "rich and inspiring experience working with student government." In their news release, they congratulated the student senate for voting to support HYC and UMAS with the Emergency Educational Assistance Fund.

Shortly after that, representatives of MSC's chapter went to a statewide UMAS meeting to set up a statewide organization of Mexican-American College Students. That organization would work on the problems of the Chicano community with an emphasis on education. Out of the conference emerged the Colorado Chicano Intercollegiate Congress (CCIC).[507]

Marty Bronstein wrote an editorial about the role of professors in college dissent. He said the faculty senate at Columbia University endorsed the right to protest, but strongly condemned both the obstructive behavior and physical violence on the campus. Bronstein said the new, liberal university professor needed to be involved with the campus community, the outside community and with the world in general. He was indirectly addressing the 49 MSC faculty members who sided with Nixon against student protestors.[508]

Fall quarter began and just as every year since the doors opened, enrollment was up. There were 5,944 students in the fall of 1969, an increase of 1,315 over the previous year—a 28 percent increase. This equated to 4,688 FTE, up from 3,465 the previous year. Dr. Phillips said that MSC expected over 7,000 students the next year.

MSC rented ten buildings, including a new student lounge on Colfax, the Zook Building, and the old Press Club Building. There were problems. Some classes had size restrictions due to fire regulations.[509]

The Afro-American Student Union (AASU) held a dinner in September. Several administrators showed up. Greg Branum, head of AASU's education committee, said the purpose was to give black students the chance to meet each other and to ascertain just exactly what was going on in the AASU. He said the association was stepping up recruitment.[510]

In October, about 60 students attended the President's Roundtable. Phillips spoke about the upcoming Auraria bond issue election. Chicano students asked Phillips exactly how he would guarantee the community that the area south of Colfax would remain low income. Some asked if the college is not helping minorities now, how it would help them after splitting up the Chicano people. The students were concerned about talk that Metro had been ordered to implement a closed door policy by 1971.[511]

Phillips said he was working to have the closed door policy reversed. He mentioned the possibilities of getting the area south of Colfax into Model Cities. Phillips also said that the relocation plan would have to be approved by the council and HUD.

Also at that meeting, King Harris asked President Phillips for space to set up a day care. Phillips said he would look into it. Harris did not get space from MSC for the day care.

Following the meeting, the student senate passed a resolution to circulate petitions to retain Metro's open door, and to deliver them to the trustees and the CCHE. Many on the CCHE did not believe in the open door to begin with. The commission wanted to cap enrollments, and an open door defeated that purpose. (Many did not believe that a college education should be available to everyone.)[512]

Three weeks later, largely because of student outcry, and because a student was now sitting in on trustee meetings, the board of trustees announced that the open door policy at Metropolitan State College would be continued after all. The trustees had backed down.

During the fall of 1969, three very big things were happening that involved almost everyone on campus in one way or another: The bond issue for Auraria; the movement to end the war in Vietnam; and intercollegiate athletics.

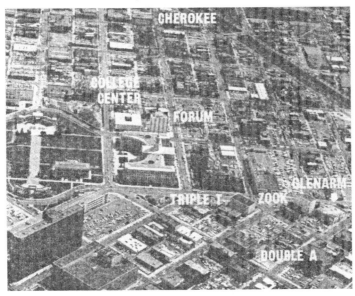

By 1969, MSC had grown to seven buildings. *Photo Courtesy of Metropolitan State University of Denver.*

THE AURARIA CAMPAIGN

In August, the city of Denver had decided to ask voters to approve a charter amendment to come up with $5.3 million to pay the city's one-third share of the land acquisition for Auraria. The matter came before the Denver City Council for final approval on September 29. Over 200 people packed council chambers, and others stood outside. Some students from MSC came to give support, others to oppose. There were also faculty members and administrators from Metro, and a few from CCD and UCD.

A large contingent of residents and business owners from Auraria showed up to learn about the proposal or oppose it. Among these were Frank Karsh and Irving Goldstein, two men who owned businesses on the Auraria site. They had formed a group called Committee for Efficient Schools.

The case for the bond issue was laid out by several speakers. Leading off was Bill Grant, a Denver attorney and co-chairman of the newly formed Citizens for Auraria committee. He gave a summary of where the site was, what was currently on the site and what the funds from the bond issue would pay for. He emphasized that this was an opportunity for Denver to achieve greatness.

Dr. Kenneth Phillips, MSC president, spoke next. He explained that the site selection committee had looked at sites throughout the city, but Auraria was the only feasible site for such a higher education complex. "This is a dream come true for our students," Phillips said.

Sterling Kahn, a member of the Denver Urban Renewal board (DURA), explained that the $12.2 million in federal funds were only available for the Auraria site. It was "use them or lose them." He pointed out that there were $2 million in federal funds available for relocation of residents and businesses, who would need to approve a compensation and relocation plan before they would be forced to vacate their property. The property tax levy would be ½ a mil, meaning the owner of a $10,000 home would pay $1.32 a year, and the owner of a $25,000 home would be assessed $3.30 a year.

Student body president Bowen was the closer. He told the council that most MSC students were sick of risking their lives crossing busy boulevards every day to attend class. He said that students at MSC were not second class citizens and deserved to have modern and adequate facilities like every other college in the state.

"If it were not for Metro State, "the average MSC student would not be going to college," Bowen said. Many Metro students worked full- or part-time and had families. They could not get a four-year education at a school outside the metropolitan area because it would mean giving up their jobs or relocating their families. Tuition at MSC was affordable, he said, but the quality of the education was equal to other institutions.

The open enrollment policy gave an opportunity to everyone to realize a dream of a college education and the higher earnings it would provide for themselves and their families. Anyone could get in, but they had to work hard to stay in, he concluded.

Then it was the opponents' turn. Dozens of speakers expressed opposition to the council. A former city councilman, Hoot Gibson, told the council to re-locate the project to the College View neighborhood in southwest Denver, saying it was also a Model Cities area.

Bal Chaves, a community activist, said he was not against re-development in West Denver but it should be postponed until more study was done on the impact it would have on the people living near Auraria.

Father Peter Garcia, pastor of St. Cajetan's church, made an appeal to save the church, saying it had been a rallying point for Denver's Hispanics since 1922. "We can be an asset if you allow us," Fr. Garcia said "But we will oppose you if you don't take us into consideration. We might even become... militant," he warned.

Councilman Irving Hook, whose district included west Denver, supported Fr. Garcia, saying St. Cajetan's should be preserved because it was more significant than the D&F Tower, which was the only structure that was spared a wrecking ball in the Skyline urban renewal project.

Then state representative Tom Bastien, a member of the legislature's Joint Budget Committee, said that he and many on his committee opposed the Auraria site. He threatened that the JBC might withhold the state's $5.3 million in financing if the project wasn't relocated to the Park Hill Golf Course. He argued that the Park Hill site would cost $1.38 million versus the $17 million for Auraria.

He was followed by numerous men and women who owned businesses on the site, including Frank Karsh and Ivan Goldstein, who vowed to fight the project in the state legislature if they lost in Denver. Several residents spoke out, some in opposition, others with questions about how they would be affected. A couple of senior citizens living in other parts of the city added that they could not afford any additional property tax.

After all the witnesses spoke, council members made comments, and then voted unanimously to put the issue on the November 4 ballot. No adjustments were made to the text of the resolution regarding St. Cajatan's.[513]

The bond election was on despite outcries from many groups, and some of the loudest came from Metro students. The two Chicano groups on campus were soundly opposed to Auraria, as was the Afro-American Student Union. They wanted the student government to oppose it, but the student senate endorsed Auraria, even if everyone felt Metro was robbed of its rightful campus and no one wanted to see a mega-campus.

The battle for Auraria was just beginning.

There was collateral damage from the proposed merger of three institutions on the Auraria site. Metro's accreditation application was put on hold for a year. The reason was the uncertainty over the forthcoming bond issue. North Central said it needed time to study the impact on Metro as part of a higher education complex, and needed to see if the funding would be approved.[514]

There were scarcely sixty days to convince voters to approve the bond issue. In recent years, bond issues had not fared that well. Even though this issue placed an ad valorum tax on property owners, the council allowed all voters to vote on it, not just property owners. That was done by making it an amendment to Denver's Charter not just an authorization for a tax increase.

That was a mixed blessing for Auraria supporters. It expanded the electorate, thus giving non-property owners, like students, the right to vote. But many non-property owners were low income Hispanics who otherwise could not have voted against it.

Passing the bond issue was not a slam dunk. There were several structural enemies to the proposal. First of all, older retired voters in northwest and southwest Denver hardly ever approved bond issues.

Second, Denver's Chicano community was nearly united in opposition, and many black community leaders were also opposed because they reasoned that if the city got away with dislocating poor Chicanos, they could do the same to poor blacks as well.

A third problem was that businesses in Auraria were organized against the bond issue. They did not want to relocate because they had low taxes, and in better neighborhoods, the land would be more expensive and taxes higher. These business owners put up money to fund a campaign against Auraria.

The Auraria issue also divided the constituency that should have been the strongest advocates for a campus: the student bodies at Metropolitan State College, the CU Denver Center, and the new Community College of Denver. The Hispano and African-American student organizations united against the bond issue in deference to the residents of Auraria and the west side. Some of Metro's most capable student leaders—Rich Castro, Virginia Lucero, Ed Lucero and John Roybal— were opposed.

Furthermore, the University of Colorado already had a downtown facility and feared that allowing Metro to have a permanent campus could threaten its Denver Center enrollment. Except for UMAS, the students at UCD and CCD generally sat on the sidelines.

Early on, the MSC the student body president said he would not support Auraria unless the rights of the displaced residents were protected. He was meeting with the Chicano leaders, the Denver planning board, DURA, Model Cities, HUD, and the CCHE and was told that assurances would be given in black and white that would protect the people of both Auraria and the west side.

A big concern of Chicanos was the encroachment of the campus and businesses into the surrounding neighborhood. The city agreed not to allow development south of Colfax. In addition, commitments were made to provide scholarships for the displaced residents and their families to the three institutions that would be located in Auraria. These commitments were acknowledged by all proponents, in every speech advocating the bond issue.[515]

Opposition from Denver's Hispanic community was being mobilized by Father Peter Garcia, pastor of St. Cajetan's church, and Waldo Benavidez, a community leader. The growing opposition made the Metro students who were supporting the bond issue nervous. They knew that, flawed as the mega-campus concept was, Auraria was the last chance for MSC to have a campus—at least one in the inner city.

Student government appointed public relations director Dave Ball to head a committee to support the bond issue. Ball recruited several other students to work on the committee, including Brian Horan, Mark Boyko, Larry Steele and Mary Renneberg, just to name a few. Eventually a team of 1,000 students was assembled to campaign for the bond issue—25 percent of the entire student body.

The student governments of the three institutions united for a newspaper photo op. Students representing the three institutions joined hands in a photo arranged by the advertising firm supporting the bond issue. Cathy Peacock, a Metro freshman and drama major; Herb Watson, a UCD graduate student with an MA in guidance; and Marjorie Richardson, a CCD freshman in secretary science appeared in the photo.[516]

The student newspaper, which had originally been skeptical of the mega- campus, came to accept it. Jon Kovash wrote that if the bond issue failed, Metro would most likely head to the suburbs. He quoted one student government official who said if the bond issue failed, Metro might as well start pasting ivy on the walls. Since the leases on all the rented buildings would expire in 1973, a move somewhere was inevitable, he wrote.

Kovash pointed out that a survey of Auraria residents, conducted by Metropolitan State College students for DURA, found most Auraria residents favored the move. That was not the consensus of the broader Chicano community, or of the Chicano students at Metro.[517]

In October, UMAS held a meeting at the Auraria Community Center for students and residents to discuss the bond issue. Virginia Lucero, a member of MSC's UMAS group, said that the only people from Metro that showed up besides UMAS were President Phillips, Bob Bowen, and six others. "Students just don't give a damn," she said. "If they vote for the bond issue it will be on information given them by big brother, without any thought as to what the bond issue is going to mean to the people who live in West Denver where Auraria sits."

Lucero speculated on what she perceived was the general attitude toward the Chicano residents who would be relocated for the new campus. "They are just a bunch of stupid Mexicans anyway. They are used to being moved. One more time isn't really going to matter to them. DURA is going to take care of them." [518]

She said that the displaced residents were proud and did not want to live in the projects. She said homeowners would get $9,000, plus a grant not exceeding $5,000, with which to buy another house. So if they find a house costing $15,000, they would have to pay the balance out of their pocket, she noted. Some people had five or six children. If they got $15,000, all they could buy would be a three bedroom house. "This is how the government plans to take care of these people," Lucero lamented.

People on the west side were concerned because they knew what would happen to their community if a college of 55,000 students was built right next door. "Only one-third of the residents in west Denver own houses. Landlords would be a fool to rent to a Chicano with children when they can rent to three or four college students who could pool their money and pay higher rent," Lucero pointed out.

West Denver was the only predominantly Chicano neighborhood with the potential of helping the people help themselves, socially, economically, culturally and politically, Lucero stated. "For the first time there is a ray of hope for the Chicano in a community that is becoming aware of its identity and is beginning to see the importance of unity," she said. "Anyone living in West Denver can feel the awakening…The young people especially…are no longer content to swallow everything that is shoved down their throats by the schools and society in general."

On the other side of the issue were students who really believed that there was no alternative to approving the bond issue. Without the city and federal money, the state would force MSC to move to the suburbs, or more likely, be merged with UCD—the goal of the regents and many legislators all along.

Dave Ball wrote an article for the "Voice of Youth" column in *The Denver Post* that told that story. "Auraria is Colorado's chance to make the nation's most brilliant innovation in higher education—an opportunity to gather in one geographical area the finest, most impressive functional and vitally necessary educational complex that can be imagined."

"Ill-informed opponents of Auraria have stated that there are better sites for the college, but they have obviously not taken the time or the effort to discover what Metropolitan State College is all about." He explained why a downtown location was essential if the school was to serve the previously un-served segments of the population.[519]

As Chicano opposition grew, Bowen, Ball and others began to feel that victory was slipping away. They met with Mayor Bill McNichols and Bill Grant, chairman of Citizens for Auraria, and voiced those concerns. They were told that everything looked good and in fact, a group of CU business students had done an un-scientific poll showing that Auraria was winning. The students did not believe the poll. Eventually they convinced the bond supporters to do a professional poll, which confirmed what the students thought. The bond issue was going down.

The Citizens for Auraria committee asked the Metro students to get more active. Ball began working with the city's PR firm to schedule speaking engagements for Bob Bowen. He spoke to several groups a week, oftentimes sharing the platform with Dean Bob O'Dell, or Larry Hamilton, who was one of the planners for Auraria. Sometimes, opponents including Waldo Benavidez, Bal Chaves, Father Garcia, Rich Castro, and Virginia Lucero presented the other side at the forums. Sometimes, the Auraria businessmen who were opposing the project showed up as well.

An army of students, faculty and staff canvassed southeast and central Denver, passing out literature, knocking on 20,000 doors and asking residents for a yes vote. If someone sounded positive, the students persuaded them to sign a pledge card. By November 4, the 1,000 volunteers had over 8,000 signed pledges. On Election Day, students staffed a phone center at the Emanuel Temple in Auraria (now an art gallery), and urged the pledged voters to get to the polls.

The other side was working also. There were several meetings in the west side in which city officials explained the bond issue and the relocation process to anxious, mostly Hispanic residents. Clearly, many were not buying the assurances. Chicanos leafleted as well.

The Citizens for Auraria committee pulled out all the stops, fearing that the bond issue was in trouble. They persuaded Denver's Catholic Archbishop Casey to write a letter which was read in all churches the Sunday before the election. He urged passage of the bond issue because it would provide educational opportunities to the poor including the Hispanic community. Father Garcia and the Chicano leaders felt like they had been stabbed in the back by their own archbishop.[520]

The Citizens for Auraria also got some Hispanic legislators to come out publicly for Auraria, including Representative Paco Sanchez, who represented the Auraria neighborhood, and Senator Roger Cisneros, who represented much of the west side[521]

On Election Day, students held a watch party in the student center. The *Rocky Mountain News* reported that the tallies were flashed on a large screen to hordes of waiting students who worked throughout the campaign in favor of passage of the Auraria issue. The crowd was quiet because most of the night, the bond issue was trailing—badly at first. As the results came in from southeast Denver, where the students had canvassed, the margin narrowed. Then as the last ballots were counted, the bond issue pulled ahead.[522]

The voters narrowly approved the bond issue by a margin of 3,773 votes. The total was 32,913 to 29,140. The 8,000 pledges the Metro students had obtained loomed very large that night. There was electricity in the air as students began celebrating what they had done.

This was student power, Metro style!

In a short victory speech, student body president Bowen said, "It's been a helluva campaign, but we've done it. Every student here deserves the credit!" He said the 8,000 vote leeway from the pledges students obtained was what was needed to carry the bond issue. He praised his fellow students for the almost 4,000-vote margin, giving Metro and its students the credit.

"We contacted nearly 20,000 people during the campaign and wound up with 8,000 written commitments from people in Denver who pledged their support at the polls," Bowen said. He heartily praised Bill Grant, the mayor, and the city council, and particularly thanked Dave Ball, who had handled the public relations campaign for Metro, and Brian Horan who had organized the canvassers, with lots of help from other students.

The Citizens for Auraria had scheduled a big election night party at the Denver Hilton. When the outcome became obvious, Mayor McNichols, Bill Grant, chairman of the citizens for Auraria group, Chamber of Commerce officers, and Bob Cameron, president of DURA, left that party and went to the humble student center on Bannock Street. They came to praise and thank the Metro students for saving the bond issue. Denver TV stations and the two Denver newspapers were there to cover it all.

"The kids had more to do with it than anyone else," Bill Grant said. "They worked like dogs out on the streets, canvassing and getting out the vote." He noted that many of the Metro students were old enough to vote. Grant said that even though the Chamber of Commerce and other business groups backed the proposal, "the students provided a new ingredient in a difficult time."[523]

The mayor and others invited the students to come over to the victory party at the Hilton, and many did. When the mayor and Grant gave victory speeches before that crowd, they repeated their praise for the students. The crowd responded with several rounds of cheers and applause for the Metro students.

Grateful politicians and businessmen bought the MSC students drinks. Although many were over 21, some were not. Larry Steele, a freshman who had worked hard in the trenches for the bond issue, said later that the party at the Hilton was the first time he tasted bourbon. He recalls having a major hangover the next day courtesy, of grateful businessmen.

In the next edition of *THE PAPER*, Ken Phillips wrote a letter to the students of Metropolitan State College saying: "Congratulations the Auraria site Bond Issue has passed. It was made possible by the efforts of you, the many students who worked long hours to provide information to the people of Denver and to get out the vote. Thank you for your support. Your efforts were outstandingly successful.[524]

A student, Peter Torsiello, wrote about the victory:

> *"In the beginning of September, the Auraria Bond Issue had been polled by an outside source (similar to any national poll of public opinion) and it had been reported that the voters would defeat the bond issue 70% to 30%. During the month of October, David Ball began to coordinate a massive and thorough campaign aimed at exposing this issue to the people. With the aid of the student body president, Bob Bowen, and other students from MSC, Denver's mass media was saturated with eager students and citizens (both pro and con) showing concern over their college and its future…MSC students and public relations were constantly fighting to change the voters' mind. And they succeeded."[525]*

Perhaps the greatest acknowledgement came in the form of an editorial published by the *Rocky Mountain News* entitled, "Dedicated Students Show the Way." The editors praised students with this tribute:

"Passage of the Denver bonds is a tribute to the hard work and dedication of students of Metro State who campaigned long and hard in the interest of a home to replace the makeshift college facilities they are now utilizing. Bill Grant, chairman of the Citizens for Auraria organization, put it this way: "The kids had more to do with it than anyone else." This dedication was all the more persuasive as none of the present students of Metro State will still be in that college when the new campus is ready. Their activities—and it should be remembered that a substantial number of students are old enough to vote—can stand as a shining example for students everywhere who want to change the status quo and stimulate action.

How much better—and more effective—was their campaign than any amount of protest marching and fist waving, not to mention violence. In this case, the earnest zeal of the students helped, we are persuaded, convinced a good many voters that they would not be inviting another disorderly college campus by helping back the Auraria complex."[26]

Until now, nothing has been written about this, no documentaries have been made; no plaques nor monuments exist; nor are their names enshrined anywhere. Nevertheless, these Metro State students probably accomplished more than any other student movement in the history of the nation. They made it possible for their alma mater, and two other institutions of higher education, to have a permanent home.

Sadly, those students' efforts have been forgotten. The institutions that benefited from what those students accomplished have swept their achievements into the dustbin of history. The early MSC students who made Auraria possible know who they are and what they have done. But will their grandchildren know? This lack of recognition is shameful.

The victory was bittersweet. Not everyone was celebrating election night. Chicano students were down. They had worked just as hard, just as effectively, and with just as much dedication as the students celebrating in the student center. They were simply outnumbered, not outworked.

MSC's Chicano students wondered how people who cared about social injustice could be so heartless and not understand their fears. These students and their supporters in the west side neighborhood deserve a tremendous amount of credit and recognition. They were underdogs, out spent by the Denver business establishment. They did not have PR firms, or newspaper ads, or even the support of their own archbishop. Yet, they nearly won.

Those students—Rich Castro, Virginia Lucero Castro, John Roybal, Ed Lucero and many others—and the community leaders Pete Garcia, Waldo Benavidez and Bal Chaves did a great service to Denver, so did the Denver GI Forum. Even if they were defeated, they raised the city's consciousness of the plight of Denver's Chicano population. They brought media at-

Students from MSC, UCD, and CCD joint to show support for the Auraria bond issue.

Left to Right: Cathy Peacock, MSC, Herb Watson, UCD, Marjorie Richardson, CCD.

Photo Courtesy of Metropolitan State University of Denver.

A jubilant Mayor Bill McNichols congratulates students on the Auraria bond election in 1960.

Left to Right: Brian Horan, Bob Bowen, Mayor McNichols, Dave Ball.

Photo Courtesy of Metropolitan State University of Denver.

tention to the struggle of La Raza in Denver. Had they not raised their voices loudly, Denver would never have heard. Their efforts must not be forgotten either.

This was student power Metro style!

An editorial put the election into perspective. *The Denver Post* said that the major factor in the size of the "against" vote was almost certainly unhappiness in the Hispano community over lack of consideration given to the neighboring west side area by city planners. "On its merits, Auraria should have won overwhelming endorsement by Hispano voters. The moral for the city fathers is clear: when a project affects a specific community as clearly as Auraria does to the west side, plan with the people affected beforehand, not as a belated, forced afterthought." How true.[527]   .

Mayor McNichols told the *News* after the election that the city of Denver would follow through on commitments made to the people in and around Auraria. He also said he would follow through to persuade the state to vote its share of the funds. A stipulation made to voters on the Auraria charter amendment was that the bonds wouldn't be issued unless the state came through with its $5.6 million share of the project. Sadly, some commitments made to the community were ignored; others still have not been fully respected.[528]

Nevertheless, the Chicano students and community leaders were responsible for emboldening a political movement that eventually brought political power for Chicanos. That movement elected Rich Castro to the legislature; Hispanics were elected mayor, US senator, Colorado lieutenant governor and as members of Congress Countless other Chicanos became officials, including members of two presidents' cabinets.

The tears of sadness that night became tears of joy on future election nights.

UPRISING: REVOLT AGAINST INTERCOLLEGIATE ATHLETICS

The second big thing in the fall of '69 was the revolt against intercollegiate athletics.

Since the trustees had approved athletics, President Phillips announced that a limited intercollegiate athletics program for men and women would begin in the fall of '69. He said the current plans included teams for basketball, baseball, swimming, field hockey, track and field, wrestling, golf, tennis and softball. There would be no football. Phillips said that the major emphasis of the school would continue to be developing a strong academic program aimed at meeting the needs of the urban community.

Keats McKinney hired Dr. James Bryant as an instructor and as the first intercollegiate men's basketball coach.[529]

Dr. Bryant had been working on his doctorate at the University of Missouri. On Superbowl Sunday, 1969, Dr. Keats McKinney met Bryant before the game in Columbia, Missouri, interviewed him, and made him an offer to teach and coach in the health, physical education, and recreation department (HPER). McKinney said something like, "No hurry, but I need your answer after the game." Bryant accepted, not because he didn't have better offers with a more suitable salary, but because he and his wife liked Colorado.

Unbeknownst to Bryant, there was some danger that the trustees could rescind their approval of intercollegiate athletics, so the coaching part of his duties could have been temporary. A student referendum was scheduled for the fall, and if the students had voted against using fees for the program, the trustees might have buckled under pressure and closed it down.[530]

As the fall quarter got underway, backlash over the newly-approved intercollegiate athletics program was coalescing. Three students, Pete Torsiello, C.G Scott and Paula Bard called for suspension of intercollegiate athletics because, they said, "it goes against the founding policies of MSC." They said they had signatures from 10 percent of the student body to force a vote on the matter. Torsiello said the wording of the question students had previously voted on was "dubious" and therefore, they wanted a new vote.[531]

At the time the trustees approved athletics few students knew what was happening. After approval, it was no longer a secret. It was out in the open and students had an opportunity to weigh in on the matter. Even though students had approved athletics 594 to 538 at spring registration the previous year, the trustees required another referendum with a higher turnout to give them political cover. The senate scheduled a referendum on athletics concurrent with class elections in the fall, as was promised to the trustees.

The issue was discussed and debated in classrooms and in the student center. Students started choosing sides. There were two camps. One thought that intercollegiate athletics would be good for building school spirit and camaraderie, and would be an excellent teaching tool for PE majors who wanted to go into coaching.

The other camp opposed athletics for two reasons. The first was fear that it would increase student fees. Already, Metro students were being forced to pay for two student centers—the tacky center they used and a big, fancy student center on Auraria that they would never get to use. Secondly, they saw the program as the camel's nose under the tent. To these students and faculty members, athletics threatened the entire notion of an urban college. They felt like it was a betrayal of Metro's mission.

The trustees were not happy hearing the anti-athletics sentiment. Trustee Betty Naugle had a meeting with the student body president and asked what had happened. Bowen assured her that despite the outcry, most students still supported athletics. He insisted that the referendum would prove that.

President Phillips was also nervous. He had recommended athletics the trustees. He called the student president in for a meeting and asked if athletics would pass. Bowen said if the turnout was big enough, it would. Phillips remained nervous. Others in the administration were secretly happy because they had opposed the student lobbying effort all along.

The student newspaper decided to air both sides of the issue so students could decide how to vote. They approached the matter like FOX News—"fair and balanced." That meant the pro side got one editorial; the con side, four.

An unidentified writer published the single pro column. He or she wrote that intercollegiate athletics would complement the physical education program and the college in general. The editorial outlined the values intercollegiate athletics promotes: developing mores, manners, morals and integrity, as well as an individual's sense of responsibility to society.

"These are the qualities necessary to perpetuate our democratic way of life. Only in the field of sports do situations exist that resemble real life situations. Thus," the writer concluded, "athletics presents numerous teaching and learning opportunities to enhance society. Sports also provide a quest for excellence, a strong-hold of the rugged life, self- discipline and self-sacrifice."

There was no planned increase in student fees, and there would not be any decrease if the program was voted out, the author said. The entire program would cost $18,950, or $2.13 per student per quarter. By contrast, the student paper cost $20,000, the student center $119,000, and the student health center, $53,500.

The first anti-athletics writer said that Metro was a new concept in education: a place where what is good from the old can be used and where the bad can be discarded and inventiveness can fill in the gaps. Somehow, that new concept had become vestigial—anatomically present, but functionally dead. There are many things needed at Metro that $19,000 could buy, the writer suggested. "How many talented people who can't afford a college education would we help?"

Peter Torsiello's article said that when the founding fathers wrote the legislation that brought Metro into existence, one of the stipulations was that there would never be any intercollegiate athletics because it was not congruous with the purpose of an urban-oriented, newly innovative institution. Now, he claimed, MSC wanted to become just another liberal arts college in Colorado with athletics.

He charged that a number of students began a program to change the minds of the trustees. "Holcombe presented the trustees with a questionnaire supposedly representative of the students, asking that intercollegiate athletics be augmented here," he alleged. "The trustees believed the presentation by Mr. Holcombe was representative of the student body as a whole." Torsiello claimed that Holcombe was acting under the omnipotent instruction of Dr. Plachy and Dr. Mehn.

He attacked the questionnaire, saying that of the 3,936 handed out, 1,000 weren't returned. "The underhandedness of the presentation to the Board to ramrod intercollegiate athletics under the noses of the students and faculty of MSC is, in my opinion, an atrocity. To manipulate the students with a questionnaire to hide all the facts and implications of intercollegiate athletics at our institution without the knowledge of the people concerned is detrimental to the college." The other articles essentially made the same arguments.[532]

Bowen fought back against accusations that Doug Holcombe and faculty members misled the trustees. It was true that the number of students who bothered to answer the questionnaire was small, he said, but "the percentage of all Americans who actually voted for Nixon was also small. Nearly half the eligible voters did not vote, and less than half of those that did, actually voted for Nixon. That did not nullify Nixon's election. If every student voiced an opinion, the majority would support intercollegiate athletics. There was no misrepresentation."

While the debate raged on, the athletic program was advancing as planned. Coaches were being hired, games were being scheduled, practice facilities were being secured, and the least possible amount of equipment was being purchased. The program was established along these guidelines:

1. No specific academic consideration would be offered any student for athletic ability; neither shall there be any discrimination against an athlete.
2. All players will be afforded the utmost protection while engaged in competitive s ports on the field and while travelling to and from athletic events.
3. Proper equipment, proper playing conditions, proper training personnel and medical attention will be available at all times.
4. No member of the staff will feel their job depends on wins and losses, although participants will still strive to the utmost and give their best to win. Nor will any job depend on gate receipts, although participants will always endeavor to present a performance worth the price of admission.
5. Strong healthy bodies, alert minds, high sense of sportsmanship, keen enjoyment, and a love of teaching should be the outcome of the athletic program at MSC. A strong attempt will be made to stress the "ingredients" of the program rather than the "embellishments."
6. The college is concerned with all its relations with the public and specifically with the development of the public perception of educational values as opposed to the commercial and publicity values of athletics.

In early November, the referendum was held with class elections. The elections were screwed up from the start. The election commissioner quit a few days before the election. Earlier, Bowen tried to postpone the election, fearing a disaster, but he was threatened with impeachment if he did, so the election proceeded.

Mark Boyko, a member of the student court and an election commissioner, who had been kept in the dark by the top election official, tried his best to conduct the election by himself. When the votes were counted, only 859 out of nearly 6,000 students voted: 412 students voted yes, 483 voted no.[533]

Immediately, the anti-athletics side began demanding that the student president notify the trustees that students did not want athletics. They insisted he tell the administration to stop spending money on a program the students turned down. Bowen replied he wanted to study the results because only 859 students had voted.

Then, Paul Marsh Jr., filed an official protest of the election with the student court. He petitioned to have the elections overturned, saying they were illegal because some ballot boxes were unmanned for hours and loose ballots were found in the student government complex. He also argued that the athletic referendum was vaguely worded.[534]

The student court met and declared that the fall elections were null and void, so the senate scheduled a new referendum on intercollegiate athletics to be carried out under stringent rules. It would cap the percentage of student fees used for athletics at five percent. That election was held at spring registration in 1970—after intercollegiate competition had begun. This time, 1,601 voted yes, 1,259 no, and 272 did not vote.[535]

Intercollegiate athletics were finally at Metropolitan State College to stay.

During all of this, the Roadrunner basketball team was playing games. The players, and even the coaching staff, were unaware of the brouhaha going on about the future of intercollegiate athletics. Dr. Bryant said that Keats McKinney never mentioned it to him. That stands to reason since McKinney wrote the "Green Report," which had promised that there would be no athletics at MSC. McKinney was in a delicate position since students had gone to the trustees to, in effect, renege on that promise.[536]

The HPER faculty was actually isolated from the rest of the faculty and the campus, since they spent their days coaching and instructing at remote facilities scattered around town. Bryant said that most of his players during those first two years worked, practiced and played, in addition to attending classes. They did not have time to get involved in campus issues. Besides, for over a year, those pushing athletics had kept their effort quiet.

Years later, it is hard to imagine that in the beginning, all the teams practiced wherever they could, had minimal equipment, no scholarships, and no team bus. They had no legacy of past championships or star players who went on to play for professional teams. They were building a program from scratch. Although victories were rare at first, those early players and teams were creating the legacy for the future championship teams at MSC and MSU Denver.

Bryant recalled that there were several times when the team would drive hours to an away game and compete that same night, or drive for hours back home after playing a night game because there wasn't any money for even a cheap motel. He remembered one match at Adams State in which the team played two games, and then drove to Denver late at night in bitter cold and snow. The station wagon was so crowded one player's head was literally out the window.

On top of that, they kept their grades up, and after defeat, they showed up at the next game and played their hearts out, even if hardly anyone came to watch. They had heart, which was the legacy they left. The glory of championships would be saved for those better financed teams that followed.

The debate continued for years. From time to time, students and others wrote editorials blasting athletics. In 1971, the father of a woman PE major wrote a letter to the editor of *The Post* saying, "If MSC is truly to serve the metro area's educational needs, it must provide a balanced program of curriculum and student activities. MSC spends $23,000 total on physical education compared with the hundreds of thousands of dollars spent at every other state institution." [537]

THE VIETNAM MORATORIUM

At the same time those issues were dividing students, there was a two-ton elephant hanging around campus: the war in Vietnam.

The first big nationwide protest called the National Moratorium Against the War was scheduled for October. MSC was the center of the movement for the entire state of Colorado. Given the involvement of Metro students in the Colorado Collegiate Association (CCA) and the 18-year-old vote, it was natural that MSC would be the leader of this effort as well.

Bob Bowen appointed Joe Taylor to coordinate the activities at MSC. The demonstration was planned for October 15. Taylor persuaded President Phillips to cancel classes on that day so that students could participate. [538] He assured Phillips the demonstration would be peaceful. To help insure this, Bowen met with a group of militant antiwar activists in Colorado, including the Weather Underground, SDS and others and asked them not to disrupt the event.

Student leaders from fifteen state colleges and universities met in the MSC student center to coordinate state-wide plans and after the meeting, they held a press conference and announced that the protests weren't going to be confined to the campuses. [539]

Represented at the meeting were: Aims Junior College, Arapahoe Junior College, Colorado College, Colorado School of Mines, Colorado State College, Loreto Heights College, Metropolitan State College, Southern Colorado State College, Regis College, Temple Buell College, CU, CSU, and the CU Denver Center. Representatives from Western State and the University of Denver were not present but endorsed the effort.

The group issued the following statement:

> *"The agony of Vietnam can hardly be calculated. The cost in American and Vietnamese lives has been staggering... We deeply believe that this cost has been a waste, that our presence in Vietnam does not represent a battle for democracy as the South Vietnamese regime our government supports is in fact nothing more than a ruthless military dictatorship. We do not believe that we are fighting aggression; Vietnam is legally one nation; the current conflict, a civil war.*
> *It is difficult to characterize the war as a struggle against communism as the*

Vietnamese are first nationalists and the communist world is not a monolith, but rather fractured groups of quarreling national entities... The moratorium will serve to maintain effective pressure for the swift extrication of American involvement in Vietnam—an involvement which recent polls indicate 60 percent of the American people believe should never have been realized. The moratorium will serve a valuable educational function, as the American people have not received the true story of Vietnam from their government."

Joe Taylor told *The Post* there was considerable support for protest activities at MSC. Afternoon classes were dismissed and professors were urged to discuss the war in their classes. He said MSC students were going to circulate antiwar leaflets in downtown Denver.[540]

The day before the demonstration, Colorado's senior Republican senator, Gordon Allott, told the press that the moratorium had been planned in East Berlin by a communist youth group. This made the front page of the newspapers, and was the top story on the morning news. Allott apparently said this to discredit the event and dampen participation. As the newspapers reported, he made the statement without any documentation to back it up. When asked by reporters, he declined to identify his source.[541]

Bowen and Taylor immediately responded, saying that Allott's statements were false. Neither had been to Berlin, and the national moratorium had not been planned by communists, either. "Allott issued this without giving any apparent proof or documentation. The charges made are serious and cast a suspicion on the loyalty on the persons participating in and planning the Moratorium," they said.

They also released a copy of a telegram they sent to Senator Allott which said: "Senator Allott: You have issued a serious charge concerning the origin of the October 15th Moratorium stating that the plans were laid by communists in East Berlin. You have failed to substantiate your remarks. We on the Moratorium Committee of Metropolitan State College hereby demand that you immediately prove and document your allegations or retract the statement admitting either that you were in error or you were deceiving the American people, whichever the case may be."

The press then asked Allott to reveal his sources, and all he said is that the information came from classified intelligence. Several local politicians spoke in defense of the Metro students, demanding that Senator Allott either document the charges, or retract them. He refused. Among those speaking out were two Republican legislators: Floyd Haskell and Kay Schomp.

Marge Sklencar, one of the coordinators of the national Vietnam moratorium, said that plans were not made by communists in June, but rather by patriotic Americans in January, 1969. The idea for the moratorium came from Jerome Grossemen, president of a Massachusetts Envelope Company. From January to June, an office was opened and plans were finalized. Sklencar said she wished to see documentation of the allegation.[542]

Following publication of that story, FBI agents questioned Bowen and Taylor's neighbors and coworkers, asking if they had noticed anything suspicious.

Years later, it was discovered that Allott's information came from information filed by an informant, but the FBI did not consider it to be credible. Allott, however, chose to release the information as though it were fact. Bowen and Taylor were not aware of that at the time, nor did they know how pervasive the FBI's use of moles on campus was.[543]

On the eve of the moratorium, the Colorado VFW urged residents to fly the American flag as a silent protest of the war demonstrators. The VFW's Colorado Commander, Victor Peterson, said the moratorium was the work of "a vocal minority of dissidents keyed toward immediate capitulation to the communist demands in Vietnam." He urged the silent majority to fly the flags at homes and businesses to counteract the "shameful" demonstrations.

Taylor responded, "Some people in this country are paranoid. They think anything pertaining to change has to have a communist behind it. I respect the VFW's right to say what it believes but we have the same right. We're not against this country, we're not anti-American. We are as American and patriotic as they are. We simply are against a war very few people want." He added that 2,000 MSC students would attend a prayer vigil on steps of the Capitol and would all be carrying American flags.[544]

On the day of the moratorium, Denver was hit by a snowstorm. Despite the weather about 1,000 people gathered on the steps of the state Capitol. A block long procession of marchers circled the capitol grounds three-abreast where the names of all the Colorado servicemen and women killed in Vietnam were read. The snow and cold had failed to stop them. Then protestors then marched single file to Governor Love's office.[545]

Fourteen members of the Clergy and Laymen Concerned About Vietnam and the American Friends Service Committee met with Love for 45 minutes after the vigil to try and get his support, but were unsuccessful. Mountain Bell allowed its employees take the day off, depending on workloads. The Episcopal Cathedral rang its bells every hour.[546]

The speakers in the MSC student center included Bob Bowen, who spoke on how to get out of Vietnam; Professor Bob Clifton, who gave a message of mourning; and Professor Wilt Flemon, who discussed the racial issues pertaining to Vietnam. Dr. Abramson, another MSC professor, spoke about the roots of the problem and the politics of Vietnam.

Rev. Craig Hart, a Catholic priest, spoke about peaceful resistance. Jim LoSasso, a Vietnam veteran, discussed what Vietnam was really like. That evening, St Thomas Seminary observed the moratorium with a peace forum, followed by a prayer vigil in the chapel.

After it was over, students weighed in. Tom Cadwallader wrote an editorial in the student newspaper thanking President Phillips for closing the school so students and faculty could participate in the moratorium.

Student leaders for across Colorado met at MSC to plan activities for the Moratorium against the war in Vietnam. Joe Taylor, center right, led activities at MSC.

Photo Courtesy of Metropolitan State University of Denver.

A large crowd participated in MSC's Moratorium protesting the Vietnam War in 1969.

Photo Courtesy of Metropolitan State University of Denver.

"It shows sensitivity on your part not common in administrators of state institutions," he wrote. "Your decision to cancel classes was not simple; that it came in the face of some high-level opposition...the moratorium did not, (as some people would suggest) represent a minority view conceived of and participated in by some radical element. The facts bear out your decision—the protest was peaceful, support for it was unbelievably widespread."

A student, Dean Secord, strongly disagreed with Phillips's decision. "I don't take exception with the moratorium, but with the way it is being conducted at MSC," he wrote. "Was the student body polled to determine their feelings on the issue? No. Perhaps the desires of a few mainly radicals, will be enforced on the entire student body and faculty."

He asked who paid for the films and use of the facilities. "I believe students who want to participate in the moratorium should be allowed to, but not permitted to disrupt the classes." Since instructors were being paid to instruct courses, the moratorium should have been conducted off campus, Secord concluded.[547]

Right after the October moratorium, Denver organizers began preparing for moratoriums in November and December. A city-wide moratorium had been scheduled for November ninth. A two-day moratorium would follow on Nov 15 and 16, and plans call for a three-day demonstration of antiwar sentiment in December.

The November Moratorium took place on the campus green as planned. Former Attorney General under LBJ, Ramsey Clark, was one of the speakers. This time, it drew one of the largest crowds ever assembled in Civic Center Park. Joan Baez sang.

A threat on Bowen's life was phoned in that morning and the college notified the police. Dr. Phillips asked Bowen not speak for his own safety, but Bowen declined and spoke as planned without incident. A phalanx of volunteer bodyguards including Dennis Schell, Junior Potter, Jerry Coleman and student body vice president Jim Cavoto surrounded him every step he took. For weeks, Coleman, who was known as Jericho, had been going everywhere with Bowen due to threats. Either the bodyguards foiled the attempt or it was just a hoax.

MEANWHILE, BACK AT THE RANCH

In October a major controversy arose over funding for recruitment of minority students. Representatives of three minority groups held a news conference to air a variety of grievances against the college. They accused officials of maintaining the "status quo at the predominately Anglo school" by failing to support minority recruitment efforts.

What set it off was the failure of the student-faculty Student Affairs Board to approve a budget request of $3,600 for the Hispano Youth Congress (HYC), the United Mexican Americans Students, and the Afro-American Student Union to use for recruitment.

A motion to approve the requests was made by Bob Bowen at the Student Affairs Committee meeting. The meeting was adjourned before action was taken, angering about 20 Chicano students who were had missed class to attend. About 10 percent of Metro's 5,900 students were black and Chicano, about the same as when the school had opened four years earlier.

Ed Lucero, vice president of the Hispano Youth Congress (HYC), said minority students had taken the initiative in recruiting other minority students and the burden should be shared by the college. A vice president of the Afro-American Student Union, Gregory Branum, also leveled complaints at the college's Student Affairs Committee. "Of about $400,000 collected each year in student fees," he said, "we haven't seen a cent of that money." Branum added that the college was "bigoted and racist."

John Roybal, president of the HYC, also charged that a Spanish teacher, Dr. Jean Fair, had systematically marked points off all Hispano students' grades on the grounds they had an advantage over other students. Hispanic students had picketed the college earlier that month demanding Dr. Fair be fired. Ed Lucero said readmission procedures for students suspended for low grades were "arbitrary."

Dr. Fair told *The Denver Post* it wasn't true. "If I had done it, I would never have given an A or B to a Hispano student, and I have done so many times. These particular students just didn't get good grades."

Another grievance was the use of the $30 a quarter student fees to host beach parties, which Lucero said minority students didn't have time to attend. He also objected to paying for health insurance they didn't need. "Many Hispano students are eligible for free healthcare at the West Side Health Center so their $7 per quarter health fee is wasted," Lucero contended.

An Anglo member of the Student Affairs Committee, Phil Henrikson, attended the news conference and criticized the Afro-American group's proposed budget, because it included money to buy an 8mm camera to make recruiting films. He said the meeting had adjourned because Branum was using profanity and there were ladies present. Henrikson announced he was withdrawing from school because he received three anonymous telephone threats, and the pressure had caused him to fail two recent tests.[548]

When asked about the complaints, Phillips said, "We have been working very closely with all the minority groups" He said the college had black and Hispano recruiters, and he estimated that half to two thirds of minority students came to Metro because "the college was convenient, and they were contacted in the usual manner. "The others were recruited by minority students."

A new student was appointed to replace Henrikson and consequently the $3,600 appropriation was approved at the next meeting with the help of a yes vote from the dean of students, Dr. Bob Thompson.

Shortly after this incident, student president Bowen was assaulted in the alley behind the student center by four angry men. One was a student who later admitted they had been drinking at the American Legion. They were angry over the Vietnam moratorium and Bowen's activities on behalf of the minority students.

When asked about the incident by *THE PAPER*, Bowen said there was some white back-lash to the minority students' news conference and the widespread disagreement over the moratorium. He attributed the incident to fabrications that were circulating around the school. "Compared to the $25,000 minority recruitment budget at UCD," Bowen said, "$3,600 was a drop in the bucket." He added that no camera was purchased.[549]

In November, a Student Bill of Rights was adopted. It began with this statement:

"Academic Institutions exist for the transmission of knowledge, for the cultural, social, and academic development of the students for the improvement of society, and for the pursuit of truth. For these reasons, academic institutions must be free and democratic, protective of the rights and dignity of human beings. Therefore, we the students of Metropolitan State College do ascertain these following rights to be among our rights as human beings."

It set forth written policies and procedures for dealing with student discipline, especially in light of the get-tough measures the legislature and trustees were proposing.[550]

The Afro-American Student Union provided Thanksgiving turkeys to needy families in the Denver area. Both Denver newspapers published photos of MSC students Brady Turk and Isetta Rawls delivering turkeys.

November ended with another student protest, this time by MSC business students. The issue was the state's IBM-biased purchasing policies for computers, and the CCHE's discrimination against MSC. Students from MSC and CCD picketed the state purchasing office demanding they speed up the acquisition of computers needed for use in classes. George Knochel, who headed students from MSC, said bureaucratic red tape was holding up the needed computers.

At a news conference, the students said they would graduate without having any actual computer training. "Basically we are asking for an investigation into computer acquisition. Studies showed a Xerox computer would cost $36,000 a year less. We don't want to demonstrate but we have no alternative." Frank Abbott, executive director of the CCHE, told the press the CCHE had approved Metro's request, but students asked, "Where's the computer?"[551]

The Roadrunners, under coach James Bryant, played their first official basketball game against Black Hills College. Unfortunately, they lost on the road 92-86. The team had to drive to South Dakota in private station wagons since the budget did not provide funds for a team bus. At home, they practiced at the National Guard Armory on wooden backboards. The Roadrunners finished their first season with a 0-24 record.

The Broncos tied the Houston Oilers in a shoot-out in Denver, thus ending the season 5-8-1. The Colorado Buffalos under Eddie Crowder rolled to another winning season with an 8-3 record. They lost to rival Nebraska in Lincoln, however.

The top single of 1969 was "Sugar, Sugar" by The Archies, but the top album was "Aquarius/Let the Sunshine In," by The 5th Dimension. Top movies were "The Wild Bunch" and "Butch Cassidy and the Sundance Kid."

In 1969, 11,780 young American men and women died in Vietnam. On December 1, 1969, the first lottery to determine the order of call for induction during 1970 was held. The 366 blue plastic capsules containing birth dates were drawn to assign order-of-call numbers to all men within the 18-26 age range. Still, 283,556 young men were drafted in 1969; most of them went to Vietnam.

MSC business students demonstrate to protest CCHE's failure to provide a computer for data processing students. *Photo Courtesy of Metropolitan State University of Denver.*

CHAPTER 13

A Bad Moon Rises

I see a bad moon arising'
I see trouble on the way
I see earthquakes and lightnin'
I see bad times today
Don't go around tonight
Well, it's bound to take your life
There's a bad moon on the rise
"Bad Moon Rising" Creedence Clearwater Revival[552]

New Year's Day brought in a new decade, but in many ways, it was just a continuation of the year before. The Vietnam War raged on, men were still being drafted, and there was still uncertainty about whether MSC would get a new home, despite passage of the bond issue in November. There were unresolved issues regarding historical structures on the Auraria site, and racial tensions on campus were still high.

WINTER OF 1970: FOX BUILDING, LOANS, AND DAY CARE

At the beginning of winter quarter, 5,141 students were enrolled at MSC, down from the 5,944 in the fall. Of these, 426 students transferred from other schools. Of the transfer students, 260 came from Colorado schools and 320 transferred from colleges outside the state. There were 1,265 veterans enrolled, including 41 women. Most of the veterans, 1,037, were using educational benefits from the Cold War GI Bill. An additional 111 were receiving war-orphan benefits.[553]

Metro State leased an additional 51,700 square feet of space, bringing the total to 282,700. The library moved to a new prefabricated metal building at 1421 Elati. The school also opened the Fox building, another prefabricated structure near the White Mule. Space was also leased on the top floor of the Woodman of the World building on Speer, near the Burger Chef, and MSC leased space in the Aaron stationary building, too.[554]

In early January, eighteen Hispano men and women from Metropolitan State College and the University of Colorado Denver Center were honored for scholastic achievement. UMAS announced their names as it opened a drive to raise $100,000 to finance four-year scholarships for about 25 Hispano students. All those honored had a 3.0 or higher GPA during the first two quarters. The MSC students were: Angelina Martinez, Belinda Lopez, Barbara Martin, Alberta Crespin, Richard Montano and Norman Pacheco.[555]

KBTV and MSC announced a radio and TV internship program in January. Six interns were appointed, including Jim Saccamano, Donald Lowe, Donald Wimberley, Mario Padilla, Bill Minckler and Mark Johnson. They did their internships at Channel 9 (KBTV as it was known then) or KBTR radio. Professor Thomas Cook, head of the MSC speech department, and Jim Petersen, of KBTR news, made the program possible.

Alvin Flannigan, the president of Mullins, which owned the stations, said, "It is the desire of Mullins Broadcasting Company to serve the total community and in particular to open the doors of opportunity in communication to those who are from minority or disadvantaged backgrounds who need practical training to qualify. It is our feeling this new internship program will meet a definite need in the Denver area."[556]

The winter quarter began with the same racial tensions with which the fall quarter had ended. In the fall, student government had begun a program to provide financial assistance to students who needed help to cover emergencies so they could stay in school. The measure was controversial.

Students could apply for a loan at the student government office, or if they were a Chicano student, they could apply at either the UMAS or HYC office; African-American students could apply at the African American Student Union (AASU). The rationale was that white students should not decide which minority students got assistance. The students signed a note requiring them to repay the loan by the end of the quarter or the administration would put a hold on their registration.

At the end of fall quarter, there was an incident involving an unpaid note by an officer of the African-American Student Union. The student held a news conference at the AASU offices and accused both Bowen and Metropolitan State College of institutional racism. The incident polarized the campus and gave certain administrators, who were against the loan program to begin with, a reason to crow, "I told you so." Nevertheless, the program continued.

Bowen had been attacked earlier by whites who were angry that he sided with the AASU; then he was attacked by a few individuals in the AASU and accused of institutional racism because he did not bend the rules for them. Those were interesting times.

After that incident, King Harris, Sherman Hamilton and others forced a new election for officers of the AASU, and new leadership took over. King Harris was elected chairman; Tony Harris, vice chairman; and Herb Sanders, office manager. Sidney Johnson, Craig Bowman, Sherman Hamilton and Louis Fisher were elected to the board. Greg Branum was appointed education officer; Elmer Officer, information manager; Louis Jean Pierre finance officer; and Geri Butler, secretary.[557]

Brady Turk formed a new black student organization. He wrote an open letter addressed to all "Black Brothers and Sisters," saying that because of the present form of servitude that black people were subjected to, the United Black Students of Colorado, with cooperation from the Metro Denver Fair Housing Center, were in the process of establishing a college-wide liaison commission for the purpose of counteracting "racism" and "exploitation" of black students in their quest for decent housing.

"Housing discrimination was something that we frequently read about," Turk wrote, "but unless we can relate to such an experience personally many of us in the past have attempted to escape or evade the real issues behind discrimination by kidding ourselves, 'Oh it won't happen to me.' Soul Brothers and Soul Sisters, I am here to tell you it can and will happen to you. True bigotry has no boundaries."[558]

In January, MSC opened its new child care facility. King Harris and his wife, Ernestine, scraped the funds together to open the center in the basement of St. Mark's Episcopal Church at 12th and Lincoln.[559] Ernestine Harris ran the center with a budget of $4,500 for the year, which was used to lessen costs for MSC students. The rate for one child was 35 cents an hour, two or more children was just 50 cents an hour. Eighteen Metro students started using the center immediately.[560]

On January 23, the college was shaken. Someone threw a smoke bomb into

King Harris organized and opened MSC's first
Child Care Center with his wife Bernice in 1970.
Photo Courtesy of Metropolitan State University of Denver.

one of the classrooms. The building was evacuated, but the suspects got away. Bomb throwing was beginning to become a somewhat regular occurrence at MSC.

AURARIA THE SEQUEL: SLUM UNIVERSITY...SERIOUSLY?

The big issue in 1970 was whether Metro would get a home. The legislature still had to appropriate the state's share of the money, or the federal and city funds would be lost. In the waning days of the 1969 session, the position of the legislature and the governor was that no state funds would go toward the land purchase. There were still legislators, like Rep. Tom Bastian (D-Denver) and George Fentress (R-Jefferson County), who wanted the college located on less expensive real estate in their districts.

An old opponent had entered the fray—disgruntled Auraria businessmen Frank Karsh and Ivan Goldstein. Their group, Citizens for Efficient Education (CEE), was actively lobbying against Auraria at the Capitol. Karsh, CEE co-chairman, called Auraria "an education sham which will cause a serious dollar drain on all higher education primarily for the benefit of a handful of downtown Denver merchants."

"If the state opens the doors on Auraria, the taxes of every citizen in Colorado will be literally earmarked for years to come to the detriment of all higher education, just to pay for the pet project of the Denver Chamber of Commerce and the Downtown Denver Master Planning Committee," Karsh said, adding that the $5.6 million requested to purchase land at Auraria amounted to $43,560 per acre.[561]

Auraria backers caught a break. Governor Love broke his silence and threw his support to funding the state's share for Auraria. In his State of the State message, Love said, "It seems clear to me that there are tremendous potential gains educationally and important savings fiscally in solutions which call for a maximum sharing of courses, students, teachers, administrative and library services, and facilities. The commission has recommended to me that Metropolitan State College and the central campus of the Community College should be located at the Auraria site, sharing it with the Denver Center."[562]

Two days later, with Harper gone, the CCHE reversed course and recommended that the Joint Budget Committee fund the state's $5.6 million share. "The Denver metropolitan area needs a higher education complex, and the Auraria urban renewal development is the best site for it," CCHE chairman Don McKinley told the committee. The commission presented a report endorsing Auraria and recommended that lawmakers appropriate a substantial amount of the $5.6 million needed to acquire the land.[563]

The next day, the Joint Budget Committee heard from opponents of the Auraria site, including Frank Karsh who said, "Auraria is the wrong site and its development would have disastrous implications." He labeled the complex as "Slum University" and claimed it was contrived for the advantage of the Denver downtown area. Karsh also mentioned traffic problems, flooding danger, social problems for the Hispano community and loss of tax revenue.[564]

Metro student Wayne Talmage entered the debate. He wrote a letter to the editor, arguing against the Auraria complex. "MSC was set up as an urban-oriented college, with an open-door policy, low tuition, and a technology division, and was to serve underprivileged and poor students," he wrote, "But MSC is traditional in philosophy, curriculum, faculty and grading. It has no visible relationship to the Hispanic or African-American communities. The majority of students aren't from the urban area, nor are they poor or underprivileged."

Talmage went on, saying MSC had a remedial program which was mostly useless because it reinforced failure with traditional methods and curriculum. MSC would destroy the Hispano community instead of serving it, he asserted.[565]

While the legislature was grappling with funding Auraria, the Landmark Preservation Commission took up two historical structures on the Auraria site: St. Cajetan's and the Tivoli. St. Cajetan's church had not previously been declared a landmark, and thus was not protected from demolition. Whether it was a landmark or not, the 1,500 who attended mass there on Sundays would no longer be allowed to do so because it would not be allowed to remain open as a functioning church, unlike St. Elizabeth's.

St. Cajetan's was consecrated in 1926. During its construction members of the congregation provided much of the labor, including the carvings on the wooden pews and altar. "If St. Cajetan's could be incorporated into the Auraria plan," the Rev. Peter Garcia said, "others might benefit too from the spirit and touch of another culture."[566]

The landmark commission was set to make recommendations on the fate of the Tivoli Brewing complex as well. A developer, Sidney J. Hollister, put forth a proposal to develop the Tivoli and the surrounding block as a commercial and community service center. Hollister, who had an option to buy the Tivoli, announced his plan to restore the building as a cultural center and opera house. He would also re-open the brewery as part of the deal.[567]

The landmark commission approved both St. Cajetan's Catholic Church and the old Tivoli Brewery as landmarks. The commission then notified the city council, which would make the final decision whether to preserve or deny landmark status. Without that, both buildings were scheduled to be demolished as crews prepared the land for the Auraria complex.[568]

When the issue came before city council, they killed the proposal to designate the Tivoli Brewery and the West Denver Turnhalle Opera House as landmarks by a 6-3 vote. Two weeks prior, a CCHE spokesman said the Auraria complex might be able to use the buildings as a student union, but an operating brewery would never be allowed on campus.

Sadly, an innovating teaching opportunity went down the tubes. The CCHE did not foresee the future craft beer industry that Metro could have been on the cutting edge of with an operating brewery on campus. The move prompted Larry Steele to start a SOB campaign— "Save Our Brewery."[569] (In 2015, a craft brewery/teaching facility opened in the Tivoli.)

To the surprise of no one but Frank Abbott, the CU regents tried to throw a new monkey wrench into Auraria. CU had been missing in action during the Auraria bond issue campaign, but in late January, the regents released a statement hinting that UCD might not be part of the Auraria complex and it would not pay its assigned share of the cost for facilities either. The statement said that CU had been excluded from the planning process and under the state constitution, and it had the authority to spend its funds as it saw fit.

Immediately, the CCHE pushed back. Chairman Donald C. McKinlay criticized the CU regents, saying, "The regents' expressed concern is wholly without merit. From the very beginning, the Denver Center of the university had been an integral part of Auraria." He also said that two university vice presidents and university staff had been directly involved in the Auraria planning.

McKinlay said the actions of the regents, and statements coming from CU, indicated that the university regarded itself as being above and beyond the Colorado system of higher education, and the university seemed to want a favored position in the planning and coordinating activities of the commission.[570]

The *Rocky Mountain News* said this had "all the pawmarks of a spirited cat fight." The article detailed several statements by the regents and the commission's responses. One example was the regents' claim that the commission didn't identify the Denver Center's plan for $1.1 million in land acquisition as an essential component of the complex when it had made its presentation to the legislature.

McKinlay declared, "At two separate hearings, the commission chairman carefully explained that the center's request for $1.1 million land acquisition adjoining the center has been endorsed by the commission as a number one priority budget item. It is inconceivable that the regents did not know this."

The regents' credibility was further called into question by Frank Abbott, who said that "the vice president now in charge of the Denver Center appeared with the president of Metropolitan State College and the Denver Community College when Auraria was presented to the legislature." He added, "The regents' charge amazed me. I wouldn't have expected it there. The prospect of not going ahead with Auraria is so horrendous I don't even want to think about it."[571]

Abbott noted there was some opposition to Auraria in the legislature, and he blamed it on a feeling by some out-of-Denver legislators that financing Auraria would cut funds from institutions in their own districts. Abbott said this wasn't a valid concern, as construction was financed by a 5 percent diversion from the general fund, which had grown recently at an annual rate of 8.5 percent to 10 percent. "What the legislature does," Abbott said "depends on what the governor does. Based on the governor's statements, I think he has thought it through."[572]

The regents' power play did not surprise MSC students, faculty, or administrators. CU had spent a decade doing everything in its power to kick Metropolitan State College in the gut.

This was just another day at the office for the regents. This foreshadowed the rocky road ahead for the three institutions on the Auraria campus.

Representative Palmer Burch (R-Denver), one of the prime sponsors of the legislation that had created MSC, introduced a resolution in the legislature to remove CU's constitutional power to spend its money as it chose. Burch said that CU had complete independence as to how to spend funds, unlike any other educational institution in Colorado.

"Once it gets the money, CU can thumb its nose at the general assembly, the governor, and almost anybody extant." Burch added, "They counsel only with God." CU had become one of the biggest supplicants for state appropriations, Burch said, adding, and "Their autonomy in spending is unique— and no longer justified."[573]

Tom Grimshaw (R-Jefferson County) introduced a bill to strengthen and redefine the powers of the CCHE in light of the regents' power play. "Existing institutions, their boards, staffs, students and alumni are all very jealous of institutional autonomy," Grimshaw said. "For this reason, the bill to strengthen the CCHE is controversial and unpopular. But the Legislature has a duty to Colorado citizens to provide the best education possible at the most effective cost ratio possible."[574]

The State Board for Community Colleges and Occupational Education joined the chorus, further isolating the regents. In a statement released in response to CU's position paper, the board's chairman, C. Stan Selby, said, "The board urges moving ahead with the project now."[575]

News columnist Pasquale Marrinzino took the CU regents to task for working to derail the Auraria complex. "While the Auraria complex was in the making, the regents remained conspicuously silent," he wrote. "Now they are throwing monkey wrenches into the works at the 11th hour. We have the other institutions now and the regents are fearful that they will be doing the exact job for which the [CU] centers had been created."[576]

After seven years, the regents had finally over-played their hand.

While the regents were putting up a smoke screen, the legislative battle for Auraria went on and there was trouble ahead. The Department of Urban Development (HUD) said, "If the Colorado Legislature doesn't appropriate at least $1.4 million this year for the first-phase purchase of land for the Auraria complex and indicate its intent to complete the purchase later, a $12.6 million federal grant will be lost by next August." A HUD spokesman said that at least ¼ of the estimated $5.6 million should be appropriated by the state to help guarantee that the state would buy the land from DURA.[577]

Even though Governor Love had strongly endorsed Auraria in his State of the State address, the footnotes of budget documents he actually submitted to the General Assembly failed to recommend any appropriation that year for Auraria land. This was yet another case of John Love saying one thing but doing another. Love's footnote said "land acquisition funding would be premature." His budget recommended only $300,000 for planning Auraria buildings, which would, in effect, be for planning on a site that might not be acquired.

Meanwhile, the anti-Auraria group Citizens for Efficient Education kept up its fight. They claimed the legislature never intended Auraria as the site for a university complex, and the CCHE represented the Downtown Denver Improvement Association, rather than the higher education needs of the state. A CEE spokesman, George Burke, cited the recent CU statement as evidence that the CCHE was ignoring the wishes of the people.

"CU is not convinced that a joint home for different institutions is the answer," Burke wrote. "The commission itself has reversed its stand for higher education with every passing breeze, having been on record saying that no state funds should be used to acquire the site," he added.[578]

The Post responded to CEE with an editorial stating, "The Colorado general assembly must answer a fateful question, which will affect the course of higher education in the state for decades to come: whether to build a big, unique three-college center in the Auraria section of downtown Denver. *The Denver Post* believes the answer is unquestionably yes; that this center will be a tremendous educational asset to all kinds of Denver area young people and will be widely admired and copied throughout the nation."[579]

Fortunately, Governor Love flip-flopped yet again. He now said that he would support "a specific bill for a specific amount of money for a start on land acquisition for the proposed Auraria college complex." Love said it was his understanding that HUD only wanted a commitment and the money wasn't needed right away, and that the 25 percent figure for appropriation was "a recent thing and I will support whatever amount is needed whether it is $1.4 million, $2 million, or whatever." Love added that the matter should be in a separate bill for debate and passage.[580]

Senators Joe Shoemaker (R-Denver) and George Brown (D-Denver) responded by co-sponsoring SB67 to put up the $1.4 million down payment for Auraria plus $125,000 in planning money. Almost immediately, the bill was caught up in a vote-trading controversy. The charges were denied by Republicans who controlled the Senate. Republicans said that they merely wanted to take a long and careful look at a group of important bills with some far-reaching financial implications. But it seemed the Senate wanted to keep a firm trading position with the House on Auraria.[581]

The Auraria bill was poised for passage in the Senate, but Speaker Vanderhoof (R-Garfield) said the Auraria measure could not pass the House as things stood.[582]

The MSC student lobbyists, including Bob Bowen, Dave Ball, Brian Horan and Larry Steele, were at the Capitol every day, lobbying for passage of the bill. At the annual legislative dinner held in February in the MSC student center, students pressed legislators to support passage of the bill before the federal and city funds disappeared.

Legislators had been impressed by the great work MSC students had done to convince Denver voters to approve the bond issue, and many felt guilty about letting Auraria die in the legislature, especially after students had put forth the effort of working through the system rather than rioting in the streets.

After a couple of weeks of arm twisting by Senator Joe Shoemaker, the Senate approved SB67 on a 28-5 vote. It committed $1.9 million, more than originally asked for, to develop the Auraria complex. Hugh Fowler (R-Littleton) said he was concerned about "the misrepresentation made to minorities and high school dropouts about their proposed ability to move among the three Auraria institutions at will." Fowler added, "That sounds great, but you know and I know, that the administrative and organizational problems of maintaining accreditation make such a plan impossible."[583]

Before the Auraria bill was heard in the House, a group of Auraria businessmen filed suit in Denver District Court to void the Auraria election and to stop the sale of bonds that would provide money to buy the land. Attorney George Creamer, representing the Auraria business-men Frank Karsh, Ivan L. Goldstein, Jack E. Jensen, Otto Bolton, Moses and Eunice Katz, Louis and Grace Binderup and Glen A. Fisher, claimed the election was illegal. Creamer cited a section of the State Constitution which says no bonds can be issued unless there is a vote of qualified electors which, "in the year next preceding such election, have paid a property tax."[584]

The news of the lawsuit, coupled with opposition from Speaker John Vanderhoof, resulted in a 6-6 deadlock on SB67 in the House Appropriations Committee. Upon hearing this, Governor Love went to the Republican legislative offices to persuade members to pass the bill. "We need that one," Love told reporters. One member of the committee was absent when the vote was taken, and only 12 of the 14 members present cast votes.[585]

Senator Shoemaker was not pleased at the news. He threatened a showdown until Christmas between the Colorado Senate and the House of Representatives over his bill. Shoemaker said he had been led to believe the House Rules Committee (controlled by the Speaker) had decided to block movement of the Auraria bill, even if it cleared the House Appropriations Committee.[586]

The Appropriations Committee brought SB67 up for reconsideration. Rep. Tom Bastien, (D-Denver), who had opposed the bond issue, saying the higher education complex should be moved to the Park Hill Golf Course, entered the fray. He added a major amendment, which that required that a branch of the Denver Community College be located somewhere in or near his district. It was supposed to be located on the Auraria site. After that amendment was added, the bill went to the Rules Committee, passed, and was sent to the House for second reading—with Bastiens's poison pill attached.[587]

When the bill came up for second reading, the House removed the Bastien amendment and several other crippling amendments. Then, despite Vanderhoof's predictions that the bill would not pass, the House approved SB67 on a 41-17 vote. It took all weekend and a lot of lobbying, however, before the House reached agreement.

An amendment, sponsored by Palmer Burch, (R-Denver) and Paco Sanchez, (D-Denver) was adopted. It stated that the $1.4 million for land acquisition could only be spent upon approval of the governor. That guaranteed that the state would not spend money to buy land until the lawsuit regarding Denver's bond issue was decided.[588]

Finally, on March 11, 1970, SB67, which had gone back to the Senate for concurrence on House amendments, became law. The lone vote in the Senate against the re-passage of the Auraria bill was cast by Sen. Hugh Fowler (R-Littleton). In spite of Senator Fowler and John Vanderhoof, MSC was about to have a permanent home.[589] The Champaign was flowing.

After the vote, Dave Ball, director of public relations for MSC student government, wrote a letter to the editor of *The Post*, thanking it for supporting Auraria. "On behalf of the Associated Students of Metropolitan State College, I would like to take this opportunity to thank *The Denver Post* for its whole-hearted and active support of the Auraria Higher Education Center." Ball added that he was confident the future would prove correct the contention that Auraria was the best site, and that thousands of students would owe their education to the foresight of Denver's citizens.[590]

Like it or not, CUDC was now forced to be part of the Auraria Higher Education Center.

SPRING: IN LIKE A LAMB, OUT LIKE A LION

Back on campus, spring enrollment was 5,011, with an FTE of 3,918. This meant that 2,592 students who had enrolled in September had been lost by spring. The silver lining was that women students now made up about a third of the student body. Men only outnumbered women by two to one, down from the three to one a year earlier. There were 1,267 veterans enrolled, about a quarter of the student body.[591]

Shortly after spring registration, Metro was one of three schools that applied for federal funds to start programs designed to motivate dropouts to continue their education. The schools were CCD, CU Denver, and Metro State College. The request was for $100,000 for the program called "Talent Search," and $1 million for the "Special Services for the Disabled" program.

The project was designed by the Special Services Office at MSC, headed by Dr. Richard A. Hildreth. Each of the three schools would get an equal share of the money. The colleges would contract with the Denver city government, which would then contract with the federal government for the block grant funds. The Talent Search program would utilize recruiters, who would try to motivate potential students to go back to school.[592]

Early that spring, President Nixon had invited approximately a hundred college and university presidents and student body presidents to the White House to discuss Vietnam and the protests against the war. President Phillips and Bob Bowen were invited, and they attended the two-day meeting, which included a photo op with the president. Even though it was a small school, MSC was undoubtedly chosen because of the significant role its students had played in Colorado's antiwar movement.

President Phillips set up a committee to review proposals and make recommendations on the plans for an urban studies program at MSC. Committee members included Dr. Eugenia Berger, Margaret Dickens, James Drugger, Steven Leonard, Stanley Love, Emmett McBroom, Dr William Rhodes, Edward Schenck, Dr. Donald Taylor and Gary Walker.[593]

Dr. Daniel Valdes recommended that the college set up an urban life center. He worked on the proposal with Welton Rotz, sociology professor; Don Taylor, sociology professor; Dennis Farhar, psychology professor; Robert Scbheeder, also a professor of psychology; Wilton Flemon, chemistry professor; and John Trujillo, Spanish professor. He said the proposal was the starting point of one working paper for a college-sponsored urban affairs and studies committee.

He proposed two divisions: ethnic studies and urban studies. Ethnic studies would contain departments of Afro-American studies, Hispano studies, and Indian studies with an ethnic studies internship program. The urban studies division would include urban studies, community services and information, counseling, and recruitment."

A student, Roger Steele, wrote a letter to the editor, saying the college bookstore was not the only commercial establishment taking advantage of Metro State students. "Until a year ago," he wrote, "the White Mule was just another dive. Then students began to patronize the place because it was convenient and reasonable. This is past history. Mr. White Mule soon realized what a goldmine he had going for him... Mr. White Mule showed his appreciation by jacking up prices."[594]

Three faculty members (Bob Clifton, political science; Morton Ohlson, economics, and Donald Taylor, sociology) appeared on the TV program "Labor's Language" and discussed forming a faculty union at MSC. Clifton said Metro was supposed to be unique but had lost that idea.

"When I say we, I mean all of the people at Metro, faculty, administration, student body," he said. "We have lost sight of our ideals and the idea of an urban oriented college with geographic and psychological accessibility for minority students and people who had a hard time in high school and would otherwise not go to college." Metro looked like a fresh start and the idea of an urban school was exciting, he added. "It was like getting in on the ground floor of something," Clifton said, and stated 40 faculty members were in support.[595]

The business fraternity, Mu Beta Chi, picked Playboy Bunny Heather to be its nominee for MSC Sweetheart Queen. Everyone now knew where the fraternity had been holding its meetings. As one can imagine, this sparked a controversy. Many women students were already beginning to question the Miss Sweetheart contest entirely. By nominating a non-student who worked as a bunny at the Denver Playboy Club, some said, Mu Beta Chi was being disrespectful to the women of Metro.[596]

There was some good news for data processing students. Bernard E. Teets, Colorado's director of administration, said he was taking steps to resolve problems with the state's controversial computer policy. Teets arranged to have computers installed at MSC for 90 days at bargain rates to give students some hands-on programming experience. MSC students had picketed Teets' offices the previous fall, complaining that they'd been promised computers but hadn't received any. MSC got a Xerox Data Systems Sigma 5 system at a cost of $5,000 per month, half the normal rate.

Teets said that he believed the CCHE had taken too long to come up with recommendations on which computers should be provided. This was another victory for students. They had demanded a Xerox computer, questioning why the state was forcing them to buy IBM equipment. It took a few months, but the students won. Student power Metro style! [597]

Shortly after the announcement, Frank Abbott, executive secretary of the CCHE blasted Teets for his decision. In a letter to Teets, Abbott wrote, "I think I can understand and in some respects I applaud your action. In some other respects I think the procedure you have followed is intolerable."

Abbot suggested that Teets failed to recognize the three years of planning that went into developing a statewide policy on computers for higher education. Abbot also denied the CCHE was the reason for the delays in getting computers for the schools. He blamed it, naturally, on Metro. [598]

At the root of the problem was an institutional bias in favor of IBM. It was alleged by many at the time, including the students, that when IBM moved its operation to Boulder County, promises were made that all state agencies would buy IBM equipment.

Auraria was not the only event at the Capitol that session that involved the MSC student lobbyists. The 18-year old vote was back. The previous session, it had passed the House, but not the Senate. The bill was re-introduced, but this time other players joined the battle to push the legislation onto the November ballot.

Former Representative Rich Gephardt of Boulder, who had voted against Metro several times at the behest of the CU regents, decided to help. He raised some money for lobby efforts and hired Steve Hogan, a DU graduate, to help lobby for the bill. Gephardt made a deal to change the bill to the 19-year-old vote.

Bob Bowen, who had begun the battle to lower the voting age in 1968, and the Colorado Collegiate Association (CCA), went along, hoping it would solve the legislative logjam. Once again, the House passed the bill. The Senate judiciary committee held a hearing on the bill. Gephardt had arranged for CU's star running back, Bobby Anderson, who had just been drafted by the Denver Broncos, to testify, hoping he could convince a few Republicans to switch sides. Anderson testified, as did MSC students Dave Ball and Bob Bowen. [599]

Dave Ball said that as the student campaign manager for the Auraria bond issue, he had learned that students were ready and qualified to vote. He noted that recent US presidents had endorsed the lower voting age, and Nixon had reiterated his support just a few days prior. Bowen reminded senators that not all young people were in college and some 25,000 Colorado residents under 21 were working and equally interested in the right to vote.

The senate judiciary committee unanimously passed the bill; it passed the full Senate and finally appeared on the November ballot. It became moot, however, because Congress passed a bill, sponsored by Senator Ted Kennedy which lowered the voting age to 18 nationwide.[600]

Things got hot in the spring. Rich Castro, an MSC student and leader in UMAS, was one of five men jailed following a minor auto accident and disturbance at 32nd and Curtis. Castro had stopped at the scene of the accident because he saw a policeman beating a Chicano youth in the course of making an arrest. After Castro intervened, he was handcuffed and taken to the station house with another handcuffed prisoner. Castro said the police addressed them as "dirty, slimy scum" and "stupid sons of bitches."

A crowd, including UMAS students from Metro, gathered at the Auraria Community Center after Castro's release from jail. Denver Police Chief George Seaton and Denver Safety Manager William Koch showed up. The crowd demanded the immediate suspension of the four patrolmen on charges that they had kicked, beaten and sprayed a handcuffed prisoner with Mace after the arrest. Chief Seaton walked out when the group demanded a citizen panel conduct a review instead of the DPD Internal Affairs. "You're not going to get a citizens' review board," Seaton snapped. "We are capable of handling our own investigations."[601]

Mayor Bill McNichols promised a full investigation, and appointed Safety Manager Koch to conduct it. He refused to comply with Chicano demands that George Seaton and the four officers involved be suspended pending the investigation. McNichols said there wasn't a need for a civilian review board because Koch was a civilian and he represented the city administration and the community at large, not just the police.

Waldo Benavidez, a member of the West Side Coalition, said the incident highlighted a double standard in police relations with Denver residents. He maintained the police used different tactics in apprehending Anglos than they did when arresting minorities.[602]

A week later, Rich Castro took a polygraph and passed. Both Denver Safety Manager William Koch and Castro's attorney, Bal Chaves, confirmed that an independent polygraph operator had detected no untruthfulness in Castro's answers to questions probing his brutality charges against the four Denver patrolmen. Mayor McNichols announced he was seeking a grand jury investigation of the charges.

Chicanos held a news conference at the Cento Cultural, in which speakers renewed calls to have the patrolmen submit to lie detector tests. They criticized the DPD's Internal Affairs Bureau for conducting their investigation in secret and without divulging the names of witnesses or their testimony. The proposed grand jury investigation was labeled unacceptable for the same reasons.[603]

While Chicanos were awaiting the results of the grand jury, a conference on mass media and the Spanish-surnamed was held in Denver. The conference was sponsored by the US Dept. of Justice and the MSC Department of Speech and Communication. It was intended to examine the relationship between the press and the Hispano community, but it ended with the media being condemned. Former MSC student Joe Fuentes covered it for the *News*.

At the conference, over 200 representatives of the Hispano community confronted 50 members of the mass media with threats and demands for better relations, Fuentes wrote. They repeatedly rebuked the media for discrimatory hiring practices, racially prejudiced news dissemination, programming bias and a general lack of interest in the needs and culture of the minority group.[604]

MSC professor Dr. Daniel T. Valdes chided the media for failing to report with fairness and objectivity, saying, "The tortilla curtain has been lifted." Valdes said the media had played a role in lifting the curtain, which it had helped create. However, many news workers didn't like the complexities of stories about the Hispano community, Valdes added.

"Mass media people often seek consensus, when consensus among such a diversified ethnic group is simply not available," Valdes said, adding that Hispanos may be black, white or mulatto, with Spanish, Mexican, Puerto Rican, Cuban or South American backgrounds.[605]

Meanwhile, MSC students had been demanding to know how their student fees were being spent, but the administration had refused to release a breakdown. The student president had a meeting with President Phillips and Business Manager Curt Wright. Bowen said students had been asking long enough. If the information was not forthcoming, he said, student government would retain an attorney and sue to force release of the information.

The next morning, an envelope appeared on Bowen's desk. In it was a complete breakdown of the $400,000+ student fee expenditures. It was immediately released to THE PAPER, which promptly printed it. Students discovered they were paying more for a future student center than the one they used.

Spring always brings student government elections. Rich Hall, a student senator announced his candidacy for student president. He said student government needed to be a student- oriented organization that meets the interests of students. He maintained that student government failed to provide student comforts and lounges and said he would establish a committee that only worked with students to find out their complaints and interests.[606]

Dave Ball also announced his candidacy for president. He had been student government's director of public relations and had managed the successful student campaign for the Auraria bond issue. He was interviewed by THE PAPER and said he was running because Metro was young and hadn't received accreditation, and that strong leadership from student government was necessary and the other candidates running had not shown that leadership in the past.

When asked what he thought of current student government, he said, "I think it is great in many areas. The student government had accomplished a great deal...we accomplished things that will benefit students in the long run, working in areas such as the state legislature and city council. And we have been working to make public relations more effective so that our students hopefully can find better jobs when they graduate from MSC. If a student chooses to transfer, it will be easier because people would have a higher opinion of MSC."

Ball said the main objective of his administration would be to make a degree from MSC worth more in terms of actual educational value and prestige as compared to CU or DU or any other college in the region.

The campaign was memorable for an interview THE PAPER had with student president candidate Gary Pickett. He dressed up as Adolf Hitler, swastika armbands and all, for the interview. Only he knew why.[607]

When Election Day came, Ball and his running mate David Sonnenberg were easily elected, no runoff required. Ball/Sonnenberg received 777 votes; Hall/Lawson, 411; Picket/Gilmore, 55; Hertlein/Keith, 55; Fierestein/Dawkins 32; and Esparza/ Isberg received 4 votes.[608]

Rich Hall congratulated Ball and commended him for the fine ethical campaign he had conducted. "During the course of the campaign," Hall said "I gained a new respect for Dave. He has proven to me that he does in fact have the interests of the students at heart. Even though he admits in a quite frank manner that his main interest lies in politics, he has guaranteed to me that he will lay that interest aside for the sake of the students at MSC. I will personally help Dave make Metro a better school for the students from all walks of life."[609]

Ball also thanked the students, saying, "I would like to extend my sincere appreciation to all those people who helped Dave Sonnenberg and me on this campaign. It is my hope that their enthusiasm will carry over into next year's activities. If we can obtain a total commitment to those priorities, which were outlined in the campaign, we will be successful in making a degree from MSC worth more in terms of actual educational value received and prestige, than one from any other college in the region. It is to this end that we are committed. Again many thanks for your support."[610]

That spring the two-year old MSC Young Democrats (YDs) was up to fifty members, making it the fourth largest delegation at the state YD convention held at Regis. MSC members dominated the convention. MSC professor Robert Pugel was re-elected for a two-year term as national committeeman. Sonja Eldeen, MSC chapter president, was elected to the executive board and Dennis Schell was elected college coordinator.

Speakers at the convention included presidential hopeful Senator Birch Bayh, Mark Hogan, Rich Gephardt, Ken Monfort and Sam Brown, the national chairman of the National Vietnam Moratorium Committee. The other delegates from MSC were Brian Horan, Pat Scott, Dan Beck, Dorothy Byers, David Ball, Larry Steel, and Elke Pugel.[611]

The MSC College Republicans had lost a great deal of steam from the previous year, when the MSC delegation was not seated at their state convention. After the election of Nixon, the

MSC chapter of the College Republicans was on the decline. Also, it was lacking the leadership of Wanda Graham.

History professor Charles Angeletti was appointed Director of the In-Service Ethnic Studies Program for Office of Economic Opportunity in Denver. Angeletti was teaching a course on Racism in American History to the employees of Denver Opportunity. In announcing his appointment, the director of Denver Opportunity said Angeletti's courses at MSC showed how race occupied a central place in the history of the US.[612]

Greg Branum and Bernard Robinson formed a second African-American organization called the Black Student Alliance. They were unhappy with the AASU and their diminished roles in the restructured organization.[613]

In April, former student body president Doug Holcombe announced his candidacy for the Democratic nomination for the State House of Representatives from Denver's District 6. Holcombe had been one of three candidates who staged an unsuccessful write-in campaign for legislative seats two years earlier. Holcombe was a part-time elementary school teacher as well as an assistant dean of students at MSC. He said he was running to try and solve the sad frustration of young people, Hispanos and the poor of his district.

Holcombe had been named an outstanding student at MSC and was listed in Who's Who in American Colleges in addition to serving as student body president. Bob Bowen was named as his campaign manager. Many MSC students worked on the campaign.[614]

Student power again. CCHE caves and gives MSC a new ZDS computer.
Photo Courtesy of Metropolitan State University of Denver.

KENT STATE AND JACKSON STATE

The war was still an issue. Another moratorium was held that spring at the state Capitol, and Jane Fonda spoke. THE PAPER noted that conspicuously absent from the assembly was the large number of straight, middle class people that had turned out for previous moratoriums. The young, black, power coalition was all that was left, THE PAPER said.[615]

Things were about to change.

A little over a week after the moratorium, the nation was stunned. National Guard troops killed four unarmed, peaceful student demonstrators on the campus of Kent State University in Ohio. That morning, 500 students had demonstrated against the US invasion of Cambodia. The governor called in the National Guard because he and the university president were determined to maintain law and order.

When students did not disperse, the National Guard raised their weapons. Someone threw rocks, the Guard opened fire and unarmed students were mowed down. Student observers were horrified. Immediately, the university president closed school and told all 20,000 students to leave campus. The bodies of Jeffrey Miller, Alison Krause, William Schroeder and Sandy Scheur lay dead on the grass of their university.[616]

Word hit MSC early that Friday morning. Emotions on campus ranged from shock to rage. Around the nation, riots were breaking out on college and university campuses. President Phillips refused calls to close the school. Many faculty members cancelled classes; others used the class to discuss what had just happened. Nixon was on TV demanding law and order be preserved.

Governor Love was in Europe trying to cajole the Olympic Committee to designate Denver as the site for the Winter Olympics. Lieutenant Governor Mark Hogan was acting governor. He called MSC student body president Bob Bowen, and asked him to come to the governor's office. Newly elected but not sworn in student president Dave Ball was working to keep the Metro campus calm. The two students had put out a joint statement urging students to remain non-violent.

Hogan wanted to keep students around the state from rioting like early reports indicated was happening around the nation. Bowen told Hogan if he called out the National Guard, like many were calling for, there would certainly be violence. It was Guardsmen who had just killed students. Their very presence would illicit an angry response. Hogan agreed. Governor Love had already phoned Hogan, telling him to call out the National Guard at college campuses, but Hogan refused.

The acting governor set up a command center in the his office. Student leaders from the major colleges came to the Capitol and met with Hogan to see what could be done to keep things quiet. The leaders that could not get to Denver spoke to Hogan on the phone and received assurances that the Guard would not be called out. Bowen spoke to the militant leaders he had earlier asked not to disrupt the moratorium and begged for restraint. Some spoke on the phone with Hogan, who gave them assurances that Colorado would deal with the massacre appropriately.

At the University of Denver, students assembled on the campus green in angry protest and refused to leave. The University's Chancellor, Maurice Mitchell, wanted the Guard called in. When Hogan refused, he contacted Denver Police Chief George Seaton and arranged for the police to forcibly remove the students just before dawn on the following Sunday.

Seaton gave Lt. Governor Hogan a heads-up. At 4 am, Hogan went to the DU campus where a phalanx of police in riot gear was already lined up. He told the commander, "If you want to remove the students, you need to take me first." The police stood down since TV cameras were there, ready to record the event. No arrests were made and no one got hurt.[617]

When Governor Love returned the next week, he called out the Guard to clear the DU campus. By then, the anger had subsided and there was minimal bloodshed. DU Chancellor Mitchell told the press that students asked him to call in the Guard, fearing for their safety. Students told a different story, however.

Colorado was one of the few places in the nation where there was no violence in the aftermath of the attack by the National Guard on the students at Kent State.

In the next issue of THE PAPER, on the front page, there was a quote: "The streets of our country are in turmoil. The universities are filled with students rebelling and rioting. Communists are seeking to destroy our country, Russia is threatening us with her might and the republic is in danger. Yes danger from within and without. We need law and order!" It was written by Adolph Hitler.[618]

Students also provided their reactions to Kent State. Gordon Hollis wrote:

"What did you do last week? While the country's students and faculties were marching, talking, and even burning what did you do? Did you generally go about your business as if nothing was happening? If so, you are a dullard...It makes no difference what side you are on; it only matters that you are on a side... To say, in effect, that my class today is more important than my help in solving a national crisis is stupid. You are not participating in "education." You are participating in a diploma mill with you, yourself, a piece of paper at the other end" [619].

R.G. Weaver, a business student who had earlier picketed the state over computers, wrote:

"In a recent speech Spiro Agnew told his audience, "Radical campus demonstrators should be treated as if they were wearing brown shirts or white sheets. What role did this speech play in the decisions of one guardsman to fire on a crowd of demonstrators? How easily it must be—in the madness of a mob—to apply the required pressure to a trigger to end the life of four people if this action is condoned or encouraged by the vice-president. The greater blame must not lie on the irre-

sponsible trigger finger of the guardsman—but on the irresponsible tongue of the man who controls thousands of fingers."[620]

Bob Smith, a member of the MSC chapter of the SDS, wrote:

"*The surest test of leadership quality is the reaction of a leader to a crisis. The moral crisis generated by the invasion of Cambodia and the massacre at Kent State was the moment to test our leaders here at Metro. They all failed. The recently elected student government, by its evasion and paralysis, has given us a sneak preview of what to expect from them in the coming months....We truly deserve the label of "second-rate" school that students at other schools pinned on us.*"[621]

Pete Klismet spoke for the conservative students by attacking Marty Bronstein:

"*The actions by the National Guardsmen at Kent state were extremely unfortunate; but obviously spontaneous. How anyone can summarily state that this was a plot of the Nixon Administration to overthrow anti-war dissidence is totally unbelievable to me. What I say is Guardsmen were driven by a natural human response to a threatening situation—self-preservation. Take facts into consideration before you run around shooting your mouth off about student radical annihilation plot. In the first place who in the hell besides a bunch of similarly inclined, mental invalids is going to be naive enough to fall for something this absurd?*"[622]

Then, Eduardo Lucero had more to say about the reaction to Kent State than the killings:

"*Where were all these people when my people needed them? How come over 400 US colleges can protest the killing of four Kent State students, and yet, when a Chicano gets his head busted for protesting the inhumanity of the great and powerful United States, nobody cares, and nobody is concerned enough to close down even one college. Chicanos have been killed by the National Guard as well as the Police... Is a Chicano not worth as much as a Kent student? What is the difference between a berserk national Guardsman and a berserk Denver Cop? Ask Rich Castro or Tony Ornelas. No hermanos, I don't think they really care about us.*"[623]

The following week, students nationwide were calling for a national student strike to protest the killings. MSC was divided over the idea.

Carol Stuckey interviewed former student president Bob Bowen about the incident. He stated that Kent State was tragic and "if it is proven that the National Guard was not fired upon first, they should be tried for manslaughter. Until we change the political system that we live in, and the present leadership, we're forced to play by the rules set down by the establishment. I think the peace movement has failed because they haven't successfully taken over the political system. Ten people in a voting booth are more effective than 100 people in Civic Center," he asserted.[624]

On the Thursday after Kent State, 800 students from MSC and UCD gathered at the Capitol to protest Kent State and the expansion of the war in Indochina. After various factions fought over the loudspeaker, two or three hundred took to the streets carrying a black casket. Then 200 demonstrators marched to UCD and closed down the school. The demonstration finally dissipated when the police broke it up. MSC organizers said the march was taken over by radicals.

The next day, classes were suspended for a few hours so students could attend a memorial service in the student center. Many students didn't agree with the fact classes were suspended, and they took their dissatisfaction out on the memorial by not attending and persuading others not to attend.[625]

Then, shortly after midnight on May 15, just eleven days after the murder at Kent State, two students were killed and twelve wounded at Jackson State College in Jackson, Mississippi. At least 140 rounds were fired by 40 police officers on about 100 unarmed African-American students who were protesting the war. This was a flash point, and rioting spread across campuses and cites around the nation.

This set off another firestorm of protests across the nation. Students and some faculty went on strike on 441 campuses around the country. At Metro, the MSC Concerned Committee had a meeting to discuss joining the strike, and students who were both for and against showed up.[626]

During a discussion in Bob Clifton's political science class, students kept asking, "What difference does it make?" It became apparent that there was a need to do something immediately, so the students walked out of the class and went to President Phillips's office. Other students joined them and about 70 or 80 students crammed into Phillips's office for a 30-minute silent memorial.

Phillips allowed the group to use his office but he left, saying he had a meeting to attend. Clifton later wrote in THE PAPER that Phillips "might have stayed and learned how to share his feelings, which would have demonstrated that he understood the students' feelings." Clifton added, "If the leaders of the nation understand there might be hope again and life will be meaningful."[627]

King Harris, Al Lewis, Wilt Flemon and others stormed the *Rocky Mountain News* to protest the way the *News* downplayed the killings at Jackson State. The group received a promise from Jack Foster, editor of the *News*, that it would carry a page one story about the slayings at Jackson State College.

The *News* had printed the story about the Jackson State killings on page 14; whereas the story about the Kent State killings was printed on page one. The students asked city editor Michael Howard about the placement. He replied, "You don't know what time that story came on the wire," saying it came out after 1:00 p.m. and page one had already been finished.

The group left and went back to MSC, but returned to the *News* at 3 p.m. with Rachel Noel, assistant professor of sociology. The group of 50 was met at the door by Howard, Vincent Dwyer (managing editor) and William Fletcher (business manager). A group of about 15 were ushered into editor Jack Foster's office. While that meeting took place, Howard went to the MSC student center to talk with the remainder of the protestors for 45 minutes. The paper did print a 10-inch story on the front page, plus related articles.[628]

President Phillips called an emergency meeting of the faculty at the Denver Auditorium. The purpose was to decide what policy the school would follow concerning those students who wanted to leave school for the balance of the quarter and work in the community against the war and the violence being inflicted on students. Phillips gave speakers of the MSC Concerned Committee and those in opposition to the strike two minutes each to express their views. Beth Brimmer spoke for the opposition; Pete Bonaker spoke on behalf of the MSC Concerned Committee.[629]

After debate, which was hot at times, the Faculty Senate endorsed a resolution that condemned the use of violence to quell peaceful demonstrations. In addition, the resolution asserted, "Because the President of the United States has exceeded his constitutional authority by invading a foreign country without a Congressional Declaration of War; We suggest that the president is in violation of the trust bestowed upon him by the people of the United States, and we request the immediate withdrawal of all American troops from Cambodia."

They also called for the withdrawal of troops from Vietnam, saying, "Furthermore, since the issue of the Vietnamese War is clouded with rhetoric; and since former presidents have made it quite clear that the United States involvement in Southeast Asia was to stop communist expansion abroad in order to prevent communist aggression on American soil, we request that the President of the United States and the Joint Chiefs' of Staff either justify the presence of US troops in Southeast Asia as necessary for the protection if the American people at home, or order their immediate withdrawal."

The faculty resolution added, "We condemn the insulting, polarizing rhetoric used by the officials of the national Government as divisive, inexcusable and demeaning not only to the university and college communities, but also to the people of the United States. We also condemn the similar insulting, polarizing rhetoric used by that small minority of students, which is likewise divisive, inexcusable, and demeaning to university and college community and the people of the United States."

The faculty also supported the request of a number of students to leave school without penalty for the remainder of the quarter, stating, "If a student feels he can better himself by taking part in activities other than those in the classroom, that he be enabled to take his grade in a class as of May 5 or take a WP or an Incomplete in a course without prejudice."[630]

There was a rally by the Afro-American Student Union (AASU). Jeff Thomas, an AASU leader, told the gathering, "When you walk on campus today your life isn't worth a plugged nickel." He said a way to stop the killings was to "put the clubs down" and start looking at others as individuals. He urged the group to start doing something constructive.

King Harris told the mostly white crowd that many of them were liars and hypocrites. "You dig the rhetoric," he said, "but are you willing to get off your ass? I challenge each of you to stand up and tell the ruling class that no longer will you tell me how to run my life, that a black man is less than human. The day has arrived when black people and brown people are no longer defined. We define ourselves."

Professor Gwen Thomas recalled an old saying that instead of landing at Plymouth Rock, the rock should have landed on the Pilgrims. "It's not a bad idea," she said. "The Puritan ethic started with hypocrisy and never once admitted to itself its basic hypocrisy." Norm Pacheco, an MSC student, urged students and faculty to participate in a weekend fast in front of the Denver police headquarters to protest police brutality.[631]

Later, four hundred students crammed the student center to voice their support for the faculty resolution. MSC closed at noon the next day so students could attend a memorial at the Denver Auditorium for the students killed and injured at Jackson State. Dean of students, Dr. Robert Thompson, said the college suspended classes in memory of the students killed at Kent State, so it would be fair to suspend classes in memory of the Jackson students.[632]

The veteran's student group at MSC was not happy that classes were called off. They protested and wrote letters to the editor. King Harris joined them, but for different reasons. He said that closing the school is what the "bigoted establishment wants us to do."[633]

In the spring of 1970, a bad moon had indeed risen.

In the midst of all the anger and protests over Kent State and Jackson State, MSC landed a new wrestling coach. Frank Powell, who had been head wrestling coach at Adams State College, resigned and accepted that position at MSC, effective in September. Dr. Powell had worked with Dean McKinney at Adams State. Later, Powell became head of the HPER department. Fortunately, the cloud over the future of intercollegiate athletics had been lifted after the third student vote on the matter earlier that spring[634]

Also in May, AHEC was established to oversee development of the Auraria higher education complex. This new board replaced the Auraria Working Committee which was established earlier by the CCHE. The members of the first Auraria board were: Leigh Norgren, Leland Luchsinger, Betty Naugle, Dr. Kenneth Phillips, Joseph Coors, Dr Joe J. Keen and Dr. Frank Abbott.[635]

Senator Gale McGee (R-Wyoming) gave the commencement address for 379 Metro State graduates. He told the audience, "Extremists today are no different than in the McCarthy era. Both deny their opponents the right to speak. They are no more interested in real dialogue and communication than their right-wing counterparts a couple decades ago. This is not only intolerant, it is illiterate," he said.

He added that the atmosphere surrounding Vietnam was no different than before World Wars I and II. But it was much more difficult to make intelligent decisions in 1970 than it was ten or twenty years earlier. The reason, he said, was that "people were confronted with too much information." They can't digest the tremendous volume of fact and opinion that is poured on them daily by newspapers, magazines, radio, and television.

It seemed strange to hear a speaker at college commencement badmouth information. (If he thought people received too much information then, what would he say about the Internet and 24-hour cable news today?)[636]

This was how the spring quarter ended, with the pall of death and violence hanging over every college and university in the nation, and deep divisions between students who were at odds over what the appropriate response should be, not only to the murders of their fellow students on campuses, but to the war in general. Kent State and Jackson State changed things significantly. Many students who previously were not radical found themselves radicalized by those events and the nation's lack of response.

MSC Faculty Senate met at the Denver Auditorium and passed a resolution demanding an end to the Vietnam war and criticizing the violent crackdown on demonstrators at Kent State and Jackson State. *Photo Courtesy of Metropolitan State University of Denver.*

CHAPTER 14

Riding Out the Storm

Riders on the storm, riders on the storm
Into this house we're born, into this world we're thrown
Like a dog without a bone, an actor out on loan
Riders on the storm
"Riders on the Storm" The Doors[637]

Things in America changed after Kent State and Jackson State, and things changed at Metropolitan State College as well. There was a new student government facing a new set of challenges. The once small, intimate college was growing. The days where nearly every student knew the names of all his or her fellow students were gone forever.

MSC was soon to have a permanent home—albeit a home it reluctantly had to share with its longtime nemesis. Planning was finally underway for Auraria and many decisions needed to be made but students were going to be involved. After the turmoil of spring quarter, most students were hoping for a bridge over troubled waters.

SUMMER AND FALL OF '70

MSC enrolled 2,146 students that fall, beating the previous year's enrollment of 1,771. Those students had 214 courses to choose from. Eighteen new faculty members were added, including two former students: Bernie Valdez and Jim Waggoner.[638]

Peter Boyles signed up for a single course that summer—a history class taught by Professor Steven Leonard. Boyles admitted in a 2013 interview that he was lost before he enrolled in Metro. Dr. Leonard suggested he take that class. At the end of the summer, Boyles picked up his grades and while walking down West Colfax it hit him: he actually had a college class credit. That was a really big deal. Boyles went on to get his degree at MSC and his MA at DU. Today he is host of a popular radio talk show.

The Post published a feature story on Steven Edwin Zimmerman, who was the last graduate to get a diploma at MSC's spring commencement. Zimmerman had been stricken with polio at 2 1/2 years of age and was wheeled onto the stage to get his degree. As a student, he carried a full class load and worked as a cartographic technician for the US Forest Service. To get his teaching certificate, he taught psychology at Lakewood High School for a quarter. He planned to get a master's degree in rehabilitation counseling.[639]

Charlie Roos of *The Post* gave a hearty endorsement to an article written by MSC student Robert Boyce about the college's parking problem. "I am sure that the 5,000 MSC students can't understand why the state has provided no money for student parking," Roos wrote, noting Boyce was a student with a part-time job and a very small income, and that parking fees and tickets had taken a large portion of his finances.

Roos noted that the police had been very zealous in ticketing students who are parked just a few minutes over the allotted time. The DPD's budget might be better spent on other things than to harass students, he suggested, adding that maybe the legislature should provide some money for a few student parking lots. Fat chance! [640]

There was a break in the investigation to find whoever threw the smoke bomb into a MSC classroom on January 23. A bench warrant was issued in June for the arrest of Eileen Samols, charging her with arson and conspiracy. Police alleged she was among four persons who tossed a phosphorous explosive into the classroom. Samols failed to appear for her preliminary hearing so Judge James Urso ordered her $1,500 bond forfeited and set a new bond of $10,000. Her co-conspirators, Daniel H. Cohen, David J. Gilbert and a third person also failed to appear. No motive was disclosed in the warrant.[641]

At the beginning of June, the Southern Baptists held their convention in Denver, and 15 African-American students from MSC confronted the delegates, demanding that they "live up to the precepts of Jesus Christ." Jefferson Thomas, one of the protestors, said, "Christians don't have any backbone in their Christian precepts." Thomas and others felt that the Baptists were still giving comfort to avowed segregationists, contrary to the teachings of Jesus.[642]

So what was the MSC community thinking in the summer of 1970? We can get an idea by reading what some students and faculty members published in *THE PAPER* at the time.

A student, Isetta Rawls, wrote an insightful editorial about population and environmental problems and what to do about them. She offered suggestions of what other things could be done, short of Chinese-style population control. Her ideas were revolutionary for 1970, suggesting things like high-efficiency furnaces, lead-free gas, compacting trash, recycling, and ending wasteful packaging including disposable bottles. The most far-out proposal of all: green roofs on buildings (like the one currently on MSU Denver's Student Success Building).

"I would love to hear a botanist and ecologist discuss the effect of those on the environment," she wrote. Too bad it took 40 years before people listened to her.[643]

History professor Charles Angeletti wrote a guest editorial entitled, "Myths I have heard," which summed up what many thought at MSC in 1970. He listed several myths and corrections to each.

Myth One: "Violence has never accomplished any good for American Society." He said that the history of our country is replete with examples of times when violence had been the indispensable instrument of social, economic, or political change.

Myth Two: "Our legal and political systems are open; therefore, conditions can be remedied and changes can occur from within." He called this absurd, saying many of our institutions were less open to change and reform than the political and legal systems of some of the so-called 'socialistic' countries.

Myth Three: "There is no place for violent revolution today." This is wrong, he said. "Read the Declaration of Independence. Many, if not all of the conflicts in our present strife-torn society could be resolved of only the democratic system would prove itself to deeply held equalitarian values.

Myth Four: "All power to the people, they know where it's at." There are rights which belong to all men, which need never be put to a popular plebiscite, or an elitist veto, he wrote.

Myth Five: "A revolution is no gentleman," Angeletti said. "The struggle may be a moral one; or it may be a physical one or it may be a moral and physical [one]; but it must be a struggle. Power concedes nothing without a demand. It never did and it never will."[644]

Julie Linicome, a 27-year-old married student with a husband and children, expressed the view held by many older, married students when she wrote a letter published in *THE PAPER*:

> *"A young girl directed an inner hostility at me…That girl could not understand my expression of fear in the face of extremism. She could not understand my plea for sanity, for sanity, in her eyes is evidently equated with apathy. I am amazed at the number of men and women who are involved in life to the extent that they would spend forty or more hours a week on the job and still enroll themselves in classes, and be active and involved members. I see people here at Metro night after night, who are a great inspiration to me. These people have set goals for themselves, and for the most part, see their own lives as part of the solution."[645]*

Summer also brought changes to *THE PAPER*. Not only was there new staff, but the publication was going high-tech. It acquired some cutting-edge technology to set the type.

THE PAPER had been relying on the *DU Clarion* to set its type, since PCs had not yet been invented. However, they acquired a new system consisting of two units: an IBM Selectric typewriter and a Selectric composer. The copy was typed on the Selectric typewriter and print-ready type came out the other end.

And there was more technology news that summer. In August, MSC finally got the new Xerox Sigma 5 computer it had been trying to get for more than a year. Earlier in the year, students had picketed the state to demand the computer.[646]

Curtis Wright, MSC business manager, announced that a new 54,000 square foot building was being built at 1350 Fox Street. It would house 37 classrooms, 51 faculty offices, and would have a 90-car parking lot. Wright said the college would use the building until after the completion of the Auraria project, which was at least four years out.[647]

During the summer, an educational program called *La Academia Del Barrio* had been organized by two MSC students, Virginia Lucero and Betty Castro. The program provided courses for young people living in the Westside. Instruction was offered in math, creative writing, English, reading, Mexican history, Spanish, dance, art and swimming. It was a success with about 55 students attending daily classes from June 22 through August 28.[648]

Another racial killing ripped the community in August, and it put MSC students in the news once again. A black educator named Roosevelt Hill was shot by a white soldier, Army Specialist 4th Class Ellis Leon Little, during a scuffle at a Mobile gas station in Colorado Springs following a dispute over a credit card. Little, who worked at the gas station, was cleared of wrongdoing by an El Paso county grand jury on the grounds it was self-defense. The African-American community was up in arms, saying the killing was murder.[649]

King Harris, chairman of the MSC Afro-American Student Union, announced that blacks would conduct their own investigation into the murder. He said that the AASU, the Black Student Union at the University of Colorado and Black United Denver (BUD) were all backing the probe, along with other members of the black community.[650]

In an attempt to prejudice public opinion against Hill, the district attorney released credit information supposedly obtained from the department store May-D&F. Eleven MSC students and faculty members picketed May-D&F to protest the alleged release of that credit information. Jerome Nemiro, president and general manager of May-D&F, responded that the store did not release the information and said, "No one ever asked us." Hearing that, District Attorney Russell back peddled at a press conference saying that the problem with Hill's May-D&F account had been straightened out but didn't explain how he got that credit information.[651]

Harris announced an economic sanction against the Mobil Oil Co which would include harassment of selected Mobil stations and they would continue until Mobil capitulated. In a full page ad, Mobile said the company didn't hold itself to blame for the shooting, and refused a demand of money to help the black community in Hill's honor. Eventually, the issue faded away.[652]

One thing this situation proved was that there were no walls between the community and this urban-oriented college.

In August, the summer commencement was held and 190 students received degrees. Rondie Keith, a recent MSC graduate, delivered the commencement address. There were 134 students who received bachelor's degrees, and 56 who received their associate degrees.[653]

The fall quarter started off with a new controversy. The MSC chapter of the SDS decided to run Metro's law enforcement program off the campus. The group applied to have a booth at registration to hand out literature and to obtain signatures on a petition demanding the program's elimination.[654]

Student president Dave Ball turned down the SDS's application for a booth. He was immediately criticized by SDS chapter president Bob Smith and others, who said Ball was denying the officially-recognized campus organization of its First Amendment rights. In an editorial, Smith said that Dean Thompson had approved the SDS table at registration. They said that by overruling Thompson, Ball was doing the dirty work for the administration.

Smith said that there was an organized effort to kick SDS out of Metro and he blasted Ball for "using every trick he can think of to prevent anyone from rocking the boat at Metro." Ball denied that he turned down the SDS the table under orders from the administration.[655]

SDS held a meeting and afterwards affirmed that they were not a terrorist organization and never had been. Bob Smith said that a group of students had left SDS in June of 1969 and formed the Weathermen, which was a terrorist group. But, Smith stated that the Metro SDS was not part of that group. He said that the SDS condemned terrorism and was only interested in building mass student struggles to fight the war, racism, and male chauvinism (e.g. ROTC, police science, war research, and racist low paying college employers) in concrete ways.[656]

Other students and faculty, calling themselves the silent majority, pushed back against efforts to get rid of police science. They said that there was no truth to the claim that police science courses lead to oppression. The answer, they asserted, was not to fight police repression with student oppression. The law enforcement department was there to educate policemen, not eliminate the ignorant cop, they said, adding, education makes cops more humane.[657]

No sooner had that controversy subsided when another one boiled over. An article appeared in *THE PAPER*, entitled "Damn the Bookstore." It mentioned how the bookstore ripped kids off in the selling of used books. (The bookstore was owned by Bargain Bookstore operating on contract with MSC.) The article pointed out how students were given just cents on the dollar when they sold a book back, then that same book would appear on the shelf with a huge markup.[658]

The bookstore manager, Gordon Johnson, said that the cost of books had remained fairly stable in view of the price increases in other segments of society. He said given the laws of supply and demand, used books had little value.[659]

Mike Bell, Tim Redfern, Bob Smith, and Fayez Abedaziz wrote a joint editorial that criticized what they called "legalized robbery" in the college bookstore and other abuses. They pointed out that a cop had beaten up a student in the bookstore and they connected that beating to the law enforcement department, even though that seemed to be a stretch.

They also blasted the fact that work-study students only made $1.40 an hour at the college, and they likened that to slavery, saying work-study should start at $2.00 per hour. "This school and all others are service stations for the US economy pure and simple," they wrote. "We are sick and tired of it, too! We think massed student power confronting the big shots is the answer to cutting these cancerous growths out of Metro."

They finished, writing, "Keep after the bookstore, but direct your outrage at the guys responsible: The Metro administration! Informing the students is the most critical step; they'll take it from there Cops out of Metro! Decent wages for students! Check out Recruiters! Dare to struggle! Dare to win!"[660]

Unbeknownst to the administration or the bookstore, some students were getting retribution that year. A student took book orders from trusted students. Then at night, he entered the bookstore by climbing through the ceiling in the adjacent college center and stole the ordered books. He then sold them at a discounted price to his student customers.

(Several years later it was revealed that Tim Redfern, one of the authors of the "legalized robbery" article, was arrested in conjunction with a Watergate-style burglary in the Socialist Workers Party offices, and the offices of Congresswoman Pat Schroeder. It was revealed he had been an informant for the FBI, and he was paid to keep quiet about the Schroeder burglary.) There is no published evidence that Redfern was an informant while he was a student at Metro, but suspicions were high at the time that he was.[661]

(The Watergate investigation later revealed that much of the radical rabble-rousing on college campuses was actually instigated by FBI plants. These paid informants would incite trouble and sometimes entrap students to participate in order to build a case against them, or justify a crackdown by authorities. Many who otherwise might not have crossed the radical line were caught up in this practice. This was done to disrupt and discredit the anti-war effort. Unfortunately, some innocent MSC students had their reputations wrongly damaged.)

The fall enrollment continued to beat expectations. A total of 7,212 students enrolled, up from 5,944 in 1969, making MSC the fifth-largest school in the state. Of those, 4,808 were men and 2,404 were women. The number of women students increased by 642 (36 percent) over 1969. The number of women in Denver was only slightly less than men in 1970, but they still only made up only 33 percent of Metro's student body. Women were still under- served in higher education.

The number of veterans fell to 972 from the 1,165 who enrolled in 1969. The declining number of draftees accounted for that. Freshmen accounted for the largest number of students.

As was always the case, most students (3,607) came from Denver, with Jefferson County a distant second (1,108). A total of 1,336 transferred in from another college, many from a junior college. There were 50 foreign students, and 241 who signed up for the weekend college.[662]

About 1,000 students received financial aid that quarter, totaling around $630,000 in scholarships, grants, loans and work-study. The school had 27 baccalaureate degree majors, 18 minors and 16 associate degree voc-ed programs. There were 236 faculty members that quarter. In addition, the administrators, secretaries, clerks, etc. working for the school brought the payroll to $415,000 a month.

MSC occupied space in 16 buildings in a five-block area and the payments to owners for rent, utilities, plant operation and maintenance totaled $1.1 million in the 1970-71 fiscal year.

At the beginning of the quarter, the Denver City Council named four new interns from MSC: David M. Sonnenberg, Robert E. McRae, Albert Martinez and Stephen Cantrell.[663]

The new editor of *THE PAPER*, Frank O'Neil, tested the waters by writing an editorial stating that America was the world's best example of the double standard. He cited that Adams County District Attorney Floyd Marks sued a Denver company for polluting the Platte River and the judge accepted the company's word that they wouldn't do it again.

He went on blasting TV and newspaper coverage of the possible danger to a small group of American Jews in Jordan, while at home an equal number of Black Panthers were being killed and arrested daily. And he wrote, "You Indians hold on, we're going to help you now. That's why we still have all those cowboy heroes on TV killing you." Dr. Phillips received many angry calls after the article appeared. O'Neil did not realize it, but this was the beginning of the end for *THE PAPER*, as MSC knew it."[664]

The first archeological expedition in MSC's history happened in the fall of 1970. Dr. Jiri Vondracek, MSC anthropology professor who was originally from Prague, led the dig and salvage operation on property owned by the Woodmore Corporation west of Denver. The purpose was to improve the school's archeology curriculum, contribute to the archeology of the region and build a collection of archeological material at MSC. They expected to recover ancient bones.[665]

The newly formed MSC Faculty Federation held its initial fall quarter business session Oct. 14. Bob Clifton was elected the federation's executive secretary; Dr. Morton Ohlson, treasurer; Dr. Peggy Walsh, public relations; Dr. Donald Wall, membership. Dr, Warren Weston of the political science department presented the committee reports for Dr. Taylor. Dr. John Spradley and Elaine Cohen were selected to serve on the elections committee.[666]

Some other things happened that quarter. The parking committee met with Mayor McNichols about the parking problem at MSC. Dan Beck, the new committee chairman, told the mayor that MSC accounted for 4,000-4,500 vehicles in downtown Denver each day. Dean Thomson said, "The unavailability of adequate student parking space was one issue that could lead to Metro's ultimate failure as an urban institution. If we can't accommodate our current students' needs, it is doubtful we will be able to attract students in the future."

Beck threw out a proposal to allow students to park at Mile High Stadium and ride a shuttle bus to campus. He said that UCD students might participate as well. McNichols said it was basically a sound idea, but city would have to be reimbursed. After the cameras left, the students were shuffled to the office of the public works director, Richard Shannon. Without media pressure, it was clear the city was going to stall, not act.[667]

While MSC students were trying to get approval to park at Mile High Stadium, DURA was proposing parking lots for 6,000 cars in the Skyline project. MSC professor Joe Megeath called that plan a suicidal path. "Someone is confused," he wrote in a letter to the editor of *The Post*. "Mass parking is not synonymous with mass transportation. We must get people out of their automobiles," he added.

Professor Megeath sarcastically pointed out the fallacy of the policy. "The City is so committed to this concept of cleaner air, lighter traffic and a better downtown that they have proposed making room for 6,000 more cars. At a cost of $27 million, a mere $4,500 per parking space, it's a bargain." Then he explained the logical extension of this was a suicidal path. More parking spaces mean more cars, which lead to wider streets, and more cars, then more parking spaces "ad nauseum," he contended.

Megeath stated the solution to smog and congestion lay in the opposite direction. If no parking is available, people will demand and use an efficient mass transit system, he wrote. We have to stop self-destructive plans like taxpayer-supported massive garages," he asserted.[668]

Professor Megeath was doing what an urban college is supposed to do—finding solutions to the problems of the city. Unfortunately, it took eighteen years before anyone acted on his suggestion and started a mass transit system. Not surprisingly, the prime mover of the mass transit system was an MSC graduate.

Also that fall, Dr. Keats McKinney threatened to dismiss Dr. Gary Michael, assistant professor of philosophy, for not signing the loyalty oath. Michael said it set a bad precedent and legislators might try to amend the oath to imperil academic freedom. It was not oppressive but a step toward oppression, he said. McKinney docked his pay and said that he would be better off at a private institution. Professor Michael said he backed down because "it was the wrong cross to die on, and not worth losing a job over."[669]

MSC was the target of two more bomb threats in October that caused the evacuation of five of the 16 buildings of the invisible campus. The first threat was received at 9:05 a.m. The caller told the operator that a bomb had been placed in one of the newer buildings near the 500 block of W. Colfax. College officials evacuated the Gold and Fox buildings, the library and the student activities center. Police searched the buildings but no bomb was found.

A second call came in around noon. That caller said a bomb had been placed in the college book store. That building was also evacuated and searched, but no bomb was found either. Was there a connection to the warrants issued over the January bombing?[670]

In November, a recent graduate, Ralph W. Ege, class of 1970, began working to form an Alumni Association at MSC. He put together a meeting that included Roger Braun, James Kirtland, Margaret Haberland, Susan Holcombe, Ruth McEwen and Marvia Valdez. He said that three faculty would be appointed to advise the group. The group met, but unfortunately, nothing came of that effort.[671]

Once again, the Afro-American Student Union (AASU) distributed gift certificates to needy families for the holidays. Jill Wells and Donald Lowe were pictured in the *News* presenting a holiday gift certificate to Mrs. Fannie Leatherman. The certificate was a gift from Safeway Stores Inc. In addition, the AASU gave away 26 turkeys before Thanksgiving to deserving families.[672]

Ten members of the MSC police sciences club set up a blood pool at the Belle Bonfils Blood Bank, from which police officers and their families could draw blood without charge. Barry R. McCauley, chairman of the group, said the club had written to all municipal police departments and state and federal law enforcement agencies in the state, outlining the plan, but only the ATF replied. Personnel there applauded the plan, McCauley said. "With this pool, a police officer can get the blood he needs," McCauley said.[673]

White Mule welcomes students back
to the invisible campus.
*Photo Courtesy of Metropolitan State
University of Denver.*

THE 1970 ELECTIONS

Elections were held in November 1970, and as in past elections, MSC was involved. Many students were supporting Doug Holcombe's candidacy for state representative. The district he was running in had been ruled by a political boss, Mike Pomponio, for over thirty years. Only candidates supported by Pomponio made it on to the ballot. Needless to say, Holcombe was not supported by Pomponio having run against the machine as a write-in candidate two years earlier.

Students working for Holcombe discovered that Pomponio did not live in the district he controlled. Holcombe supporters challenged his residency at the Democratic credentials committee and won. Pomponio was disqualified as a delegate. With Pomponio politically wounded, Doug Holcombe narrowly missed getting top line in his primary against the incumbent, Dominick Coloroso.

Larry Steele wrote an editorial saying that this was unheard of in a district run by one man. "If change can come, this is the means by which it would take place," Steele wrote. "No one, not even the revered silent majority, can condemn the many students who want to promote change in this manner." (Pomponio was later replaced as the Democratic district leader by the former student body president, Bob Bowen.)[674]

Holcombe came close, but lost his primary bid in September. The fact that he had come close opened the door for other candidates, including other MSC graduates, to get elected to office.

Also in the summer of 1970, MSC journalism professor and former Marine, Greg Pearson, ran for Congress on the Republican ticket. He abandoned his previous hawkish views, and ran as a dove. Pearson only received 131 out of 1,200 votes at the pro-war Republican assembly. Pearson was asked how he felt about working within the system and he replied, "I made several absolute strategic blunders in this thing—I should not have waited until May 7 to get in."[675]

Pearson told *THE PAPER* that the people who were going to make changes were the people in the so-called establishment, the people who control the processes by pulling levers on voting machines. "And the people who are going to affect pulling of those levers are people like Bob Bowen and Frank O'Neil [new editor of *THE PAPER*], and I can cite 40-50 students here, who went through the mundane and lonely process of getting elected as a delegate. They've got a candidate [referring to Democrat Craig Barnes]," Pearson said.[676]

Later that summer, GOP congressional candidate Mike McKevitt spoke for an hour in Bob Clifton's national government class. He said that 70-80 percent of the crimes committed by juveniles are due to narcotics. "These modern-day Huck Finns are also involved in such activities as prostitution, assaults, even murder," adding that a poor upbringing and a permissive society were the reasons. One can only imagine how that indictment went over in a Bob Clifton class. At least McKevitt showed up for his one and only time on campus.[677]

Many students who had worked on the Holcombe campaign shifted their focus to Mark Hogan's gubernatorial campaign, Craig Barnes' congressional campaign and for the La Raza Unida candidates. Hogan was a consistent supporter of MSC, unlike the flip-flopping governor. He had played a pivotal role in passing the bill that allowed the college to open.

The MSC Young Dems held a rally for Mark Hogan organized by club president, Sonja Eldeen. He addressed the recent SDS controversy, saying, "don't keep the SDS out—let them meet and discuss their ideas openly." He also said, "I don't want to make the automobile the number one citizen in Colorado," advocating a mass transit program for Denver.[678]

Another candidate, George Garcia, the La Raza Unida candidate for lieutenant governor, came to Metro to seek student support. In 1968, Garcia had received his Associate degree in math at MSC. He said the La Raza platform was for localized government and local control of schools. He said La Raza would declare all of Denver's ghettos disaster areas and then ask for federal assistance to rebuild them.

Garcia said that Chicanos were worse off in Denver than blacks, noting that 82 percent of Chicanos who entered high school did not finish. He pointed out that the median education for the Chicano was 8.1 years, but for blacks it was 11.1 years. He said less than one percent of Chicanos went to college and less than half of them graduated.

Garcia said Metro was one of the better colleges in the state and it was not afraid to apply theory to reality. He said Metro could more do more for minority groups, but considering the age of the school at that point, criticism would be premature. One of the best things about Metro was the open door policy, he said. Elimination of the open door would deprive many people from at least having a chance at a college education.[679]

Meanwhile, an article in *THE PAPER* speculated that the Republican Party was dead on campus. It said the Republicans no longer had a liaison, and the author reminded students that Governor Love and other candidates would not even come to the campus. And, the article stated, "the two lonely souls at GOP headquarters said they knew of no Republicans at MSC, and didn't care if Republicans showed up there to speak."[680]

Even though Governor Love did not accept an invitation to come to MSC, student president Ball criticized him at a news conference for his campaign literature, which described MSC as a community college. "The governor makes all appointments to the Board of Trustees, signs all bills pertaining to education and approves all appropriations, yet he still does not know who governs this major state institution."

The statement to which the students objected was found in a brochure put out by the Committee for John Love and John Vanderhoof. It read, "The State Board for Community Colleges and Occupational Education governs a brand new system of community colleges, including such new schools as Metropolitan State in Denver, El Paso Community College in Colorado Springs, and the Auraria Higher Education Center and Denver Community College." Almost nothing in that statement was accurate.

"Perhaps Gov. Love had been too busy hunting bandits in Eastern Colorado, antelope in WY, Kudus in Africa and federal appointments in Washington," Ball said. "He is the only major state official who has not taken the minimal time or trouble to look over facilities or talk to students and faculty," Ball stated. Perhaps Governor Love did not read the bill he signed into to law that created Metro in the first place.

Ball's statement was endorsed by the student senate, and by presidents of several MSC campus organizations, including the MSC Republicans, MSC Business Club, MSC Pre-Med Club, UMAS, MSC Drama Club and MSC Young Democrats. Dave Zimmerman, speaking on behalf of the stealthy MSC Republican club, said the campaign statement "doesn't speak too well of the Republican Party or the leadership."[681]

Just before the November election, a series of candidate forums were held in the student center, and they were well attended. In addition to Hogan, Craig Barnes and other Democratic candidates spoke. One day, however, Larry Steele invited J.D. MacFarlane, the Democratic candidate for attorney general, to address students. Only Larry Steele showed up.[682]

It seemed like speaking at MSC was the kiss of death for candidates that year. None of the candidates who courted the votes of MSC students won on Election Day. All the candidates who stayed away were elected. Yikes.

The student government held its class elections that fall as well. Dave Ball requested a referendum to raise student fees $2.00 per quarter to provide funds to provide emergency assistance to students. The referendum would provide more money for the program established the previous year.

Ball explained the fee increase, saying, "The purpose of the referendum is to accomplish what should have been accomplished long ago for the students of the college. The money generated will go into a student support committee fund, administered by students, and will be used to finance emergency and short term loans, book rentals, and tutorial programs for students who find themselves in academic or financial difficulty at one time or another during their college career."[683]

Ball said he hoped to get matching funds from government or private sources. "It is time to show in a concrete way that we are committed to the ideal upon which this college was founded—that every student who has the motivation and the ability to get an education can go as far and as fast and as high as he can," Ball said, "regardless of financial of ethnic considerations. I do not believe that $2.00 is too much to ask of our students because the money is so urgently and justly needed. We cannot let even one more student flunk out because they do not have money for textbooks."

J. Nicholas McCammon, aka The Militant Mugg-Wump, wrote an editorial against Ball's proposal calling Ball a "con artist."

On MSC Election Day, students defeated the student fee referendum 934 to 594. There were several reasons. One was the program had a bad name because the year before, Greg Branum did not repay his note and ended up being accused of assaulting the student body president. In addition, students were not happy paying fees for a student center at Auraria they would never see, and were wary of fees.

Dave Zimmerman, head of the College Republicans and a member of the Ball administration, wrote an editorial about the referendum saying, in an urban-oriented college he was baffled that students who voted to approve intercollegiate athletics did not approve the loan program. That may have been the last time a Republican would publicly advocate raising fees and giving the money to disadvantaged students.[684]

Class officers were elected. They were: senior senator, Ken Sherwood; junior president, Dan Beck; junior senator, Virginia Lucero; sophomore president, Sonja Eldeen; sophomore senator, Russ Barrows; freshman president, Greg Huntzinger; freshman senator, Sharon Jones. Kathy Rosengrant and Susie McDougal were elected to the curriculum committee.[685]

Dr. Stephen Leonard announced in December that the MSC Center for Urban History had been listed in the *National Oral History Report*, an annual publication. The Center was established in 1967 and it sought to preserve local historical data of all types. Inquiries came from many publications, including *The NY Times*, he said.[686]

A HORSE WITH NO NAME

I've been through the desert on a horse with no name
It felt good to be out of the rain
In the desert you can remember your name
Cause there ain't no one for to give you no pain
  - "A Horse with No Name" America[687]

Winter enrollment was down to 6,123 students from the 7,212 in the fall. Of those, 117 were in the weekend college. According to forecasts, there should have been 6,500 students winter quarter. Enrollment was up, however, from the 5,303 of a year earlier. Jim Waggoner reported that most of the 1,706 students who failed to return said it was because they transferred to another school. Other reasons were financial problems or a work conflict.[688]

In December, Dan Beck, chairman of the parking committee, announced that a tentative agreement had been reached with the city of Denver and the Tramway Corporation to permit students at Metropolitan State College, the University of Colorado Denver Center and Community College of Denver to park their cars at Mile High Stadium while they attended classes. Students could park at the stadium and ride shuttle buses to the downtown facilities of the colleges. Fares would be 40 cents round-trip and the buses would run every 15 minutes from 7 a.m. to 10:30 p.m. Monday through Friday.

Students of the three schools would vote at January registration if they wanted to participate in the parking program. If enough interest was indicated and arrangements could be completed, the stadium will be open to student parking on Jan. 15. Students who park there will be charged a $2.50 parking fee per quarter. Beck said that money would be used to pay lot attendants and other costs of using the facility.[689]

Also, beginning in the fall quarter of 1971, MSC would begin a four-year B.A. program in early childhood education. The program was authorized by the CCHE and would train specialists in the education of preschool-age children and toddlers enable directors of nursery schools and day care centers to obtain their licenses and provide kindergarten teachers with necessary credentials for teacher certification.

Students who enrolled in the program would train in MSC's Child Day Care Center, which was then comprised of two buildings, one at 1038 Cherokee and the other at 1044 Cherokee. The two buildings accommodated 30 children—10 toddlers and 20 preschoolers. A budget of $17,500 had been allotted from student fees to help operate the center. The MSC students were part of a group of 40 area residents studying under a grant to become day care workers. The grant provided for 125 students to be trained through August 1971 at MSC or CCD.[690]

Another name change controversy surfaced, more serious than previous attempts. Dr. John Plachy, chair of the division of science and mathematics, started a name change campaign to counteract the mistaken impressions many people had about the college. "Our name doesn't indicate we have state status," Plachy said, "and for years we've been treated as a second-rate institution. We are a state college and I think the new name would be better as far as our relationship to the community and the state is concerned."

Plachy presented a petition to Dr. Ken Phillips, signed by seven of the eight deans at MSC, eight of nine division chairmen, and most of the 25 department chairs, in addition to 70 percent of the faculty and staff.

Mayor McNichols weighed in and endorsed the plan, following a meeting with a representative of a faculty committee which presented a petition urging the change. "In my opinion," McNichols said, "the name Colorado State College at Denver is superior to Metropolitan State College, and would be a desirable change." State Rep. Anthony Mullen (D-Adams County) and State Senator Roger Cisneros (D-Denver) had agreed to sponsor the proposed legislation in the coming session.[691]

President Phillips said that he neither supported nor opposed the change because the trustees hadn't met yet, but he said that the current name implied that MSC was a junior college supported by the city rather than the state. Betty Naugle, new chair of the trustees, said she believed there was a lot of merit in the request because of the confusion over the college's name, but said she didn't know if the petition would be on the board's agenda for the Jan. 15 meeting in Pueblo.

Student president Dave Ball said he opposed the proposed name change until students had a chance to weigh in on the matter. He said that the change had been considered by everyone except the MSC students. He indicated that a poll of student opinion would be taken at winter quarter registration.[692]

These annual name-change battles made going to Metropolitan State College seem like riding through the desert on a horse with no name.

ANOTHER NEWSPAPER CONTROVERSY

Just when it seemed like a quarter would pass without a controversy involving *THE PA-PER*, the editorial staff made sure that did not happen. The student newspaper published an excerpt from a book by Leah Fritz called "From Adam's Rib to Women's Lib: A Woman's View of the Clitoris."

Fritz wrote, "Once our eyes opened up in our long somnambulism, we found all around us vivid signs that we are all regarded as legitimate objects of men's pleasure—like food and wine; and that our pleasure, if permitted at all, is conceived of as an automatic out-growth of the male's: the lamb enjoying its slaughter! In many cases men freely admitted their sexual pleasure was increased to the extent that the female partner showed she was not enjoying the act and to be forced into it."

The newspaper did the unthinkable. It printed the words clitoris and orgasm. But when they printed the following paragraph from the book, they crossed the line: "Keeping women, who in early years exhibit superior intellectual abilities, chained to menial chores and the fine craft of aggravating men's egos, men can assure themselves that Beethoven is the final accomplishment in music, Shakespeare in poetry, Michelangelo in sculpture."[693]

Immediately, there was a firestorm of ferocity over "clit-gate" not seen since the Lauren Watson interview. Students attacked Frank O'Neil for printing it. Debra Winkleplick, the newly crowned Miss Metro State, wrote an editorial questioning whether "From Adam's Rib to Women's Lib: A Woman's View of the Clitoris" 1) belonged in *the paper*; 2) really represented woman's liberation (in its true sense); and 3) whether most women felt as Leah Fritz did toward sexuality and men. Winkleplick defended traditional male/female roles. "Men are stronger," she wrote, adding she felt this book was an attack on men.[694]

Men also took offense at the "filth and promiscuity" in the article. They were highly offended that *THE PAPER* printed the word clitoris. None of them had ever received any complaints about their sexual performance from the women in their lives.

The publication's problem was not the disgruntled men whose egos were bruised, or women standing by their men. It was the reaction of the administration. President Phillips said that he was getting all kinds of negative comments from Capitol Hill over the clitoris article. "This could cost us as much as a half to a full million dollars in the budget," he feared.

"The Board of Trustees has a very negative reaction to *THE PAPER* right now, mostly because of the kind of articles that have been written," Phillips said adding, that the Watson interview also concerned the trustees.

When asked if it was obscenity, Phillips replied, "I don't want to get myself in the position of declaring whether it is obscene or not. That's not the kind of argument anybody ever wins. It's the sort of thing that doesn't do us any good." He went on, "We've been working like hell for the past five and a half years to build the reputation of being an upright sort of college, and this sort of thing loses that kind of reputation very quickly…I've had business people stop me downtown, some very important business people, and tell me they just object to our newspaper."

Phillips cautioned, "The truth is if this persists on student newspapers of the campuses in the state college system the legislature will take over control of student funds." Phillips said that "if we had no newspaper, we'd have less trouble than we're having now."[695]

Earlier in the year, the CU regents had shut down the *Colorado Daily* because they did not like the editorial direction the paper was taking. The *Daily* was then taken over by private businessmen who operated it as a public newspaper.

The SDS criticized President Phillips for his comments and accused him of threatening to violate academic freedom just because the business community got him uptight. "We say shut it [*THE PAPER*] down right now or force Keats McKinney to hire young innovative teachers," the new SDS spokesman Tim Redfern wrote.[696]

The publications board held a hearing on five formal complaints it received on Leah Fritz's article. George Brunner, head of the business club, decried the overall content of *the paper*. Other complaints came from the Baptist Student Union and the Newman Club, a Catholic organization. Orson Brinker, associate professor of mathematics, filed a letter signed by 25 faculty members blasting the extreme political and social positions of *THE PAPER* and suggested that the student and faculty senates establish guidelines.

The tone of the discussion prompted the editor, Frank O'Neil, to retain an attorney. Dean Bob Thompson suggested that a referendum on *THE PAPER* be held in lieu of censorship.

On November 16, on a 4-1 vote, the board of publications dismissed all charges against *THE PAPER* but one. During the two-and-a-half hour meeting, *THE PAPER*'s staff presented petitions, letters of support and a statistical content analysis of the publication in their defense. The Police Science Club even supported the student paper. The board ruled that the charges didn't detail specific examples of alleged "unsound journalism and indecency," and were beyond its scope of authority.

The remaining charge, brought by George Bruner, dealt with alleged violations in the canon of journalism in connection with the story on the women's lib movement. The writer of that story, Leah Fritz, spoke of female sexual response. Bruner cited a Masters' and Johnson's book, "Human Sexual Response," and said the story lacked truthfulness and accuracy. The board called the issue "medical" and didn't rule on it. The board took no action on the remaining charge. A bullet was dodged but only for the time being. [697]

Shortly after the Fritz article was published, three MSC students announced they were going to bring the woman's liberation movement to Metro. Trudy Sauter, Ann Bennett and Claudia Guiet were heading the effort. Their main objective was education of the local female population.

"Before anything can be accomplished, women must be educated about oppression, suppression and about woman's lib—its function and goals," Guiet asserted. "The woman's frustrations must be brought out to the point where they want action and are willing to act." The women said this might take a long time and the major goal of any woman's organization is to restore to women their respect and their rights.

"Wake up, look around us and see the image of women as shown in movies, TV, pop music, commercials," Guiet stated. "Take note of some common phrases pertaining to you—'just like a woman,' 'apple pie and motherhood' and 'a woman's place is in the home.' Is the plastic image of a Vogue woman all there is to you? Are you really as dumb and helpless as they say? We have been fed this bullshit for generations," Guiet declared, "and it is time to come together." [698]

And so the battle for gender equality began at MSC.

It seemed like it would never end, but the year 1970 finally drew to a close. The Denver Broncos finished their first season in the new NFL with a 5-8-1 record. They had started out 3-0 but faltered after that. The highlight was that attendance at their final game at Mile High Stadium that season was 51,001. From then on, it became very hard to get a ticket to a Broncos game in Denver.

The Colorado Buffaloes posted a winning 6-5 record and ranked 19th in the AP poll. The bad news is they lost at home to their rival, the Nebraska Cornhuskers. The Buffs played three televised games and lost two of them.

The Roadrunner basketball team finished the first season with a 0-26 record. Despite their record, the Roadrunners played their hearts out, but not many people watched.

"M*A*S*H" and "Five Easy Pieces" were the top movies that year. Simon and Garfunkel's "Bridge over Troubled Water", The Carpenters' "(They Long to Be) Close to You" and "American Woman" by The Guess Who were the top three songs.

In 1970, 6,081 Americans died in Vietnam. While students, faculty, and staff of MSC celebrated New Year's Eve in 1970, 334,600 young American men and women were still fighting in the jungles of Indochina, two years after Nixon promised to end the war.

CHAPTER 15

Changes...

Ch-ch-changes
Pretty soon now you're gonna get older
Time may change me
But I can't trace time
I said that time may change me
But I can't trace time
"Changes" David Bowie[699]

It seems that big announcements always seem to happen around New Year's. The year 1971 was no different.

A BIG CHANGE IS COMING

In January, MSC President Ken Phillips suddenly announced that he would resign his position at the end of spring quarter. He said his resignation was due to the pressures of the times and of the position. "I have been here five and a half years and the pressures have been mounting. It has been a strenuous job." He said it had nothing to do with recent student criticism of him detailed in *THE PAPER*, or nothing to do with any group.[700]

(At the time, there were whispers around campus that some African-American students threatened to throw him out his tenth floor window. Phillips never confirmed that, no evidence ever surfaced and no one ever apologized for, or took credit for, such a threat.)

Phillips was in a no-win situation during much of his last two years at Metro because of the times, as he said in his explanation for the resignation. The Vietnam War, the fight by minorities for social justice and the rising women's movement all meant that he was under constant pressure from some group making demands or complaining about a policy or about a certain faculty member. He always listened carefully, and more often than not, sided with students on the issues.

Nevertheless, Phillips was almost always blasted by someone over every decision he made. When he closed the college to allow students to attend memorials for Dr. King and the students at Jackson State, he was attacked. When he wouldn't close the school for other events, he was blasted. He was regularly accused of institutional racism by minority students, and occasionally by some faculty members. At the same time, he was attacked by some white students who thought he gave in to minorities too often.

Phillips was under immense pressure from the trustees, legislators, and members of the business community. They objected to things that were published in the student newspaper, and to things that occurred on campus, like the antiwar protests and other demonstrations. Many in the community wanted him to expel the rabble rousers and criticized him for not doing so. Phillips became the scapegoat for the times.

In a 2013 interview recorded by his son, also named Ken Phillips, Dr. Phillips added a little clarity to the reason for his resignation. There had been threats to him and his family. This became too much. Here are his words:

"Well, as you know, the '60s was a very difficult time. We started in '65, and we were every so often getting bomb threats and fire bombs thrown into windows... It was a very trying time; kind of a stupid time, but very trying. I was getting threats that people were going to shoot me and people were going to blow up my car and stuff like that. And they threatened my family and threatened me with bombs and things like that. So it got to be quite a pain in the neck and strenuous."[701]

Besides the personal threats, there was another factor in his resignation: the bomb scares and bomb incidents. Phillips reflected on the fact that he could not catch a break when it came to bombs. He was criticized for evacuating buildings, but knew if he didn't, he'd be blasted for that as well. He said this:

> *"And then, of course, every time we'd get a bomb threat we'd empty the buildings that the bomb threat was in; and we got a lot of criticism from some of the key people in the area. They felt we didn't need to empty the buildings. And in discussing this with some of them, they said 'you are over-reacting.' And I'd say ok, let's assume that there is a bomb in there and it goes off, and we lose a lot of college age students. Who do you think is going to get criticized for that? I said 'you won't, but it will be us.' So anyway, it was a very trying time."*

His son, Ken, said that his father believed that if he didn't get another job, he would soon be dead from the pressure. The job would kill him.[702]

Shortly after the announcement of his resignation, President Phillips was named recipient of the 1970 Ralph M. Schwab Memorial Award for Citizenship by the Metro Denver Board of Realtors. He was honored for his work in getting Metropolitan Sate College up and running in a short time, and for getting it accredited in five years. This was the first of many awards he would receive after announcing his resignation.[703]

The resignation shocked the college, but it also created a new challenge: how to pick a replacement. When Dr. Phillips was hired, the trustees made the decision alone. They had a search committee, but they did not have to contend with existing faculty and staff, who had a vested interest in the outcome. And they did not have to deal with students. The college existed, at the end of the day, to serve students, whether anyone besides students understood that or not.

The trustees began setting up a selection committee comprised of members of the trustees, administrators, faculty, students and others. This group, called the Institutional Advisory Committee, would interview candidates and make recommendations to the trustees. The debate over the make-up of the committee was not unlike the battle going on at the Paris peace talks, which were stalled over the shape of the table. Many faculty and students were concerned that their voices were not adequately represented on the Institutional Advisory Committee.

On February 3, the MSC Faculty Federation announced the creation of a faculty-student committee designed to acquaint the board of trustees with a broad spectrum of opinion that was not found on the selection committee as it was proposed. This faculty-student committee would tender advice on the selection of the new MSC president. The federation was joined by other concerned faculty members in the meeting held at the Wyler Auditorium in the basement of the Denver Public Library.

A committee of seven faculty members was chosen, including: Dr. John Spradley, English; Dr. Brooks Van Everen, history; Dr. Donald Taylor, sociology; Dr. Peggy Walsh, history; Dr. William Rhodes, philosophy; Dr. Wilton Flemon, Afro-American Studies; and Mr. David Sandoval, Hispano Studies. Students were invited to select seven students to sit on the committee. Those would be chosen through normal student processes.

Dr. Van Everen, the federation's executive secretary, said it was important to preserve the integrity of faculty and student opinion. He said that federation members did not believe that the Institutional Advisory Committee would reflect the true constituency of MSC. He stated that students should have more than two members on the committee of ten, and that a committee which excludes representation from minorities can't be considered democratic or representative.[704]

The next day, Feb. 4, the MSC faculty senate approved a motion to enlarge the committee to include a total of 10 student representatives. The following day, Dr. H. Grant Vest, executive secretary for the trustees, quickly kicked that idea to the curb. He reaffirmed the trustees' position that the committee should include only two students and not exceed 12 members. So the faculty had to either fight or surrender.

Dave Ball, MSC student body president, asked the faculty senate to reaffirm its original position and increase the size of the committee by naming 10 students. He argued that the trustees were making a mistake because they had failed to take into consideration the diversity of MSC's population.

There was immediate pushback to Ball's request. One unnamed college administrator described the situation as a question of whether the trustees or the students were going to run the college. Dr. Lloyd K. Herren, chairman of MSC's music department, sided with the unnamed administrator and argued that two students on a 12-member committee amounted to *more than* equal representation.

Herren said the faculty was caught between a rock and a hard place—one being the trustees; the other a few loud students. He said there were some faculty members acting like students and some students acting like faculty members. In reply, some students suggested that Dr. Herren take a remedial math class and learn about percentages, ratios and proportion.

A new proposal to bring the advisory committee into conformity with the trustees' requirements was presented to the faculty senate. It called for nine faculty, two students and one administrator to serve on the committee. As proposed, two of the nine faculty members were to represent the Hispano and black communities of the college. Opponents characterized this as "one token black and one token Hispano in a college founded to provide an education to the underserved minorities."

A motion to table that proposal and thus reaffirm the faculty's previous decision to have larger student representation failed 90-59 in secret balloting. A motion to allow the student representatives to accompany the committee on trips to interview prospective presidents also failed.[705]

Ball denounced the faculty senate's actions to essentially exclude students from any meaningful input into the selection of the president of the college. "The rationale of the trustees," he said, "seems to be that what was good enough for Southern Colorado State College, a suburban residential college, is good enough for MSC, an innovative, urban, commuter college. This is not true. The trustees seem to be under the impression that what will work at one state college will work at them all."

Ball stated that minority faculty members were also underrepresented and that students had been effectively excluded from the selection process. "In a day in which there is growing disorder on college campus, this is a serious mistake. On the one hand the trustees say they favor more student dialogue and involvement in the decision-making processes, and on the other hand they exclude students from any effective role in selecting the man who will rule their college for years to come." He stated that the representation of two students was only a token gesture at best.

He also mentioned that it was imprudent for a committee to be traveling around the country, interviewing candidates in the midst of a financial crisis, but if the committee persisted in taking the trips, at least one student should go, too.

Ball said MSC students had been in touch with legislators and were seeking to have them introduce a resolution which would affirm the need for greater student participation. In addition, students were meeting with the trustees in an effort to convince them to re-evaluate their position. A meeting with Gov. Love was being sought so students could express themselves regarding the selection of the three new members on the board of trustees.[706]

The students and the Faculty Federation lost the battle. The Institutional Advisory Committee was set up the way the trustees and faculty senate wanted it. Nine faculty members, one administrator and two students were selected. The faculty members were: Dr. John Mirich, chairman; Dr. George C. Becker; Dr. Lloyd K. Herren; Dr. Roy A. Hinderman; Dr. Harry A. Temmer; David M. Abbott; Dr. Oscar H. Schuette; Dr. Wilton Flemon and David Sandoval. Dr. Robert V. Thompson, dean of students, represented the administration and served as secretary. Dave Ball appointed Andy Esparaza and King Harris as the student members.[707]

This was a return to the old ways. Previously, students had won a seat on the CCHE and the trustees.

During the kerfuffle, Professor Charles Allbee was featured in an article in *The Post* on MSC's Weekend College (WC), which was funded by a Model Cities grant. A Weekend College student, Juanita Leon, was shown in a photo with a caption explaining that the program helped her reach her goals by providing incentive, advice, tutoring, and a free college education.

Allbee, the weekend college director, said, "There are no shoddy goods sold here. There's no lowering of academic standards." He explained that the classes and even the faculty were tailored to the students' needs. "But the system fails sometimes when a student is so beset by problems, he has to move on. Then we help him so withdrawal is least damaging."

The weekend college program was geared toward "at-risk" students or students who had already dropped out. To get accepted, students went through an extensive acceptance routine where interviews lasted anywhere from 45 minutes to two hours. Students ranged in age from 17 to 61. Gary Trujillo, an MSC student as well as counselor and tutor for WC, said his job required him to go out into neighborhoods and talk up the program.[708]

There was some closure on the earlier smoke bomb incident. One of the women who had failed to show in court to face charges for tossing a bomb into a classroom in the Glenarm

Building in 1970 finally appeared in court. Miss Diana L. Hooten, an eighteen-year-old from West Denver, was granted one year's probation.[709]

The aerospace science program got a boost when the CCHE approved two new baccalaureate majors. The new programs would be offered in the fall of 1971. These two majors were aviation maintenance management and air traffic control.[710]

In January, the child care center opened a new facility at 1038 Cherokee, funded by a grant of $106,000 from the US Department of Labor and $17,500 from student fees. "We like to have children explore things for themselves and we stress the importance of undergoing the actual experience as the way to learn something," head teacher Brenda Lanier said.

"Students are very concerned about whether their children are getting a good education," MSC education professor Winnona Graham said. "I think the mothers are very relieved that because of the day care center their children are sharing in their educational effort." At that time, 85 percent of the student body worked and 35 percent were married with children.[711]

THE AURARIA BATTLE CONTINUES

At the beginning of 1971, Dave Ball, one of the students most responsible for the bond issue passing, had second thoughts about Auraria. He took a new position saying, Auraria would be detrimental to the CU Denver Center. Ball and the student body president of UCD, Jack Hefestay, held a press conference and said, "It is our belief that the present plans for the perimeters of Auraria are detrimental to the goals of UCD and Auraria residents." Ball admitted that he had worked for the project, but now had concerns. "It is too large and the concerns of residents were not being met."[712]

During the Auraria campaign, commitments were made to residents about relocation. In February, the Interim Policy Board for Auraria voted unanimously to establish a task force for housing the dislocated residents. The ten-member task force was composed of Auraria residents, a member of DURA and others involved with planning and relocation. The board also reaffirmed that demolition of existing structures within the Auraria site would not begin until adequate and acceptable housing was available for displaced Auraria residents.[713]

A bill to extend the deadline for spending the money appropriated to buy land for the Auraria complex was introduced in the House of Representatives. This bill was necessary since the deadline was approaching and the state was not in a position to buy the land because the relocation plan had not been approved by the residents, and because the lawsuit by the group of businessmen led by Frank Karsh was still pending.[714]

A few weeks later, however, Judge George M. McNamara dismissed the Auraria businessmen's lawsuit without a trial, saying that their legal arguments lacked substance. The suit contended that the voters' approval of a $6 million bond issue was illegal because it allowed non-property taxpayers to vote. Attorney George Creamer, who represented the plaintiffs, said a City Charter provision limited bond election voting privileges to residents who had paid property tax. The city's position was that the voters amended the charter in the election.[715]

Judge McNamara ruled that recent Supreme Court decisions found that public issues cannot be confined to approval from property owners alone.[716]

The *News* wrote an editorial after the dismissal, urging the state to get on with the project. Auraria was a well thought out and progressive approach to the college education explosion that had taken place in Denver, the *News* said. "MSC—sprawled in a tangle of departments and buildings—had grown beyond expectations and will continue to grow." The *News* said it understood the sentiments of those who must vacate the site. "We are certain that they will be satisfied that relinquishing their property will have been a civic contribution."[717]

Paul Cormier, relocation director for DURA, suggested that it might start buying property in August and September, and he estimated the entire relocation effort would take 45 months. "One hurdle was cleared when the lawsuit was dismissed," Cormier said, adding though that the businessmen did appeal to the Colorado Supreme Court on March 15.[718]

Another problem holding up Auraria was that it hadn't received approval for the loan and grant from HUD, which was expected to provide 2/3 of the funds—about $12.3 million. The HUD delay had caused DURA to postpone a public hearing before Denver City Council. Even though voters had approved $6 million in bond sales, the council had to approve the project after holding another a public hearing.

Soon, Congress approved legislation which gave residents a better deal. Previously owner-occupants were to be paid $5,000 toward a home purchase. Now that was increased to $15,000.[719] Most residents were tenants, however, so for them, the rent subsidy of $1,000 over two years was increased to $4,000 over four years. This meant that tenants could receive an $80 per month subsidy for the next four years. Many residents, however, wanted housing near where they lived because many of them worked downtown.[720]

Despite these issues, officials from the three institutions (CCD, CU Denver and MSC) vowed to move directly ahead with planning for the Auraria project. Dr. Owen Smith of CCD said that clearance of the 169-acre tract awaited only a relocation plan suitable to current residents and that construction would proceed in stages as the tract was cleared and residents relocated. He announced that relocation and clearance was scheduled to begin in the summer and ground would be broken in the summer of 1972.

He said that MSC would be the first to occupy its new buildings in fall of 1974, and CCD and CU Denver would move in by the following spring. Smith said MSC is running out of space it can lease for classroom area and that some leases were due to expire in 1973. Smith estimated that under present circumstances, the site would be totally developed by 1980, at a cost ranging from $50 million to $60 million.[721]

Included in the estimates was $368,000 for land acquisition within the Skyline Urban Renewal site for the CU Denver Center expansion on the east side of Speer, $250,000 for planning of shared facilities and $180,000 for the first CCD unit and the second MSC unit.[722]

Despite all of the optimism expressed by the Auraria planners, the legislature's Joint Budget Committee was sending signals the project might be delayed. The JBC was hinting it might only appropriate $100,000 that year for planning.

The *Rocky Mountain News* shot off an editorial blasting the legislature's delay. "The Auraria Higher Education Center in downtown Denver has the potential for providing a great deal of higher education at comparatively low cost—and with great efficiency. It is, therefore, hard to understand why the General Assembly's Joint Budget Committee gave Auraria the back of its hand," the *News* wrote.

"Unless the assembly changes Auraria will be delayed drastically," the News wrote. "The committee had recommended only $100,000 for projects needed to move three institutions toward joint use of the site. The project should have at least $250,000 in planning funds to get physical construction started. If planning is delayed, MSC's move will be delayed. MSC now rents space at a cost of $1 million per year. We hope the assembly takes a closer look at Aurania's needs," the *News* added.[723]

On August 3, Governor Love signed an executive order creating a new Auraria Higher Education Commission and appointed Phil Milstein, Shelby Harper, and Max Morton to serve on it. The new board could appoint an executive director, and until the legislature created it by statute, staffing would be provided by CCHE.[724]

Even though the legislature had passed SB67 to fund Auraria in 1970, the war was not over. On December 17, at a Joint Budget Committee hearing for the 1972 fiscal year's budget, Senator Don Friedman (R-Denver) expressed doubts about the wisdom of committing to construction at Auraria. He asked, "Why not a university without walls?" He noted that a college named Metropolitan State College had just been authorized in the Twin Cities. Even though he was in the legislature during the entire Auraria debate, Friedman asked if alternative sites had been studied.[725]

At that hearing, two students from Metro and UCD spoke. Dave Ball shocked many when he said, "Academic planning had been ignored in favor of buildings. The concept had been pushed and propounded principally for economic reasons rather than educational ones." UCD student president Tom Hyland added, "We've been excluded from most of the major planning."

Joe Shoemaker (R-Denver), one of the strongest supporters of Auraria in legislature, exploded, saying, "There has been more planning done on this site than a combination of all the other sites in Colorado...I am tired of hearing opinions and ten minutes of testimony charging that there has been no planning or cooperation." The committee took a bus tour of the site following the meeting.

"Let's End the nonsense on Auraria," *The Denver Post* editorialized after the meeting. They charged Senator Friedman, Dave Ball and Tom Hyland with taking ill-informed pot-shots. *The Post* said Friedman was doing so much talking he hadn't been listening to what's going on.[726]

Ultimately, the money was appropriated and the Auraria Higher Education Center was built.

While the Auraria debate was going on at the Capitol, life on campus moved on. Former U.S. Attorney General Ramsey Clark gave a talk to 400 MSC students at Phipps Auditorium as part of the Creative Arts Festival. He advocated the creation of "new rights," which included: a right to health, a right to all the education one can absorb and a right to meaningful and expanding employment. "Until we do that," Clark said, "we will be breeding crime." [727]

A 10-person delegation from Colorado Cares, including William Daniel Chase, president of the Metro State Veteran Student Association, met with members of the North Vietnamese delegation in Paris. The group delivered more than 250,000 letters protesting treatment of American POWS by North Vietnam.[728] The North Vietnamese promised to relay information about the missing men.[729]

There was mixed news for MSC's teachers' education program. The Colorado State Board of Education approved MSC's training program for elementary teachers, but it refused to approve the training program for secondary teachers. The approval permitted state certification of teachers who completed the programs. The excluded majors were behavioral sciences, economics and political science.

The commission stated that the majors were adequate themselves, but they hadn't been well adapted as teaching majors. The commission stated that the secondary education program was in urgent need of study and revision. "The MSC education department apparently has little influence in affecting teacher education programs in the academic departments," the commission said. MSC secondary education students could continue to take Adams State College extension courses to qualify for state certificates.[730]

Harold Ironshield, president of the American Indian Students at Metropolitan State College, called a press conference in March to express their displeasure about a bill pending in the Colorado legislature. The bill would have limited free tuition at Fort Lewis College in Durango to Native Americans who were from Colorado. Traditionally, all native Americans had received free tuition at the college under the terms of a Congressional land grant, which gave the Fort Lewis College to the state.

Ironshield indicated this was "the same problem which had faced the red man throughout United States history—the white man controls the Legislature and the Legislature has the power." Ironshield stated that education was the only way Indians could advance themselves, but Dunbar's ruling and the bill indicated that the white people "just don't want us in college." The free tuition cutoff was just another example of the white man breaking a treaty with the Indians, Ironshield added.[731]

MSC made its mark on Denver's spring elections. Professor David Sandoval and two MSC graduates, W.L. Stuart and Phil Henrikson, were running for the Denver School Board. In addition, Bill Wilson, who was in charge of MSC's mail facility, was running for Denver councilman at large.

MSC IS ACCREDITED

Finally, there was some great news. MSC had been granted full accreditation by the North Central Association of Colleges and Secondary Schools. NCA's regulations required that a new institution couldn't be fully eligible for accreditation until one class had been graduated. The first baccalaureate degrees were awarded by MSC in June 1969.

Dr. Kenneth Phillips expressed great satisfaction that this high achievement was attained in the sixth year of the college's operation. Phillips said, "In six hectic years, during which an ever-swelling tide of students has put a strain on faculty, facilities and funds, MSC had risen from nothing to become the biggest state college in Colorado, and was now a full member of the club of accredited institutions."[732]

The Denver Post wrote an editorial commending Metro and Dr. Phillips on the accreditation:
> *"To the public, this means MSC can give its students a standard-quality college education. To the students, this means credits from MSC are more acceptable at any other college or grad school they attend. To potential students, MSC will now be listed in catalogs as an accredited school. For administrators and faculty, accreditation is a welcome and hard-earned symbol of status.*
> *We hope that staff will start working to make the college as 'metropolitan' in inner essence as in name. We don't feel that the college has yet used the city's resources as fully as it might to enrich its educational program. Now that MSC is 'in the club,' we hope it will feel free to experiment and innovate more, to become much more than a standard state college. Meanwhile, though, President Phillips and everyone else involved are entitled to congratulations on a big job well done."[733]*

SALARIES, WOMEN, INTERIM PRESIDENT

The quarter did not end with a celebration over accreditation. A new flap occurred over faculty pay for the summer session. The MSC Faculty Federation accused the governor, the trustees and the college administration of breach of contract in connection with the lowering of summer salary schedules.

The executive secretary of the 45-member Faculty Federation, Dr. Brooks Van Everen, said that he believed the governor, trustees and administration had taken "a terribly regressive action dictated by a false sense of economics." The federation's statement was in response to the administration lowering summer faculty salaries from 28 percent to 25 percent of the teachers' annual salaries. The 28 percent salary was provided for in the teachers' yearly contracts and was paid to all who taught in previous summers' sessions.

Van Everen said the federation felt so strongly about this arbitrary action that it hired an attorney to give advice on what action could be taken. "We are quite prepared to take this issue into the courts. We believe that the time has come to stop manipulating college faculty members and using them as easy fall-guys," he said.

Dr. Harold Benn, dean of the summer quarter, replied, saying the summer salary schedule reflected what was in Governor Love's 1971-72 annual budget, which indicated summer salaries in the state college system must be fixed at 25 percent of the academic year's salary. Benn said the administration was told to put a statement in the summer school contract noting that summer teachers waive any rights to payment at the 28 percent rate of the previous academic year's salary and the attorney general's office said that such a procedure was legal.

"We're very sorry we had to do it," Benn said, "but when you're told to pay 25 percent by the attorney general's office, you have no choice." H. Grant Vest, executive secretary of the trustees, said he would not comment until he had seen a copy of the federation statement. A federation member said the contracts with the 25 percent salary schedule would be signed, but under protest.[734]

Women at MSC fared somewhat better than at other colleges and universities around the nation. In 1971, the national percentage of women on college facilities was 19 percent. At MSC it was nearly 25 percent. The number of female department and division heads at MSC had also increased rapidly. The number of women in administration, on the other hand, was below the national average. However, 90 percent of the civil service staff were women.

The percentage of men and women admitted was the same as it had been since day one. The overall acceptance rate was 62 percent, lower than the 73 percent in 1966-67. One reason was the men fared better on ACT tests than women, in part because high schools did a better job preparing boys for ACT tests on the presumption that boys would go to college. The average composite score for male students was 19.6, but it was 17.7 for females. Males did better in math and science, and this was the reason for women having lower composite scores.

Women, however, fared better on mean high school GPA than men. The female mean GPA was 2.52 versus 2.21 for males. GPA, however, is a better predictor of college success than standardized ACT tests.[735]

Just as that news about women at MSC came out, Joan McCoy wrote a feature article in the *News* about business professor Dr. Patricia L. Duckworth, the new chair of the business division, who succeeded Dr. Forkner, who had stepped out of administrative duties to work on his book.[736]

"Women's lib doesn't like me," Duckworth said, adding that her recipe for success was, "be qualified, marry the right man, work hard, don't remind your peers you are a woman, but always act like a lady."

Duckworth said the division she headed, which included the accounting, marketing, business systems, management and business teacher education departments, had 1,300 students, which was 20 to 25 percent of the student body. It had twenty one faculty members, five of which had doctorates. She would have liked to have more women on staff, but the ones who applied weren't qualified, she asserted.

"We cater to a slightly different breed. They are concerned with earning a living. They have come here because they realize the value of education. With just one year of college, they can move from their $1 to $1.25 an hour at a hamburger stand to a job giving them $2.35 to $2.65 an hour," Duckworth said. She noted that after the Kent State "occurrence," it was the business majors who demanded that the school be kept open. "They know why they are in school, they study hard and they don't want to lose out on something they have paid for." She said.[737]

Spring enrollment was 6,160, including 250 enrolled in the weekend college. Of those, 5,182 were continuing students. This was down 1,413 over winter quarter. Furthermore, 3,107 students had dropped out since the fall. This constituted a 44 percent attrition rate. The dropout rate for the weekend college was 38 percent.

The high dropout rate, however, was a national trend. A study by the Department of Health Education and Welfare found that only half of all students entering four-year colleges made it for two years and only 15-25 percent ended up graduating.[738]

In April, Carleton E. (Pat) Reed, professor of law enforcement at MSC, estimated that as many as 100 Denver Police Department officers were enrolled as part-time students at Metro, and most of them, he said, were good students, intelligent, a cut above the average. "The day of the big, dumb, thick-soled cop is over," Reed added. "Like other young people, the police students we get are interested in relevance: psychology, sociology, political science. They want to improve society without overturning it."

"Sure, some of them have their prejudices," he admitted. "But you've got to remember one thing: They're down there in the mud, seeing life as it is, sometimes at its worst, and not just reading about it in textbooks."

The MSC debate program under Gary Holbrook won again. Judy Knapp and David Litschel were shown in a photo in the *News* after they clutched the Colorado-Wyoming Forensic Association junior division debate championship for having the best competitive record that academic year. The award was given annually to persons who had two years' or less experience in organized intercollegiate debate competition. The association included all four-year institutions in Colorado and the University of Wyoming.[739]

At the end of April, at a luncheon at the Brown Palace Hotel, Arnold McDermott, head of Denver's Career Service Authority, presented Dr. Phillips with a special award for his outstanding accomplishments. McDermott was filling in for Mayor McNichols, who was out of town.[740]

In May, the trustees announced that Dr. Keats McKinney would serve as the interim college president until a new president was hired to replace Ken Phillips.

CRISIS AT *THE PAPER*

The quarter could not end, however, without yet another controversy involving the student newspaper. On May 4, student body president Dave Ball was named the new editor of *THE PAPER* effective at the end of his term as student president. The publications committee wanted Ball as editor over Jon Kovash, the current managing editor. The administration and many faculty members had decided that they would no longer tolerate four-letter words and controversial articles in the student paper.

Upon his appointment, Ball said he was opposed to use of four-letter words and vindictive attacks on individuals. He promised to publish more news about college activities and programs, conduct opinion polls, and run articles which would have a specific academic appeal. Ball had been a reporter for *THE PAPER* prior to joining the administration of student body president Bob Bowen in 1969.

Ball's appointment set off a firestorm of protest from the existing staff of *THE PAPER* and some other campus groups including SDS. Paul Hutchinson wrote an article entitled, "Paper Gets Balled." He pointed out that Ball was chosen on a 2-1 vote with two abstentions, with one member absent. He acknowledged that Ball had a journalism background, but indicated that none of the other staff members Ball had brought in had any experience at all. Hutchinson said Dean Thompson played the role of prosecuting attorney at the publications meeting.[741]

The issue simmered for two weeks but on May 20, *THE PAPER* published an article written by Fred Pollard entitled, "Stay Home and Masturbate." In the article, written as a sarcastic metaphor to describe the meeting where Ball was selected, Pollard used sexual metaphors to describe members of the board of publications including, Dean Thompson and faculty member Joy Yuthas, as well as the student members. One of the student targets was Fred Estey, who Ball had appointed to the publications board just two weeks earlier. He voted for Ball.

The student publication had already printed words like clitoris and orgasm in a previous issue, but now they used the word masturbation in relationship to faculty members and students on the committee. This could not stand. Professor Yuthas filed a formal complaint and students lined up on both sides of the issue.[742]

Dean Thompson reportedly said that if the publications board did not close *THE PAPER*, the administration would. On the same day that Dr. McKinney was named the interim president, the publications committee met and voted 5-1 to suspend *THE PAPER*. In addition, they denied the newspaper funds, and denied editor, Frank O'Neil and the staff, access to their offices except to remove their personal belongings, under supervision.[743]

On June 3, the fired staff of *THE PAPER* put out a last unofficial copy. They told their side of the story, explaining that the Pollard article was a metaphor. Editor Frank O'Neil wrote a goodbye in long hand addressed to the staff (those who are here, those who have gone, and those who hurt.) This was what he wrote:

> *"It is rare in a group of people that creativity, courage, happiness and concern for each other all come together. They did. I was part of it. Because of it, I have changed. Because of it I have learned. Not the shallowness of the classroom, but the gut-level learning of the spirit. We are not without our bruises but they will mend. I am happy to be part of you. We are alive and have only started."*

There was no way Dr. Phillips would intervene. The trustees and the legislature had been on him for years over the student newspaper. There was no way Dr. McKinney would take the side of *THE PAPER* either. The administration, and many powerful faculty wanted a different type publication, and they seemed to have gotten it.

Under Ball, *THE PAPER* had a new professional look. After his graduation in 1972, Ball went on to earn his master's degree in journalism from Columbia University. He graduated with honors and was offered a job writing for Newsweek upon graduation. Today, he is an accomplished author.

Student government elections were held and students elected MSC's first black student body president. Haile Zamadie was elected president on a ticket with two running mates: Sam Arnold and Elaine Bland. They received 498 votes. Their closest opponent, Dan Edwards and Dave Birge received 369 votes. Dave Ball and most student government officers supported Edwards. Zamadie was endorsed by Isetta Rawls. Sonja Eldeen was elected Justice.[744]

One unidentified student wrote that students voted for the wrong reasons. He or she wrote that blacks voted for Zamadie because he was black; Chicanos voted for Edwards because his running mate was Chicano.[745]

At the banquet where the new officers were installed, awards were issued to various students. Mark Boyko received the President's Award. The Outstanding Students were: Alen Lewis III, George Brunner, Ken Sherwood, Andrew Esparza, Peggy Valdez, Carol Trombetta, Neysha Humphreys, David Ball, Susan Treece and Catherine Joy.

The students named to Who's Who in American Colleges and Universities were: Dave Cooper, Janet Malloy, John Mollock, and Don Lowe. The outstanding faculty honors went to: Elaine Cohen, reading; Robert Schenkein, faculty news editor; and Winona Graham, education. Bernardo Valdez, assistant dean of students, was named one of the five Outstanding Young Men in America.

THE END OF AN ERA

Commencement was held at Currigan Hall on June 6. Dr. Ken Phillips bestowed Associate degrees on 148 graduates, and Bachelor's degrees on 477. Dr. Peggy Walsh gave both the invocation and benediction. The commencement address was given by John Kellogg, president of Kellogg-Hartman-Walton, Inc.

President Richard Nixon sent a form letter to each graduate, saying that the "continued success of the American Experiment depends on the qualities of heart, mind and spirit of our young people." He said the graduates had the responsibility to build the kind of society that would make future generations proud to identify with their accomplishments.

"The destiny of our nation," Nixon said, "is not divided into yours and ours. We share it. There can be no generation gap in America. We must all keep an open mind and forthright spirit, balance the courage of our convictions with the courage of our uncertainties, triumph over bigotry and prejudice and recapture the unity of purpose that has always been our strength."

After degrees were bestowed, Stuart McLaughlin, chairman of the Board of Trustees, presented Dr. Ken Phillips with a Doctor of Laws degree in recognition of his tremendous achievements. He also read a citation honoring Phillips. This was the last commencement for Dr. Phillips as president. No other person had presided over a commencement as president of MSC in its brief history.[746]

Phillips was the first permanent president of the college, replacing interim president Dr. Harlan Bryant in the summer of 1965. Phillips, and his staff, pulled off an astonishing feat by getting a brand new college up and running in just five months, with few resources and little money. Phillips himself had only two and a half months after he was hired to open the doors. On top of that, he was able to obtain accreditation for the new school in five years. That was the first time a new institution was accredited in that short of time.

President Phillips led the school during the most difficult period for a college president in history. Often, he was praised and vilified on the same day. One cannot look back at what was accomplished in those years, under trying circumstances, with few resources and little support and not give credit Dr. Ken Phillips and the other faculty, staff and administrators on his team.

The citation read, in part, that "From the day he arrived in Denver, Dr. Phillips' trademark has been an extended hand and an infectious smile. Always willing to listen to others, he maintained an open office door for all students, faculty and the public." It listed his achievements and enumerated the number of community organizations Phillips belonged to.

Among the students receiving degrees that day were: Dave Sonnenberg, Sherman Hamilton, Alex Delgado, Mark Boyko, George Brunner, Al Martinez, Rick Reeser, Bob Bowen and Joe Taylor. These were just a few of the students who played a role in furthering Metropolitan State College during the previous four years. They joined the ranks of others who graduated before them, and those who would graduate afterwards. Without their service, MSU Denver would not be what it is today.

> *One morning I woke up and I knew*
> *You were really gone*
> *A new day, a new way, I knew*
> *I should see it along*
> *Go your way, I'll go mine*
> *And carry on*
> *Rejoice, rejoice, we have no choice but*
> *To carry on*   ·
> *Carry on*

- "Carry On" Crosby Still Nash and Young[747]

Metropolitan State College carried on, and life went on.

In August, the trustees hired Dr. James Palmer as the new president of MSC. Palmer had been dean of science and engineering at Union College in Schenectady, NY. He would be the fourth person at MSC with the president's title, but only the second permanent president. Palmer would be replaced by Dr. Richard Netzel.

This was the end of an era. Metropolitan State College began with a vision. It endured through years of tough and often bitter struggle. The odds were stacked against Metro from the very beginning. Powerful forces tried to prevent it from coming into existence, they tried to close it after it opened, tried to convert it to a junior college, and they tried twice to merge it with UCD. Nothing came easy, but MSC endured and prospered.

Were it not for MSC, thousands of students would never have received a college education, and our community would have been robbed of the countless contributions those thousands of graduates have made. It was only possible because of a vision and the perseverance to endure the struggle.

At last this story has finally been told.

-To Be Continued-

Epilogue

On May 18, 1991, 25 years, twelve days and 54 minutes after Governor John Love signed HB349 into law creating Metropolitan State College, Dr. Kenneth Phillips, the college's first permanent president, delivered the commencement address at McNichols Sports Arena for the graduates of Metropolitan State College. The hundreds of grads that day were a far cry from the 28 in MSC's first commencement in 1967.[748]

Dr. Phillips made note of some events that, as he put it, were particularly critical to the establishment and success of the college. "Had they [the visionaries] not been successful, it would have resulted in the failure of the entire idea. What a discouraging thought—there would be no graduation today," he asserted.

He recalled that he and his team had two and a half months to organize programs and courses; rent facilities and convert them to educational use; buy the necessary furnishings and equipment; hire fifty excellent faculty members to teach the required courses; and print the catalogue, course schedules and necessary forms. "To say it was a hectic time, is an understatement," he said, adding "and we did open on time."

"There is no greater service to humanity or to society than the man or woman who instructs the rising generation," he said quoting Cicero. Then, addressing the graduates, he said that they must consider the "challenge of change," noting that fifty years ago, change occurred more slowly, but today, the profile of change is getting steeper. He challenged them to a lifetime of learning, quoting the Chinese proverb, "Like rowing upstream, not to advance is to fall back."

Sadly, while recognizing Roy Romer, Betty Naugle, Grant Vest and Mayor McNichols for their significant roles in creating the college and establishing the Auraria Higher Education Center, Dr. Phillips failed to mention the significant role students and faculty played in that history even though as president, he always acknowledged the students unique contributions.

What began with feasibility studies in 1958 and continued through tough battles until the doors opened in 1965, was amazing. It is hard to quantify the impact Metropolitan State College had on the community. That impact lives on through the accomplishments of those who taught, those who administered and most importantly, those who benefited from the knowledge they only received because men and women cared enough to endure the struggle to create this institution.

Those visionaries did not want just another state college nor did they just want a college in Denver. They wanted and created something special, something unique—a new experiment in education for all who were willing to work to get it, regardless of race, nationality, gender, and especially, economic condition. That vision recognized that everyone has something to contribute, and through education, they are empowered to make those contributions. It was going to teach city kids to live in the city and solve its problems.

The visionaries saw MSC as a place where business and community leaders would come to the college on a regular basis and be involved in the education there. Likewise, students were to be encouraged to get involved in the community.

In the beginning, before it had a campus, there were no walls between Metropolitan State College and the city. What happened in the city, happened on the campus. Students and faculty members were actively involved in the issues of the day; involved in all the problems and struggles of the city. There were no lines, no boundaries, and no barriers. That is the way an urban grant college was supposed to be.

Those who were there in the beginning, started from scratch; they had no legacy to build on, no collective learning experience. They had to wing it. Students, administrators and faculty at MSU Denver today, have a rich legacy on which to build; they have a collective learning experience to guide them.

As MSU Denver prepares for its 50th anniversary in 2015, it must acknowledge and embrace its complete history, the history of all the men and women, inside and outside the school who made MSU Denver what it is today, and who gave this university the promise it holds for the future. That includes former students who are now alumni. Without the vision and struggle of all these individuals, there would be no 50th anniversary for MSU Denver to celebrate.

The challenge facing the entire MSU Denver community—the current administration, faculty, students, benefactors, and alumni—is to make sure that the vision that gave rise to this institution endures without compromise; that the struggle was not in vain; that the institution embraces everything an urban-oriented institution must embrace.

Will we accept that challenge?

Tables

Table I: The First Faculty and Administrators at MSC (1965-66)

Faculty

Lorene Adcock, Business; Charlene Alexis, Library Science; Charles Allbee, English; Dr. Donald Baldwin, History; Dr. Harold Benn, Biology; Dr. Jean Bowles, Biology; Dr. Phillip Boxer, English; Dr. George Brooke, Psychology; Dr. Thomas Cook, Speech; Walker Edwards, Political Science; Dr. Jeanne Fair, French, Spanish; Dr. Irvine Forkner, Business; Perlita Gauthier, Business; Ronald Graham, Math; Dr. Vernie Iazzetta, Psychology; F.D. Lillie, Psychology; Dr. Keats McKinney, Education; Dr. Milliard McLallen, English; Robert Mangold, Art; Dr. Peggy Mulvihill, History; Dr. Morton Olson; James Parker; Dr. Gail Phares; Ken Phillips; Dr. Jon Plachy; Robert Rhodes; Dr. Keith Roper; Dr. Melvin D. Spurlin; Robert Sullenberger; Dr. Harry Temmer; Gwen Thomas; Dr. Lester Thonssen; Ronald Wahl; Raymond Willms; Dr. Jerry Wilson

Administrators

Dr. Kenneth Phillips, President; Dr. Keats McKinney, Dean of Instruction; F.D. Lillie, Dean of Student Services; Curtis Wright Business Manager; Keats McKinney Acting Dean Arts and Sciences; Dr. Gail Phares, Dean Applied Sciences; Charlene Alexis, Librarian

Metropolitan State College Catalogue 1965

Table II: First Graduates Metropolitan State College, June 1967

Roger Braun AAS, Mike Brigman AA, Charles Brock AA, Heather Ann Cowan AA, Lynn Davis AA, Elizabeth Enenbach AAS, Billy Gorelick AA, Margaret Haberland AA, Bill Hester AAS, John Hallerstein AA, Ion Doug Holcombe III AA, Suzanne Williams Holcombe AA, Samuel Huddleston AA, Margaret Isenhart AS, Carol Kirchler, AA, Thomas Lamb AAS, David Leiker AAS, Lonnie McCartt, William Mizer AA, Donald Newman AA (with honors), Donald Odiorne AA, Hilda Orum AA, Linda Lee Ruhoff AA, Ester Meyers Runge AA (with honors), Leo Schenkeir AA, Douglas Schuck AA, James Sheets AAS, Barbara Montano Vialpando AA.

The Metropolitan June 5, 1967

Table III: First Baccalaureate Graduates of MSC 1969

Constance Johnson, Arthur Adams, Mickey Bland, Michael Brigman, William Crandall, John Greene, Edna Mosley, Thomas Rossolillo Jr., Margaret Isenhart, Edmon Adams, Gary Austin, Jerrie Berge, Frederic Boyce, Kenneth Degener, Louise Gold, Ida Sue Harrison, John Hellerstein, Suzanne Holcombe, Donald Neuman, Hilda Orum, Joseph Pagliascotti Jr., Michael Richards, Kathleen Roberto, William Roper Jr., Esther Runge, Sarita Schneebeck, Roseanne Schwartz, Carol Virginia Smiley, Donna May Soderlun, William Stuart, Fred Trentaz, Marilyn Wilson, Robert Young, Heather Sheets, James Sheets, Geneva Isted, Patricia Stone, Margaret Haberland, Richard Hildreth, John Mendenhall, Charlotte Hoyer.

Bibliography

FOR FURTHER READING

Gould, Richard, (2007) *The Life and Times of Richard Castro: Bridging a Cultural Divide*
. (2007) Colorado Historical Society, Denver, Colorado U.S.A

Abbott, Frank C. (1999) *The Auraria Higher Education Center: How it came to be Auraria
Higher Education Center,* Denver, Colorado U.S.A.

Magdalena Gallegos (2011) *Where the Rivers Meet*, Denver, Colorado U.S.A

McEnroe, Betty, (1992) *Denver Renewed: A History of The Denver Urban Renewal Authority,*
Edited by Dick Johnston; Underwritten and produced by The Denver Foundation and
the Alex B. Holland Memorial Fund Denver, Colorado U.S.A

Goodstein, Phil, (2003) *A Peoples History of Early Colorado Denver from the Bottom Up; Volume One From Sand Creek to Ludlow,* New Social Publications, Denver Colorado U.S.A

Self, Robert O. (2012) *All in the Family The Realignment of American Democracy since the
1960s,* Hill and Wang, New York, New York U.S.A.

May, Gary (2013) *Bending Towards Justice: The Voting Rights Act and the Transformation of
American Democracy* Basic Books, New York, New York U.S.A.

Notes

Prologue

1. Morrison, Berny (1988 February 12) "Vote set today for 1988 start on rapid transit" *Rocky Mountain News*,

2. *Where the Rivers Meet*, Magdalena Gallegos Denver, CO., 2011

Chapter 1

3. Http://extras.denverpost.com/snapshot/part2a.htm, accessed January 13, 2014

4. U.S. Census Bureau Colorado 1960

5. *Trustees Report on the Plan of Operation for Metropolitan Sate College*, Board of Trustees, December 30, 1963 (Green Report) p. 15, Auraria Library Archives

6. Reed, Carson and Hawk, Doug "The Colorado Community College and Occupational System: A Silver Anniversary History", Denver Community College 1994, 16-50, Auraria Library Archives

7. Zinke, George (1964) "The Special Needs of Low Income and Minority Persons in *the Metropolitan* Area, University of Colorado; *Trustees Report on the Plan of Operation for Metropolitan Sate College* (Green Report) p.2 Auraria Library Archives

8. Gaskie, Jack (1963, February 9) "College Plans Depend on Pupil Background" *Rocky Mountain News*, "MSC Newsclippings" (Vol. I) Auraria Library Archives

9. *Trustees Report on the Plan of Operation for Metropolitan Sate College*, Board of Trustees, December 30, 1963 (Green Report) p. 16, Auraria Library Archives

10. *Colorado House of Representatives Journal* 1958 Denver Public Library

11. Rosenburg, Jennifer, "President John F. Kennedy Gives Man on the Moon Speech" *20th Century History*, http://history1900s.about.com/od/1960s/a/jfkmoon.htm, accessed Sept. 2012

12. Author unknown (1963, February 13) "Report Issued by Task Unit on Education," *The Denver Post*, "MSC Newsclippings" (Vol. I) Auraria Library Archives

13. Interview with Sheldon Steinhauser 2012, Transcript in author's files

14. Author unknown (1962 November 25) "New College for Denver Considered," *The Denver Post* p.3A, "MSC Newsclippings" (Vol. I) Auraria Library Archives

15. Gaskie, Jack (1962 December 2) "Denver College Feared Mecca for Rejects" *Rocky Mountain News*, "MSC Newsclippings" (Vol. I) Auraria Library Archives

16. Chase, Robert L. (1962 December 6) "Back Door Sneak" Robert L. *Rocky Mountain News*, "MSC Newsclippings" (Vol. I) Auraria Library Archives

17.   Author unknown (1962 December 2), "Regents Oppose MSC" *Rocky Mountain News* "MSC Newsclippings" (Vol. I) Auraria Library Archives

18.   Author unknown (Editorial), (1962 December 16) "State Junior College for Metro Area Better Now than New 4-Year School" *The Denver Post*, Newsclippings (Vol. I) Auraria Library Archives

19.   Author unknown (1962, December 19) "Board Opposes New Denver State College" *The Colorado Daily*, "MSC Newsclippings" (Vol. I) Auraria Library Archives

20.   Rose, David (1962, December 19) "CU Faculty Unit Rips Denver College Plan" *Rocky Mountain News*, "MSC Newsclippings" (Vol. I) Auraria Library Archives

21.   Author unknown (1962 December 22) "Extension Students Nix Denver College" *Rocky Mountain News*; Newsclippings (Vol. I) Auraria Library; also, Author unknown (1962, December 22) "CU Extension Students Prefer Degrees, Oppose New School" *The Denver Post* "MSC Newsclippings" (Vol. I) Auraria Library Archives

22.   Gaskie, Jack (1963 January 1) "Accreditation Unit Says CU Might Peril Standing," *Rocky Mountain News*, "MSC Newsclippings" (Vol. I) Auraria Library Archives

23.   Price, Max (1963, January 1) "New College Urged CU in Error Burch Insists *The Denver Post*, "MSC Newsclippings" (Vol. I) Auraria Library Archives

24.   Author unknown (1962, December 28) "Education 'Blueprint' Called a Step Forward," *Rocky Mountain News*, "MSC Newsclippings" (Vol. I) Auraria Library Archives

25.   Gaskie, Jack (1962, January 3) "Colleges Ask Ban on Admission Rule," *Rocky Mountain News*, "MSC Newsclippings" (Vol. I) Auraria Library Archives

26.   Thomasson, Dan (1963, January 8) "4-Year CU Branch Is Ruled Unconstitutional," *Rocky Mountain News*, "MSC Newsclippings" (Vol. I) Auraria Library Archives

27.   Author unknown (1963, January 11) "Extension Students Challenge New School" *Rocky Mountain News*, "MSC Newsclippings" (Vol. I) Auraria Library Archives

28.   Author unknown (1963 January 11) "Here is Text of Gov. John A. Love's State of the State Message to the Legislature" *The Denver Post* p. 14, "MSC Newsclippings" (Vol. I) Auraria Library Archives

29.   Thomasson, Dan (1963, January 12), "Demos Disagree with Love's Proposals," *Rocky Mountain News*, "MSC Newsclippings" (Vol. I) Auraria Library Archives

30.   Price, Max (1963, January 16) "Romer Stresses Need to Act Fast on New College in Denver," *The Denver Post*, "MSC Newsclippings" (Vol. I) Auraria Library Archives

31.   Rose, David (1963, January 22) "Love Predicts Denver To Get Institute of Higher Learning," *Rocky Mountain News*, "MSC Newsclippings" (Vol. I) Auraria Library Archives

32.   Author unknown (1962, February 13) "Report Issued by Task Unit on Education," *The Denver Post*, "MSC Newsclippings" (Vol. I) Auraria Library Archives

33.   Author unknown (1962, January 22) "Mackie Raps Plan for Denver College" *The Denver Post*, "MSC Newsclippings" (Vol. I) Auraria Library Archives

34.   Price, Max (1963, February 18) "State Education Group Backs New State College in Denver" *The Denver Post*, p. 1, "MSC Newsclippings" (Vol. I) Auraria Library Archives

35.   Author unknown (1963, February 20) "College Urgency Stressed," *The Denver Post*, "MSC Newsclippings" (Vol. I) Auraria Library Archives

36.   Author unknown (February 25), "Legislature Report: Metropolitan State College Measure Offered in House," *The Denver Post* "MSC Newsclippings" (Vol. I) Auraria Library Archives

37.   Author unknown (1963, February 26) "Burch Introduces Bill Asking Denver Area State College" *Rocky Mountain News*, "MSC Newsclippings" (Vol. I) Auraria Library Archives

38.   Author unknown (1963 March 9) "CU Amendment Might Delay College in Denver Two Years" *Rocky Mountain News*, p.28, "MSC Newsclippings" (Vol. I) Auraria Library Archives

39.   Author unknown (1963, March 23) "Future of CU Extension is Jeopardized" *Rocky Mountain News*, "MSC Newsclippings" (Vol. I) Auraria Library Archives

40. Author unknown (Editorial) (1963, March 25) "Denver College Plan Gets Boost," *The Denver Post*, "MSC Newsclippings" (vol. I) Auraria Library Archives

41. Gaskie, Jack (1963 March 26) "Love Backs Bill on Metro College Study, *Rocky Mountain News* p. 5, "MSC Newsclippings" (Vol. I) Auraria Library Archives

42. Author unknown (1963 March 30) "House Action Threatens CU Extension Unit" *Rocky Mountain News*, "MSC Newsclippings" (Vol. I); also, Gavin, Tom (1963 March 30) "CU Denver Center Gets Death-Knell Vote" *The Denver Post*, "MSC Newsclippings" (Vol. I) Auraria Library Archives

43. *Colorado House of Representatives Journal 1963*, April 1, 1963 Denver Public Library

44. Price, Max (1963, March 30) "CU Aids Asks Denver College Facility Talks" *The Denver Post*, "MSC Newsclippings" (Vol. I) Auraria Library Archives

45. Gaskie, Jack (1963, April 2) "CU Extension Students Protest Metro College" *Rocky Mountain News*, Page 1, "MSC Newsclippings" (Vol. I) Auraria Library Archives

46. Author unknown (1963, April 4) "Metro College Study Deferred" *The Denver Post*, "MSC Newsclippings" (vol. I) Auraria Library Archives

47. Schantz, Tom (1963, April 4) "Regents Oppose Phase-out of Denver Center" *Colorado Daily*, "MSC Newsclippings" (Vol. I) Auraria Library Archives

48. *Colorado House of Representatives Journal* 1963, May 5, 1963 Denver Public Library

Chapter 2

49. "Knockin' On Heaven's Door," Bob Dylan 1973 Soundtrack film: Pat Garrett and Billy the Kid

50. Author unknown (1963, May 30) "Education Expert to Make Colorado Study" *The Denver Post*, "MSC Newsclippings" (Vol. I) Auraria Library Archives

51. Gaskie, Jack (1963, June 30) "Junior College Costs AS High as Other Units" *Rocky Mountain News*, "MSC Newsclippings" (Vol. I) Auraria Library Archives; Gaskie, Jack (1963, June 30) "More Colleges or Not? That is the Question" *Rocky Mountain News*, p. 14, "MSC Newsclippings" (Vol. I) Auraria Library Archives

52. Author unknown Editorial (1963, June 12) "Horse Back Before the Cart" *Rocky Mountain News*, "MSC Newsclippings" (Vol. I) Auraria Library Archives

53. Gaskie, Jack (1963, July 18) "4-Year College Could Trigger Dollar Squeeze," *Rocky Mountain News*, "MSC Newsclippings" (Vol. I) Auraria Library Archives

54. Gaskie, Jack (1963, July 21) "Love Asked to Release Funds for Tax-Run College in Denver," *Rocky Mountain News*, "MSC Newsclippings" (Vol. I) Auraria Library Archives

55. Author unknown (1963, July 27) "CU President Fears People Think Too Much of Degree," *Rocky Mountain News* p. 5-7, "MSC Newsclippings" (Vol. I) Auraria Library Archives

56. Coffman, Don (1963, August 2) "Sen. Hewitt Raps Separate College" *Colorado Daily*, "MSC Newsclippings" (Vol. I) Auraria Library Archives

57. Coffman, Don (1963, August 12) "Panel to Advise End of Extension," *Colorado Daily*, Front Page, "MSC Newsclippings" (Vol. I) Auraria Library Archives

58. Thomasson, Dan (1963, August 10) "College Planning Funds OKd," *Rocky Mountain News* also: Ayers, Rendell, (1963, August 10) "Love Releases College Funds," *The Denver Post* Page 1, "MSC Newsclippings" (Vol. I) Auraria Library Archives

59. Author unknown (1963, November 5) "Smiley Attacks Metro College Plan," *The Denver Post*, "MSC Newsclippings" (Vol. I) Auraria Library Archives

60. Brown, Fred (1963, December 18) "Smiley Says Extended CU Better Answer For Area," *The Denver Post*, "MSC Newsclippings" (Vol. I) Auraria Library Archives

61. Gaskie, Jack (1963, November 18) "CU Seeking Denver Technical Institute" *Rocky Mountain News*, "MSC Newsclippings" (Vol. I) Auraria Library Archives; also Lindenmann, Walt (1963, November 19) "Regents Draft Metro Post High School Plan," *The Denver Post*, "MSC Newsclippings" (Vol. I) Auraria Library Archives

62.   Interview with Sandi Jones, notes in author's files

63.   Gaskie, Jack (1963, December 11) "Plan Seeks Start of Metro College By September '64," *Rocky Mountain News*, "MSC Newsclippings" (Vol. I) Auraria Library Archives

64.   Author unknown (1963, December 19) "State labor Leader Backs MSC," *Colorado Daily*, "MSC Newsclippings" (Vol. I) Auraria Library Archives; Author unknown (1963, December 20) "A College of Promise," *Littleton Independent*, "MSC Newsclippings" (Vol. I) Auraria Library Archives

65.   Author unknown Editorial (1963, December 22) "Start Two-year Metro College in 1964," *The Denver Post* p. 2AA, "MSC Newsclippings" (Vol. I) Auraria Library Archives; Author unknown Editorial (1963, December 22) "Opposes Four-Year Metro College," The Open Forum, *The Denver Post*, "MSC Newsclippings" (Vol. I) Auraria Library Archives

66.   Walt Lindenmann (1963, December 23) "Metro College Plan Draws New Criticism," *The Denver Post*, "MSC Newsclippings" (Vol. I) Auraria Library Archives

67.   Lindenmann, Walt (1963, December 29) "Lawmakers Warm Up Metro College Dispute," *The Denver Post*; also: Gaskie, Jack (1963) December 30) "2 Denver Legislators lambaste Opponents of Metro College," *Rocky Mountain News*, "MSC Newsclippings" (Vol. I) Auraria Library Archives

68.   Lindenmann, Walt (1963, December 31) "Metro College Problem for Assembly," *The Denver Post* p.32, "MSC Newsclippings" (Vol. I) Auraria Library Archives

69.   Thomasson, Dan (1964, January 1), "House Speaker Nixes Denver Metro College" *Rocky Mountain News*, Front page, "MSC Newsclippings" (Vol. I) Auraria Library Archives

70.   Gaskie, Jack (1964 January 4) "Denver C of C Wants Vocation High School," *Rocky Mountain News*, Front Page, "MSC Newsclippings" (Vol. I) Auraria Library Archives

71.   Lindenmann, Walt (1964, January 5) "C of C View Puzzles Metro College Aides," *The Denver Post*, also: Author unknown (1964, January 5) "Romer Protests Rejection of Metro State College," *Rocky Mountain News*, "MSC Newsclippings" (Vol. I) Auraria Library Archives

72.   Author unknown (1964, January 9) "Degree-Granting CU Branches Outside Boulder Are Proposed," *The Denver Post*; also Unknown (1964 January 10) "Off Campus Degree Proposals Pushed" *Rocky Mountain News*, "MSC Newsclippings" (Vol. I) Auraria Library Archives

73.   Author unknown Editorial (1964, January 12) "Lift Doubt From Off-Campus Degrees" *The Denver Post*, "MSC Newsclippings" (Vol. I) Auraria Library Archives; Author unknown Editorial (1964, January 13) "Which Will Give The Most Higher Education for the Money?" *Daily Camera*, "MSC Newsclippings" (Vol. I) Auraria Library Archives

74.   Author unknown, (1964, January 22) "Metro College Killed: Premature Love Asserts" *Denver Post* Front Page; also Thomasson, Dan (1964, January 22) "Love Labels new College Premature" *Rocky Mountain News* p. 5, "MSC Newsclippings" (Vol. I) Auraria Library Archives; Author unknown (1964, January 23) "College Plan Killed While In Print shop," *The Denver Post*, "MSC Newsclippings" (Vol. I) Auraria Library Archives

75.   Lindenmann, Walt (1964, January 22) "Love's Metro College Delay Draws Attacks," *The Denver Post*, "MSC Newsclippings" (Vol. I) Auraria Library Archives

76.   Author unknown Editorial (1964, January 23) "Realistic and Promising," *Rocky Mountain News* p. 48, "MSC Newsclippings" (Vol. I) Auraria Library Archives

77.   Author unknown editorial (1964, January 24) "Metro College Gap Needs Filing," *The Denver Post*, "MSC Newsclippings" (Vol. I) Auraria Library Archives

78.   Gaskie, Jack (1964, February 3) "State 'Needs' Metro College," *Rocky Mountain News* p. 37, "MSC Newsclippings" (Vol. I) Auraria Library Archives; Author unknown (1964, February 6) "Planners will ask 1965 Metro Opening," *Rocky Mountain News*. p.26, "MSC Newsclippings" (Vol. I) Auraria Library Archives

79.   Author unknown (1964, February 13) "School Board Wants Metro College Opened" *Rocky Mountain News* p. 27, "MSC Newsclippings" (Vol. 1) Auraria Library Archives

80.   "Don't let the sun catch you crying", Gerry and the Pacemakers, written by Joe Greene, April 1964, EMI Columbia (UK).

81. Author unknown (1964, March 3) "Trustees Pushing Plans to Establish Metro College," *Rocky Mountain News* p. 28, "MSC Newsclippings" (Vol. I) Auraria Library Archives: Author unknown (1964, March 4) "Record of the 44th", *Rocky Mountain News* p. 38, "MSC Newsclippings" (Vol. I) Auraria Library Archives

82. Lindenmann, Walt (1964, July 11) "Governor's 'New View' on Junior Colleges Cited" *The Denver Post* "MSC Newsclippings" (Vol. I) Auraria Library Archives

83. Gaskie, Jack (1964, September 3) "Metro State Endorsement is Attacked" *Rocky Mountain News* p. 24, "MSC Newsclippings" (Vol. I) Auraria Library Archives

84. Gaskie, Jack (1964, September 23) "State's Senior College Heads Demand Special Metro Plan" *Rocky Mountain News* p.8, "MSC Newsclippings" (Vol. I) Auraria Library Archives; Author unknown (1964, October 13) "Opposition On Metro Unit Told" *The Denver Post*, "MSC Newsclippings" (Vol. I) Auraria Library Archives

85. Author unknown (1964, November 1) "McVicker Advises 2-year Denver College" *The Denver Post*, "MSC Newsclippings" (Vol. I) Auraria Library Archives

86. Author unknown (1964, October 10) "Metro College Draws Attack" *The Denver Post*, "MSC Newsclippings" (Vol. I) Auraria Library Archives

87. Larson, Leonard (1964, December 31) "Super Board in Works For All State Colleges" *The Denver Post*, "MSC Newsclippings" (Vol. I) Auraria Library Archives

Chapter 3

88. Kingston Trio; "A Worried Man" Album: The Kingston Trio 1958; Written by Gordon Mills

89. Larsen, Leonard (1965, January 21) "Bill Spurs Metro College *The Denver Post* p.45, "MSC Newsclippings" (Vol. I) Auraria Library Archives

90. Author unknown (1965, January 27) "Bill would Modify Metro College Plan" *The Denver Post* p.65, "MSC Newsclippings" (Vol. I) Auraria Library Archives

91. Author unknown (1965, February 5) "2 CU Regents Ask College Fund Delay" *Rocky Mountain News*, "MSC Newsclippings" (Vol. I) Auraria Library Archives

92. Logan, William (1965, February 6) "Metro State College Assured Floor Debate" *Rocky Mountain News*, "MSC Newsclippings" (Vol. I) Auraria Library Archives; also Larsen, Leonard (1965, February 6) "Debate Due on Metro College" *The Denver Post*, "MSC Newsclippings" (Vol. I) Auraria Library Archives

93. *The Colorado Community College and Occupational System: A Silver Anniversary History* Carson Reed and Doug Hawk Denver Community College 1994, p 16-50

94. Larsen, Leonard (1965, February 8) "Metro College Change Offered" *The Denver Post*, "MSC Newsclippings" (Vol. I) Auraria Library Archives

95. Author unknown (1965, February 15) "Junior College In Denver Endorsed by CU Alumni" *The Denver Post* p.2, "MSC Newsclippings" (Vol. I) Auraria Library Archives

96. Author unknown Editorial (1965, February 16) "Junior College Can Serve Best" *The Denver Post* p.18, "MSC Newsclippings" (Vol. I) Auraria Library Archives

97. Gaskie, Jack (1965, May 3) "Undergrad Dropout Rates at CU Studied" *Rocky Mountain News* p. 57, "MSC Newsclippings" (Vol. I) Auraria Library Archives

98. Author unknown (1965, February 17) "New Bill Seeks Curb on College" *The Denver Post* p.38, "MSC Newsclippings" (Vol. I) Auraria Library Archives

99. Author personally heard the remarks at legislative proceedings; Interview Doug Holcombe

100. Author unknown (1965, February 26) "Degree-Granting CU Branches Defeated Narrowly in House" *Rocky Mountain News*, "MSC Newsclippings" (Vol. I) Auraria Library Archives

101. Edwards, Cliff (1965, March 2) "Hearing on Metro College Bill Marked by Note of Urgency" *Rocky Mountain News* p.62, "MSC Newsclippings" (Vol. I) Auraria Library Archives

102. Larsen, Leonard (1965, March 2) "Lawmakers Told to Act on Metro College" *The Denver Post*, "MSC Newsclippings" (Vol. I) Auraria Library Archives

103. Author unknown (1965, March 13) "CU Regents Urge 2-Year Limit on Metro College" *The Denver Post* p.16, "MSC Newsclippings" (Vol. I) Auraria Library Archives: Author unknown (1965, March 2) "Smiley, Regents Want Denver JC, *Colorado Daily*, "MSC Newsclippings" (Vol. I) Auraria Library Archives

104. Author unknown (1965, March 11) "Fight Erupts on Metro College Bills" *Rocky Mountain News*, "MSC Newsclippings" (Vol. I) Auraria Library Archives

105. Interview Mark Hogan by Robert Bowen, October 24, 2013. Transcript in author's files

106. Logan, William (1965, March 12) "House Gives First Approval to 4-year Metro College" *Rocky Mountain News* p.8, "MSC Newsclippings" (Vol. I) Auraria Library Archives

107. Interview Mark Hogan by Robert Bowen, October 24, 2013. Transcript in author's files

108. *Colorado House of Representatives Journal 1965*, March 11. 1965

109. Author unknown (1965, March 11) "Fight Erupts on Metro College Bills" *Rocky Mountain News* p.8, "MSC Newsclippings" (Vol. I) Auraria Library Archives

110. Author unknown (1965, March 23) "State College in Denver to Be a 4 year institution" *The Sentry*, CU Denver Center p.1 "MSC Newsclippings" (Vol. I) Auraria Library Archives

111. Giblin, Mary Louise (1965, April 18) "Denver Metro College Plan Seen As Threat to JC Movement" *The Daily Sentinel* Grand Junction, p.1, "MSC Newsclippings" (Vol. I) Auraria Library Archives

112. Author unknown (1965, April 20) "Plan Beaten Down to Make Metro State a Junior College" *Rocky Mountain News* p.13, "MSC Newsclippings" (Vol. I) Auraria Library Archives

113. Larsen, Leonard (1965, April 20) "Foes of Metro College Set Back" *The Denver Post* p.12, "MSC Newsclippings" (Vol. I) Auraria Library Archives

114. Kelley, Donald E (Senator) (1965, April 20) "Reply on Metro College" *The Denver Post* p.19, "MSC Newsclippings" (Vol. I) Auraria Library Archives

115. Author unknown Editorial (1965, April 22) "What a "Metro College" Should Be" *The Denver Post*, "MSC Newsclippings" (Vol. I) Auraria Library Archives

116. Moran, Martin (1965, April 23) "Bill to Open Metro College Killed" *Rocky Mountain News* p. 113; also Author unknown (2965, April 23) "Senate Panel Kills Pay Hike" *The Denver Post* p.2, "MSC Newsclippings" (Vol. I) Auraria Library Archives

117. *Colorado Senate Journal 1965*, Denver Public Library

118. Author unknown (1967, February 20) "What Can Be Done" *MSC Faculty-Staff Newsletter* p.2 (Vol.2) No. 21 Auraria Library Archives

119. Author unknown Editorial (1965, May 5) "Argument on Metro College is Over" *The Denver Post*, "MSC Newsclippings" (Vol. I) Auraria Library Archives

120. Author unknown (1965, May 6) "The End of the Session" *Rocky Mountain News* p.84, "MSC Newsclippings" (Vol. I) Auraria Library Archives

Chapter 4

121. "It's a Wonderful World," Louis Armstrong; 1965; Written by: George David Weiss, George Douglas, and Bob Thiele

122. U.S. Census 1960; U.S. Census 2010; U.S. Census update 2012 Denver Public Library

123. Dr. Joseph Lowery in an interview with Rev Al Sharpton on MSNBC broadcast live on the 50th anniversary of Dream Speech August 28, 2013

124. Stonewall Inn National Historic Landmark Register Number: 99000562 National Parks Service: http://www.nps.gov/diversity/stonewall.htm, accessed December 2, 2013

125. *Trustees Report on the Plan of Operation for Metropolitan Sate College*, Board of Trustees, December 30, 1963 (Green Report) p. 2 Auraria Library Archives; The six Studies of the Legislative Committee and the Task Group are summarized in: *Individual Opportunity and Economic Growth in the Denver Metropolitan Area February 1963*.

126. *Trustees Report on the Operation of Metropolitan State College*, December 30, 1963, p.3 Auraria Library Archives

127. Tillson, Dr. William (1970, February 2) "The Extroverted, urban Oriented College : Some Concept Definitions" *THE*

PAPER p.5 3(17) Auraria Library Archives

128. *Trustees Report on the Operation of Metropolitan State College*, December 30, 1963, p.5, 6 Auraria Library Archives

129. Curtis, Olga (1969, February 2) "Metro State: Denver's Invisible College *Empire Magazine*, "MSC Newsclippings" (Vol. X) Auraria Library Archives

130. Interview Dr. Charles Angeletti by Robert Bowen, Jan. 23, 2014. Transcript in author's files

131. Interview Dr. Gwen Thomas October 23, 2012. Transcript in author's files

132. Interview Larry Steele by Robert Bowen November 21, 2013. Transcript in author's files

133. Harnell, Gaylord P. (1967, April) "College and University Business," April 1967, reprinted in part in *MSC Faculty-Staff Newsletter* (1967, May 15) p.2 , Vol.2 (No.32) Auraria Library Archives

134. Howe, Howard (1967, October) "Higher Education and the Challenge of the Urban Crisis" *Phi Delta Kappan Magazine*; Reprinted in part *MSC Faculty-Staff Newsletter* (1967, October 30) p.2 Vol.3 (No.10) Auraria Library Archives

135. Kerr, Dr. Clark (1968, January) "A Call for the Urban Grant College" *Phi Delta Kappa Magazine*, Reprinted in part (1968, January 15) *MSC Faculty-Staff Newsletter* p. 1, Vol. 3 (No. 17) Auraria Library Archives

136. Kerr, Dr. Clark (1968, September) "Objectives of Urban University." *Phi Delta Kappan Magazine*; Reprinted in part (1968, January 15) MSC Faculty Staff Newsletter p.1, Vol.3 (No. 17), Auraria Library Archives

137. *Trustees Report on the Plan of Operation for Metropolitan Sate College*, Board of Trustees, December 30, 1963 (Green Report) p. 17& 18 Auraria Library Archives

138. Interview Sheldon Steinhauser, 2012. Transcript in author's files

139. "Report of the Legislative Committee on Education Beyond High School" 1960, presented to the Legislature State Capitol Archives

140. "Women's role in contemporary society: A report of NY 'commission on Human Rights" *1969* Library of Congress

141. "Women's role in contemporary society: A report of NY 'commission on Human Rights" *1969* Library of Congress

142. Self, Robert O, *All in the Family The Realignment of American Democracy since the 1960s*, Hill and Wang, New York

143. *Trustees Report on the Plan of Operation for Metropolitan Sate College*, Board of Trustees, December 30, 1963 (Green Report) p. 17 Auraria Library Archives

144. http://www.pbs.org/newshour/bb/study-finds-high-sat-act-scores-might-not-spell-success/ accessed February 18, 2014

145. Excerpt from *Phi Delta Kappan Magazine* re-printed (1966, May 16) *MSC Faculty-Staff Newsletter* (Vol.1) Auraria Library Archives

146. Interview Courtney Cowgill Nov. 2, 2012. Transcript in author's files

147. Interview King Harris Nov. 2, 2012. Transcript in author's files

148. Interview Larry Steele Nov. 21, 2013. Transcript in author's files

149. Author unknown (1966, May 2) "Statement on College Objectives" *MSC Faculty-Staff Newsletter* p. 1, 2 Vol.1 (No.17), Auraria Library v

150. Huff, Larry & Linton, William (1963). "*Easier Said than Done.*" Album: Easier Said Than Done United States, Roulette Records

Chapter 5

151. Downtown" Petula Clark, 1964 United Kingdom, Songwriters: Astasio, George / Cano, Christopher Thomas / Jen, John Bent. / Pebworth, Jason Andrew / Rachild, Chad/ Michael / Roentgen, Kevin M.

152. Author unknown (1965, May 7) "President Named for Metro College" *The Denver Post*, "MSC Newsclippings" (Vol. I) Auraria Library Archives

153. Author unknown (1965, May 10) "Adams State Official Named First Dean of Metro State" *Rocky Mountain News* p. 43, "MSC Newsclippings" (Vol. I) Auraria Library Archives

154. Author unknown (1965, June 9) "Metro College Gets 12 Applications a Day" *The Denver Post*; also Author unknown (1965, June 9) "81 Apply for First Year Class at Metro State" *Rocky Mountain News Post* "MSC Newsclippings" (Vol.1) Auraria Library Archives

155. Author unknown (1966, February 14) "Mrs. Bentley First MSC Secretary" MSC Faculty and Staff Newsletter p.1 Vol.1

(No. 8), Auraria Library Archives

156. Pinney, Greg (1965, August 11) "The Rise of Metro College for the Fall Semester" *The Denver Post* p.80ff, "MSC News-clippings" (Vol. II) Auraria Library Archives

157. Author unknown (1966, February 14) "Mrs. Bentley First MSC Secretary" *MSC Faculty-Staff Newsletter* p.1, Vol.1 (No 8) Auraria Library Archives

158. Pinney, Greg (1965, August 11) "The Rise of Metro College for the Fall Semester" *The Denver Post* p. 80ff "MSC News-clippings" (Vol. II) Auraria Library Archives

159. Author unknown (1966, March 28) "Mrs. Crosby Brought Varied Experience to Metro" *MSC Faculty-Staff Newsletter* Vol.1 (No. 13), Auraria Library Archives; also, Author unknown (1966, April 25) "Miss Elwell is Both Counselor and Student" *MSC Faculty-Staff Newsletter* Vol.1 (No. 16), Auraria Library Archives; also Author unknown (1966, November 21) "Mrs. Louks Came to Colorado From Iowa" *MSC Faculty-Staff Newsletter* p.1 Vol.20 (No. 12) Auraria Library Archives

160. Author unknown Editorial (1965, May 11) "Vote No on the Junior College" *The Denver Post* "MSC Newsclippings" (Vol.1) Auraria Library Archives

161. Author unknown (1965, May 20) "New CU Center Policy Urged" *The Denver Post*; also Unknown Editorial (1965, May 27) "New Role for CU in Denver" *The Denver Post* p.24 "MSC Newsclippings" (Vol.1) Auraria Library Archives

162. Author unknown (1965, June 9) "Instruction in Culinary Arts Advocated for Metro State" *The Denver Post* "MSC Newsclippings" (Vol.1) Auraria Library Archives

163. Author unknown (1965, June 13) "First Six Members of Faculty Appointed For Metro State" *The Denver Post* "MSC Newsclippings" (Vol.1) Auraria Library Archives

164. Johnston, Dick (1965, June 11) "Inner City Site urged For College" *The Denver Post* "MSC Newsclippings" (Vol.1) Auraria Library Archives

165. Gaskie, Jack (1965, June 15) "Metro College Leases Space" *Rocky Mountain News* p.6 "MSC Newsclippings" (Vol.1) Auraria Library Archives

166. Author unknown (1965, June 16) "College Site Fails City Test" *The Denver Post* "MSC Newsclippings" (Vol.1) Auraria Library Archives; also Gaskie, Jack (1965, June 17) "Metro College's Forum Bldg. Use Argued" *Rocky Mountain News* p.15 "MSC Newsclippings" (Vol.1) Auraria Library Archives

167. Author unknown (1965, June 16) "Metro College's New Headquarters" *The Denver Post* "MSC Newsclippings" (Vol.1) Auraria Library Archives

168. Gaskie, Jack (1965, June 15) "Metro College Leases Space" *Rocky Mountain News* p.6 "MSC Newsclippings" (Vol.1) Auraria Library Archives

169. Interview Charlene Alexis 10/19/2011. Transcript in author's files.

170. Author unknown (1965, June 16) "Metro State Accused of Wasting Money" *Rocky Mountain News* "MSC Newsclippings" (Vol.1) Auraria Library Archives

171. Author unknown (1965, June 21) "Board OKs Use of Forum Bldg. For College" *Rocky Mountain News* "MSC Newsclippings" (Vol.1) Auraria Library Archives

172. Author unknown (1965, July 16) "Metro unaffected By Forum Lawsuit" *The Denver Post* "MSC Newsclippings" (Vol. II) Auraria Library Archives

173. Author unknown (1965, July 8) "Metro State: College President Appointed" *The Denver Post* p.3 "MSC Newsclippings" (Vol. II) Auraria Library Archives; also, author unknown (1965, February 7) "Dr. Phillips Brought Broad Background to MSC" *MSC Faculty- Staff Newsletter* p.1 Vol.1 (No. 7) Auraria Library Archives

174. Interview Dr. Ken Phillips by Andrew Phillips. Transcript in author's files

175. Author unknown (1965, July 9) "Californian named head of Metro State" *Rocky Mountain News* p.36 p.1 "MSC Newsclippings" (Vol. II) Auraria Library Archives

176. Interview Doug Holcombe by Robert Bowen December 2013. Transcript in author's files

177. Author unknown (1965, July 9) "Metropolitan College Gets New Staffers" *Rocky Mountain News* "MSC Newsclippings"

(Vol. II) Auraria Library Archives

178. Interview Dr. Jerry Wilson Sept. 14, 2011. Transcript in author's files

179. Gaskie, Jack (1965, July 17) "Higher Education Panel Sets Guidelines for 'Battle'" *Rocky Mountain News*; also author unknown (1965, July 18)"Metro is Topic: State Panel Confers" *The Denver Post* "MSC Newsclippings" (Vol. II) Auraria Library Archives

180. Author unknown (1965, July 18) "Metro is Topic: State Panel Confers" *The Denver Post* "MSC Newsclippings" (Vol. II) Auraria Library Archives

181. Gaskie, Jack (1965, July 18) "New Metro State To Up Requirements" *Rocky Mountain News* "MSC Newsclippings" (Vol. II) Auraria Library Archives

182. Chase, Robert L. (1965, July 21) "Different Picture of Metro College" *Rocky Mountain News* "MSC Newsclippings" (Vol. II) Auraria Library Archives

183. Pinney, Greg (1965, July 20) "Kenneth Phillips: Metro Chief Vows 1st-Rate College" *The Denver Post* "MSC Newsclippings" (Vol. II) Auraria Library Archives

184. Pinney, Greg (1965, August 11) "The Rise of Metro College for the Fall Semester" *The Denver Post* p.80ff "MSC Newsclippings" (Vol. II) Auraria Library Archives

185. Interview Dr. Ken Phillips by Andrew Phillips. Transcript in author's files

186. Pinney, Greg (1965, August 11) "The Rise of Metro College for the Fall Semester" *The Denver Post* p. 80ff "MSC Newsclippings" (Vol. II) Auraria Library Archives

187. Pinney, Greg (1965, August 22) "698 Apply: Metro College List Goes Up" *The Denver Post* "MSC Newsclippings" (Vol. II) Auraria Library Archives; also, Gaskie, Jack (1965, September 4) "Metro Accepts 1st 600 Students" *Rocky Mountain News* "MSC Newsclippings" (Vol. II) Auraria Library Archives

188. Pinney, Greg (1965, September 4) "New Denver College to Offer Training in 4 Technical Fields," *The Denver Post* "MSC Newsclippings" (Vol. II) Auraria Library Archives

189. Author unknown (1965, September 9) "Metro College Enrolls 1,000th Student" *The Denver Post* "MSC Newsclippings" (Vol. II) Auraria Library Archives

190. Author unknown (1965, September 28) "Metro College Begins With a Test" *The Denver Post* "MSC Newsclippings" (Vol. II) Auraria Library Archives

191. Lalendorf, Fritz (1965, September 30) "Metro Library in Quite a State," *Rocky Mountain News* "MSC Newsclippings" (Vol. II) Auraria Library Archives

192. Interview Tony Ledesma May 17, 2012. Transcript in author's files

193. Interview Charlene Alexis Oct 19, 2011. Transcript in author's files

194. Metropolitan State College Catalogue 1965-66 Auraria Library

195. Gaskie, Jack (1965, November 14) "Metro State's Blueprint Changes" *Rocky Mountain News* "MSC Newsclippings" (Vol. II) Auraria Library Archives

196. Interview Roger Braun by Robert Bowen December 2013. Transcript in author's files

197. Tharp, Marty (1965, November 25) "Thonssen Scores Metro First: 16th Book Shows College Tie" *The Denver Post* "MSC Newsclippings" (Vol. II) Auraria Library Archives

198. Interview Larry Strutton, Feb. 15, 2013. Transcript in author's files

199. Gaskie, Jack (1965 November 14) "Metro State's Blueprint Changes" *Rocky Mountain News* "MSC Newsclippings" (Vol. II) Auraria Library Archives

200. Author unknown (1965, December 4) "Metro State's Role Questioned By Commission" *Rocky Mountain News* "MSC Newsclippings" (Vol. II) Auraria Library Archives

201. Author unknown (1965 December 5) "Assembly Wishes At Issue: Official Defends Metro College Role" *The Denver Post* also; author unknown (1965, December 5) "Metro Criticism Blamed on Legislature" *Rocky Mountain News* "MSC Newsclippings" (Vol. II) Auraria Library Archives

202. Roos, Charles (1965, December 10) "Education referee needs to Scramble" *The Denver Post* p.34, "MSC Newsclippings" (Vol. II) Auraria Library Archives

203. Pinney, Greg (1965, December 16) "Site Funds Sought By Metro College" *The Denver Post* "MSC Newsclippings" (Vol. II) Auraria Library Archives

204. Gaskie, Jack (1965, December 2) "Area Surveyed for Metro College Site" *Rocky Mountain News* "MSC Newsclippings" (Vol. II) Auraria Library Archives

205. Author unknown (1965, December 21) "Study Requested of College Sites" *The Denver Post* "MSC Newsclippings" (Vol. II) Auraria Library Archives

206. Author unknown (1965, December 22) "Don't Lose Metro By Default" *The Sentry Jefferson County* "MSC Newsclippings" (Vol. II) Auraria Library Archives

207. Evans, Pat (1966, January 20) "What Do They Think of Metro?" *The Sentry* CU Denver Center; also reprinted (1966, January 31) MSC Faculty-Staff Newsletter, "MSC Newsclippings" (Vol. III) Auraria Library Archives

208. Author unknown (1965, December 5) "Board Honors by Official Resolution" MSC Faculty–Staff Newsletter p.1 Vol.1 (No 1) Auraria Library Archives

Chapter 6

209. "Catch Us If You Can" Dave Clark Five, Album: The Dave Clark Five: The Hits. Written by Dave Clark; Lenny Davidson 1965

210. Author unknown (1965, December 26) "300 Okayed As Metro Students" *The Denver Post* p.1 "MSC Newsclippings" Vol. II Auraria Library Archives

211. Gaskie, Jack (1966, January 12) "Metro Loses 38% of First Quarter Students *Rocky Mountain News* "MSC Newsclippings" (Vol. III) Auraria Library Archives

212. Chase, Robert L. (1966, January 13) "Metro State's Purpose" *The Denver Post* "MSC Newsclippings" (Vol. III) Auraria Library Archives

213. Author unknown (1966, January 15) "Resolution Clarifies Metro State's Role" *Rocky Mountain News*; also Unknown (1966, January 15) "Metro College is Target of Resolution" *The Denver Post* "MSC Newsclippings" (Vol. III) Auraria Library Archives

214. Author unknown (1966, January 16) "Board Reaffirms Metro 4-Year Plan" *The Denver Post* "MSC Newsclippings" (Vol. III) Auraria Library Archives

215. Author unknown (1966, January 17) "Metro College: Plan Drawn to Give Aerospace Courses" *The Denver Post* "MSC Newsclippings" (Vol. III) Auraria Library Archives

216. Chase, Robert L. (1966, January 18) "Spell Out Plan Before Election" *The Denver Post* "MSC Newsclippings" (Vol. III) Auraria Library Archives

217. Author unknown (1966, January 20) "Downtown Campus Detailed Study Slated" *The Denver Post* "MSC Newsclippings" (Vol. III) Auraria Library Archives

218. Author unknown (1966, January 23) "Metro College Officials Face Assembly Quiz" *Rocky Mountain News* "MSC Newsclippings" (Vol. III) Auraria Library Archives

219. Pinney, Greg (1966, January 27) "Metro College Officials Agree To Work With Other Schools" *The Denver Post* "MSC Newsclippings" (Vol. III) Auraria Library Archives

220. Pinney, Greg (1966, January 30) "Nine Campuses: Love Receives College Critics" *The Denver Post* "MSC Newsclippings" (Vol. III) Auraria Library Archives

221. Author unknown (1966, February 1) "Mackie Denies 2-Year Limit" *The Denver Post* "MSC Newsclippings" (Vol. III) Auraria Library Archives

222. Author unknown (1966, February 7) "Credit Hour Jump For New Semester" *Rocky Mountain News* "MSC Newsclippings" Vol. III (No. 4) Auraria Library Archives

223. Author unknown (1966, March 21) "MSC Bombers Second in Basketball League" *MSC Faculty-Staff Newsletter* p.1 Vol. III1 (No. 12) Auraria Library Archives; Author unknown (1966, February 14) "Metro State to Publish Quarterly" *The Denver Post* "MSC Newsclippings" (Vol. III) Auraria Library Archives

224. Author unknown (1966, February 10) "Metro Debate Opens; Fund Misuse Charged" *The Denver Post*; also; Unknown

(1966, February 10) "Metro College Additional Money Bill Clears House" *Rocky Mountain News* "MSC Newsclippings" (Vol. III) Auraria Library Archives

225. Author unknown (1966, February 14) "A Valentine Present For MSC" *MSC Faculty-Staff Newsletter* p.1, Vol.1 (No. 8) Auraria Library Archives

226. Gaskie, Jack (1966, March 9) "Era Ends for Big Increases in High School Graduates *Rocky Mountain News* p. 5 "MSC Newsclippings" (Vol. III) Auraria Library Archives

227. Author unknown (1966, March 21) "Social Activities" *MSC Faculty-Staff Newsletter* p.2 Vol.1 (No. 12) Auraria Library Archives

228. Pinney, Greg (1966, April 23) "Enrollment Boom Feared: Cold War GI Bill Worries State's Colleges" *The Denver Post* "MSC Newsclippings" (Vol. III) Auraria Library Archives

229. Gauss, Gordon G (1966, May 9) "Student Wave Under GI Bill Is Minimized" AP *Rocky Mountain News* "MSC Newsclippings" (Vol. III) Auraria Library Archives

230. Pearce, Ken (1966, May 27) "Six More Programs Planned for Metro College" *The Denver Post* "MSC Newsclippings" (Vol. III) Auraria Library Archives

231. Author unknown (1966, May 1) "Police Training Plan at Metro State Hit" *Rocky Mountain News* "MSC Newsclippings" (Vol. III) Auraria Library Archives; Author unknown (1966, June 17) "Duplication Ruling Angers Metro State" *Rocky Mountain News* "MSC Newsclippings" (Vol. III) Auraria Library Archives

232. Interview Doug Holcombe by Robert Bowen November 25, 2013; Interview Roger Braun by Robert Bowen December 2013. Transcript in author's files

233. Pinney, Greg (1966, June 14) "Suspension Rate Called Low: One Third at Metro Failing" *The Denver Post* "MSC Newsclippings" (Vol. III) Auraria Library Archives

234. Author unknown (1966, June 8) "Metro State Meets Needs of Denver Area Student" "The Open Forum" *The Denver Post* "MSC Newsclippings" (Vol. III) Auraria Library Archives

235. Author unknown (1966, August 1) "Use of Sumer School for Probationary Admission or Marginal Students" *MSC Faculty-Staff Newsletter* p.1 Vol.2 (No. 2) Auraria Library Archives

236. Author unknown (1966, June 27) "Welcome to the Summer Quarter" *MSC Faculty-Staff Newsletter* Vol. 1 (No.21); Author unknown (1966, June 27) "Enrollment Data" *MSC Faculty-Staff Newsletter* Vol.1 (No. 22) Auraria Library Archives

237. Author unknown (1966, June 16) "Six Metro Courses Approved" *The Denver Post* "MSC Newsclippings" (Vol. III) Auraria Library Archives; Author unknown (1966, June 1) "Duplication Ruling Angers Metro State" *Rocky Mountain News* "MSC Newsclippings" (Vol. III) Auraria Library Archives

238. Chase, Robert L. (1966, June 19) "Education Plan Needed" *Rocky Mountain News* "MSC Newsclippings" (Vol. III) Auraria Library Archives

239. Johnston, Dick (1966, June 2) "Plans Board Reviews Metro College Sites Study" *The Denver Post* "MSC Newsclippings" (Vol. III) Auraria Library Archives

240. Johnston, dick (1966, July 7) "Economic Gain Stressed: Auraria Campus Urged" *The Denver Post* "MSC Newsclippings" (Vol. IV) Auraria Library Archives

241. Harding, Del (1966, July 7) "Auraria is Favored as Metro Site" *Rocky Mountain News* "MSC Newsclippings" (Vol. IV) Auraria Library Archives

242. Author unknown (1966, July 19) "Developments Regarding a Site for the College" 7 *MSC Faculty-Staff Newsletter* p.1 Vol.2 (No.1) Auraria Library Archives; also, Gaskie, Jack (1966, August 28) "Mayor Asks College Trustees to Select Auraria for Metro" *Rocky Mountain News* "MSC Newsclippings" (Vol. IV) Auraria Library Archives

243. Author unknown (1966, July 27) "Police Science Programs OK'd" *The Denver Post* "MSC Newsclippings" (Vol. IV) Auraria Library Archives; also, Author unknown (1966, August 24) "Law Enforcement Expert Named as Metro Professor" *Rocky Mountain News* "MSC Newsclippings" (Vol. IV) Auraria Library Archives

244. Sandoval, Joseph G. (2013) "A Short History of the Department of Criminal Justice and Criminology at MSC Denver" p.2,3, Auraria Library Archives

245. McCoy, Joan (1969) "Program Builds Concept of Justice" *Rocky Mountain News*, P. 56 (Vol. XI) Auraria Library Archives

246. Interview Joseph Sandoval by Robert Bowen, February 13, 2014. Transcript in author's files

247. Sandoval, Joseph G. (2013) "A Short History of the Department of Criminal Justice and Criminology at MSU Denver," p. 9. Auraria Library Archives

248. Author unknown Photo Caption (1966, September 25) "If You Think Metro College Isn't Popular Just Take a Look at This" *The Denver Post* p. 29 "MSC Newsclippings" (Vol. IV) Auraria Library Archives

249. Author unknown (1966, October 9) "Enrollment Doubles at Metro State" *The Denver Post* "MSC Newsclippings" (Vol. IV) Auraria Library Archives

250. Interview Roger Braun by Robert Bowen November 2013. Transcript in author's files

251. Author unknown (1966, October 17) "Candidates to Visit MSC" *MSC Faculty-Staff Newsletter* p.1 Vol.2 (No.8) Auraria Library Archives

252. Author unknown (1966, November 14) "MSC Presents First Opera" *MSC Faculty-Staff Newsletter* p.2 Vol.2 (No.11) Auraria Library Archives; Author unknown (1966, November 21) "Report on Speech Program" *MSC Faculty-Staff Newsletter* p.1 Vol. 2 (No. 12) Auraria Library Archives

253. Author unknown (1966, December 12) "AWS Moves Ahead" *The Metropolitan* 1(2) Auraria Library Archives

254. Author unknown (1966, December 12) "Democrats and Republicans Organize" *The Metropolitan* 1(2) Auraria Library Archives; Author unknown (1966, December 12) "Board to Decide on Policies" *The Metropolitan* 1(2) Auraria Library Archives

255. (1966, November) "Strengthening Higher Education in Colorado" CCHE Archives, State of Colorado, State Capitol Archives

256. Author unknown (1966, December 12) "Christmas Dance Highlights Winter Festival" *The Metropolitan* 1(2) Auraria Library Archives

257. *Argument without End: In Search of Answers to the Vietnam Tragedy,* Robert McNamara, New York 1999

Chapter 7

258. "Purple Haze," written by Jimi Hendricks; Released on a single by The Jimmy Hendricks Experience, January 1967

259. Author unknown (1967, January 16) "Winter Quarter Enrollment" *MSC Faculty-Staff Newsletter* Vol.2 (No.15) Auraria Library Archives

260. Gaskie, Jack (1967, January 5) "College Budget Requests Cut Sharply" *Rocky Mountain News* "MSC Newsclippings" (Vol. V) Auraria Library Archives

261. Author unknown (1967, February 20) "What Can Be Done" *MSC Faculty-Staff Newsletter* p. 2, 3 Vol. 2 (No. 21) Auraria Library Archives

262. Interview Doug Holcombe by Robert Bowen November 2013. p. 2, 3. Transcript in author's files.

263. Interview Roger Braun, December 2013. Transcript in author's files.

264. Author unknown (1967, January 16) "Metro Grand Opening Held for New Student Center" *Rocky Mountain News* "MSC Newsclippings" (Vol. V) Auraria Library Archives

265. Carter, Charles (1967, January 27) "Negro Panelists Defend Black Power Goals" *The Denver Post* "MSC Newsclippings: (Vol. V) Auraria Library Archives

266. Author unknown (1967, January 27) "Metro State Literary Review Too Good Looking, Critic Says" *The Denver Post* "MSC Newsclippings" (Vol. V) Auraria Library Archives

267. McCartt, Lon (1967, February 13) "Legislators Face Student Forum" *The Metropolitan* (1) 3 Auraria Library Archives

268. Author unknown (1967, February 13) "Spanish Surnamed Attend Metro" *Rocky Mountain News* "MSC Newsclippings: (Vol. V) Auraria Library Archives

269. Author unknown (1967, February 13) Letters to The Editor," *The Metropolitan* 1(3) Auraria Library Archives

270. *Columbine, Metropolitan State College* Denver, Colorado Vol. 1 (No. 1) 1967 Auraria Library Archives

271. Author unknown (1967, February 17) "Metro State College Sweetheart Candidates" *Rocky Mountain News* "MSC

Newsclippings" (Vol. V) Auraria Library Archives

272. Author unknown (1967, February 27) "67 Sweetheart Crowned" *The Metropolitan* 1(4) Auraria Library Archives

273. Author unknown (1967, February 27) "Lecture Recital Slated" *The Metropolitan* 1(4) Auraria Library Archives

274. Arnold, Clarence (1967, February 27) "Why Insurance?" *The Metropolitan* 1(4) Auraria Library Archives

275. Horton, John (1967, February 27) "An Aye on Sports" *The Metropolitan* 1(4) Auraria Library Archives

276. Author unknown (1967, February 20) "A Call to Vision" *MSC Faculty-Staff Newsletter* p 2 Vol.2 (No. 21) Auraria Library Archives

277. Author unknown (1967, February 20) "What Can Be Done" *MSC Faculty-Staff Newsletter* Vol. II (No. 21) Auraria Library Archives

278. Author unknown (1967, February 17) "C of C Backs 4-Year Metro College" *Rocky Mountain News* "MSC Newsclippings" (Vol. V) Auraria Library Archives

279. Brown, Fred (1967, February 27) "More College Funds Asked" *The Denver Post*; also, Unknown (1967, February 14) "Legislature Gets Education Report" *Rocky Mountain News* "MSC Newsclippings" (Vol. V) Auraria Library Archives

280. Author unknown Editorial (1967, March 8) "Time to Move Ahead on Metro State" *The Denver Post* "MSC Newsclippings" (Vol. V) Auraria Library Archives

281. Author unknown (1967, March 20) "Currigan Urges 4-Year for Metro College" *Rocky Mountain News* p. 20 "MSC Newsclippings" (Vol. V) Auraria Library Archives; Becker, George (1967, March 18) "Metro State Goals" *The Denver Post* "Open Forum" "MSC Newsclippings" (Vol. V) Auraria Library Archives

282. Brown, Fred (1967, March 23) "Love Urges Buildup of 2-Year Colleges: Legislators Told Need is 'Urgent'" *The Denver Post* "MSC Newsclippings" (Vol. V) Auraria Library Archives

283. Author unknown (1967, March 25) "Love Backed On Colleges" *Rocky Mountain News* "MSC Newsclippings" (Vol. V) Auraria Library Archives

284. Author unknown (1967, March 3) "4 Years for Metro State and Student's Appeal" *The Denver Post* "MSC Newsclippings" (Vol. V) Auraria Library Archives; Author unknown (1967, March 26) "Metro College Gears for a 4-year Operation" *The Denver Post* "MSC Newsclippings" (Vol. V) Auraria Library Archives

285. Moran, Martin (1967, March 25) "Senate Oks Upper Division Classes for Metro State" *Rocky Mountain News* "MSC Newsclippings" (Vol. V) Auraria Library Archives: *Colorado Senate Journal 1967* (March 3) Denver Public Library; also, Gavin, Tom (1967, March 25) "Senate Oks College Expansion" *The Denver Post* "MSC Newsclippings" (Vol. V) Auraria Library Archives

286. Carter, Charles (1967, March 27) "Metro State in Denver Senate Oks College Expansion" *The Denver Post* "MSC Newsclippings" (Vol. V) Auraria Library Archives

287. *Colorado House of Representatives Journal* 1967 Denver Public Library

288. Phillips, Ken "Express Gratitude" (1967, April 24) *The Metropolitan* p.1 (1) 6Auraria Library Archives

289. Author unknown (1967, April 14) "Prospectus: Rights Discussion Lively Topic" *The Metropolitan* p.1 1(6) Auraria Library Archives

290. Myers, Bill (1967, March 1) "Civil Rights Situation in Denver 'Not ideal'" *The Denver Post* "MSC Newsclippings" (Vol. V) Auraria Library Archives

291. Interview Doug Holcombe by Robert Bowen, November 25 2012. Transcript in author's files.

292. Cusimano, Paul (1967, March 14)"Letter to the Editor" *The Metropolitan*, 1(5) Auraria Library Archives

293. Author unknown (1967, April 5) "You Know It's The Silly Season" *The Denver Post* Front Page "MSC Newsclippings" (Vol. V) Auraria Library Archives

294. Author unknown (1967, April 24) "Student Elections" *The Metropolitan* 1(6) Auraria Library Archives

295. Author unknown (1967, April 24) "Inaugural Meeting Held" *The Metropolitan* 1(6) Auraria Library Archives

296. Horton, John (1967, April 24) "An Aye on Sports" *The Metropolitan* 1(6) Auraria Library Archives

297. Author unknown (1967, May 8) "Metro Wins College Bowl" *The Metropolitan* Front Page 1(7) Auraria Library Archives

298. Author unknown (1967, May 8) "LSD in Colorado" *The Metropolitan* Front Page 1(7) Auraria Library Archives

299. Author unknown (1967, May 8) "Greg Pearson Added to MSC Faculty" *The Metropolitan* 1(7) Auraria Library Auraria

Library Archives

300. Author unknown (1967, May 29) "Prospectus Forum: Prospectus Hosts Question–And-Answer" *The Metropolitan* Front Page 1(8) Auraria Library Auraria Library Archives

301. Author unknown (1967, May 29) "Miss Metro" Metropolitan p.1 (1)8; also, Unknown (1967, June 5) "Miss Metro Crowned" *The Metropolitan* p.2, 1(9) Auraria Library Auraria Library Archives

302. Author unknown (1967, May 29) "Metro Receives Police Grant," *The Metropolitan*, p.1, 1(8) Auraria Library Auraria Library Archives

303. Sandoval, Joseph G, (2013) "A Short History of Department of Criminal Justice and Criminology at MSU Denver" page 3 Auraria Library; and, Author unknown Editorial (1967, September 1) "Two New Ideas Can Aid Police," *The Denver Post*, p.22 "MSC Newsclippings" (Vol. V) Auraria Library Archives

304. Author unknown (1967, June 5) "President's Message" *The Metropolitan* p.1 1(9) Auraria Library Archives

305. Author unknown (1967, June 5) "May Festival Rounds Out Year," *The Metropolitan* 1(9) Auraria Library Archives

306. Author unknown (1967, June 5) "Library Moves Home" *The Metropolitan* 1(9) Auraria Library Archives

307. Author unknown (1967, June 5) "Denver's Tennis Champ: Metro Sports Shots" *The Metropolitan* p.4 1(9) Auraria Library Archives

308. Author unknown (1967, June 5) "College 'Hawks and Doves': Viet War Polled" *The Metropolitan* 1(9) Auraria Library Archives

Chapter 8

309. Bob Dylan, "The Times They are a Changin'", Album (same name), Columbia Records Jan. 13, 1964

310. "Somebody to Love," Jefferson Airplane Surrealistic Pillow Album written by Darby Slick, February 1967

311. Anderson, T.H (1995) The *Movement and the Sixties: Protest in America from Greensboro to Wounded Knee*, (Oxford University Press), p.172

312. (March 14, 2007) "Transcript American Experience" documentary on the Summer of Love *PBS* and *WGBH*

313. Leary, Timothy (1983) *Flashbacks: A Personal and Cultural History of an Era* p. 253 Published: Jeremy Tarcher, Los Angeles, 1983

314. *Itchycoo Park*, a psychedelic pop song written by Steve Marriott and Ronnie Lane, first recorded by the Small Faces, August 1967.

315. Author unknown (1967, April 16) "Many Draft Cards Burned - Eggs Tossed at Parade," *New York Times*, p.1, 38

316. Whitburn, Joel (2004). The Billboard Book of Top 40 Hits: Eighth Edition Record Research p. 415.

317. Gail Dolgin; Vicente Franco (2007). "The Summer of Love," *American Experience* (PBS). Retrieved 2007-04-23

318. "White Rabbit" Jefferson Airplane, written by Grace Slick, Album: Surrealistic Pillow, RCA, United States 1967

319. Chenoweth, Lawrence. "The Rhetoric of Hope and Despair: A study of the Jimi Hendrix Experience and the Jefferson Airplane." American Quarterly 23 (1971): 25-45. JSTOR. University of Arizona Library, Tucson.

320. "Give Peace a Chance" Plastic Ono Band; written by John Lennon, performed with Yoko Ono while Lennon was still with the Beatles; Apple Records, 1969

321. Interview Roger Braun by Robert Bowen December 1, 2013. Transcript in author's files.

322. Unknown (1967, October 9) "Un-Titled" *You're Choice* Front Page (1)1 Auraria Library Archives

323. Author unknown (1967, October 9) "President Welcomes Students" *Your Choice* Front Page 1(1) Auraria Library Archives

324. Author unknown (1967, October 9) "Metro Begins Third Year," *Your Choice* Front Page 1(1) Auraria Library Archives

325. Interview Larry Strutton February 15, 2013. Transcript in author's notes.

326. Interview Rick Reeser May 18, 2013. Transcript in author's notes.

327. Megeath, Joe (2014, March) *History of the Computer Information Systems (CIS) Department* Auraria Library Archives

328. Author unknown (1967, October 9) "Holds Meeting" *Your Choice* p 3 1(1) Auraria Library Archives

329. Author unknown (1967, October 3) "Metro College Sites are Narrowed to 3" *Rocky Mountain News* "MSC Newsclippings" (Vol. VI) Auraria Library Archives

330. Author unknown (1967, October 23) "The Bitch-In" *Your Choice* Front page 1(2) Auraria Library Archives; Author unknown Editorial (1967, October 23) "Bitch-In" *Your Choice* 1(2) Auraria Library Archives

331. Author unknown (1967, October 23) "Goff Visits" *Your Choice* 1(2) Auraria Library Archives

332. Author unknown Editorial (1967, October 16) "Metro State a City College" *The Denver Post* "MSC Newsclippings" (Vol. VI) Auraria Library Archives

333. Author unknown (1967, October 18) "Arvada Won't Bow Out of Site Race" *Cervi's Journal* "MSC Newsclippings" (Vol. VI) Auraria Library Archives

334. Author unknown (1967, October 29) "Trustees Recommend Auraria Site for Metro" *Rocky Mountain News* "MSC Newsclippings" (Vol. VI) Auraria Library Archives

335. Carter, Charles (1967, October 29) "1st Choice for College: Auraria Picked for College Site" *The Denver Post* "MSC Newsclippings" (Vol. VI) Auraria Library Archives

336. Author unknown Editorial (1967, October 31) "Auraria is Right For Metro" *The Denver Post* "MSC Newsclippings" (Vol. VI) Auraria Library Archives

337. Author unknown (1967, November 9) "Auraria Site For Metro is Endorsed by SPARC" *Rocky Mountain News* "MSC Newsclippings" (Vol. VII) Auraria Library Archives

338. Author unknown (1967, November 11) "Metro College Urged to Study Park Hill Site" *Rocky Mountain News* "MSC Newsclippings" (Vol. VI) Auraria Library Archives; also, Pinney, Greg (1967, November 11 "Golf Links Proposed as Metro Site" *The Denver Post* "MSC Newsclippings" (Vol. VII) Auraria Library Archives

339. Author unknown Editorial (1967, November 14 "Metro State and the Golf Course" *The Denver Post* "MSC Newsclippings" (Vol. VII) Auraria Library Archives

340. Author unknown (1967, November 19) "College View Location Suggested for College" *The Denver Post* "MSC Newsclippings" (Vol. VII) Auraria Library Archives

341. Author unknown (1967, October 29) "Metro gets on Cultural Caravan" *The Denver Post* "MSC Newsclippings" (Vol. VI) Auraria Library Archives

342. Fuentes, Joseph (1967, October 30) "Puff Goal Set: Looking Out for MSC Majority" *Neoteric Puff* 1(2) Auraria Library Archives

343. Author unknown (1967, November 6) "Name *the paper* Contest Winners" *Metro Gadfly* 1(3) Auraria Library Archives

344. Author unknown (1967, November 6) "Student Government Makes Plans And Spends Money" *Metro Gadfly* 1(6); and, Unknown (1967, November 6) "Senate Appointments" *Metro Gadfly* 1(3) Auraria Library Archives

345. Author unknown (1967, November 6) "Mexican-American Conference," *Metro Gadfly* 1(3) Auraria Library Archives

346. Graham, Wanda (1967, November 20) "Frosh Cast Most Votes, Count Low" *Neoteric Puff* 1(2) Auraria Library Archives

347. Author unknown (1967, November 15) "The Election" *Metro Gadfly* 1(4) Auraria Library Archives

348. Author unknown (1967, November 15) "Senate Defeats House Bill" *Metro Gadfly* 1(4) Auraria Library Archives

349. Author unknown (1967, November 15) "Unequal Law Enforcement Debated" *Metro Gadfly* Front Page 1(4) Auraria Library Archives

350. Author unknown (1967, November 15) "LSD Effects Debated" *Metro Gadfly* 1(4) Auraria Library Archives

351. Author unknown (1967, November 15) "MSC Students Support Boycott *Metro Gadfly* 1(4) Auraria Library Archives

352. Author unknown (1967, November 5) "A March For Freedom" The *Neoteric Puff* Front Page 1(2) Auraria Library Archives

353. Author unknown (1967, November 20) "Protest a Favor?" The *Neoteric Puff* 1(2) Auraria Library Archives

354. Author unknown (1967, November 20) "Nursing School Starts with 39 in MSC Class" The *Neoteric Puff* 1(2) Auraria Library Archives

355. Author unknown (1967, October 26) "Only male in Nursing Class" *Rocky Mountain News* "MSC Newsclippings" (Vol. VI) Auraria Library Archives

356. Author unknown (1967, November 15) "Cheerleaders Chosen" *Metro Gadfly* 1(2) Auraria Library Archives

357. Untitled Editorial (1967, November 29) *Metro Gadfly* 1(5) Auraria Library Archives

358. Author unknown (1967, December 6) "Raise in Student Fees Necessary Says Dean" *Metro Gadfly* 1(6) Auraria Library

Archives

359.   Author unknown (1967, December 6) "A Penny's Worth of Now to Play at S.G, Dance" *Metro Gadfly* p.1 1(6) Auraria Library Archives

360.   *The Life and Times of Richard Castro: Bridging a Cultural Divide* Richard Gould 2007 Colorado Historical Society

Chapter 9

361.   "Revolution" The Beatles, Album: "White Album", Apple Records, written by John Lennon, 1968

362.   Author unknown (1968, January 17) "Public Apathy Imperils Metro" *Cervi's Journal Post* "MSC Newsclippings" (Vol. VIII) Auraria Library Archives

363.   Author unknown (1968, February 5) "Student Statistics" *MSC Faculty-Staff Newsletter* p.1 Vol. III (No. 20) Auraria Library Archives

364.   Author unknown (1969, February 5) "Plans For Student Newspaper" *MSC Faculty-Staff Newsletter* p.3 Vol.3 (No.20) Auraria Library Archives

365.   "Love is all you Need" The Beatles, written by John Lennon and Paul McCartney, Album: Love Album, Parlophone, 1967.

366.   Author unknown (1968, March 4) "New Programs Authorized" *MSC Faculty-Staff Newsletter* p.1 Vol. 3 (No. 4) Auraria Library Archives

367.   "Simple Song of Freedom;" written by Bobby Darin; Album: Aces Back to Back (2004)

368.   Krasner, Paul (2007, January 28) "'60s live again', minus the LSD" *Los Angeles Times*

369.   Hill, Gladwin (1962, November 8) "Nixon Denounces Press as Biased" Gladwin Hill, *New York Times*

370.   Cunningham, Alan (1968, April 8) "Student Power in Colorado" *Rocky Mountain News Post* "MSC Newsclippings" (Vol. VIII) Auraria Library Archives

371.   Graham, Wanda (1968, April 1) "Voting Group Forms" *THE PAPER* 1(1) Auraria Library Archives

372.   Donahue, Bernie (1968, April 1) "Bobby Casts His Spell; Student Power Speaks" *THE PAPER.* 1(8) Auraria Library Archives

373.   Lucas, Spencer (University of Wisconsin) and Medhurst, Martin J. (Texas A & M University) "100 American Speeches of the 20th Century"; Scarborough, Joe (2005, November 19) "RFK: Bending History" *Scarborough Country*

374.   Bloomhower, Ray E. (2008) *Robert F. Kennedy and the 1968 Indiana Primary,* Bloomington, IN: *Indiana University Press.* Page 68

375.   Howard, Michael (1968, April 6) "Metro College Memorial for Dr. King is Symbolic" *Rocky Mountain News* "MSC Newsclippings" (Vol. VIII) Auraria Library Archives

376.   Unknown (1968, April 8) "I Have a Dream: Mankind Mourns King" *THE PAPER* 1(9) Auraria Library Archives

377.   Bronstein, Martin (1968, April 15) "All Denver Mourns Dr. King" *THE PAPER* 1(10) Auraria Library Archives

378.   Richard, Bobby E. (1968, May 6) "Afro-American Student Group Active" *THE PAPER* p.3, 1(13) Auraria Library Archives

379.   Author unknown (1968, April 22) "200march on Capitol" *THE PAPER* 1(11) Auraria Library Archives

380.   Author unknown (1968, April 22) "Spring Quarter Enrollment" *MSC Faculty-Staff Newsletter* p.3 Vol.3 (No.28) Auraria Library Archives

381.   Author unknown (1968, March 25) "College Hosts College Bowl Hopes to Defend Championship" *THE PAPER* 1(7) Auraria Library Archives

382.   Author unknown (1968, March 25) "22 Groups Active at MSC" *THE PAPER* 1(7) Auraria Library Archives

383.   Author unknown (1968, April 21) "Improved Race Relations Urged on State Campuses" *The Denver Post* "MSC Newsclippings" (Vol. VIII) Auraria Library Archives

384.   Donahue, Bernie (1968, March 25) "Why Have half a College" *THE PAPER* 1(7) Auraria Library

385.   Carter, Charles (1968, April 21) "Metro College Students Urge Athletic Program" *The Denver Post* "MSC Newsclippings" (Vol. VIII) Auraria Library Archives

386.   Stefan Bradley, (2009). *Harlem vs. Columbia University: Black Student Power in the Late 1960s* New York, New York:

University of Illinois. pp. 5–19, 164–191

387. Author unknown (1968, May 6) "Two Views Right Left" Editors Page *THE PAPER* 1(13) Auraria Library Archives

388. Author unknown (1968, April 15) "Constitution Ratified" *THE PAPER* p.1 1(10) Auraria Library Archives

389. Author unknown (1968, April 15) "MSC Needs Books to Fill Library for Library" *THE PAPER* 1(10) Auraria Library Archives

390. Author unknown (1968, April 29) "Bomb Threat Closes School Mid-Terms Postponed" *THE PAPER* p.1 1(12) Auraria Library Archives

391. Author unknown (1968, May 6) "AH Women" *THE PAPER* p.6 1(13) Auraria Library Archives

392. Author unknown (1968, May 20) "King, Queen Crowned" *THE PAPER* 1(15) Auraria Library Archives

393. Author unknown (1968, May 20) "Students Cast Votes Elect Government" *THE PAPER* p.1 1(15) Auraria Library Archives

394. Fuentes, Joseph and Bronstein, Martin (1968, May 27) "Two MSC Clubs Air Problems of Minorities" *THE PAPER* p.1 1(16) Auraria Library Archives

395. Clifton, Robert (1968, May 27) "There is More Democracy in the Soviet Union" *THE PAPER* 1(16) Auraria Library Archives

396. Engle, Mark (1968, May 27) "Colorado Collegiate Association Explained, Necessary for MSC" *THE PAPER* p.6 1(16) Auraria Library Archives

397. Author unknown (1968, June 3) "Phillips, Lillie Speak at Meet" *THE PAPER* 1(17) Auraria Library Archives

398. Engle, Mark (1968, May 27) "Colorado Collegiate Association Explained, Necessary for MSC" *THE PAPER* p. 6 1(16) Auraria Library Archives

399. Author unknown (1968, June 3) "Paper Plans Future" *THE PAPER* p.1 1(17) Auraria Library Archives

400. Fuentes, Joseph (1968, June 3) "We Want Willms" *THE PAPER* p.4, 1(17) Auraria Library Archives

401. Bronstein, Martin (1968, June 3) "Johnson Suggests Lower Voting Age" *THE PAPER* p.5 1(17) Auraria Library Archives

402. Moran, Martin (1968, June 2) "Atypical President" *Rocky Mountain News* "MSC News Clippings" (Vol. VIII) Auraria Library Archives

Chapter 10

403. "For What it's Worth" Buffalo Springfield written by Stephen Stills 1965, released 1967 album: Buffalo Springfield

404. Anderson, Byron (1968, June 24) "Feedback" *THE PAPER*. 1(18) Auraria Library Archives

405. Wolford, Rodney (1968, July 15) "Rights Must Not Fall Stop Gun Legislation" *THE PAPER* 2(1) Auraria Library Archives

406. Bronstein, Martin (1968, June 2) "Parents Are You Hypocrites? Or, Rather Are Your Children? *THE PAPER* p.4 1(17) Auraria Library Archives

407. Author unknown (1968, June 23) "American Negro Literature Course Being Offered" *MSC Faculty-Staff Newsletter* p.1 Vol.3 (No.35) Auraria Library Archives

408. Author unknown (1968, July 2) "Negro Literature Class Set" *Rocky Mountain News* "MSC Newsclippings" (Vol. IX) Auraria Library Archives

409. Author unknown (1968, July 15) "Beach Party Success, Dear Lillie Gets Wet" *THE PAPER* 2(1) Auraria Library Archives

410. Maureen* (1968, July 15) "What's happening" *THE PAPER* 2(1) Auraria Library *last name unknown Auraria Library Archives

411. Bronstein, Martin (1968, July 15) "Law Enforcement Teacher Lacks Quality Due MSC" *THE PAPER* 2(1) Auraria Library Archives

412. Jennings, Peter and Brewster, Todd (1998) *The Century*. New York: Doubleday, p 413

413. Farber, David Chicago '68 p.196, Chicago: University of Chicago Press, 1988.

414. Gitlin, Todd *The Sixties: Years of Hope, Days of Rage* p.332, Toronto: Bantam Books, 1987

415. Farber, David, *Chicago '68* Chicago: University of Chicago Press, 1988.

416.   Author unknown (1968, October 6) "Another Record—Another Accurate Prediction" *MSC Faculty-Staff Newsletter* p.2 Vol. 4 (No. 6) Auraria Library Archives

417.   Interview Jett Conners, 2012. Transcript in author's files.

418.   Taylor, Tom (1968, September 23) "Week Events Planned for All Students" *THE PAPER* 2(2) Auraria Library Archives

419.   Moran, Martin (1968, September 7) "Educational Complex Idea is unveiled for Auraria" *Rocky Mountain News* "MSC Newsclippings" (Vol. IX) Auraria Library Archives

420.   Bronstein, Martin (1968, September 23) "Questions Presented On Commission Move" *THE PAPER* 2(2) Auraria Library Archives

421.   Author unknown (1968, September 30) "Lillie leaves MSC, Will Return; Students, School are Great" *THE PAPER* Front page 2(3) Auraria Library Archives

422.   Graham, Wanda (1968, September 23) "Campus Clubs Are Busy Seeking New Members" *THE PAPER* 2(2) Auraria Library Archives

423.   Author unknown (1968, September 23) "HPER Sports Program Expands" *THE PAPER* 2(2) Auraria Library Archives

424.   Author unknown (1968, September 30) "MSC's CCA Rep To Attend Meet" *THE PAPER* p.2 2(3) Auraria Library Archives

425.   Author unknown (1968, September 30) "Campus SDS Represented at Nixon Rally" *THE PAPER* 2(3) Auraria Library Archives; also, Author unknown Editorial (1968, September 30) "Nixon and the Rally" *THE PAPER* 2(3) Auraria Library Archives

426.   Author unknown (1968, September 30) "Dr. Henry Bagley—Professor of English" *MSC Faculty-Staff Newsletter* p.2 Vol.4 (No.5) Auraria Library Archives

427.   Talmage, Wayne (1968, October 10) *Declare Your Position:* Essay *THE PAPER* 2(4) Auraria Library Archives

428.   Author unknown (1968, October 14) "Senate News" *THE PAPER* 2(5) Auraria Library Archives

429.   Author unknown (1968, October 21) "CCA News" *THE PAPER* 2(6) Auraria Library Archives

430.   Joseph Fuentes (1968, November 4) "3 MSC Students Seek Write-Ins" *THE PAPER* p.1 2(8) Auraria Library Archives

431.   Interview Doug Holcombe 2013 by Robert Bowen. Copy of transcript in author's files; personal knowledge

432.   Holmes, Jane (1968, November 11) "Election Results Show Different Story" *THE PAPER* p.1 2(9) Auraria Library Archives

433.   Author unknown (1968, November 25) "Bowen Wins CCA Office" *THE PAPER* p.1 2(11) Auraria Library Archives

434.   Bronstein, Martin (1968, November 11) "Give Nixon Time" *THE PAPER* p.2 2(9) Auraria Library Archives

435.   Cadwallader, tom (1968, November 18) "Morality Legislation" *THE PAPER* Editor's Page 2(10) Auraria Library Archives

436.   Cadwallader, Tom (1969, February 24) "Polemics" *THE PAPER* 2(20) Auraria Library Archives

437.   Bowen, Bob (1968, December 14) "Why is Image of the Student so Bad?" *The Denver Post* "Voice of Youth" MSC Newsclippings" (Vol. X) Auraria Library Archives

438.   Cadwallader, Tom (1969, January 20) "Polemics" *THE PAPER* p.1 2(15) Auraria Library Archives

439.   Author unknown (1969, February 17) "Editor asked to resign" *THE PAPER* 2(16) Auraria Library Archives

440.   Cadwallader, Tom (1960, March 3) "Polemics: Cadwallader Blasts Student Government" *THE PAPER* 2(21) Auraria Library Archives

441.   Fuentes, Joseph (1969, March 10) "My Final Editorial" *THE PAPER* 2(22) Auraria Library Archives

Chapter 11

442.   "Aquarius/Let the Sunshine In" The Fifth Dimension, 1969; Album: "The Age of Aquarius" Label: Soul City, Written by James Rado, Gerome Ragni, and Galt Mac Dermot

443.   Author unknown (1969, January 20) "Winter Quarter Enrollment" *MSC Faculty- Staff Newsletter* Vol. IV (No.14) Auraria Library Archives

444.   Cadwallader, Tom (1969, January 6) "Student Interviews Otto Preminger" *THE PAPER* p.1 (2)13 Auraria Library Archives

445. Fuentes, Joseph (1969, January 13) "2 Students Attend Symposium in DC." *THE PAPER* p.1 2(14) Auraria Library Archives

446. Author unknown (1969, January 13) "MSC Student Speaks" *THE PAPER* p.6 2(14) Auraria Library Archives

447. Author unknown (1969, November 18) "Bowen heads up CCA Legislative Affairs" *THE PAPER* 2(10) Auraria Library Archives

448. Author unknown (1969, January 13) "CCA gets seat on Board" *THE PAPER* 2(14) Auraria Library Archives

449. Author unknown (1969, January 9) "Campus Disorder Bill is Introduced" *Rocky Mountain News* "MSC Newsclippings" (Vol. X) Auraria Library Archives; also, Logan, Bill (1969, January 24) "Colo. Senate Group Launches Probe of Campus Disorder" *Rocky Mountain News* (Vol. X) Auraria Library Archives

450. Author unknown (1969, January 25) "Senators to Quiz College Officials" *Rocky Mountain News* p 52, "MSC Newsclippings" (Vol. X) Auraria Library Archives

451. Roos, Charlie (1969, January 31) "Joint Committees Draft New Campus Disorder- Bill" *The Denver Post* "MSC Newsclippings" (Vol. X) Auraria Library Archives

452. Author unknown (1969, February 3) "New Draft Law" *THE PAPER* p.2 2(17) Auraria Library Archives

453. Author unknown (1969, January 6) "Campus Cops Coming" *The Paper* p.1 (2)12; also, Unknown (1969, January 13) "Welcome Campus Security" *THE PAPER* p.1 2(13) Auraria Library Archives

454. Ball, David W. (1969, February 3) "CCA hears Abbott, McKinley; Plan Bargains for Students" *THE PAPER* 2(17) Auraria Library Archives

455. Author unknown (1969, January 16) "Model City Grant to spur MSC Plans" *The Denver Post* "MSC Newsclippings" (Vol. X) Auraria Library Archives; also, Author unknown Editorial (1969, January 16) "Auraria College Project Comes Alive" *The Denver Post* "MSC Newsclippings" (Vol. X) Auraria Library Archives

456. Cooper, Gene (1969, January 25) "Joint Efforts Urged to Get College Site" *The Denver Post* "MSC Newsclippings" (Vol. X) Auraria Library Archives

457. Author unknown (1969, February 20) "$5 million bond Issue proposed for Auraria Site" *Rocky Mountain News* "MSC Newsclippings" (Vol. X) Auraria Library Archives

458. Author unknown (1969, January 12) "Board Candidate is Student" *The Denver Post* "MSC Newsclippings" (Vol. X) Auraria Library Archives

459. Author unknown (1969, February 24) "Hispanic Culture Week" *THE PAPER* p.1 2(20) Auraria Library Archives; Ball, David W. (1969, March 3) "Torres Speaks to Students" *THE PAPER* 2(21) Auraria Library

460. Author unknown (1969, May 24) "Hispano Youth Counseled on College" *The Denver Post* "MSC Newsclippings" (Vol. X) Auraria Library Archives

461. Author unknown (1969, February 17) "Baez Speaks, Harris Answers" *THE PAPER*.2 (19) Auraria Library Archives

462. Author unknown (1969, March 3) "Reason is Answer to Generation Gap" *MSC Faculty-Staff Newsletter* p.1 Vol. IV (No. 20) Auraria Library Archives

463. Author unknown (1969, January 13) "Not all College Students are at the Point of Rebellion Against Society" *MSC Faculty-Staff Newsletter* p.2 Vol. 4 (No.15) Auraria Library Archives

464. Author unknown (1969, January 27) "A Different Kind of Student Publicity" *MSC Faculty-Staff Newsletter* p.2 Vol. 4 (No.7) Auraria Library Archives; Charles Angeletti (1969, January 27) "Ouch" *THE PAPER* 2(16) Auraria Library Archives

465. Interview Doug Holcombe by Robert Bowen Nov 2013. Transcript in author's files

466. Author unknown (1969, February 3) "Brawl erupts, MSC loses" *THE PAPER* 2(17) Auraria Library Archives

467. Bowen, Bob (1969, April 2) "Sports Survey, *THE PAPER* p.2 2(23) Auraria Library Archives

468. Author unknown (1969, April 21) "Athletic Proposal to Trustees" *THE PAPER* 2(24) Auraria Library Archives; also, Fuentes, Joseph (1969, April 21) "Students Present Athletic Proposal to Trustees" *THE PAPER* p.5, 6 2(24) Auraria Library Archives

469. Author unknown (1969, March 10) "Basketball Team Ends Losing Season" *THE PAPER* p.7, 2(22) Auraria Library Archives

470.   Canino, Dale (1969, March 10) "Editorial-On Sports" *THE PAPER* p. 8, 2(22) Auraria Library Archives

471.   Author unknown (1969, March 3) "Bomb scare empties Bldg." *THE PAPER* 2(21) Auraria Library Archives

472.   Interview Gary Holbrook, Dr. Steve Leonard Dec. 9, 2013. Transcript in author's files.

473.   Bell, Dan (1969, March 5) "Mayor Prefers Big Bond Issue" *Rocky Mountain News* "MSC Newsclippings" (Vol. X) Auraria Library Archives

474.   Author unknown (1969, March 100 "CCA Elects New Officers" *THE PAPER* 2(22) Auraria Library Archives

475.   Author unknown (1969, March 17) "Congrats to MSC Students" *MSC Faculty-Staff Newsletter* p.2 Vol. 2 (No. 21) Auraria Library Archives

476.   Bronstein, Martin (1969, April 7) "Lillie Resigns" *THE PAPER* 2(22) Auraria Library Archives

477.   Author unknown (1969, April 14) "CCA Drug Research" *THE PAPER* p.1 2(23) Auraria Library Archives

478.   Fuentes, Joseph (1969, April 14) "Senate Interpretation" *THE PAPER* p.2, 2(23) Auraria Library Archives

479.   Author unknown (1969, April 14) "Bill Introduced to Limit Enrollment at MSC" *THE PAPER* 2(23) Auraria Library Archives

480.   Personal recollection; also, Interview Doug Holcombe by Robert Bowen 2013. Transcript in author's files.

481.   Author unknown (1969, April 21) "CCA Art Show" p.1 *THE PAPER*. 3(24) Auraria Library Archives

482.   Personal Recollection; also, Interview Doug Holcombe by Robert Bowen 2013. Transcript in author's files

483.   Curtis, Olga (1969, February 2) "Metro State: Denver's Invisible Campus" *Empire Magazine* Cover "MSC Newsclippings" (Vol. X) Auraria Library Archives

484.   Author unknown (1969, April 21) "Enrollment Above Predictions" *MSC Faculty-Staff Newsletter* p.1 Vol. 4 (No. 24) Auraria Library Archives

485.   Moran, Martin (1969, May 24) "CU Board of Regents Oks Disaffiliation for SDSers" *Rocky Mountain News* "MSC Newsclippings" (Vol. XI) Auraria Library Archives

486.   Ball, David W. "Bob Bowen Raps on campus issues" *THE PAPER* p.2, 3,4,5,6 2(22) Auraria Library Archives

487.   Author unknown (1969, May 5) "Metro YRs Snubbed" *THE PAPER* 2(28) Auraria Library Archives

488.   Author unknown (1969, May 5) "Paper endorsed Bowen-Cavoto" *THE PAPER* p.1 2(28) Auraria Library Archives

489.   Ball, David W. (1969, May 19) "Boyko Praised, Senate Absent" *THE PAPER* 2(30) Auraria Library Archives

490.   Cadwallader, Tom (1969, May 12) "The Rhetoric of Violence" *THE PAPER* p.1 2(29) Auraria Library Archives

491.   Author unknown (1969, May 23) "MSC Players Set Miller Work" *The Denver Post* "MSC Newsclippings" (Vol. XI) Auraria Library Archives

492.   Author unknown (1969, May 26) "MSC Students Honored" *THE PAPER* p.1 2(31) Auraria Library Archives

493.   Author unknown Photo (1969, May 19) "Spring" *THE PAPER* p.1 2 (30) Auraria Library Archives.

494.   Author unknown (2969, June 15) "Metropolitan State College Degrees Are Listed" *The Denver Post* "MSC Newsclippings" (Vol. XI) Auraria Library Archives

495.   Interview Dennis Heap Feb. 14, 2013. Copy transcript in author's files.

Chapter 12

496.   "Easy To Be Hard" Three Dog Night, Album: Suitable for Framing Dunhill Records *1969*, written by" Gerome Ragni, James Rado, Galt Mac Dermot.

497.   Author unknown (1969, July 14) "New Record for Summer Enrollment" *MSC Faculty-Staff Newsletter* Vol. 5 (No.1); also, Author unknown (1969, August 4) "You Can't Beat This" *MSC Faculty-Staff Newsletter* Vol. 5 (No.2) Auraria Library Archives

498.   Author unknown (1969, May 5) "Report Warns of Racial Polarization in Denver" *Rocky Mountain News* "MSC Newsclippings" (Vol. XI) Auraria Library Archives

499.   Author unknown (1969, July 26) "Commission Plans Enrollment Control" *The Denver Post* p.26, "MSC Newsclippings" (Vol. XII) Auraria Library Archives

500.   Debber, Dale (1969, June 2) "Angeletti, Valdes, to Teach At Area Consortium" *THE PAPER* p.2 2(32) Auraria Library Archives

501.   Author unknown (1969, June 16) "Professors Back Nixon Stand" *The Denver Post* The Open Forum "MSC Newsclip-pings" (Vol. XI) Auraria Library; also, Author unknown (1969, August 4) "Quote of Note" *MSC Faculty- Staff Newsletter* p.2 Vol.5 (No. 2) Auraria Library Archives

502.   Author unknown (1969, July 1) "Group of Teachers Files Suit Over Education Oath" *Rocky Mountain News* (Vol. 5) No.2 Auraria Library Archives

503.   Author unknown (1969, July 7) "Can Faculty and Students Work Together" *THE PAPER* p.6 3(1) Auraria Library Archives

504.   Author unknown (1969, July 7) "Sports School" *The Denver Post* "MSC Newsclippings" (Vol. XII) Auraria Library Archives

505.   Interview Joe Megeath, Nov. 1, 2012. Copy of transcript in author's files.

506.   Author unknown (1969, August) "Bowen, Books, and Money" *THE PAPER* p.5 3(2) Auraria Library Archives

507.   Author unknown (1969, August) "Hispano News" *THE PAPER* p.7 3(2) Auraria Library Archives; also, Lucero, Virginia (1969, September 5) "UMAS Represented at Meet, Planning For Big Year" *THE PAPER* p.3 3(3) Auraria Library Archives

508.   Bronstein, Martin (1969, August) "The Role of the College Professor in Campus Dissent" *THE PAPER* p.4 3(2) Auraria Library Archives

509.   Author unknown (1969, October 6) "Latest enrollment Figures" *THE PAPER* p.1, 2 3(5) Auraria Library Archives

510.   Robinson, Bernard (1969, September 29), "Dr. Phares Talks at A.A.S.U. Dinner" *THE PAPER* p.1. 3(4) Auraria Library Archives

511.   Author unknown (1969, October 6) "Pres. Explains 'Open Door' To Hispano Students" *THE PAPER* p.1 3(5) Auraria Library Archives

512.   Author unknown (1969, October 6) "Open Door" Major Issue" *THE PAPER* p.1 3(5) Auraria Library Archives

513.   Lyle, Don (1969, September 30) "Council OKs Bond Issue for Ballot" *Rocky Mountain News* "MSC Newsclippings" (Vol. XII) Auraria Library Archives

514.   Author unknown (1969, September 22) "Accreditation Application Not Acceptable-Now" *Rocky Mountain News* p.1 (Vol. XII) Auraria Library Archives

515.   Bowen, Bob (1969, October 6) "Student Body President Column" *THE PAPER* p.7 3(5) Auraria Library Archives

516.   Author unknown (1969, November 3) "All for Auraria" *THE PAPER* 3(9) Auraria Library Archives

517.   Kovash, Jon (1969, October 6) "It's Heads of Tails for MSC" *THE PAPER* p.2 3(5) Auraria Library Archives

518.   Lucero, Virginia (1969, October 27) "Auraria Questioned" *THE PAPER* p 2 3(8) Auraria Library Archives

519.   Ball, David W. (1969, November 1) "Metro Student Defends Auraria" *The Denver Post* Voice of Youth "MSC Newsclip-pings" (Vol. XIII) Auraria Library Archives

520.   Author unknown (1969, October 26) "Archbishop Casey Urges Voters to OK Auraria Plan:" *Rocky Mountain News*; also, author unknown (1969, October 30) "Archbishop Urges Citizens to Support Auraria Issue" *Denver Catholic Register* "MSC Newsclippings" (Vol. XIII) Auraria Library Archives; also author unknown (1969, October 30) "Auraria Meet Generates More Heat Than Light" *Rocky Mountain News* "MSC Newsclippings" (Vol. XIII) Auraria Library Archives

521.   Author unknown (1969, November 2) "Tuesday Election Issue: 21 Denver Legislators Favor Auraria" *Denver Post* p. 33, "MSC Newsclippings" (Vol. XIII) Auraria Library Archives

522.   Tucker, Richard (1969, November 11) "City Voters Give Okay to Auraria" *Rocky Mountain News* p. 5 ("MSC Newsclip-pings" (Vol. XIII) Auraria Library Archives

523.   Tucker, Richard (1969, November 11) "City Voters Give Okay to Auraria" *Rocky Mountain News* p. 5 ("MSC Newsclip-pings" (Vol. XIII) Auraria Library Archives

524.   Phillips, Dr. Kenneth (1969, November 10) "To: All Students of Metropolitan State College" *THE PAPER* page 1 (3)10 Auraria Library Archives

525.   Torsiello, Peter M. (1969, November 10) "To victors go the spoils" *THE PAPER* p.4 3(10) Auraria Library Archives

526.   Author unknown Editorial (1960, November 6) "Dedicated Students Show the Way" *Rocky Mountain News* "MSC

Newsclippings" (Vol. XIII) Auraria Library Archives

527. Author unknown Editorial (1969, November 5) "Auraria: Fine but Too Close" *The Denver Post* "MSC Newsclippings" (Vol. XIII) Auraria Library Archives

528. Lyle, Don (1969, November 6) "Mayor Vows Auraria Follow Through" *Rocky Mountain News* "MSC Newsclippings" (Vol. XIII) Auraria Library Archives

529. Author unknown (1969, July 18) "Metro State Sets Limited Athletic Program" *Rocky Mountain News* "MSC Newsclippings" (Vol. XII) Auraria Library Archives

530. Telephone interview of Dr. Bryant by Robert May 27, 2014. Transcript in author's files.

531. Torsiello, Peter (1969, September 29) "The Ball Controversy" Editorial *THE PAPER* p.43(4) Auraria Library Archives

532. Author unknown (1969, October 20) "Speaking Out on the Athletic Question: Pros and Cons" *THE PAPER* p.5, 6, 7 3(7) Auraria Library Archives

533. Author unknown (1969, November 19) "Election Results" *THE PAPER* p.1 3(11) Auraria Library Archives

534. "Election contested" Marsh Jr., Paul. (1969, November 24). Elections Contested. *The Paper* 3(12), pages 1 and 3. Auraria Library Archives

535. Author unknown (1970, March 30). Athletics Passes" *The Paper 3(22)*, page 1. Auraria Library Archives

536. Telephone Interview Dr. James Bryant by Robert Bowen May 27, 2014. Transcript found in author's files.

537. Ashton, Jack (1971, February 16) "Need for Varsity Athletics at Metro State" *The Denver Post* Open Forum, "MSC Newsclippings" (Vol. XII) Auraria Library Archives

538. Author unknown (1969, October 13) "Classes Closed Oct 15: Philips" *THE PAPER* p.1 3(6) Auraria Library Archives

539. Author unknown (1969, October 31) "Student Leaders State Position: Moratorium to Educate All" *THE PAPER* p.1 3(6) Auraria Library Archives.

540. Green, Chuck (1969, October 7) "State Students Corner: Campus War Protests Planned" *The Denver Post* "MSC Newsclippings" (Vol. XII) Auraria Library Archives.

541. Author unknown (1969, October 20) "Bowen versus Allott" *THE PAPER* p.1, 3, 3(7) Auraria Library Archives

542. Author unknown (1969, October 20) "Bowen, Taylor Demand Allot Document Charges" *THE PAPER* p.1 3(7) Auraria Library Archives.

543. Personal inspection of the FBI file on my activity during the antiwar protests at MSC in the 1960s *after* it had been de-classified for the Watergate investigation. I was able to see information reported by informants (moles) identified only by code names.

544. Kane, George (1969, October 15) "Moratorium, Viet War Find Opponents in Colorado" *Rocky Mountain News* "MSC Newsclippings" (Vol. XIII) Auraria Library Archives

545. Dunning, John (1969, October 15) "Snow Doesn't Halt Moratorium: 1,000 at Capitol Protest War" *The Denver Post* "MSC Newsclippings" (Vol. XIII) Auraria Library Archives

546. Stuckey, Carol (1969, October 20) "Moratorium Impressive Sight" *THE PAPER* p.1 3(7) Auraria Library Archives

547. Secord, Dean (1969, October 20) "Letter to Editor" *THE PAPER* 3(7) Auraria Library Archives

548. Carter, Charles (1969, October 29) "Minority Groups List Grievances at MSC" *The Denver Post* "MSC Newsclippings" (Vol. XIII) Auraria Library Archives

549. Author unknown (1969, November 10) "Chain Letter" *THE PAPER* p 5 3(10) Auraria Library Archives

550. Author unknown (1969, November 24) "Proposed Student Bill of Rights Metropolitan State College" *THE PAPER* p.2 3(12), Auraria Library Archives

551. Kane, George (1969, November 26) "Students Demand Computer Probe" *Rocky Mountain News*; also, Jain, Bob (1969, November 25) "Students Will Press for Class Tools" *The Denver Post* "MSC Newsclippings" (Vol. XIV) Auraria Library Archives

Chapter 13

552. "Bad Moon Rising" Creedence Gold, 1969 John Fogerty

553. Author unknown (1970, February 9) "Veterans Program at MSC" *MSC Faculty-Staff Newsletter* Vol.5 (No.15), Auraria Library Archives

554. Author unknown (1970, February 23) "New Facilities for the Fall of 1970" MSC Staff and Faculty Newsletter p.1 Vol. 5 (No.17) Auraria Library Archives

555. Jain, Bob (1970, January 8) "18 Hispanos Receive Honors" *The Denver Post* "MSC Newsclippings" (Vol. XV) Auraria Library Archives

556. Author unknown (1970, January 12). KBTV and MSC Announce Radio/TV Internship Program. *THE PAPER* p.1 3(14), Auraria Library Archives

557. Author unknown (1970, February 9) "A.A.S.U. Election; New Exec. Board" *THE PAPER* p. 3 3(18), Auraria Library Archives.

558. Turk, Brady (1970, January 12) "Open Letter To All Black Students," *THE PAPER* p. 5 3(14), Auraria Library Archives

559. Author unknown (1970, January 12) "MSC Students Can Bring Their Children To College" *THE PAPER* p.1 3(14) Auraria Library Archives

560. O'Neill, Frank. (1970, February 2) "MSC Daycare Center: Playpen" *THE PAPER* p.3 3(17), Auraria Library Archives

561. Author unknown (1970, January 8) "CEE To Oppose State Funding Of Auraria Educational Center" *Denver Herald-Dispatch* "MSC Newsclippings" (Vol. XV) Auraria Library Archives

562. Author unknown (1970, January 11) "Text of Governor Love's General Assembly Message" *The Denver Post* "MSC Newsclippings" (Vol. XV) Auraria Library Archives

563. Brown, Fred (1970, January 13) "State Hears Auraria Plan" *The Denver Post* "MSC Newsclippings" (Vol. XV) Auraria Library Archives

564. Brown, Fred (1970, January 14) "Auraria Site Hit at Hearing" *The Denver Post* "MSC Newsclippings" (Vol. XV) Auraria Library Archives

565. Talmage, Wayne (1970, January 12) "Auraria Impact on Urban Area" (letter to the editor) *The Denver Post* "MSC Newsclippings" Auraria Library Archives

566. Buresh, Dave Photos (January 8, 1970) "ST. CAJETAN'S: to be or not to be" *The Denver Post*; also, Ditmer, Joanne (1970, January 8) "Raising the Roof: St. Cajetan's; Future Still Precarious" *The Denver Post* "MSC Newsclippings" (Vol. XV) Auraria Library Archives

567. Author unknown (1970, January 6) "Landmark Board to Decide Fate of Brewery and Church" *The Denver Post* "MSC Newsclippings" (Vol. XV) Auraria Library Archives; also, Chase, Robert L. (1970, February 18) "A brewery on the campus?" (editorial) *Rocky Mountain News* "MSC Newsclippings" ((Vol. XVI) Auraria Library Archives

568. Lyle, Don (1970, February 17) "Church, brewery designated landmarks" *Rocky Mountain News* "MSC Newsclippings" (Vol. XVI) Auraria Library Archives

569. Lyle, Don (1970, April 14) "Council kills preservation of brewery, opera house *Rocky Mountain News* "MSC Newsclippings" (Vol. XVII) Auraria Library Archives

570. Author unknown (1970, February 1) "Commission Head Raps Statement By Regents" *Boulder Daily Camera* "MSC Newsclippings" (Vol. XVI) Auraria Library Archives

571. Author unknown (1970, February 1) "Education unit disputes regents' paper" *Rocky Mountain News* "MSC Newsclippings" (Vol. XVI) Auraria Library Archives; also Author unknown (1970, February 2) "College Commission Says CU Regents Seek Preference" *The Denver Post* "MSC Newsclippings" (Vol. XVI) Auraria Library Archives

572. Author unknown (1970, February 20 "Abbott Defends CCHE Action" *The Denver Post* "MSC Newsclippings" (Vol. XVI) Auraria Library Archives

573. Author unknown (1970, February 5) "House unit approves CU spending curb" *Rocky Mountain News* "MSC Newsclippings" (Vol. XVI) Auraria Library Archives

574. Grimshaw, Tom (1970, February 4) "Higher Education Prime Topic" (editorial) *Lakewood Sentry* "MSC Newsclippings" (Vol. XVI) Auraria Library Archives

575. Author unknown (1970, February 5) "Support Repeated For Auraria Center" *The Denver Post* "MSC Newsclippings" (Vol. XVI) Auraria Library Archives

576. Marrinzino, Pasquale (1970, February 7) "The song is a little bit off key" *Rocky Mountain News* "MSC Newsclippings" (Vol. XVI) Auraria Library Archives

577. Johnston, Dick (1970, February 5) "Price to Save U.S. Funds: Auraria Need: $1.4 Million in '70" *The Denver Post* "MSC Newsclippings" (Vol. XVI) Auraria Library Archives

578. Burke, George (1970, February 5) "Education And The Commission" *Denver Herald-Dispatch* "MSC Newsclippings" (Vol. XVI) Auraria Library Archives

579. Author unknown (1970, February 6) "Auraria Is the Only Right Answer To Pressing Urban Education Needs" (editorial) *The Denver Post* "MSC Newsclippings" (Vol. XVI) Auraria Library Archives

580. Johnston, Dick (1970, February 6) "Love Vows Auraria Fund Bill Support" *The Denver Post* "MSC Newsclippings" (Vol. XVI) Auraria Library Archives

581. Tucker, Richard (1970, February 8) "School plan depends on horse trading" *Rocky Mountain News*; Larson, Leonard (1970, February 8) "Auraria Project Reported in Vote-Trading Deal" *The Denver Post* "MSC Newsclippings" (Vol. XVI) Auraria Library Archives

582. Logan, Bill (1970, February 11) "Senate GOP maps horse trading on major bills" *Rocky Mountain News* "MSC Newsclippings" (Vol. XVI) Auraria Library Archives

583. Logan, Bill (1970, February 26) "State Senate approves Auraria funds" *Rocky Mountain News* "MSC Newsclippings" (Vol. XVI) Auraria Library Archives s

584. Lyle, Don (1970, February 28) "Businessmen challenge legality of Auraria vote" *Rocky Mountain News* "MSC Newsclippings" (Vol. XVI) Auraria Library Archives

585. Roos, Charles (1970, March 7) "Auraria Appropriations Bill Blocked in House" *The Denver Post* "MSC Newsclippings" (Vol. XVI) Auraria Library Archives

586. Author unknown (1970, March 8) "Showdown is threatened over Auraria" *Rocky Mountain News* "MSC Newsclippings: (Vol. XVI) Auraria Library Archives

587. Author unknown (1970, March 9) "House Unit Oks Plan for Auraria" *The Denver Post* "MSC Newsclippings" (Vol. XVI) Auraria Library Archives

588. Tucker, Richard (1970, March 10) "Auraria complex wins preliminary approval" *Rocky Mountain News* "MSC Newsclippings" (Vol. XVI) Auraria Library Archives

589. Author unknown (1970, March 11) "Auraria Measure Cleared" *The Denver Post* "MSC Newsclippings" (Vol. XVI) Auraria Library Archives

590. Ball, David W. (1970, March 27) "Support for Auraria Site" Open Forum *The Denver Post* "MSC Newsclippings" (Vol. XVI) Auraria Library Archives

591. Author unknown (1970, May 11) "Registrar's Report on Spring Enrollment" *MSC Faculty-Staff Newsletter* p.1 (Vol. 5) No. 18 Auraria Library Archives

592. Author unknown (1970, April 8) "Help and Hope for Denver 'Dropouts" Denver *Cervi's Journal* "MSC Newsclippings" (Vol. XVII) Auraria Library Archives

593. Author unknown (1970, April 13) "Urban Studies Program" *MSC Faculty-Staff Newsletter* p.1 (Vol. 5) No. 24 Auraria Library Archives

594. Steele, Roger. (1970, February 2). Letter to the Editor. *The Paper 3(17)*, page 5. Auraria Library Archives.

595. Walsh, Bob. (1970, February 16). "Metro Professors on TV", Union is Subject *THE PAPER* p.1 3(19), Auraria Library Archives.

596. Author unknown (1970, February 16). Bunny Heather Runs for Mu Beta Chi. *THE PAPER* p. 3 3(19), Auraria Library Archives.

597. Author unknown (1970, March 19) "2 Denver Colleges to Receive Computers" *The Denver Post* "MSC Newsclippings" (Vol. XVII) Auraria Library Archives

598. Brown, Fred (1970, March 21) "Computer Decision Challenged" *The Denver Post* "MSC Newsclippings" (Vol. XVI) Auraria Library Archives

599. Tucker, Richard (1970, February 18) "CU's Anderson aids vote at 19 efforts" *Rocky Mountain News* "MSC Newsclippings" (Vol. XVI) Auraria Library Archives

600. Larsen, Leonard (1970, February 18) "19-Year Old Vote Endorsed" *The Denver Post* "MSC Newsclippings" (Vol. XVII)

Auraria Library Archives

601. Crawford, James (1970, April 17) "Group angered over alleged police beatings" *Rocky Mountain News* "MSC Newsclippings (Vol. XVII) Auraria Library Archives

602. Author unknown (1970, April 17) "Probe Promised of Alleged Police Brutality" *The Denver Post* "MSC Newsclippings" (Vol. XVII) Auraria Library Archives

603. Crawford, James (1970, April 30) "Castro passes polygraph test in questioning" *Rocky Mountain News* "MSC Newsclippings" (Vol. (XVII) Auraria Library Archives

604. Fuentes, Joseph (1970, May 3) "Hispanos claim media display bias" *Rocky Mountain News* "MSC Newsclippings" (Vol. XVII) Auraria Library Archives

605. Lane, George (1970, May 3) "'Tortilla Curtain Lifted' at Media Conference *The Denver Post* "MSC Newsclippings" (Vol. XVII) Auraria Library Archives

606. Author unknown (1970, April 6) "Hall Platform" *THE PAPER* pages 1, 4 3(23), Auraria Library Archives

607. Author unknown (1970, April 27) Interview with Gary A Pickett *THE PAPER* p.6 3(27), Auraria Library Archives;

608. Author unknown (1970, May 4) "Election Tabs" *THE PAPER* p.2 3(28), Auraria Library Archives

609. Hall, Richard (1970, May 4) "Hall Congratulates Ball" *THE PAPER* p.2 3(28), Auraria Library Archives.

610. Ball, David W. (1970, May 4). "Ball: Priorities Outlined in Campaign" *THE PAPER* p.2 3(28) Auraria Library Archives.

611. Author unknown (1970, May 4) "Metro State YD's Make Presence Felt at State Young Demo Convention" *THE PAPER* p. 4 3(28), Auraria Library Archives

612. Author unknown (1970, May 18) "Angeletti directs Ethnic Program" *MSC Faculty-Staff Newsletter* p.5 Vol. V (No. 29) *THE PAPER*

613. Branum, Gregory (1970, May 4) "Second Black Club on Campus" *THE PAPER* p.5 3(28), Auraria Library Archives.

614. Author unknown (1970, April 25) "Metro State grad enters House race" *Rocky Mountain News* "MSC Newsclippings" (Vol. XVII) *THE PAPER*

615. Author unknown (1970, April 20) "Fonda in Denver Protest" *THE PAPER* p.1 3(26), Auraria Library Archives.

616. Author unknown (1970, May 11) "Four Students Murdered By National Guard on Kent State Campus" *THE PAPER* p.1 3(29), Auraria Library Archives.

617. Interview Mark Hogan by Robert Bowen. Transcript in author's files

618. Hitler, Adolph. (1970, May 11) Quote from 1932 cited in *THE PAPER THE PAPER* p.1 3(29) Auraria Library Archives

619. Hollis, Gordon (1970, May 11) Editorial Page *THE PAPER* p.3 3(29) Auraria Library Archives.

620. Weaver, R.G. (1970, May 11) Editorial Page *THE PAPER* p.3 3(29), Auraria Library Archives

621. Smith, Bob (1970, May 11) "Nixon has pinned on us" Editorial Page. *THE PAPER* p.3 3(29), Auraria Library Archives.

622. Klismet, Pete (1970, May 11) Editorial Page *THE PAPER* p.3 3(29), Auraria Library Archives.

623. Lucero, Eduardo (1970, May 11) Editorial Page *THE PAPER* p.3 3(29), Auraria Library Archives

624. Stuckey, Carol (1970, May 11) "Bowen Thinks Peace Movement has Failed; Needs to Take over Political System" *THE PAPER* pages 1, 3 3(29), Auraria Library Archives.

625. Kovash, Jon (1970, May 11) "Thursday Protest" *THE PAPER* p.6 3(29), Auraria Library Archives; O'Neil, Frank (1970, May 11) Editorial *THE PAPER* p. 4 3(29), Auraria Library Archives

626. Author unknown (1970, May 18) "Largest-Ever Student Strike Hits 441 Campuses" *THE PAPER* pages, 1-2, 4.6 3(30), Auraria Library Archives; also, Author unknown (1970, May 18) "Two Students Killed, Eleven Wounded at Miss." *THE PAPER* p 1 3(30), *THE PAPER* Auraria Library Archives.

627. Clifton, Robert L. (1970, May 16) "Students' Desperate Need," letter to the editor *The Denver Post* "MSC Newsclippings" (Vol. XVIII) Auraria Library Archives

628. Jain, Bob (1970, May 16) "MSC Students Protest at News" *The Denver Post*; also, Smith, Christopher (1970, May 16) "150 protest News' report on 2 slayings" *Rocky Mountain News* "MSC Newsclippings" (Vol. XVIII) Auraria Library Archives

629. Author unknown (1970, May 18) "Emergency Faculty Meeting Today" *THE PAPER* p.1 3(30), Auraria Library Ar-

chives.

630. Author unknown (1970, May 18) "Senate Endorses Resolution" *THE PAPER* p.1 3(30) Auraria Library Archives.

631. Moran, Martin (1970, May 16) "Metro to mark deaths of two black students" *Rocky Mountain News* "MSC Newsclippings" (Vol. XVIII) Auraria Library Archives

632. Author unknown (1970, May 18) "School Closes at Noon" *THE PAPER* p. 1 3(30), Auraria Library Archives

633. Author unknown (1970, May 18) "Don't Close Schools, MSC Group Urges" *The Denver Post* "MSC Newsclippings" Vol. XVIII) Auraria Library Archives

634. Author unknown (1970, May 13) "Powell Accepts Wrestling Position at Metro State" *Alamosa Valley Courier* "MSC Newsclippings" (Vol. XVIII) Auraria Library Archives

635. Author unknown (1970, May 5) "Two Groups Named For Auraria Project" *The Denver Post* "MSC Newsclippings" (Vol. XVIII) Auraria Library Archives

636. Author unknown (1970, June 22) "Some Thoughts About Senator Gale McGee" *MSC Faculty- Staff Newsletter* p.1 Vol. 5 (No, 32)

Chapter 14

637. "Riders on the Storm" The Doors, Album: LA Woman, 1971, written by Jim Morrison, Robby Krieger, Ray Manzarek, John Densmore

638. Author unknown (1970, May 25 "214 Summer Courses" *THE PAPER* p. 1 3(31), Auraria Library Archives.

639. Author unknown (1970, June 9) "He Rode as Others Walked, But MSC Grad Isn't Lazy" *The Denver Post* ("MSC Newsclippings" (Vol. XVIII) Auraria Library Archives

640. Roos, Robert (1970, May 26) "City Aid on MSC Parking" letter to the editor *The Denver Post* "MSC Newsclippings" (Vol. XVII) Auraria Library Archives

641. Author unknown (1970, June 15) "Warrant Out for Woman Charged in MSC Arson" *The Denver Post* "MSC Newsclippings" (Vol. XVIII) Auraria Library Archives

642. Author unknown (1970, June 3) "Live Up to Christian Ideals, Blacks Urge" letter to editor *The Denver Post* "MSC Newsclippings" (Vol. XVIII) Auraria Library Archives

643. Rawls, Isetta (1970, May 25) Editorial Page, *THE PAPER* p. 4 3(31), Auraria Library Archives

644. Angeletti, Charles (1970, June 1) Guest Editorial *THE PAPER* p.4 3(32), Auraria Library Archives

645. Linicome, Julie (1970, June 1) Letters to the Editor *THE PAPER* p. 5 3(32), Auraria Library Archives.

646. Author unknown (1970, August 5) "Metro Awarded New Equipment" *THE PAPER* p. 4 4(2), Auraria Library Archives

647. Author unknown (1970, August 16) "Metro State Addition Set" *The Denver Post* "MSC Newsclippings" (Vol. XVIII) Auraria Library Archives

648. Author unknown (1970, August) "La Academia Del Barrio Is Summer Success" *West Side Recorder* "MSC Newsclippings" (Vol. XVIII) Auraria Library Archives

649. Author unknown (1970, July 27) "Community' Trial Called In Hill Case" *The Denver Post* "MSC Newsclippings" (Vol. XVIII) Auraria Library Archives

650. Author unknown (1970, July 27) "Blacks to hold own 'investigation' of Hill slaying" *Rocky Mountain News* "MSC Newsclippings" (Vol. XVIII) Auraria Library Archives

651. Lane, George (1970, August 21) "May-D&F Is Picketed As Protest in Hill Case" *The Denver Post* "MSC Newsclippings" (Vol. XVIII) Auraria Library Archives

652. Author unknown (1970, August 28) "Denver Black Group Plans Mobil 'Sanction'" *The Denver Post* "MSC Newsclippings" (Vol. XVIII) Auraria Library Archives

653. Author Unknown (1970, August 10) "190 get degrees at Summer Commencement" MSC Faculty and Staff Newsletter (Vol.6) No.4) Auraria Library Archives

654. Smith, Bob. (1970, September 28). Abolish MSC's "Cop" Department. *THE PAPER* p. 3 4(3), Auraria Library Archives.

655. Smith, Bob. (1970, October 8) Letters: "Smith Again" *THE PAPER* p. 4 4(4), Auraria Library Archives.

656. Smith, Bob (1970, October 8). Letters: "And Again" *THE PAPER* p. 4 4(4), Auraria Library Archives.

657. Cline, Frank S. et al (1970, October 8) "SDS: No Cause & Effect" *THE PAPER* p. 8 4(4), Auraria Library Archives

658. Rothman, Bonnie (1970, October 8)."Damn It!" *THE PAPER* p. 1 4(4), Auraria Library Archives

659. Hutchinson, Paul (1970, October 14) "Book Rep Answers Back" *THE PAPER* p.4 4(5), Auraria Library Archives

660. Abedaziz, Fayez, et al. (1970, October 28) "Dare To Strike!" *THE PAPER* p.5 4(7), Auraria Library Archives

661. http://tvnews.vanderbilt.edu/program.pl?ID=492418 accessed May 2014. These reports on coverage on NBC news by David Brinkley on the Red Fern situation.

662. Author unknown (1970, November 9) "Fall Enrollment" *MSC Faculty-Staff Newsletter* Vol.6 (No.9) Auraria Library Archives

663. Author unknown (1970, September 29) "Councilman advises interns" (photo by Mel Schieltz) *Rocky Mountain News* "MSC Newsclippings" (Vol. XIX) Auraria Library Archives

664. O'Neill, Frank. (1970, September 28) "A Note From our Beloved Editor" *THE PAPER* pages 1, 5 4(3), Auraria Library Archives.

665. Author unknown (1970, October 25) "We Dig" *MSC Faculty-Staff Newsletter* Vol. 6 (No. 7) Auraria Library Archives

666. Author unknown (1970, October 26) "Federation members Meet" *MSC Faculty-Staff Newsletter* Vol. 6 (No 7) Auraria Library Archives

667. Hutchinson, Paul. (1970, October 28). Parking: There Is Hope. *THE PAPER* p. 2 4(7); also, "Parking Committee Meets with City" *THE PAPER* p. 2 4(7), Auraria Library Archives.

668. Megeath, Joe (1971, April 28) "City Transit Problems" (letter to editor) *The Denver Post* "MSC Newsclippings" (Vol. XX) Auraria Library Archives

669. Hutchinson, Paul and Scott, Chuck (1970, October 14) "The Loyalty Oath Hassle" *THE PAPER* p. 3 4(5), Auraria Library Archives.

670. Author unknown (1970, October 15) "Metro buildings target of 2 phone bomb threats" *Rocky Mountain News* "MSC Newsclippings" (Vol. XIX) Auraria Library Archives

671. Author unknown (1970, November 16) "Proposed MSC Alumni Association" *MSC Faculty- Staff Newsletter* Vol. 6 (No. 11) Auraria Library Archives

672. Author unknown (1970, November 24) "Holiday gift certificate" (photo by Mel Schieltz) *Rocky Mountain News* "MSC Newsclippings" (Vol. XIX) Auraria Library Archives

673. Author unknown (1970, November 26) "Colo. Law Agencies Blood Bank Opened" *The Denver Post* "MSC Newsclippings" (Vol. XIX) Auraria Library Archives

674. Steele, Larry (1970, June 1) (Letters to the Editor) *THE PAPER* p. 5 3(32), Auraria Library Archives.

675. Larsen, Leonard (1970, May 14) "Greg Seeks 'Fantastic Upset'" *The Denver Post* "MSC Newsclippings" (Vol. XVIII) Auraria Library Archives

676. Kovash, John. (1970, July 22) (Interview with Greg Pearson) "Working Within the System" *THE PAPER* p .1 4(1), Auraria Library Archives.

677. Hutchinson, Paul. (1970, August 5) "McKevitt Speaks" *THE PAPER* p. 2 4(2), Auraria Library Archives

678. Romfh, Peter (1970, September 28) "Hogan: 'Don't Keep SDS Out'" *THE PAPER* p. 3 4(3), Auraria Library Archives

679. Snyder, Michael (1970, November 3) "MSC Graduate Offers New Leadership for the State" *THE PAPER* p. 1 4(8), Auraria Library Archives.

680. Author unknown (1970, October 14) "Campaign Schedule" *THE PAPER* p. 3 4(5), Auraria Library Archives.

681. Author unknown (1970, October 23) "We are embarrassed: "MSC Students Criticize Love" *The Denver Post* "MSC Newsclippings" (Vol. XIX) Auraria Library Archives

682. Author unknown (1970, November 23) "Underwhelmed at College Reception" *MSC Faculty- Staff Newsletter* Vol. 6 (No. 12)

683. Ball, David. (1970, October 28) "Ball: In Support of Fee Increase" *THE PAPER* p. 4 4(7), Auraria Library Archives.

684. Zimmerman, David. (1970, November 11). ASMCS on the Failure of the Referendum. *The Paper* 4(9), page 5. Auraria Library Archives

685. Author unknown (1970, November 11) "ASMSC Election Results" *THE PAPER* p. 1 4(9), Auraria Library Archives

686. Author unknown (1970, December 7) "Center for Urban Studies and History" *MSC Faculty-Staff Newsletter* Vol. 6 (No. 12) Auraria Library Archives

687. "A Horse With No Name" America, Album: *America, 1972* written by Dewey Bunnell

688. Author unknown (1970, December 7) "Reasons Given for Failed to return" *MSC Faculty-Staff Newsletter* Vol. 6 (No. 12) Auraria Library Archives

689. Author unknown (1970, December 10) "Stadium-Bus Use Planned As Student Parking Solution" *The Denver Post* "MSC Newsclippings" (Vol. XIX) Auraria Library Archives

690. Author unknown (1970, December 13) "Metro College to Offer New Education Degree" *The Denver Post* "MSC Newsclippings" (Vol. XIX) Auraria Library Archives

691. Author unknown (1960, December 27) "McNichols backs Metro State name" *Rocky Mountain News* "MSC Newsclippings" (Vol. XIX) Auraria Library Archives

692. Williams, Jerry (1970, December 28) "College Name Change Sought" *The Denver Post* "MSC Newsclippings" (Vol. XIX) Auraria Library Archives: also Author unknown (1970, December 31) "Name-Change Position Told" *The Denver Post* "MSC Newsclippings" (Vol. XIX) Auraria Library Archives

693. Fritz, Leah (1970, October 28) "From Adam's Rib to Women's Lib: A Woman's View of the Clitoris" *THE PAPER* pages 8-9 4(7), Auraria Library Archives.

694. Winkleplick, Debra (1970, November 3) "Miss Metro On Women's Lib" *THE PAPER* p. 7 4(8), Auraria Library Archives.

695. Hutchinson, Paul et al. (1970, November 11) "Phillips Discusses *The Paper*" *THE PAPER* p. 9 4(9), Auraria Library Archives.

696. Redfern, Timothy (1970, November 23) "SDS on *The Paper* and Contents" *THE PAPER* p. 1 4(10), Auraria Library Archives.

697. Hutchinson, Paul (1970, November 11) "Pub Board Hears Complaints" *THE PAPER* p.1 4(9), Auraria Library Archives; also Author unknown (1970, November 17) "MSC's '*The Paper*' Survives Board Vote" *The Denver Post* "MSC Newsclippings" (Vol. XIX) Auraria Library Archives

698. Butterfield, Jennifer (1970, October 28) "Local Chapter to educate MSC women" *THE PAPER* p. 9 4(7) Auraria Library Archives

Chapter 15

699. "Changes" David Bowie, Album: Hunky Dory Album, RCA Records, 1971, written by David Bowie

700. Author unknown (1979, January 28) "Leaving MSC Phillips Says" *The Denver Post*; also, Moran, Martin (1970, January 29) "Metro President resigns effective at summers end" *Rocky Mountain News* "MSC Newsclippings" (Vol. XIX) Auraria Library Archives

701. Interview Dr. Ken Phillips by Ken Phillips 2013, copy in author's files

702. Interview Professor Ken Phillips by Robert Bowen May 28, 2014. Transcript in author's files

703. Author unknown (1971, February 9) "Dr. Kenneth Phillips" Denver *Daily Journal*, "MSC Newsclippings" (Vol. XX) Auraria Library Archives

704. Author unknown (1971, February 17) "Metropolitan State College Forms Joint Committee" *Cervi's Journal* "MSC Newsclippings" (Vol. XX) Auraria Library Archives

705. Moran, Martin (1979, February 18) "Faculty at MSC debates selection" *Rocky Mountain News* "MSC Newsclippings" (Vol. XX) Auraria Library Archives

706. Author unknown (1971, February 19) "Selection method of Metro chief hit" *Rocky Mountain News* "MSC Newsclippings" (Vol. XX) Auraria Library Archives

707. Author unknown (1971, March 8) "12 Named To Help Pick MSC Head" *The Denver Post* "MSC Newsclippings" (Vol. XX) Auraria Library Archives

708. Nellhaus, Arlynn (1979, February 4) "Weekend College' Helps Get Ex-Dropouts Back on Track" *The Denver Post* "MSC

Newsclippings" (Vol. XX) Auraria Library Archives

709. Author unknown (1971, February 5) "Probation Granted in MSC Arson" *The Denver Post*, "MSC Newsclippings" (Vol. XX) Auraria Library Archives

710. Author unknown (1971, February 6) "Metro State Offers 2 New Majors" *Pueblo Chieftain* "MSC Newsclippings" (Vol. XX) Auraria Library Archives

711. Smith, Christopher (1971, February 8) "Metro State Day Care Center busy" *Rocky Mountain News* "MSC Newsclippings" (Vol. XX) Auraria Library Archives

712. Smith, Christopher (1971, January 15) "Students Tell of Fears About Auraria Project" *Rocky Mountain News* "MSC Newsclippings" (Vol. XIX)

713. Author unknown (1971, February 11) "Auraria task force plan on housing OKd" *Rocky Mountain News* "MSC Newsclippings" (Vol. XX) Auraria Library Archives

714. Author unknown (1971, February 11) "Bill Delays Deadline on Auraria Site" *The Denver Post*, "MSC Newsclippings" (Vol. XX) Auraria Library Archives

715. Author unknown (1971, March 3) "Auraria Protest Suit Killed" *The Denver Post* "MSC Newsclippings" (Vol. XX) Auraria Library Archives

716. Lyle, Don (1971, March 3) "Suit against Auraria site is dismissed" *Rocky Mountain News* "MSC Newsclippings" (Vol. XX) Auraria Library Archives

717. Author unknown (1971, March 4) (editorial "Get on with Auraria" *Rocky Mountain News* "MSC Newsclippings" (Vol. XX) Auraria Library Archives

718. Author unknown (1971, march 16) "Appeal On Auraria Suit Filed" *The Denver Post* "MSC Newsclippings" (Vol. XX) Auraria Library Archives

719. *The Auraria Higher Education Center: How it came to be*, Frank C. Abbott 1999 Auraria Higher Education Center Denver p.75

720. Author unknown (1971, March 8) "Auraria Uncertainty Remains" *The Denver Post* "MSC Newsclippings" (Vol. XX) Auraria Library Archives.

721. Author unknown (1971, March 8) "Auraria College Officials Vow To Move Ahead With Plans" *The Denver Post* "MSC Newsclippings" Auraria Library Archives

722. Moran, Martin (1971, March 9) "Auraria work to start in 1972" *Rocky Mountain News* "MSC Newsclippings" (Vol. XX) Auraria Library Archives

723. Author unknown (1971, April 1) "Costly Delay For Auraria" editorial *The Denver Post* "MSC Newsclippings" (Vol. XX) Auraria Library Archives

724. *The Auraria Higher Education Center: How it came to be*, Frank C. Abbott 1999 Auraria Higher Education Center Denver

725. *The Auraria Higher Education Center: How it came to be* Frank C. Abbott 1999 Auraria Higher Education Center Denver

726. Author unknown (1971, November 17) "Lets end the nonsense on Auraria" editorial *The Denver Post* "MSC Newsclippings" (vol. XXII) Auraria Library Archives

727. Williams, Jerry (1971, February 17) "Clark Favors 'New Rights'" *The Denver Post* "MSC Newsclippings" (Vol. XX)

728. Author unknown (1971, March 14) "Coloradans Talk With North Viets" *Rocky Mountain News* "MSC Newsclippings" (Vol. XX) Auraria Library Archives

729. Author unknown (1971, March 14) "Colorado Cares Group Returns" *The Denver Post* "MSC Newsclippings: (Vol. XX) Auraria Library Archives

730. Parmenter, Cindy ('97', March 10) "Board Imposes Limit on MSC" *The Denver Post* "MSC Newsclippings" (Vol. XX) Auraria Library Archives

731. Author unknown (1971, March 31) "Two Students Protest College Tuition Cutoff" *The Denver Post* "MSC Newsclippings" (Vol. XX) Auraria Library Archives

732. Author unknown (1971, April 1) "Metro State is granted full accreditation" *Rocky Mountain News* "MSC Newsclippings" (Vol. XXI) Auraria Library Archives

733.   Author unknown (1971, April 8) "Metro State Has 'Arrived'" editorial *The Denver Post* "MSC Newsclippings" (Vol. XXI) Auraria Library Archives

734.   Williams, Jerry (1971, April 13) "Summer Salary Cuts Rile Metro Federation" *The Denver Post* "MSC Newsclippings" (Vol. XXI) Auraria Library Archives

735.   Author unknown (1971 April 12) "The Status of Women at MSC" MSC Faculty and Staff Newsletter Auraria Library Archives

736.   Megeath, Joe (2014) *History of the Computer Information Systems (CIS) Department,* Section II, Auraria Library Archives

737.   McCoy, Joan (1971, April 22) "Patricia Duckworth's success recipe" *Rocky Mountain News* "MSC Newsclippings" (Vol. XXI) Auraria Library Archives

738.   Author unknown (1971, April 26) "Spring enrollment" MSC Faculty-Staff Newsletter; also, (1971, May 10) "College Dropouts" MSC Faculty and Staff Newsletter Auraria Library Archives

739.   Unknown (1971, April 19) "Debaters honored" (photo) *Rocky Mountain News* "MSC Newsclippings" (Vol. XXI) Auraria Library Archives

740.   Prieto, John (1971, May 1) "MSC President Honored for Service to Denver" photo *The Denver Post* "MSC Newsclippings" (Vol. XXI) Auraria Library Archives

741.   Hutchinson, Paul (1971 May 5) "Paper Gets Balled" Paul Hutchinson *THE PAPER* p.3 4(26) Auraria Library Archives

742.   Pollard, Fred A. (1971, May 20) "Stay Home and Masturbate" *THE PAPER* p 2 4(28) Auraria Library Archives

743.   Edwards, Dan (1971, June 3) "Thumbs Down" *THE PAPER* p.2 4(29)

744.   Author unknown (1971, May 13) "ASMSC" *THE PAPER* p.3   4(27) Auraria Library Archives

745.   Author unknown (1971, May 13) "You Apathetic Bastards" *THE PAPER* 4(27) Auraria Library Archives

746.   Dr. Ken Phillips Dr. of Laws Degree awarded in June 1971. Given to author by Professor Ken Phillips

747.   "Carry On" Crosby Still Hash and Young, Album: Déjà Vu (1970), written by Steven Stills

748.   Hand written original text of the commencement address delivered by Dr. Ken Phillips in June 1991 given to me by Professor Ken Phillips.

Index

AA Building 105, 205

Aaron Stationary Bldg. 246

AASU 168, 220, 240, 242, 277

Abbott, David 291

Abbott, Dr. Frank 102, 182, 242, 250, 266

Abedaziz, Fayez 274

Abramson, Dr. 238

Academic retention 92

Accreditation 13, 213, 296

Adair, Barbara 112, 203, 215

Aerospace Program 292

AHEC 294

Alexander, Milroy 63

Alexis, Charlene 72, 80, 82

Albi, Joseph Rep. 14

Allbee, Chuck 107, 291

Allott, Gordon Senator 237

Alumni Association 277

Anderson, Byron 178

Anderson, Doug 192, 197, 206

Angeletti, Charles xviii, 54, 144, 189, 202, 260, 271

Angus, Charles 168

Antinomianism 140,

Archuleta, Katherine xvii,

Armstrong, Bill Sen. 158

Arnold, Clarence 107, 118, 127, 145, 150, 152, 187

Arnold, Gary 192, 213, 218

Arnold, Sam 300

Associated Women Students (AWS) 107

Athletics Intercollegiate 159, 168, 169, 203, 231-236,

Athletics Intramural 183, 204

Auraria xix, 94, 101, 102, 146, 148, 157, 182, 198, 206, 221--231, 248-254, 266, 292-295

Austin, Gary 168

Avram, Vic 128

Baby Boom 5, 7, 31, 50, 97, 134

Baez, Joan 200, 240

Bagley, Dr. Henry 118, 130, 184

Bain Jean 14, 121

Baker, Cheryl 183

Ball, Dave 197, 206, 224, 226, 227, 230, 252, 254, 256, 258, 259, 273, 279, 280, 282, 290, 294, 295, 299, 300

Barbour, Karen 145

Bard, Paula 232,

Barnhill, Steve 185

Barrows, Russ 281

Bartel, Vivian 106, 115, 117, 124, 145, 150, 151, 168, 187

Bastien, Tom 223, 248, 253

Baucus, Dean 213

Beck, Dan 173, 259, 275, 281

Becker, Dr. George 121, 291

Behr, John 40

Be-In 135, 136, 137

Bell, Mike 274

Benavidez, Waldo 224, 226, 229, 257

Benn, Dr. Harold 123, 297

Bennett, Ann 285

Bentley, Ferne 68

Berger, Falk 189

Berman, Bruce 213
Bernaman, Rae 107, 108, 112
Biddick, Mildred 217
Birge, David 300
Black Panthers 144, 166, 175, 190, 197, 212, 214
Black Student Alliance 260
Bland, Elaine 300
Bland, Mickey 306
Blansett, Barbara 149
Bleecher, Mary xviii
Bombers MSC 96
Bonaker, Pete 265
Bookstore 116, 273
BOPPI 128
Bottomly, Dr. Forbes,
Bowen. Robert xvii, 104, 163, 164, 173, 174, 182, 183, 189,
    190, 194, 202, 203, 206, 213, 222, 226, 234, 236- 238,
    240, 241, 256, 258, 261, 278, 301
Bowman, Craig 191, 247
Boyce, Robert 270
Boyko, Mark 214, 215, 225, 234, 300, 301
Boyles, Peter 270
Branum, Greg 191, 247, 260
Braun, Roger xviii, 10, 79, 85, 96, 108, 112, 113, 117, 118,
    127, 144, 146, 150, 168, 171, 187, 203, 215, 277
Brigman, Mike 117, 168, 171, 192
Brimmer, Beth 265
Brinker, Orson 284
Brock, Chuck 108, 127, 130, 168, 186, 187, 203
Bronstein, Martin, 166, 170, 174, 179, 180, 186, 189, 193,
    207, 220
Brown, George 96, 252
Brown, Irving 197
Brown, Judi 129
Brown, Maurice 171, 192, 213
Brunner, George 284, 300, 301
Bryant, Dr. Harlan 68, 70, 71, 73, 77, 79
Bryant, Dr. James 231, 232, 242
Bulger, Jean 153
Burch, Palmer xvii, 11, 14, 15, 36, 39, 121, 251, 254
Burns, Forrest Rep. 12
Butler, Geri 192, 247

Cadwallader, Tom 185, 189, 190, 191, 192, 206, 211, 213,
    214, 238
Caldwell, Gregory 149
Canino, Dale 205

Cantrell, Stephen 275
Carrillo, Carl 218
Casey, Archbishop 227
Castro, Betty 272
Castro, Richard xviii, 10, 104, 143, 145, 183, 199, 226, 229,
    231, 257
Cavoto, Jim 170, 183, 213, 214, 224, 240
Caywood, Star 36, 121
CCA 130, 174, 183, 186, 189, 196, 206, 207
CCHE 70, 74-76, 86, 95, 99, 100, 108, 111, 112, 120, 148, 160,
    174, 218, 221, 242, 248
Chase, William 295
Chaves, Bal 223, 226, 229
Chicano students 221, 222, 224, 229
Choppock, Betsey 117
Circle K 117
Cisneros, Roger 227, 282
Clark, Dee 171, 187, 192
Clark, Ramsey 240, 295
Clark, Ruth Rep. 15, 41,
Clifton, Bob 173, 189, 238, 255, 264, 275, 278
Coleman, Jerry 213, 240
Cohen, Elaine 275, 300
College Bowl 128, 168
College Republicans of MSC 107, 110, 118, 162, 213, 259, 281
Columbine, The 116, 117
Committee Education Beyond High School 7, 9, 12, 13, 15, 22,
    23, 51, 55, 60, 203
Conners, Jett 174, 181
Conrad, Pam 192
Cook, Tom 70, 246
Cooper, Dave 300
Coors, Joe 266
Cotton, Ranaye 153
Coulson, Charles 106, 168, 214
Cowan, Heather 82, 107
Cowgill, Courtney 63, 64
Cox, Deanne 118
Crespin, Alberta 246
Cronk, Jerry 118, 171, 174, 188, 192, 194
Crosby, Dorita 69
Crowley, Liz 145
Counterculture 141,
CU 10, 11-17, 23, 32, 212, 250
CU Denver Center 12, 14, 17, 18, 37, 69, 75, 87, 96, 250
Cultural Caravan 149
Currigan, Tom 88, 94, 102, 121

Cusimano, Paul 127

Dameron, Thomas Rep. 14
Daniels, Dave 112, 187, 203
Davis, Lynn (Spike) 99, 105, 108, 117
Dawkins, Dave 259
Dazey, Nancy Jo 171
Debate Team, MSC 206, 298
Debber, Dale 209
Delgado, Alex 168, 213, 301
DeBerard, Faye 11
Denny, Richard 215
Denver Public Library 72, 80
Des Jardins, Marcia 128
Dines, Allen Representative xvii, 7, 14, 29, 36, 39, 121
Dolan, Pat 184
Donahue, Bernie 170, 174
Dowell, Donna 171
Drama Club 117, 170
Droll, Bini 171
DU Administration bldg. 71
Dubman, Elene 171
Duckworth, Dr. Patricia 297, 298
Dunbar, Duke 12
Duncan, Beth 153
DURA 222, 224, 225, 227, 293

East, Chris 189
Edwards, Dan 300
Edwards, Walker 77
Ege, Ralph 277
Eighteen Year Old Vote 163, 175, 202, 256
Eldeen, Sonja 173, 259, 279, 281, 300
Elliot, Denise 206
Ello, Jim 108, 187
Elwell, Kay 69
Emily Griffith Opportunity School 71, 81
Enrollments 79, 83, 91, 97, 100, 104, 111, 126, 145, 158, 179, 195, 211, 217, 245, 254, 269, 274, 281, 298
Esparza, Andy 168, 171, 192, 259, 291, 300
Estey, Fred 192
Evans, Frank 14,
Eversole, William 183, 197

Faculty Federation 275, 296
Fair, Dr. Jean 168, 241
Fentress, George Rep. 121, 158, 248

Ferguson, John 197
Fisher, Louis 247
Fitzgerald, Michael 213
Flemon, Wilt xviii, 238, 255, 264, 289
Forkner, Irv 146, 219, 297
Forum Building 69, 71, 81
Fowler, Hugh Sen. 112, 253
Fox Building 245
Friedman, Don 14, 294
Frisbie, Dick 96
Fritz, Leah 283
Fuentes, Joseph 82, 96, 107, 149, 174, 183, 187, 192, 193, 215, 257

Gadfly 148, 150, 159
Garcia, Father Peter 224, 226, 227, 229
Garcia, Anthony xix
Garcia, George 279
Garnsey, Bill 121
Gephardt, Rich 37, 42, 256, 259
Gibbs, Walter 127
Gill, Ted 121, 197
Gilmore, Patricia 99
Gold, Louise 170, 183, 215
Goldhan, Jo Ann 168
Goldstein, Irving 223, 253
Gonzales, Rodolfo "Corky" 104, 143, 151, 172
Gonzalez, Pearl 153, 187
Graduation (Commencement) 129, 174, 216, 266, 301
Graham, Wanda107, 162, 168, 187, 213
Graham, Winnona 300
Grant, William 222, 226, 227
Green Report 28, 51, 52, 58, 60, 65, 71, 153, 159, 174, 203, 235
Green, Jackie 118
Greenfield, Glenda 171
Greenwell, Belle 171
Greenwood, Bob 186
Gregory, Nancy 191
Griffith, William Rep. 14
Grimshaw, Tom, Rep 197, 251
Grout, Judee 107, 108,118, 128
Gude, Chris 108
Guiet, Claudia 285

Haberland, Margaret 171, 183, 192, 215, 277
Hall, Richard 258, 259
Hamilton, Larry 226

Hamilton, Sherman 82, 166, 171, 184, 247, 301

Harper, Shelby 9, 27, 30, 70, 71, 75, 76, 86, 88, 95, 99, 112, 128, 148, 14, 189, 248, 294

Hardegree, Reverend 106

Harmon, Shirley 152

Harris, Ernestine 247

Harris, King 64, 181, 221, 247, 264, 266, 272, 291

Harris, Tony 247

Hart, Craig 238

Haskell, Floyd Rep. 121

Hawley, David 129

HB349 1, 2, 14, 15, 16, 17, 18, 19, 50

HB 1101 36, 38, 39, 40, 43

Heap, Dennis 216

Hegger, Frankie 171

Henrikson, Phil 241, 296

Herren, Dr. Lloyd 290, 291

Hertlein, Peter 174, 184, 259

Hester, Bill 128

Hildreth, Dr. Richard 254

Hildreth, Richard Jr. 168, 174, 187

Hill, Duke 128

Hinderman, Dr. Roy 291

Hispano Club 172, 183

Hispano Youth Congress 198, 199, 219, 220, 240

History Dept. 54

Hogan, Mark xvii, 9, 14, 36, 39, 40, 41, 45, 113, 121, 209, 259, 261, 262, 279

Holbrook, Gary 206, 298

Holcombe, Doug xviii, 10, 81, 96, 99, 105, 108, 112, 113, 117, 119, 122, 127, 145, 159, 163, 164, 168, 171, 173, 179, 186, 188, 194, 201, 202, 203, 209, 215, 216, 233, 260, 278

Holcombe, Suzanne 186, 215, 277

Hollis, Gordon 262

Holmes, Dr. Darrell

Horan, Brian 225, 227, 230, 252, 259

Horton, John 118, 128

Houtchens, Bernard 24

Howard, Kathy 118, 145, 171, 187, 192, 213

Howe, Harold 54

Hull, Jeanette 108

Humphreys, Neysha 300

Hunter, Kirk 108

Huntzinger, Greg 281

Hurricane, Omar xviii

Hutchinson, Paul 299

Iazzetta, Vernie 77

Imatami, Becky 112, 171, 215

Ironshield, Harold 295

Isberg, Carl 187, 207, 259

Jackson, John 215

Jean Pierre, Louis 247

Johnson, Mark 246

Johnson, Sidney 168, 247

Jones, John Paul 168, 187

Jones, Judi 108, 112, 117, 118, 129

Jones, Rick 186

Jones, Sandi 68, 72

Jones, Sharon 281

Joy, Katherine 214, 300

Kammerzell, Karen 116

Kangiesser, Jim 107

Karins, Dave 108, 187, 213

Karsh, Frank 223, 248, 253, 292

Keen, Dr. Joe 266

Keifer, Dieter 174

Keith, A.A. 205

Keith, Rondie 174, 259, 273

Kelley, Andrew Rep. 16

Kelley, Don Sen.42

Kellogg, John 301

Kemp, Frank xvii, 36, 39, 40, 87, 121, 202

Kenna, Betty xviii

Kerr, Dr. Clark 54

Kessel, Marc 130

Kiley Pat 69

King, Dorothy 166

Kirtland, James 170, 187, 277

Klein, Ben Rep. 121

Klismet, Peter 262

Knapp, Judy 298

Knochel, George 242

Konrad, Marsha 218

Knox, Wayne 95, 115, 121

Kovash, Jon 225, 299

Kummerlin, Al 171, 187, 192

Lamplighters 117, 192

Langendoerfer, Jim

Leary, Timothy 135, 137

Ledesma, Dr. Antonio 64, 81, 82

Lennox, William Rep. 15, 16, 28, 38

Leonard, Stephen 76, 189, 255, 270, 281

Lesser, Roger 192

Lewis, Al 214, 264, 300

Lewis, David 207

Library (MSC) 80, 82, 131

Lillie, Forrest D. Dean 70, 74, 76, 85, 89, 113, 115, 153, 183, 185

Linicome, Julie 271

Lininger, Brian 106

Litschel, David 298

Loyalty Oath 276

Locke, Harry Sen. 17, 18, 43

Lopez, Belinda 246

Louks, Faye 69

Love, John Governor 1, 13, 18, 21, 23, 24, 27, 28, 33, 108, 121, 248, 251, 279, 294

Lowe, Donald 246, 277, 300

LSD 136, 152

Lucero, Ed 151, 198, 220, 224, 229, 241, 262

Lucero, Virginia 143, 224, 225, 226, 229, 272, 281

Luchinger, Leland 266

Mackie, John Rep. 7, 10, 14, 28, 37, 40, 86, 88, 92, 95, 115

Maestas, Mary 206

Maldonado, John 183

Malloy, Janet 300

Mano 172

Markert, Molly xviii

Marsh, Paul Jr. 235

Martin, Barbara 246

Martinez, Al 275, 301

Martinez, Angelina 246

Martinez, Daniel 150, 172

Martinez, Jess 151

Martinez, Manny 124

Massari, Vince Rep. 14. 40, 41

Mau Mau Underground 144

May Fest 171

McBride, Mary 108, 146, 187, 215

McCauley, Barry 277

McDivitt W. L. 26, 31, 74

McDougal, Susie 281

McEwen, Ruth 277

McFarlane, J. D. 36, 38, 87, 96, 121

McKinlay, Donald 248, 250

McKinney, Dr. Keats. 25, 65, 68, 70, 78, 89, 142, 175, 231, 235, 266, 276, 284, 299

McLallen, Millard 70

McLaughlin, Stuart 148, 169, 196, 301

McNichols, Bill 226, 227, 230, 231, 257, 282

McRae, Robert 275

McVicker, Roy 26, 32

Megeath, Joe 219, 276

Meier, Joan 71

Mehn, Dr. Duane 169, 197, 203, 233

Mendenhal, John 168

Mennenga, Virginia 64

Metropolitan (Student Newspaper) 107

Meyers, James 199

Michel, Dr. Gary 276

Militant Mugg Wump 280

Milligan, Dr. Merle 197

Milstein, Phil 294

Minckler, Bill 246

Mirich, Dr. John 291

MLK Assassination 165

Mollock, John 300

Monfort, Ken 121

Montano, Barbara 82

Montano, Richard 246

Moody, Vern 118, 127, 166

Moratorium, Vietnam 236-240

Morreale, Don 149

Morton, Max 294

Mosley, John 151

Movimiento, El 143, 150

MSC Bombers 96

Mumma, William 197

Music Program 106, 118

Mu Beta Chi 255

Mu Sigma 117

Mustangs, (Mascot) 128

Myneeder, Mildred 117

Name Change 282

Naugle, Betty 70, 75, 76, 79, 86, 92, 128, 148, 167, 266, 282

Neoteric Puff 149, 152, 159

Netzel, Dr. Richard 301

New Campus Review (NCR) 114, 150

Nicholson, Will 121

Noel, Rachel xvii,

Norgren, Leigh 266

Nursing Program 105, 153

Oberholtzer, Kenneth 13, 39
Officer, Elmer 247
Ogle, Ray 107, 126
Ohlson, Morton 255, 275
O'Neil, Frank 174, 207, 275, 278, 284, 299
O'Dell, Robert 183, 226
Open Door 60, 62, 63, 221

Pacheco, Norman 198, 246
Padilla, Marco 246
Palmer, Dr. James 301
Paper, The 167, 174, 299, 300
Park, Don 149, 174
Parker, James 107
Pasco, Bonnie 128, 149
Paslay, Bob 128
Peacock, Cathy 225
Pearson, Greg 32, 128, 278
Peiner, Mary Elizabeth 215
Peterie, Richard 117
Petersen, Ginger 171
Phares, Dr. Gail 79, 96, 98
Phi Beta Lambda 117
Phillips, Dr. Kenneth 53, 64, 73, 74, 78, 80, 83, 86, 87, 95,
    99, 117, 122, 123, 142, 145, 166, 167, 168, 175, 187,
    209, 218, 221, 222, 227, 232, 241, 255, 265, 282, 284,
    287- 289, 296, 298, 301
Philosophy Club 117
Pickett, Gary 151, 171, 179, 192, 213, 259
Pierre, Louis Jean 247
Placky, Dr. Jon 77, 197, 2 82
Plastino, Phyllis 206
Police Science 102, 273, 277
Pollard, Fred 299
Polemics 192, 214
Porter, Ralph Rep. 121
Potter, W. T "Junior" 84, 197, 202, 240
Pouraghabagher, Ali 96
Powell, Frank 266
Prophets (Mascot) 151
PROSPECTUS 106, 115, 117, 124, 129, 146, 150, 151, 152
Publicity Club 117
Pugel, Elke 259
Pugel, Robert 259

Quinlan, Clarence 121
Quinn, Shannon 106, 107,108, 112, 203

Rawls, Isetta 196, 242, 270, 271, 300
Redfern, Timothy 274, 284
Reed, Dr. Carleton "Pat" 102, 129, 298
Reed, Carson 81
Reeser, Richard 145, 171, 186, 188, 191, 194, 207, 301
Reeves, Betty 69
Regents, CU 12, 17, 23, 25, 36, 38, 42, 62, 251
Renneberg, Mary 225,
Rhodes, Robert 115, 119, 120
Rhoades, Dr. William 255, 289
Richard, Bobbi 171
Ricketts, Dick 170, 186
Rios, Richard 107, 117
Roadrunners 204, 205, 216, 235, 242
Roberto, Kathy 170, 187, 214
Robinson, Bernard 168, 260
Rogers, Keith 70
Rollins, Wayne 70
Romer, Roy xviii, 7, 10, 12, 13, 14, 15, 17, 28, 36, 44, 55, 69
Room 227 State Capitol 68, 77
Roon, Eugene 197
Rosengrant, Kathy 281
Roth, Herrick xviii, 26, 95,209
Roybal, John 224, 229, 241
Rubin, Ted Rep. 16, 17
Russell, Dr. John Dale 22,

Saccamano, James 107, 117, 118, 192, 246
Sadowski, Ed 186
Sanchez, Paco 227, 254
Sanders, Herb 247
Sandoval, David 289, 296
Sandoval, Joseph G.103, 104, 126, 143
Saunders, Allegra 121
Sauter, Trudy 285
SB 314 121, 122
SB 344 43
SCAB 107, 150
Scheifflein, Joseph Sen. 121
Schell, Dennis 218, 240, 259
Schempp, Barbara 79
Schenkein, Robert 300
Schnitker, Annette 171
Schomp, Kay 237

Schuck, Doug 82

Schuette, Dr. Oscar 291

Scott, C.G.232

Scott, Ed (Sheriff Scotty) 36

SDS/SDA 144, 162,184, 185, 190, 197, 213, 236, 273, 279, 284, 299

Secord, Dean 240

Shaw, Ken 146

Sheehan, Nancy 130

Sherwood, Ken 281, 300

Shoemaker, Joe 36, 43, 44, 96, 252, 253, 294

Simmons, Dave 117

Skiffington, L.C. 87, 88

Smilanic, Carmel 116

Smith, Robert 186, 215, 262, 273, 274

Sonnenberg, Dave 259, 275

Spanish Club 117

Spencer, Barbara 128

Spradley, Dr. John 196, 275, 289

St. Cajetan's 249

Steele, Larry 54, 64, 173, 225, 249, 252, 259, 278

Steinhauser, Dr. Sheldon vii, 219, 220

Stockton, Ruth Rep., Sen, 16, 36, 43

Strutton, Larry 84, 145

Stuckey, Carol 263

Student Center 105, 119, 170, 220

Student Government 105, 106, 127, 170

Student Lobbyists 112, 113, 115,121, 159, 202

Stuart, W. L. 296

Summer of Love 134, 135, 136, 138, 144, 151

TTT (333) Building 71, 81, 117, 187

Tager, Ken 197

Talmage, Wayne 162, 171, 184, 185, 187, 213, 249

Taylor, Barbara 118

Taylor, Don 255, 275, 298

Taylor, Joe 130, 236, 237, 238, 239, 301

Taylor, Tom 171

Temmer, Dr. Harry 291

Thayer, Ken 197

Thomas, Gwen xviii, 54, 77, 179, 266

Thomas, Jeff 266, 270

Thomsen, David 153

Thompson, Dr. Robert 183, 187, 241, 266, 275, 284, 291, 299

Thonssen, Dr. Lester 84, 206

Tillson, Dr. William 52, 54

Tivoli 249

Todd, Chick 145

Todorovick, Mike 168

Tomhave, Cindy 118, 186

Toren, Gaye 118

Torres, Father Joseph

Torsiello, Peter 232,

Treece, Susan 300

Trombetta, Carol 300

Trujillo, Gary 291

Trustees of State Colleges 15, 30, 31, 47, 146, 168, 196, 233, 284

Tumler, John 130

Turk, Brady 242, 247

Turner, Helen 153

Ulrich, Sallyann 145, 153, 174

UMAS 220, 224, 225, 240

Urban-Oriented College 52, 53, 54, 210

Urban History Center 281

Urban Studies 255

Upper Division (4-Year) 108, 120, 123

Valdes, Dr. Daniel xviii, 172, 195, 219, 255, 289

Valdez, Bernardo 174, 269, 300

Valdez, Marvia 174, 277

Valdez, Peggy 300

Van Arsdale, Jo 153,215

Vanderhoof, John Rep. 27, 92, 252, 253, 279

Van Everen, Dr. Brooks 289, 297

Van Howe, James

Vest, Dr. Grant 25, 30, 38, 297

Veteran Student Association 295

Vialpando, Barbara 82

Viewbook 103

Vigil, Wayne 96, 128

Vince, George 96

Voc-tech 53, 115

Vondracek, Dr. Jiri 275

Waggoner, George 63

Waggoner, Jim 183, 184, 269

Wall, Dr. Don 275

Walsh, Dr. Peggy 54, 189, 275, 289

Watson, Lauren 106, 107, 114, 124, 166, 175, 185, 190, 191, 214

Weaver, R.G.262

Weber, Joe 151

Weekend College 291

Wells, Jill 277

Weston, Dr. Warren 174, 275

White Mule 84, 85, 246, 255, 277

Winkler, Linda 153, 168

Winkleplick, Debra 283

Willms, Raymond 70,174

Wilson, Dr. Jerry 74

Wilson, Janet 151

Wilson, Penny 118

Wimberley, Donald 246

Wolf, Donald 103

Wolford, Rodney 178

Woman's Liberation MSC 285

Woodman of the World Bldg. 246

Woods, Marjorie 113

Woods. Rosemary 107, 108

Woodward, Bruce 79

Wright, Curtis 79, 89, 98, 153, 202, 204, 258, 272

Wright, Dr. Elizabeth 196

Y.E.S. Committee 163

York, Chris 186, 215

Young, Bob 184, 212, 215

Young Democrats 259, 279

Young, Gary 151

Younkin, Pam 153

Your Choice 145, 149

Yunker, Joy 118, 130

Yuthas, Ladessa 299

Zamadie, Haile 300

ZDS Computer 255, 260

Zimmerman, Dave 281

Zimmerman, Stephen 270

Zook Bldg. 220

About the Author

Robert E. Bowen is a news analyst, retired business owner, and former three-term Colorado State Representative. He enrolled in Metropolitan State College in 1968, where he received a BA in History.

Robert lived through the events chronicled in this book, including the lowering of the voting age to eighteen and the nationwide protests against the Vietnam War. When colleges throughout the U.S. rioted after Kent State, Robert was instrumental in preventing violence on Colorado campuses.

Since retirement, Robert continues to be involved with grass roots politics. He analyzes international, national, local, and environmental news through his two online columns. His hobbies include genealogy and writing history in the context of the times.